AWARENESS DIALOGUE & PROCESS

Essays on Gestalt Therapy

Gary M. Yontef

CONTENTS

PREFACE

─────────

Awareness, Dialogue and Process. From the vantage point of
Gestalt therapy theory everything is process — everything is
moving and changing. It is new to twentieth-century thought that
physicists regard even the universe itself as moving and changing.
Clearly, theory and practice also change.

By bringing together in one book the papers I have written on
Gestalt therapy, from the first paper I wrote in 1969 through
papers I wrote this year (1991) especially for this volume, I hope
to enable the discerning reader to see, perhaps even more clearly
than I, the continuities, discontinuities and changes in my thinking. To help in this process I wrote commentaries before each
paper to guide the reader, especially by noting the time and
context in which each paper was written.

This book is a collection of essays, and not the comprehensive
and integrated overview of the theory of Gestalt therapy that I
think Gestalt therapy needs and that I would like to write. As a
collection of essays, it does not carry through the basic principles
in systematic fashion so that they weave throughout the entire
book. It does not eliminate redundancy. It does not explicitly
enough address *Gestalt Therapy* (1951). It does not carry forth the
analysis of the figure/ground phenomena or the problems of the
self concept. On the positive side, it does contain several new
essays on clinical practice (diagnosis, treatment of character
disorders, shame, groups) and theory (a new introduction to field
theory).

I hope this collection of papers will facilitate further theoretical
dialogue. For me, dialogue is one of the most important aspects

of Gestalt therapy theory and practice, including the process of theorizing. Most of my papers were written with the attitude that theory is a dialogue, even if my writing has often fallen short of sounding dialogic.

I regard Gestalt therapy theory and practice as a living system and as such it either engages, grows and develops or stays static, self-referential and stagnates. Engaging the world in a way that fosters new developments is a vital and necessary aspect of Gestalt therapy theory. It is only by dialogic engagement of Gestalt therapists and theorists with each other, with patients, other systems of practice and thought, changing world conditions, and so forth, that we facilitate new understanding.

Theory is a form of dialogue that establishes systematic intellectual support for our clinical work. It is a way of using ideas and information to support the experimentation and the clinical relationship, both of which Gestalt therapy theory considers to be forms of dialogue. Theory is a written and systematic intellectual account arising out of human relationships. I publish my views and others react, agree, criticize, and the dialogue continues as I am affected and assimilate or reject the reactions. When I can respond, perhaps by changing some of my viewpoints, the dialogue results in the emergence of improved understanding through dialectic development. It is this process of growth that I find exciting and useful and that motivates me to continue to engage in and love theoretical discussion and to write theory papers.

Theories are not true (or false), and do not establish truth. However, they are more or less useful, consistent, insightful, stimulating, and so forth. Theories are frameworks that arise out of our clinical and didactic work and also stimulate and guide further work as well. One of the tests of good theory is heuristic. What changes as a result of the theory? Does it result in some additional understanding? When something is translated into Gestalt therapy language, does it result in some new information that wasn't present before the translation? Does it lead to new research, new ideas? Above all, does it aid clinical practice? I hope that my efforts are useful on some of these dimensions.

I want to extend my acknowledgments and thanks to Molly Rawle for her initial suggestion and encouragement in doing this project and to Molly and Joe Wysong for their work in carrying it to conclusion. Their friendship and support has been a motivating force behind this book and very important to me personally.

I especially want to thank Lynne Jacobs. Over the years, she has been open-hearted with her time in reading and editing my papers, improving my style, content, perspective, etc. As the material for this book piled up, and I needed help, she always answered the call. She has challenged me where we differ, in a manner that always respected our differences. While I can usually do this on a person-to-person level, I am afraid that in theory work I am similar to what has been said of Martin Buber: I am kind to people and cruel to ideas. For this book she has once again been a good friend, an excellent editor, and brought home to me once again the lesson that people need each other.

And finally, thanks to my most ardent supporter, my wife Judith, who has always encouraged me. She has brought me life and warmth and fun in spite of my funny obsession with writing papers. For this and for many other reasons I am very grateful that she is who she is and is in my life. Thanks, Judi.

I

THE HISTORY
AND
POLITICS
OF
GESTALT THERAPY

1

RECENT TRENDS IN GESTALT THERAPY
IN THE UNITED STATES
AND WHAT WE NEED
TO LEARN FROM THEM

═══════════════

Commentary

On June 29, 1989 I was invited to speak at the Third British Gestalt Therapy Conference in Nottingham, England on the subject of current trends in Gestalt therapy in the United States. This paper is an adaptation of that talk and will serve as an introduction to the volume. In this paper I discuss what I think we have learned, beginning with a review of the development of Gestalt therapy in the United States, the advances and some of the unfortunate aspects or "errors."

Introduction:
How do we know what works?

In the forty-year history of Gestalt therapy in the United States there have been many exciting and useful developments. And there have also been some misdevelopments, errors, misconceptions, and holes that have developed. Unfortunately, there seems to be some repetition in other countries of the mistakes we have made in the United States. There seems to be a propensity to rediscover the wheel, with countries in which Gestalt therapy got a later start repeating with enthusiasm the errors we made in the 1960s. This has often been promoted, bolstered, serviced and strengthened by expatriate Americans who use a model of Gestalt therapy that has largely been transcended in the United States. I hope that by sharing our current experience, the learning curve can be shortened elsewhere. On a positive note, some countries are already avoiding some of the errors that we made.

I have been referring to errors and mistakes. But how do we know what is an error?

For me, the test of our theory is in the practice of ongoing therapy with "real patients." "Real patients" refers to people coming to a psychotherapist for therapy rather than training. My primary professional activity is treating such people. Other activities, such as training therapists, giving lectures, or giving demonstrations are secondary. Working with other therapists in training groups and workshops is useful, but whatever happens in that context is only a secondary test of the effectiveness of practice based on our theory.

I judge the effectiveness of training in how it helps or doesn't help the practice of therapy. Our primary data come from the ongoing contact and awareness work in psychotherapy.

Of course, one way to test what we say and do is research. Unfortunately we don't do much research in Gestalt therapy, either formal or informal. We also do not do a lot of real philosophic analysis. We do a lot of "it sounds good to me" kind of analysis, without real data, phenomenological explication, philosophic analysis or intellectual debate. Even our presentation of clinical material is skimpy, i.e., meager in quantity, sparse in detail, and often merely a nominal reference to clinical description.

Presenting one's thoughts and clinical wisdom without subjecting it to the test of research or debate or phenomenological explication or philosophic analysis lends itself to the idealization of authorities, leadership by charisma, and substituting the logic and articulateness of a presenter rather than investing ourselves in careful phenomenological exploration based on actual experience, tested over time and refined by the crucible of dialogue. Advancing ideas without the support of good theory that is based on good research and good theoretical analysis is not good phenomenology.

Background I: The Early Years

Reaction Against Classical Psychoanalysis

Gestalt therapy began as a reaction to the rigidity of classical psychoanalysis by therapists who were trained in classical psycho-analysis. In the current era it is hard for some to imagine how rigid psychoanalysis had become. When I was first in training to be a psychiatric social worker in 1962, there were serious debates in clinics in which I worked and trained as to whether it was allowed to shake the hand of a patient who extends his hand as a greeting in the waiting room or whether it unduly interferes with the proper development of the transference. Some of this kind of rigidity can still be seen in some of the newer psychoanalytic schools. For example, I remember reading one of Heinz Kohut's books (in the 1970s) in which he discussed a case in which the psychoanalysis was irreparably lost after hundreds of hours of work merely because the analyst let the patient find out that he was a Roman Catholic.

Gestalt therapy also reacted against the psychoanalytic change theory, which was pessimistic about growth possibilities and had a limited sense of the available options.

The psychoanalytic stress on transference rather than on the actual relationship was accompanied by a parallel emphasis on interpretation rather than the actual experience of either the patient or the therapist. The realities of the current relationship were entered into only via transference interpretations. And the therapeutic work mostly utilized the transference as a clue to sources in the past of the current behavior of the patient. When the therapist formulated an inference about how the current behavior, as evidenced in the transference, was caused by past events, this was interpreted to the patient, often as if the inference were fact (M. V. Miller, 1988).

The entire concept of the role of the therapist was radically modified by the early Gestalt therapists. The psychoanalytic theory of change required that the therapist limit personal disclosures or any other overt presence that would reveal the person of the

5

therapist. Even the office had to be decorated in a neutral manner, e.g., without family pictures or personal mementos that would taint the blank screen and color the transference.

The analyst had to practice the rules of neutrality and abstinence. The analyst was not allowed to deviate from absolute neutrality, e.g., by taking sides in a patient's conflict, and was not allowed to gratify any wish of the patient. Either of these was seen as distorting the transference and interfering with the work of analysis. It was believed that the analyst could maintain a position that was truly neutral and hence would have no effect on the transference, as if a "neutral" stance, were such possible, would not affect the transference.

The psychoanalytic theory of change also required passivity by the patient. The basic rule for the patient was to share all associations without censoring. (Of course, it was generally ignored that this rule was not neutral, but took sides against the resistance.) Good analytic work in this model did not include phenomenological focusing. All active behavior by the patient during the session, or making changes in ones life before the analyst thought that the issues were worked through, was considered acting out and resisting the analytic work.

One of the basic aspects of psychoanalysis that was changed in the Gestalt therapy movement was that psychoanalysis was theory driven and not based primarily on actual experience. And, the theory that drove psychoanalysis was drive theory. In that theory the determinants of personality were considered largely preset, not social or existential. For example, the castration complex occurred universally in all people in all cultures because of basic drives each person is born with.

The Gestalt Therapy Revolution: Attention to Possibilities

Gestalt therapy did not just react to psychoanalysis, but started a revolution that was firmly rooted in a basic belief in the power of human capabilities.

The Power of Awareness and Presence

In the new model, both therapist and patient grow by being actively present and engaged both during therapy sessions and in the world in general.

Gestalt therapy emphasized what people knew and what people could learn by focusing their awareness. They created a new methodology that was not based on what people didn't know and couldn't know (the unconscious could not be known except through interpretation and analysis of the transference in psycho-analysis).

The Power of Experimenting

Gestalt therapy was based on the power of experimentation, of trying something new and letting awareness emerge from the new experimental behavior. Rather than a methodology limited to free association and analyzing the transference, Gestalt therapy made room for a more powerful methodology. By being free of rigid, theory-driven restrictions, Gestalt therapists and patients could try new behavior and test it with their own awareness processes.

The alternatives to this utilization of the experimental attitude were the psychoanalytic attitude of treating new behavior as acting out and the behavioristic attitude of controlling behavior using the principles of reinforcement. The experimental attitude supports a more active functioning mode by therapist and patient without the therapist becoming a behavior modifier or the patient being accused of acting out.

The Power of the Here and Now

The Gestalt therapy revolution was a key part of a movement in which the momentary here and now was the focus point for awareness work, contact and the creating of new solutions. Twentieth-century field ideas had not yet made a major impact in therapy when the Gestalt therapists, partially under Gestalt psycho-logical and Lewinian influences, made it a central part of the Gestalt therapy way of thinking. "What are you doing (or aware of) right now, and how are you doing it? " replaced "Why did you do that?" as the prototypical question.

Some described Gestalt therapy as "I and Thou, Here and Now, What and How." It was revolutionary in the therapy scene at that time for therapists and patients to engage each other based on what was actually being experienced, done, or needed at the very moment. The descriptive, process, field emphasis on what and how rather than a speculative emphasis on mechanistic causality was also new in psychology at that time.

Two Styles

Two contrasting tendencies or styles emerged in Gestalt therapy and still continue. One is a theatrical, cathartic approach in which technique is accentuated more than person-to-person involvement. Sometimes I call this boom-boom-boom therapy. The other style is a hard-working, person-to-person, contact-oriented approach. Each of these has been present in embryonic form since at least the mid-1960s. Both tendencies were pioneering. One became the forerunner, or at least an early example, of the many manipulating therapies that have blossomed in the 1980s. The other was the forerunner of a dialogic emphasis on the paradoxical theory of change that has also started to bloom in this past decade.

I was introduced to one style of Gestalt therapy in 1964 when Perls gave his annual training series at Metropolitan State Hospital in Norwalk, California. He was brought there by Arnold Beisser, now a faculty member of the Gestalt Therapy Institute of Los Angeles, then Director of Psychiatric Training at the hospital.

Perls was theatrical, outrageous, narcissistic. He both engaged and enraged people. He got a reaction from the psychiatric staff and residents in training, and also from psychotic patients that had not been reached by anyone else.

He thought of Gestalt therapy as a serious psychotherapy based on the theory expounded in Perls, Hefferline and Goodman (1951). He toured the country demonstrating Gestalt therapy. But, freed from the influence of the New York City Gestalt therapy group, his tendencies to show off, look for excitement, his suspiciousness about patients trying to make a fool of him, his theatrical background all rose to the fore. By the time he realized that he was inadvertently encouraging a style of Gestalt therapy that was more "turn on" than good therapy, it was too late to keep the popular picture of Gestalt therapy consistent with the basic theory. At the end, he did speak out against the turn-on attitude and the confusion of that with Gestalt therapy.

When I saw him, I was attracted to the possibilities in the philosophy he discussed (see the chapter "Why I Became a Gestalt

Therapist"). Personally, I didn't find Perls likable and had only a small admiration for him. But I found the possibilities intriguing.

When I worked with Jim Simkin I experienced something different, a very different style or tendency. I found him personally concerned, contactful, straight and direct. He emphasized an attitude of "no shoulds" and "there is enough room" that was pivotal in my growth (Simkin, 1974). He was an example of the Gestalt therapy emphasis on the therapist showing his or her concern by an active presence; he assertively confronted the present reality of the patient. He emphasized the existential themes of ownership of one's choices and behavior, responsibility for self-regulation, and experimenting to find out what was possible. Although his style was not dialogic by modern standards, and he was very suspicious of the concepts of empathy and inclusion, he was definitely not theatrical, cathartic or technique oriented.

Background II: Contrasting Revolutions (1950 and 1965) — Two Revolutions and Two Different Times

1947 to 1951: Rebellion Against Authoritarianism
Gestalt therapy was inaugurated in the era of the post World War II reaction against authoritarianism. It was formed by people with an aggressive attitude and a revolutionary ideology. They tried to create a whole social and political theory. The group was marked by personal, political and intellectual confrontation. No one was exempt from this, e.g., Perls was confronted and criticized for his disinclination to talk theory or enter into personal dialogue.

Since they were a revolutionary and politically aggressive group, rebelling against rigid social practices, it is not surprising that they also rebelled against the rigidity in psychoanalysis. They were connected with analysts such as Harry Stack Sullivan and Erich Fromm who were beginning to emphasize ego rather than id and social interaction rather than drive theory.

However the early Gestalt therapy group went further than the reforming psychoanalysts in that they altered the very basis of psychoanalysis when they emphasized reality contact over transference, active presence over blank screen, dialogue and phenomenological focusing over free association and interpretation, field theory over mechanistic theory and process theory over Newtonian and Aristotelian dichotomies.

1960s

In the 1960s a new model of Gestalt therapy spread throughout the world. The chief influences in this model were Fritz Perls, the Esalen Institute, and the 1960s political and social scene in the United States.

The 1960s, the era of "anything goes," was the era of the free school and of no organization. This was a rebellious movement, but a naive rebellion. It had a naive faith in uncultivated goodness and intelligence. It was anti intellectual and anti organization and anti structure.

Within the 1960s movement there was very little support for intellectual confrontation. The movement was rebellious and revolutionary, but without a post revolutionary model. It was even ignorant of its own roots.

In 1950 Gestalt therapy theory was in part a political theory of anti authoritarianism, a theory of political Anarchism. In 1965 Gestalt therapy was part of a larger movement that was anarchistic, i.e., anarchistic with a lower case a. It was a movement against organization but without a real political theory supporting Anarchism.

How Meaning is Derived

In Gestalt therapy theory meaning is the configuration of figure against a ground, the here and now figure of interest against a more general context or background.

The Gestalt therapists of 1950 knew the importance of the background when they treated a patient. Most had good clinical as well as philosophical backgrounds. They practiced and were treated in long term individual therapy, still sometimes even using the couch.

In the movement of the mid-1960s background was neglected, or even dismissed. For example, the developmental history of a patient was most often ignored. And many talked about as if knowing history was totally unnecessary.

10

In the 1980s we have learned to bring the here and now figure and the historical background into more of a synthesis. We have learned that it is important to be aware of the background. Therapy and theory have become more effective, but not as simple as before.

The Boom-Boom-Boom Style

The anti-theoretical attitude in the 1960s made possible the development of the boom-boom-boom style of therapy that many came to characterize as Gestalt therapy. In the mid to late 1960s Gestalt therapy developed this theatrical and highly catharsis oriented approach. It was arrogant, dramatic, simplistic, promising quick change. It contrasted with the early Gestalt therapy movement and was embedded in the anti-intellectual and naive rebellious attitude of the 1960s.

Many started equating Gestalt therapy with the bombastic pyrotechnics and abrasive confrontation of this style. Like Perls, this style of therapy got people's attention, it made things happen quickly. Therapists could get dramatic effects demonstrating it. Charismatic therapists using this style employed technique and encounter to move people, with a naive faith that this would result in long-term growth. (We will see later that we have subsequently learned better.)

Boom-boom-boom therapy replaced careful therapeutic exploration with gimmicks. This turn-on, quick change orientation was in marked contrast with the long term therapy of the early Gestalt therapists and even in contrast with the actual practice of skillful Gestalt therapists during the 1960s.

Patients in the quick action type of therapy frequently developed or enhanced counter-phobic resistance. Shy patients were encouraged to become expressive, even if they became brassy and bold. Without due regard for the person's overall personality and without respecting the person's resistance and the need to proceed through resistance by awareness and assimilation, the results were often unintegrated, inauthentic and inflexible.

In that era, many (critics and advocates alike) confused Gestalt therapy with encounter groups. While the theory of Gestalt therapy was phenomenological and emphasized good contact, many groups used pressure, confrontation and group tyranny in the name of "Gestalt therapy." While the careful Gestalt therapy approach was based on "no shoulds," these groups used group pressure and other programmatic efforts to bring patients into conformity with the group goals, e.g., expression of anger, or cooperativeness, or physical touching, etc. Of course, therapist and patient alike tended to perceive these new norms as more liberating than the old ones, without appreciating that introjects are introjects.

The "Is" Versus "Getting the Patient to Take the Next Step"

The mainline Gestalt therapy methodology centers on the paradoxical theory of change. This emphasizes being in contact with what is, with who one is, and allowing growth to develop naturally. The boom-boom-boom approach is a behavior-modification approach and emphasizes getting the patient to take the next step.

There is a difference between enhancement of self-support that enables the next step of growth and the behavior modification attitude of getting the patient there. In the Gestalt behavior modification mode resistance is broken down; in phenomenological Gestalt therapy the emphasis is on awareness work, i.e., contact with what is. This latter approach supports the patient growing and the next step emerging, rather than a next step being aimed at by the therapist.

The heart of Gestalt therapy is in the paradoxical theory of change. In that approach resistance is recognized and acknowledged. Resistance is named and understood. It is not understood as something undesirable, just understood. Awareness work in this model integrates the poles of impulses and resistance. But resistance is not broken down or jumped over. Self-support is enhanced so the patient may go through whatever next step fits for that person in their lifespace. But the therapist doesn't center on getting the patient to take the next step as conceptualized by the therapist.

Charismatic Leadership Style

In psychoanalysis the passive therapist interpreted to the passive patient. Gestalt therapy started with the active engagement of patient and therapist. Unfortunately, as the theatrical 1960s style was developed and practiced, it was frequently marked by the therapist leading by charisma rather than dialogic contact and phenomenological focusing.

The boom-boom-boom style was a natural medium for therapists who had a need to be charismatic. This style featured drama over substance, "peak experience" over growth. This met the narcissistic needs of the therapist rather than the therapeutic needs of the patient. For whose need were these dramatic techniques used? I think too often for the therapist's glorification.

Jim Simkin contrasted the guru and the therapist. The guru got those he worked with to love him, whereas the therapist loved those he worked with. He meant that the therapist made clear, direct, honest contact based on caring and respect for the autonomy, self-support, awareness capacity of the patient.

The early Gestalt therapists knew well the lessons of psychoanalysis, of the importance of the ongoing therapeutic relationship and of the importance of the phenomena of transference and countertransference. Their practice and theory accounted for these phenomena in an assimilated manner. However, in the 1960s and early 1970s this was sometimes omitted from the oversimplified characterization of the Gestalt therapy system. As we will discuss below, lately in the United States we have learned (or relearned) the importance of relationship and dialogue and of following the immediate experience of the patient.

The charismatic leadership style did not reap the benefit of the patient's wisdom or of interaction or of what emerges from dialogue. It was not bothered by modesty or by data. Very little attention was paid in this style to observational data that did not conform to the therapist's expectations. There has been no long-term data sought by those practicing this style, except perhaps anecdotal confirmation of the excellence of their work. What works with what kind of patients? What are the dangers? Fallout? In the mode of narcissistic grandiosity, to which we were all heir to some degree, we were blind. God, were we special!

There is some evidence emerging that therapy based on technique, charisma, and catharsis doesn't work as well as the charismatic advocates believed. Gestalt therapy did open the therapy world to new possibilities. But the theatrical version looked better than it was. People were injured in obvious and subtle ways.

Anything Goes

The environment of the 1960s, especially in Gestalt therapy, allowed these distortion to flourish. The avoidance of theory, and especially the avoidance of intellectual conflict, furthered the lack of clear thinking and went along with the "anything goes" attitude.

The horror stories abounded in the 1960s, and this was predictable. There was so much oversimplification and there was the naive faith that encouraged everyone to think they can just go out and do therapy. There were built-in excuses and rationalizations in this attitude. It was as if it was enough that the moment of therapy was dramatic, exciting, a "peak experience." Just as charismatic leaders didn't need to know history, they didn't think they needed to know the outcome of their interventions.

The theory of Gestalt therapy was sophisticated on the question of responsibility for one's own behavior. But the cliché level dogma oversimplified this and insisted that patients were responsible for their own lives, including their own therapy. And at this cliché level, the therapist was not held equally responsible for the outcome of the therapy. If the therapy didn't work, or if the workshop was too intensive for a patient, the rationalization was that the patient would simply go home and be responsible for finding whatever help was needed.

This was at the cliché level. Many spoke out on the subject of the therapist's responsibility, including Frederick Perls, Laura Perls, Walter Kempler, Jim Simkin and others.

One of my favorite horror stories: I remember Jim Simkin doing a weekend training workshop in Tucson, Arizona. One therapist with no previous training or experience in Gestalt therapy came to the workshop. He never worked during the workshop, and if memory serves correctly missed the last session on Sunday morning. On the next day, Monday morning, he declared himself to be a Gestalt therapist.

Many examples are less obvious than this. Many trained by taking workshops, without systematic supervision or theoretical understanding, practiced Gestalt therapy without knowing what they didn't know. The more aggressive of these were even contemptuous of those who took stands for more rigorous training, more rigorous theory, etc.

14

Some barely knew how to do something called Gestalt therapy, didn't know the theory, and with the passage of time considered themselves competent to train others in Gestalt therapy. Somehow practicing for a time, although without any special evidence of competence or understanding of the theory, qualified them (they thought) to do training and even start institutes.

Gestalt Therapy Literature

In the early 1950s there was only a sparse Gestalt therapy literature, but a great interest in theory production. There was *Gestalt Therapy, Ego, Hunger and Aggression*, the excellent 1948 article by Perls (Perls, 1948) and a few other minor articles. But the intellectual dialogue continued and they had a respect for theory. They were interested in good quality thought rather than oversimplified theory, commercialism, or any isms or introjects.

From 1950 to 1972 there were no advances in the Gestalt therapy literature. In 1969 when I wrote my first paper, a review of Gestalt therapy theory and practice, there were only a few unpublished introductory articles being informally circulated in addition to the pre-1951 literature, and a sparse oral tradition teaching Gestalt theory (e.g., the work of Isadore From).

In the 1960s the attitude toward theory changed. There was a loss of interest in theory, consistent with the antiintellectual attitude of the decade: "Lose Your Mind and Come to Your Senses." There was also a growing inability to do theory, i.e., more people in Gestalt therapy who not have the background, training or temperament to conduct good theoretical analysis or continue an intellectual dialogue.

That was most unfortunate. For while there was not a rich literature in Gestalt therapy, I found a rich literature in the diverse sources that flowed into Gestalt therapy, e.g., Martin Buber, Gestalt psychology, existentialism, phenomenology, Zen, etc.

The final deterioration of the era in regard to theory came with the clichés and posters. Perls and others contributed to this deterioration. *The Gestalt Prayer* posters were perhaps the worse of these. By the time Perls realized he was contributing to a bastardization of Gestalt therapy, the damage was done.

Background III: The 70s
Sobering Up And Thinking It Over

From "Turn-on" to "Tune In"

In the 1970s the humanistic psychology movement began to discover that catharsis was not enough, and there was a reaction against the turn-on attitude of the 60s. Many who had naively thought that Gestalt therapy was a simple therapy and reduced it to boom-boom-boom now discovered spirituality, finding a new interest in transpersonal concerns. And as they had distorted Gestalt therapy into a therapy that just confronted patients into externalizing their feelings, now they focused inward, using various forms of meditation, etc. Now one could hear "Gestalt therapists" talk of chakras, extrasensory perception, healing by massaging auras and the like.

But this approach to Gestalt therapy was not comprehensive, it was still Gestalt therapy, without a Gestalt therapy framework. Neither the theory nor the practice were thought through. They tuned in without any theoretical understanding of Gestalt therapy. Many left Gestalt therapy without understanding it and entered into new realms of practice and thought, still oversimplifying and without a comprehensive framework. For example, many borrowed from Buddhism, but oversimplified and distorted it as much as they had Gestalt therapy.

In the 1970s the spiritual emphasis was in personal salvation only. It was not synthesized with the fundamental Gestalt therapy theory, (I hope we are doing better now). In Gestalt therapy, of course, the self, awareness, spirituality are relational. Awareness and spirituality are not seen as emanating from going inward, but from dialogue in the individual/environment field.

In its adoption of a Protestant-like emphasis on the individual and his salvation, the tuning-in attitude treated the individual as isolated from the field with relationships added on. The idea of discovering wisdom by turning awareness inward toward oneself separates the individual and environment and separates awareness (internal) and contact. There are several ways in which this is a very serious distortion of Gestalt theory, including the loss of the vital Gestalt notion that everything and everyone is inherently relational. The Gestalt therapy notion of spirituality would be closer to Martin Buber's, in which there is no *I* apart from *I-you* or *I-it*, and in which man's dialogue with God depends on the dialogue of person-to-person and the person-to-person dialogue can exist only against the background of the dialogue between humanity and God.

This approach of the 70s deemphasized another important aspect of Gestalt theory: It had virtually no idea of social responsibility. It was essentially narcissistic and individualistic. This change in the theory had begun in the "I do my thing, you do your thing" attitude of the 60s. In the 70s it was being called spiritual.

And one could see it in the relationships in the community. One encountered the centered person who could say *I*, who had an energetic aura, who looked charismatic and spiritual, but who paid no attention to the needs of others, to the needs of the group. They would not do any work that was not personally exciting to themselves. You might want to chant with such a person, but you wouldn't want to share a kitchen with one.

Thinking It Over: Beyond Fritz

In the 70s many, Laura Perls being just one, spoke out to make clear that Perls' style was only one style of Gestalt therapy. It wasn't the only style Perls had used in his lifetime and certainly wasn't the only legitimate style of Gestalt therapy. And some were making clear that his cliché level theorizing was not representative of Gestalt theory. Some, especially Isadore From, were teaching theory according to the principles of Paul Goodman (as written in *Gestalt Therapy*).

Somehow the professional community never fully got that message. Why? One can only speculate. People like Laura and Isadore were not prolific in writing. They were also not as theatrical as Perls was. They spoke out later in time, after the theatrical demonstrations of Perls and his imitators had made an indelible impression on the professional and lay public. And they were not running with a great social tide as the boom-boom-boom Gestalt therapists were in the 60s.

It is one of those ironic twists of history that the better grounded and thought-through positions received less attention. On the other hand, their restatements, clarifications and improvements in Gestalt therapy theory did lead to the further development of Gestalt therapy in the 80s.

Literature in the 70s

From 1972 onward the dry spell in Gestalt therapy literature was relieved and more literature was produced. Much of it has been at the introductory level. While this was sometimes an improvement over the very difficult prose in *Gestalt Therapy*, the literature quickly became repetitive. And much of it did not even deal well with the basic theory of Gestalt therapy, presenting it inaccurately.

Not only was the basic theory not well treated, but there was very little attention drawn to the fit of philosophy, method and technique. There was a paucity of real clinical discussion. There was and remains a serious need for general clinical discussion at a sophisticated level and also good case material.

What is Gestalt Therapy?

Why the Question Arose

In the 1970s more attention was given to the question "What is Gestalt therapy?" The question arose because of the proliferation of styles of Gestalt therapy and the growth of the popularity of Gestalt therapy as a movement. Simultaneously, there was a continued decline in the understanding of the theory of Gestalt therapy by many of its practitioners.

And abuses of Gestalt therapy became more salient. As the therapy grew more popular, and its theory presentations and community organization did not grow, many people with poor professional background and training in Gestalt therapy practiced a lot of bad Gestalt therapy. And a lot of therapies flourished that were Gestalt therapy-like, including the infamous "Gestalt therapy and ... "

By the end of the decade many of the innovations of Gestalt therapy were assimilated into the general practice of psychotherapy. Many therapies were moving in the direction of Gestalt therapy. Psychoanalysis became more experiential with the advent of Object Relations and Self Psychology. Behavior Modification moved into cognitive behavior therapy, moving away from the remnants of the black box notion of behaviorism.

The old simple picture of psychoanalysis and Gestalt therapy that I described above became increasingly untenable. New therapies, such as structural family therapy, Ericsonian therapy, etc., presented very active alternatives to the old choice of psychoanalysis or behavior modification.

Gestalt Therapy Defined as Specified Techniques

The professional literature is filled with descriptions of Gestalt therapy in terms of specific practices or techniques. While to some of us this is the antithesis of Gestalt therapy, some Gestalt therapists have defined the therapy in terms of techniques. That became the dogma, and that is how they trained new Gestalt therapists. Gestalt therapy training in this model was training in techniques and therapy became the application of these techniques. Thus specific spontaneous techniques used by Perls became dogma: the empty chair, beating pillows, "put it into words." This definition of Gestalt therapy is even implicit in articles that recommend not using such techniques with particular patients, as if this were an exceptional modification of Gestalt therapy.

This approach to Gestalt therapy shows a lack of understanding of what psychotherapy is, and manifests a loss of depth and flexibility. In this approach being emotional replaces true understanding and catharsis replaces real creativity. Defined this way, Gestalt therapy is only another form of behavior modification, but one lacking the accountability and honesty of behavior modification.

This is Gestalt Therapy

A parallel reduction of Gestalt therapy occurs when it is defined in a way that equates it with a particular style. Whatever style is being used as a model then becomes "this is Gestalt therapy." Of course, Gestalt therapy is a general philosophy and methodology and is applied in a great variety of styles, with a great variety of patients, in a great variety of modalities and settings. Yet the literature is filled with articles in which the author confuses his or her own synthesis, conclusions, clinical experience with Gestalt therapy.

How could Gestalt therapy be reduced to one of its styles? I think this could happen because of the lack of clear thinking and theorizing. If you don't know the general theory, and your teachers don't present it, then when you see Gestalt therapy practiced in groups in a 1-1 style, it is natural to assume that Gestalt group therapy means doing 1-1 therapy in a group setting. When I did Gestalt therapy in a hospital setting with chronic and acute schizophrenics in the 1960s I didn't use empty chair techniques. It fit the context and the patients to do a lot of work in groups using psychodrama, seeing couples, ward level meetings, etc. This was Gestalt therapy in that setting as practiced by me. Without clear theory I could say "this is Gestalt therapy," or I could show how this is one of many ways of applying the Gestalt therapy attitude.

Whatever Gestalt Therapists Do

Many good people find the jurisdictional arguments about what Gestalt therapy is boring, useless and even dangerous. They want to focus on what people do rather than on belief, dogma or allegiance. These people want to take a stand that is not for a reduction of Gestalt therapy to techniques or dogma, but rather a flexible understanding of what Gestalt therapists do. I am in sympathy with this attitude. One way to accomplish this has been to define Gestalt therapy as "whatever Gestalt therapists do." I am not sympathetic with that definition.

Lamentably, there are quacks, incompetents, charlatans and misguided fools doing therapy, and some of them call themselves Gestalt therapists. Since we have no mechanism for certifying Gestalt therapists, and those who define Gestalt therapy as "what Gestalt therapists do" would not want such a mechanism, we would be saying that Gestalt therapy is what these incompetent therapists do, thus reducing Gestalt therapy to its least competent denominator.

Besides, that definition does beg the question. Good Gestalt therapy is doing what is needed according to a clear model. It is not a blank check to do whatever your impulse is and call it Gestalt therapy. Gestalt therapy is not permission to be flaky.

Gestalt therapy is freedom to do therapy with spontaneity, liveliness and creativity. But it also entails responsibility. Responsibility to know what you are doing. The responsibility to name what you are doing and share it so the effects can be studied. Responsibility to know what works, to care about best options. Responsibility to improve therapy.

All of this means more specificity about what Gestalt therapy is than "Gestalt therapy is whatever Gestalt therapists do."

80s: What Have We Learned?
Change of Times (United States)

General Social Change

The 1980s in the United States has been was a very different time and place than in the 60s and 70s. This has been the era of the Yuppie. A never ending search for easy answers has continued throughout this decade. In the 80s general narcissism has been rampant, often without the spiritual trappings of the 70s.

There has been a growing reliance on technology, with concomitant decline in reliance on person-to-person interaction. Families watch TV without talking to each other. There is a decline in the work ethic and a decline in commitment.

Change in Psychotherapy

Psychotherapy has become increasingly sophisticated.

On one hand, there has been an increased belief in and reliance on technological solutions. This is an important facet of the current context of Gestalt therapy: In this age of technology and therapy by procedure, there is an increased need for approaches that emphasize person-to-person values. I believe that while there is much more need than ever for the Gestalt therapy of dialogue and phenomenology, there is much less need for "Gestalt therapy wizardry," that is, procedure-oriented therapy. What is needed in the psychotherapy field are approaches based on the prime Gestalt therapy principles of dialogue, phenomenological awareness and field (process) theory.

Psychoanalysis

In general psychoanalysis has become less oriented to drive theory and closer to basic experience. It has become less rigid, more interpersonally oriented. It is a more formidable alternative

21

to Gestalt therapy than classical psychoanalysis ever was and closer to the true intent of Gestalt therapy than boom-boom-boom approaches that call themselves Gestalt therapy.

Yet psychoanalysis is not the answer. It still lacks much that Gestalt has to offer. It has neither a theory of consciousness nor a methodology that makes full use of the power of phenomenological focusing and experimentation. It does not have a theory that truly integrates the interpersonal and the intrapsychic. It does not have a concept of the role of the therapist that can truly encompass the variations that are clearly needed when working with disparate kinds of patients. For example, some psychoanalysts have varied from the psychoanalytic stance in working with borderline patients and moved closer to a dialogic approach. They have to find special justification for that which is routinely encompassed within Gestalt therapy practice and theory. And finally, they do not have a theory of the therapeutic relationship that is at all adequate for the changes they are making. They are moving closer to Gestalt therapy, and need something equivalent to the encompassing framework of Gestalt therapy.

Research

There has been a growth in the knowledge base of psychotherapy in general.

Research shows a generally positive effect of psychotherapy. This is less dramatic than it might be because the good effects are balanced the harm or ineffectiveness of some therapists (Bergin and Suinn, 1975; Lambert, 1989). Averaging good therapy and good therapists with harmful therapy practices and poor therapists results in a mild overall psychotherapy benefit rather than a stronger therapeutic effect.

Yalom illustrates this in his book on encounter groups (Lieberman, et al., 1973). One Gestalt therapist was very effective and got very beneficial results with no casualties. This group was effective in "emphasizing experiencing as a dominant value, a value that reflects a motif of many encounter ideologies, but which showed a significant increment only in this group "(Lieberman, et al., p. 126). Members of this group also said that the group environment offered more opportunities for open peer communication.

On the other hand, a second Gestalt therapist used a strong, aggressively stimulating, abrasive, charismatic leadership style and was in the statistical group that had the largest number of casualties (Lieberman et al., p. 126). Members of this group had a lowered sense of self-esteem, became less lenient toward themselves and saw the environment as less lenient. "Of interest is that despite the high stimulation and here-and-now orientation of [this group] ..., participants declined in their valuing of experiencing and became much more self-oriented and growth-oriented" (Lieberman, et al., p. 126).

Clearly how the therapist practices results in a wide range of results from very therapeutic to precipitating psychotic breakdown. And the label used by the therapist, e.g., Gestalt therapist, does not in itself indicate the quality of the therapy.

Of course, certain practices or attitudes work better with particular kinds of patients. There are different dangers with different kinds of patients. It has become clear how complex it is and what factors need to be considered in matching of therapist, approach and patient, e.g., the kind of patient, the kind of therapy, the personality and background match of the therapist and patient, etc. For example, working with awareness of the negative cognitive processes of depressives seems to be generally more effective than mainly emphasizing catharsis. This is as true for Gestalt therapy practice as it is for any other kind of therapy.

Increased Clinical Experience in Gestalt Therapy

Gestalt therapists have more experience as Gestalt therapists than they had decades ago. We have learned from experience doing Gestalt therapy and from our own personal therapies. I have been doing Gestalt therapy for over 24 years, 19 of which have been spent doing long-term psychotherapy in the same general location. My understanding and practice has been tempered by this experience, e.g., by seeing long term patterns unfold and how they are affected by different interventions, attitudes, matching of therapist and patient, and so forth. I have also learned by treating successive generations within the same family. So too I have learned from personal therapies over the years. And in this I am typical rather than unique.

23

One of the things we have learned is clearer recognition of patterns. We recognize more clearly different kinds of patients, and how to work with them and what the dangers are. For example, as talked about elsewhere in this volume, we have learned a lot about how to work with borderline and narcissistic character disorders, i.e., the therapeutic indications and dangers.

In general, the importance of empathy and attunement has grown in importance in my mind over the years as a result of these various factors.

Some Obvious General Lessons

There Are No Easy Answers

Clichés are often wrong (To say they are "always" wrong would be another inaccurate cliché). Searching for easy answers or being unwilling or unable to chew over statements before accepting them, using them or making them seems incompatible with individual growth or the growth of a therapy system.

We Need the Process of Producing Good Theory

Kurt Lewin said that "nothing is so practical as good theory." Without good theory, we are without good overall direction. Good theory is clear, consistent, and makes a difference.

Good theory is a process of theorizing, not permanent or thing-like and not dogma. It is a process of getting clear and consistent. It is a recognition of weaknesses and incomplete aspects. It is a process of constantly changing, testing, challenging, improving.

We need intellectual dialogue. Truth emerges from struggling with conflicting ideas, including honest and competent feedback. Ideas unexpressed or not critically commented on by others are unreliable. Professional ideas that are not presented in a forum in which colleagues struggle with it and destruct it are unreliable. We need to honor our colleagues by challenging their theoretical and clinical statements.

We need theory that is verifiable. Only in that way can we find out what is true or useful and works and what does not.

We Need Professional Knowledge From Outside Gestalt Therapy

We have learned that we need diagnosis and case description from other perspectives. We need technological information about treatment possibilities. (We will discuss this in relation to clinical work in the application section of this volume.)

And we need the stimulation of theoretical analysis and philosophical discussions from people of various perspectives. For example, over the last few years there have been a series of articles in *The Journal of Humanistic Psychology* over theoretical problems with self-actualization theory that could be important and stimulating for the development of Gestalt therapy theory and that might provide an opening for a contribution by Gestalt therapy (Geller, 1982, 1984; Ginsburg, 1984).

No Shortcuts in Training Good Therapists

There are no shortcuts in training good therapists. With shortcuts people often do not even know what they are missing. I remember many years ago teaching the first comprehensive theory course for the Gestalt Therapy Institute of Los Angeles. In that first course I had trainees with a variety of levels of experience. I was discussing how to apply Gestalt therapy in treating schizophrenics. One of the advanced trainees, a licensed psychotherapist who seemed to do acceptably well in the experiential training group, didn't even know what a schizophrenic was. She had taken too many shortcuts. How would she even know that she was seeing a schizophrenic, let alone how to treat one, if she didn't know what one is?

Need For Better Literature

We learned the hard way that demonstrations and popularity alone are an insufficient support base for a continued development of Gestalt therapy. I believe that maintaining Gestalt therapy and helping it prosper require a good literature and dialogue within the Gestalt therapy community, as well as more good material to non-Gestalt therapy audiences.

Where that has not developed, Gestalt therapy has been in trouble after a peak of popularity. When the wave of popularity recedes, when new technologies and ideas are presented, Gestalt therapy will fade to the degree that it doesn't have a good support

theory, dialogue and presentations to the general
nmunity.

..... with Our Own Root Theory

...c basic theory is still best laid out in Perls, Hefferline and
Goodman. This needs to be understood and form the basis of
future work. We don't need to agree with everything in *Gestalt
Therapy*, but a theoretical dialogue needs to take that analysis into
account in a competent way. We need to use it more in training,
theory building and dialogue. Then we need to go beyond it.

When we discuss concepts (the part) we need to discuss the
relationship of the concept or part to the whole, and that involves
the analysis of *Gestalt Therapy*.

The Paradoxical Theory of Change

What Is the Paradoxical Theory of Change?

The more you try to be who you are not, the more you stay the
same. Growth, including assimilation of love and help from others,
requires self-support. Trying to be who one is not is not
self-supporting.

A major aspect of self-support is identification with one's state.
Identification with your state means knowing your state, i.e., your
actual experience, behavior, situation. Since one's state changes
over time, identification with one's state includes identifying with
the flow of states, one into another, that is, having faith in movement and change.

Self-support must include both self-knowing and self-accepting.
One can't adequately support oneself without knowing one's self
— one's needs, capabilities, environment, duties, etc. Knowing
about oneself and not owning that it is chosen and rejecting
oneself is a form of self-deceit. Sartre discusses this as "bad faith,"
in which one confesses and in the act of making such a confession
disidentifies with that which has been confessed. For example, I do
a cowardly act, and confess to being a coward. But in the act of
confessing to being a coward, I deceive myself into a subtle belief
that I who confess am above being cowardly. It is as if the cowardly

behavior wasn't chosen, but was somehow visited upon the confessing person.

When a therapist "leads" or "heals" a patient, the therapist is actually pushing or pressuring the patient to be different. And the more the patient is aimed toward a goal, the more he or she will stay fundamentally the same. Pushing or aiming leads to resistance to the pushing. Then the patient not only has his or her original resistance to his or her own organismic functioning, but now also acquires a resistance to the intrusion of the therapist. This latter resistance is usually healthy, although it also prevents working through the original stuckness that necessitated therapy.

There is another reason for the fact that the therapist's pushing does not result in real movement. One of the ways of not coming into contact with the intrusion of the pushy therapist is to inject. The patient may outwardly conform or rebel, but in either case is likely to swallow whole that which the therapist is advocating: "If I were a competent person, I would want to do what the therapist is suggesting."

If the person changes in conformity with the push of the therapist, it will not be on the basis of autonomy and self-support. And the person will not have acquired the tools of self-support and autonomy.

Most of all, a therapist pushing, leading or aiming a patient gives the message: You are not enough as you are. This is a message that induces shame and/or guilt. In short, the therapist who pushes does not benefit the patient's self-support.

Such a therapist may be acting out of "good intentions." This does not ameliorate the situation. I believe that pushing patients generally meets therapists' needs, not patients'. Seeing rapid changes may be gratifying and exciting, but does it further the growth of the patient? I doubt if the transference and idealization produced are as enhancing to the patient as they are to the therapist. I think the patient may be the last to know that this is true. Pushing may lead to the discovery of something, but generally with no tools to do it without the therapist. At best it may give the patient the ability to keep doing whatever the therapist pushed the patient into. This has a very limited generalizability.

There is also the reverse of the paradox: the more one tries to stay the same, the more the person changes in relation to the changing environment. How do you deal with stuck patients, patients who try to stay the same and get worse in relation to the environment, if we don't push?

The method to deal with stuck patients without pushing and aiming is: dialogue, awareness and experimentation. This requires patience. It requires that the therapist have the attitude that there is "enough room" for the patient in the world the way the patient is, and it requires faith in organismic growth.

It is my experience that if this doesn't work, pushing won't either, except perhaps in the very short run. Pushing is most dangerous with patients who don't change easily. In the unusual case in which it does work, it makes dramatic reports to one's colleagues. It is more usual that pushing leads to relationship impasses. This almost always involves the therapist not taking responsibility for his/her part in the interaction. If the therapist is frustrated, the responsibility for this is the therapist's. The therapist is responsible for finding or creating a better approach. Therapists also need to know the limits of the state of the art. And mostly, the therapist needs to be able to monitor and work through his or her own countertransference.

Respecting the Patient

My picture of Gestalt therapy is one based on a horizontal relationship. As much as possible, the therapist treats the patient as an equal (albeit with a difference in roles necessitated by the therapeutic contract).

This is equally true when dealing with a patient that the therapist would call resisting. The patient's resistance is unhealthy only when it is not in awareness and part of the organism's creative adjustment. Resisting the therapist or Gestalt therapy may be a healthy reaction. Even when the patient resists his or her own awareness, it may be healthy. Our attitude in Gestalt therapy is to bring resistance into awareness so that the self-regulation of the patient is marked by better contact and awareness. An integrated and growthful completion of the psychological situation requires integration and not annihilation of the resistance.

The patient's defenses need respect from the therapist, not attack or coddling. It is helpful to know and name the defenses or avoidances, to understand and own them. Neither an attempt to eliminate the defenses nor catering to them are likely to result in improvement for that patient. The goal is to have the patient understand the resistances and take charge of them with full awareness. And this has to be at the patient's pace.

The patient knows best. Some Gestalt therapists attribute to the patient full responsibility, full power, to make themselves sick or well, but then take on themselves the decision to push the patient past their defenses. It seems to me that if patients are so capable that they are responsible for themselves (their lives, their pathology, their therapy), then their resistances need to be respected also as something they choose because it meets an important need.

Historically Gestalt therapy has been associated with rebellion against authority and promoting nonconformity. Do we not become authoritarian ourselves when we set ourselves out as the person to decide when the defenses should be battered down?

I don't think the answer is only in going easy with patients. The awareness work needs to be done, and the therapist who decides to be "supporting" and not do awareness work is also not respecting the patient and the patient's choice. The answer is in dialogue and clarity about diagnosis (both of which will be discussed later).

Respecting the patient includes noting the level of self-support that the patient is capable of. It includes knowing what the patient wants from the therapy work, the therapy sophistication of the patient, the sanity, cohesion of identity, intelligence, etc.

In groups this becomes more complicated. For the therapist has the responsibility of observing, acknowledging, respecting the needs of all individuals and the group as a whole. The individual who needs to move slowly may elicit pushing from the rest of a frustrated group. Group pushing can be even worse than therapist pushing. In this situation the group needs to learn to face frustration without being disrespectful of boundaries, differences and autonomy.

The group is not safe if it is dominated by group hostile aggression or even insistence on imposing the needs of the majority on the minority. On the other hand, the group is not safe if negative feelings and thoughts are not expressed. The therapist is responsible for defining safety needs and balance.

The Choice

The paradoxical theory of change conflicts with catharsis as a prime intervention. It conflicts with breaking down defenses and trying to annihilate resistance. It conflicts with using techniques or the personality of the therapist to directly move patients toward a preconceived outcome ("health").

The paradoxical theory also clashes with the idea of simplistic training of therapists. Good therapy according to the paradoxical theory of change requires the therapist to have a good theoretical understanding, good personal centering and good clinical understanding.

The further development of Gestalt therapy in the United States has moved "beyond charisma." Experience has taught us something of what is essential in the multiple-focused Gestalt therapy theory, i.e., a dialogic relationship and awareness based on respect for the patient's personal experience and experiential style. This requires a good knowledge of clinical patterns and necessities.

What is not essential, and in fact antithetical to good training and therapy, is the star system of trainers and therapists whereby charisma dominates. The newer approach requires hard work rather than charisma. Psychological health and maximizing human growth, like genius, is 90% perspiration and 10% inspiration.

Relationship: Engagement and Emergence

We have learned to replace Gestalt therapy based on charisma, theatrics and catharsis with an emphasis on the dialogic engagement of the patient and therapist and of patients with other patients in groups and to trust that growth emerges from such engagement.

The Social Dimension:
Relationship and Therapeutic Effectiveness

There has been a general increase in the emphasis on relationship in psychology. This is also true in Gestalt therapy and is part of a general growth in appreciation in Gestalt therapy of the social dimension.

Research on factors in therapeutic success consistently point to the importance of the relationship. In psychoanalysis there is an increased emphasis on relationship, unfortunately often using terminology that still confuses contact with transference. In Gestalt therapy there is an increasing emphasis on the therapeutic relationship and in Gestalt therapy groups an increasing relationship emphasis.

Another aspect of the amplified appreciation of the social dimension in general and on relationship in particular is an increase in emphasis on families and organizations in Gestalt therapy. Although working with family and organizational groups is not new in Gestalt therapy, it is being done more often, written and talked about more often, and discussed and practiced with more sophistication than ever before.

Part of the further development of Gestalt therapy has been an increased appreciation of Buber's "healing through meeting." Healing is a restoring of wholeness. And it was Buber's belief that only through a certain kind of person-to-person engagement could healing take place.

Full engagement takes place here and now. In the 1960s some unfortunately interpreted here and now in an exclusionary, narrow way. Now we are more inclined to share more fully in the life story of patients and to share our life story as appropriate to the therapy. Erving Polster's book *Every Person's Life is Worth a Novel* is an example of this emphasis (Polster, 1987).

But there have also been contrary trends in psychology and psychiatry, especially treatment by procedure. There has been a growth of a technological perspective. Therapy in general has moved toward an increased technical or technique-oriented approach, toward looking for the quickest route. What techniques work with depressive patients? Or borderlines? Cookbooks of therapy, often termed manuals, are more often used in research on psychotherapy.

It is interesting to me that, even with such rigorous attempts to standardize the procedures, the personality of the individual therapist and the quality of therapeutic relationship still cause very different outcomes for different therapists and for different thera-pist-patient matches (Lambert, 1989).

Historically Gestalt therapy has been in the camp of humanism and posed an alternative to behaviorism and similar control and technique-oriented therapies. Our emphasis was on working with people, not controlling or reconditioning them. But there was always some tension between our humanism on the one hand and our technology and propensity for charismatic leadership on the other. Many have raised the question of whether using empty chairs, beating pillows, clinical use of frustration and other such devices are really humanistic. More recently the question is framed in terms of whether it is consistent with a dialogic approach.

To a great extent we have learned to move beyond the tech-nique orientation. And that is a great part of my message in this paper. We have learned about the importance of dialogue and relationship, the paradoxical theory of change and allowing change to emerge rather than being aimed for, and the unimpor-tance of particular techniques. Yet in spite of this, in many places people are still trained primarily in techniques and using pressure and frustration to get people to change. I think this is a distortion of Gestalt therapy. This never was good Gestalt therapy theory, and is certainly not presently.

In this age of movement toward quick technological fixes, the real Gestalt therapy of humanism, dialogue — of the paradoxical theory of change — is needed more than ever. In family therapy there are some signs of dissatisfaction with the more manipulative family approaches and a receptivity to engagement-oriented approaches which emphasize awareness and dialogue.

For me the essence of Gestalt therapy is the integration of person-to-person engagement with general clinical and technical competence. And this is true regardless of the modality or type of patient.

Dialogic Engagement — Reality Is Relating

The dialogic view of reality is that all reality is relating. Living is meeting. Awareness is relational — it is orientation at the boundary between the person and the rest of the organismic environment field. Contact is also obviously relational: it is what happens between person and environment. Our sense of our self is relational (made most clear in *Gestalt Therapy*). I believe, with Buber, that spirituality is also relational.

We grow by what happens between people, not by looking inward. Inner and outer are only "secondary elaborations" or differentiations in the organism/environment field.

In *Gestalt Therapy*, Perls, Hefferline and Goodman say that contact is the primary reality. The person (self) is defined in terms of the interrelations between the person and the rest of the field:

2. Self is the System of Present Contacts and the Agent of Growth.

> We have seen that in any biological or socio-psychological investigation, the concrete subject-matter is always an organism/environment field. There is *no* function of any animal that is definable except as a function of such a field....

> The complex system of contacts necessary for adjustment in the difficult field, we call `self.' Self may be regarded as at the boundary of the organism, but the boundary is not itself isolated from the environment; it contacts the environment; it belongs to both, environment and organism. (p. 373)

Actualization of the self in the Gestalt therapy sense of the actual here and now relation between person and other is carefully contrasted with trying to actualize a self-image. Images, including images of oneself, are products or representations and not the actual relational event of existing in the human world. One of the things that distinguishes Gestalt therapy from object relations, and other psychoanalytic approaches (new and old), is that Gestalt therapy emphasizes actual relating rather than self-other images. The motto is: contact the actual. Contact the actual other person and also what is really true for you as a person.

There is only the I of the I-it and the I-thou. Thou, what happens at the true meeting of persons as persons. In such meetings each person is treated as a separate other; each person is treated as an end in him or herself. A person in dialogue fully knows and confirms that the other is a separate and equally special consciousness.

In the I-it relationships there is a distancing and thickening of the boundary. In the I-it something is aimed for, rather than being allowed to emerge from the engagement of persons as persons. In the I-it mode there is calculation, controlling, treating people as a means to an end. Planning, arguing, manipulating people, are all in the I-it mode. The therapist who uses his or her personality to move the patient into health operates in the I-it mode.

One cannot exist without the I-it. It is a healthy and organismically necessary mode. But there is an I-it in which the person swings between I-it and I-thou. It is an I-it in the service of the I-Thou. In previous papers I sometimes referred to this as the "I-thou relation," as opposed to the "I-thou moment." I have switched to terminology I think less confusing: reserving the I-thou terms for the peak moment of the coming together that Buber describes so poetically in *I and Thou*, and using the term dialogic for the broader relating that is a swinging between the I-it and the I-thou (Hycner, 1985; Jacobs, 1989).

Characteristics of Dialogue

In therapy dialogue means a relationship based on engagement and emergence rather than one of getting the patient somewhere or withholding presence or gratification in the service of furthering the transference neurosis.

Presence

Buber describes the existential encounter with phrases such as "living over against" and "struggle with" and "wrestle" with. This means neither being nice nor being brutally honest. It means meeting and holding your ground in a way that is contactful and practices inclusion and confirmation (see next subsection). It means bringing oneself to the boundary with the other person but not marching through the boundary or controlling the other person, i.e., not controlling what is on the other side of the boundary.

Buber refers to "genuine and unreserved communication" as a characteristic of dialogic presence. Fully present people share meaning with each other. For the therapist it means sharing meaning with the patient. Full meaning includes despair, love, spirituality, anger, joy, humor, sensuality. In the dialogic relationship the therapist is present as a person, and does not keep himself or herself in reserve as in the analytic stance nor function primarily as a technician.

One needs to be clear that unreserved communication refers to the therapist surrendering him or herself to the dialogue, and does *not* mean without discrimination. It refers to a lively involvement in which the therapist appropriately and regularly shows his or her own feelings, experiences, etc. The nature of the other person and the situation is an organic part of the dialogic contact with another. When one addresses a narcissistically vulnerable person dialogically, one does not address that person as one would address one who is not susceptible in that way.

There has been a growing realization in Gestalt therapy in the United States that it is more theoretically consistent and often more effective to tell patients how you are being affected rather than acting on the feeling by using frustration techniques and other gimmicks that may actively deal with the clinical situation and show a presence of some sort by the therapist, but that avoid dialogue. Later in this book we will discuss factors involved in making the discrimination of when and how to do this (and when not to) with different kinds of patients, e.g., with narcissistic personality disorders.

Confirmation and Inclusion
  People become unique selves by the confirmation of other people.
  Confirm: "made present" by other people. Someone is confirmed when another person "imagines the real," that is, when the person puts himself/herself in the shoes of the other and imagines, lives through, what the other person experiences.

What is confirmed in this process is the existence of the other person as a separate existing human being with an independent soul just like the perceiver's. At the most basic level it is confirming the existence of the other as a separate person. The therapist confirms that the patient exists, that the patient has an effect and is as worthwhile as any other person. The patient is not invisible, nor just an object of the other's wishes or images.

Some people have described looking into the eyes of a guru and seeing the infinite; people say that when they looked into

Buber's eyes they saw themselves being met. That is what patients need from their therapist. The master therapist responds to the unique.

Confirmation is acceptance plus. It certainly includes the message of acceptance, "there is enough room." Gestalt therapy in theory and good practice has an intrinsic respect for diversity and differences. It is one of the cornerstones of the Gestalt therapy attitude.

Confirmation also includes confirming what you are called to become. Although there can be no inclusion and confirmation without acceptance, with inclusion and confirmation there is also the affirmation of potential. Accepting people as they are does not mean that hope of growth is given up. On the contrary, it is precisely this potential for growth into what one can truly be that is the heart of confirmation.

Inclusion is the Highest Form of Confirmation.

Inclusion is feeling into the other's view while maintaining the sense of yourself. The person practicing inclusion sees the world for a moment as fully as possible through the other's eyes. And it is not confluent, since the person practicing inclusion simultaneously maintains a sense of themselves as a separate person. It is the highest form of polar awareness of self and other.

Inclusion is sometimes confused with identification and empathy. Identification is different in that a person senses an identity of self and other; it is a loss of the sense of differentness. Inclusion includes moving further into the pole of feeling the other's viewpoint than is sometimes meant by the term empathy, while simultaneously keeping a sharper awareness of one's separate existence than is sometimes implied in the term empathy. Inclusion, like the Thou that sometimes emerges when two persons are contactful in a dialogic manner, requires grace. Inclusion may fully develop when one has the support and extends oneself into contact with the other.

Inclusion in Therapy

Many Gestalt therapists have criticized empathy because of the danger of confluence, i.e., the danger of confusing self and other by believing one can actually experience exactly what the other person experiences. When I first showed a draft of an earlier paper in which I discuss inclusion in Gestalt therapy, Jim Simkin asked: "Is this your way of sneaking empathy into Gestalt therapy?" But inclusion requires awareness of separateness while one is swinging into the pole of experiencing as fully as one can the viewpoint of the other.

The practice of inclusion and a phenomenological perspective fit together very nicely. In phenomenology everything is acknowledged to be viewed from some person's time space awareness perspective. From a strictly phenomenological viewpoint every person's phenomenology is equally real. When doing therapy in a phenomenological frame, careful attention is paid to the patient's actual experience (and of course, the therapist's also) and process. Special focus is paid to what is happening between therapist and patient from the patient's perspective.

While there is much more of a sense of mutuality in a dialogic therapy than in an analytic or behavioral therapy, inclusion is not mutual. There is a limit to how mutual inclusion is in therapy. Most patients are not able to practice inclusion at the beginning of therapy. They have to develop in therapy the capacity to be in the kind of contact that is involved in practicing inclusion.

Buber claims that when the patient can practice inclusion, therapy is over. I disagree most emphatically with this. Patients do develop the capacity for inclusion, and some patients start off with that ability already developed.

However, if in a therapy inclusion is regularly practiced mutually, it is no longer therapy. The task of therapy, the structure and function of it, require that most of the time the inclusion be one way. The contract and the task is to focus on the experience of the patient for the patient's growth.

For the patient who can already practice inclusion, the therapeutic relationship can serve as a forum in which he or she can be in a relationship in which they don't have to practice inclusion unless it suits their therapeutic needs. In this context they can take care of themselves and be attended to by the therapist and not take care of the therapist. Moreover, no matter how able the patient may be in practicing inclusion, the person cannot fully view himself/herself as another person (the therapist) can view them, and this is often very important in the growth of the patient who can practice inclusion. This is often the case when therapists enter therapy.

Dialogue, Phenomenology and Psychoanalytic Advances

Some brands of psychoanalysis have moved closer to the actual experience of patients. This is a vast improvement over classical psychoanalysis and is certainly more phenomenological. It is often an improvement over the theatrical Gestalt therapy of the 1960s. As a result many who reduced Gestalt therapy in their own minds to that particular style of Gestalt therapy have moved into one of the newer psychoanalytic modes, e.g., self psychology.

But there is a limit to the phenomenological focus of even the most modern psychoanalytic therapies. They still come from the heritage of free association and interpretation, and don't expand the phenomenological emphasis to include phenomenological focusing training or experimentation. Experimental phenomenology is not yet included in the expanded psychoanalytic therapies.

There is also a limit to the amount of therapist self-disclosure. This is something that is only sometimes done, with special rationale and apologies. If the therapy of the particular patient absolutely requires it, it may be justified. But the true power of a dialogic therapy is still not appreciated and the theory and training of the analyst doesn't provide for optimal operation within a dialogic context.

It has been said that when two people sing, there is a dialogue. In Gestalt therapy we can sing with the patient. We do not have the limitations on contact, presence and creativity that is present in most psychotherapies. In this dialogue we can sing, dance, talk, emote, draw, argue. We work with and struggle with the patient.

There is also a different use of the concept of here and now in Gestalt therapy and in psychoanalytic therapies. This is still true even with the expanded and liberalized view of the here and now focus in Gestalt therapy that we discussed earlier. The here and now is entered into in psychoanalytic psychotherapy and psychoanalysis via the transference concept. However, in psychoanalysis the data of the analysis of the transference is used primarily to explicate the past rather than furthering the dialogue and experimental phenomenology of the present relationship with the patient.

One cannot do good therapy without dealing competently with the transference phenomena. One cannot do good therapy and ignore developmental issues either. However, in Gestalt therapy we do deal with both of these. Of course we do so using the dialogic and phenomenological perspectives we have been discussing and that will be discussed further throughout this book.

Dialogue and Aiming

Dialogue cannot be aimed for. Dialogue emerges from between contacting persons.

Dialogue Emerges from Between

Dialogue is what emerges when you and I come together in an authentically contactful manner. Dialogue is not you plus I, but rather emergent from the interaction. Dialogue is something that may happen when both parties make themselves present. Dialogue can happen only if the outcome is not controlled or determined by either party.

"Trying" makes the interaction not dialogic. Trying, in the sense of aiming at an outcome and finding means to reach that outcome, is a manipulation. Of course, manipulation is not a bad thing. Buber made clear that I-it was absolutely necessary for existence. In *Gestalt Therapy* manipulation is used as the word describing the motor behavior aspect of the sensorimotor activity of organisms. Clearly this can be healthy and important and it is important that each person can and does do that as needed.

But aiming is not dialogic.

Sometimes one hears of people talking of using dialogue in order to grow. This is another example of manipulating, of aiming. It uses the other person and is an example of I-it. It is using the other person in order to be oneself. The dialogic attitude is the converse: being oneself in order to meet otherness.

Trying to get a patient someplace is an I-it interaction. When Gestalt therapy uses techniques to move a patient somewhere, it becomes a form of behavior modification rather than a dialogic therapy. This is true even if the therapist is trying in good conscience and with clearly healing motivation to aim the patient to "health."

Real Contact Isn't "Made," It "Happens"

Each party can bring their will to the boundary, to the meeting — but only that far. Using will to control is not dialogic contact with otherness, it is controlling otherness. Contact to assimilate the other person to be in fact confluent with one's wants or images can be part of organismic self-regulation, but it is not dialogic contact. In organismic self-regulation that is dialogic the other person is contacted and remains an independent person, although aspects of that independent person, that otherness, is assimilated into oneself. For example, a person may have a style I don't like. I can accept that person with that style. I may learn from some aspect of how that person is and in that sense assimilate something of him or her into myself. But that is very different than manipulating to get that other person to be how I want him or her to be.

Dialogic contact starts with bringing one's will to the boundary, and the rest requires response from the other person and grace. You prepare, use your will. Then it either happens or not.

This requires faith or trust in what will happen. It requires trust in existence and a faith that the ground will support you and the other person. It requires faith that there are resources not only within the control of the person, but in the rest of the organismic/environmental field.

Paradox: You Cannot Be Yourself by Aiming at Yourself

Each person is unique, but only with human engagement is the unique self confirmed, maintained and developed. It is only in the contact of the I-Thou encounter that the uniqueness of each person develops. Only by knowing how we are with other people and how they are with us do we truly become ourselves and know ourselves.

When a person looks inward, introspects, retroflects, etc., they are not engaging with otherness. This is pointing at the self. In real encounter, the pointing is to the meeting with otherness, the meeting of me and not me.

That is why I do not consider Gestalt therapy a "Self" psychology. In self psychology there is an emphasis on pointing to the self and in dialogic therapy there is an emphasis on engagement and emergence.

Becoming yourself ("I") happens by entering into relationship. By presenting yourself as you are, other people can treat you as Thou. By treating another person as a Thou, you become more fully yourself.

2

WHY I BECAME A GESTALT THERAPIST: GOODBYE TO JIM SIMKIN

Dear Jim,

I started writing this letter and article for your Festschrift. I am finishing it as a posthumous goodbye.

My life has radically changed as a result of my interaction with you. It has been 19 years since I first worked with you and Fritz at Esalen. Since that time my life has grown richer and I have been more alive, connected with people, loving and productive than I had ever dreamed of. I love and appreciate you.

In reading the manuscripts submitted for your Festschrift I notice how many people talk of the dramatic encounter with you. Simkin the Stalwart, Simkin who follows his own drummer no matter what, Simkin the unmoveable rock, Simkin the insightful who leaps to the core of the center of the patient's character structure. Although I do remember incidents with that dramatic character, I most appreciate and love you for a more continuous, mundane attitude that weaved through your work moment by moment. What I appreciate you for most is not your unique form of dramatic abrasiveness, but rather I consider your contribution more vital and ultimately dramatic than the dramatic stories. I want to explicate and acknowledge this quality of relating, it is the reason why I became a Gestalt therapist and why I continue to be one.

I first found out about Gestalt therapy through training sessions Fritz had at Metropolitan State Hospital in 1964-1965. Although I was intrigued by the intensity of his contact, by his talk about Far Eastern thought (with a substantial amount of inaccuracy), his ability to create dramatic reactions in my colleagues, I didn't feel personally touched nor particularly attracted to be a Gestalt therapist. I merely wandered into my next experience with Gestalt therapy, the advanced group at Esalen. It was there I met you and through my contact with you that I felt deeply touched as a person and attracted to learn Gestalt therapy.

With you I got my first taste of what was possible by going from impasse to life beyond the impasse. When you invited me to be your Psychological Assistant I first realized what top-notch psychotherapy and psychotherapy training is. Much later I realized the potential in Gestalt therapy that went beyond any one style, including yours. Much later I learned how to apply what I learned from you in my own style, some by applying more rigorously what I learned from you, some by deviating from what I learned from you.

But I always look back on my work with you as the turning point, and I feel grateful, loving, warm, appreciative.

In this article I have tried to describe the essence of what I learned from you and why I became a Gestalt therapist, for they are the same thing.

Goodbye, Jim. I appreciate what you have done for me and I love you. I will miss you.

Love,
Gary
1984

When I was first exposed to Gestalt therapy I had been through a psychoanalytic psychotherapy, social work school, and was working as a psychotherapist without ever understanding what contact, experience, or awareness was. From Jim Simkin I learned what immediate, personal experience was and how essential and valuable it is. Whatever else Jim did, he always clarified my experience, and I always knew that Jim was centered in his own experience in reaction to me. He often didn't share what his experience was, but he knew and he insisted that I know my own experience. Even when he did not like a trait of mine, he honored my experience — he insisted on us both being explicit about who I was and accepting what was. "Is" replaced "should."

From Jim I learned how to know what I experienced, and the importance of knowing what else was possible. I learned the importance of clarity and responsibility about choices I actually had made and choices I have now. All the rest followed from this honest awareness of is, choice and responsibility. His observations and experiments usually left me with a fuller understanding of my own experience, and an increased discrimination of my real, immediate experience from static old learning I carried around as if it were my current experience. Jim wanted to make it as likely as possible for the patient to make his or her own discoveries (rather than be taught), to develop his or her own style (rather than be a copy of Jim), and to go beyond Jim if the potential was present.

Jim worked *with* me. When Jim was working each person's awareness and contact between therapist and patient never took a back seat to theory or anything else. He never cheated me from discovering and learning for myself by being too helpful or by his needing to teach. He suggested experiments rather than "talk-about" or behavior modification exercises. I learned how to expand by experimenting and noticing my experience.

Jim trusted the process of the awareness continuum and organismic self regulation. I learned to stay with — to continue being aware of an experience, to know how not to interrupt and avoid. Awareness of process and natural transformation replaced obsessing, reforming, trying.

When I worked with Fritz I found myself confused. Fritz confronted me with an experiment that supported him in not reinforcing my behavior of confusing myself, but left me more confused and trying. I did not feel contacted, understood, accepted or facilitated. For me it was different with Jim. When I worked with Jim and I was confused he asked me to be my confusion. I felt like I was in a fog. "Be the fog." I described the color, sensations, consistency of me as fog. "Stay with it." I really became amorphous like fog, grey like fog, moist like fog. Then I started to change, without trying. The fog became warm, I became steam. I ended up feeling alive, my color improved, I did not feel confused. By staying with my experience (awareness, feelings, sensations) without judging and avoiding, I grew and transformed into a me that embodied more of my potential for fullness. I learned it was possible to stay with my own process — I could choose to support myself.

I had believed in a pluralistic society and in self-determination. I found in social work some philosophy consistent with this, but not an intensive and effective psychotherapy methodology. From Jim and Gestalt therapy I found that. Jim said that for him doing therapy was a way of using his excess love. I regard Gestalt therapy as the therapeutic and personal equivalent to the pluralistic attitude.

I learned that it was all right to have the experience that I did have. No one had ever told me that it was okay to have my own experience, to be excited, angry, impatient, turned on, sad, questioning, etc. It was also all right for Jim to have his experience in response. Contact is appreciation of differences. I remember the workshop in Arizona in which Jim had me tell everyone in the group that "there was enough room for me and Jim."

I had never thought of accepting myself. I had only known self-rejection. I also learned to accept other people and their experience while maintaining my own experience. Before I had cared about people, but this was interfered with by my judging them and me. Instead of caring and accepting I had cared and self-righteously sought one truth instead of appreciating differences. In Gestalt therapy I learned a philosophy of "no shoulds." What is, is! I learned from Jim that I do not need to be right, best, perfect, have *the* answer — I learned I can center on what is.

Jim always considered each person as separate and equally having the right to be as they are, to have their own experience. He avoided manipulations that pulled one person into confluence with another. Jim reacted strongly (sometimes too much so) to any threat of confluence/loss of ego boundaries.

With hindsight I realize that often I would have learned more if Jim had expressed verbally, explicitly and directly who he was, especially his feelings and how I affected him. If I asked he would usually tell me. Often his face showed disapproval. Then I wasn't aware enough to ask, and he did not share spontaneously his experience or take responsibility for finding out what effect he had on me. Similarly, sometimes he left me with a dramatic statement, suggestion, observation that I remembered for years, often without knowing that I was somewhat bewildered and curious about what experience of Jim's led to his intervention. I would subliminally ask myself: what in the world did Jim have in mind?

Jim didn't follow the pied piper of popularity, but rather followed an inner drummer. I learned a lot about honesty and courage in using aggression for self definition, for defining my own boundary, for taking a stand. Before I met Jim I had thought of myself as honest and courageous on issues of ethics and morals. From Jim I learned that often I was self-righteous rather than clear and firm; from Jim I learned that I often became obsessive and indecisive rather than firmly standing up for what I believed in. When I first taught and supervised graduate students in the Psychology Department at UCLA, I supervised a graduate student who misused Gestalt therapy to control, browbeat and recondition patients. I waffled because I didn't want to injure the student. Jim: "It is because of schmucks like you that we have so many poor therapists in the field." Not gentle, but honest. I had to face my spiritual dilemma (not for the last time).

I learned to honor my own aggression. I remember learning that when I wrote I picked my scalp instead of chewing on the intellectual material in front of me. He helped me discover that I could direct my aggression outward and that might be productive and acceptable, even necessary.

I remember Jim's suggestion that had me going around the group in Oklahoma saying "I won't .... " That day I learned that I had strong "I won'ts" and went on to experiment and found out how powerful I was and could feel when I knew my won'ts (experience) and expressed them explicitly (contact).

Jim was not very good with theory. But he did know the difference between my theory building and my obsessing. Sometimes he responded honestly to the former, although often without sophistication; he did not collude with my obsessing. There was a lesson here: he could encourage me to go beyond him. He was poor in theoretical ability and intolerant of verbosity, but he encouraged my theoretical work anyway.

After I had finished my work with Jim I explored on my own and moved beyond Jim's trust of ongoing process and added a sophistication about Gestalt theory. I found field theory as a necessary support for my Gestalt therapy work and theorizing. I explored dialogic existentialism. I found out that the emphasis on direct experience was a part of an intellectual tradition in philosophy and research called phenomenology, and that dialogic existentialism, phenomenology and field theory formed a larger whole. Later I integrated my background in group work, political science, anthropology, oriental studies, individual therapy with my lessons from Jim.

From Jim Simkin I learned basics. Gestalt therapy came to be a compass guiding me through the travails of becoming a humane and effective therapist and human being. It was a framework to integrate diverse strands. Dialogic contact and the awareness continuum became the operational application of existentialism and phenomenology. "Working" became an operational application of phenomenological focusing.

I have expanded: Now I integrate psychoanalytic knowledge into what I do, I focus more on continuity and historical antecedents, I focus more on group process, I talk more about theory than Jim, I utilize body work and expression of my personal feelings, more than I ever learned from Jim. It is easy to grow and integrate when the basic framework is built on trust of individuals, individual's experience, on dialogue between individuals, on faith in ongoing process. Thank you, Jim.

3

A REVIEW OF THE PRACTICE OF
GESTALT THERAPY

═══════════════

Commentary

*I wrote this review as a part of the graduation requirements for
my doctorate in psychology at the University of Arizona. (It was not
my dissertation, which was an empirical social psychology study.) It
was first published by a California State University bookstore in
1969. The style of the paper, including the many quotations, was in
part due to the academic requirements, especially in view of the
number of unpublished papers that were then in circulation that I
wanted to make known and the paucity of published papers. It was
more widely circulated in 1975 when it was published in
Stephenson's book* Gestalt Therapy Primer. *For the historical
minded reader it can serve as a comparison of my views in later
papers with my published views in 1969.*

Psychological orientations are frequently dichotomied into
those stressing behavioral variables and those stressing
phenomenological variables. Although some psychologists have
recognized the need for both, many are not aware that Frederick
Perls founded a type of psychotherapy that does integrate both.
Perls' major works (1947; Perls, Hefferline and Goodman, 1951)

47

stress his theory and not his psychotherapy practice. Although he and his coworkers have written papers stressing the practice of therapy, these have not been sufficiently available in popular professional journals (e.g., Enright,1970a; Levitsky & Perls,1969; Simkin). The practice of this type of therapy, Gestalt therapy, is the focus of this paper. Gestalt therapy as a type of existential philosophy (Enright,1970a; Simkin; Van Dusen, 1960), as a theory of personality and research (Perls, 1947, Perls et al., 1951) and the theoretical and historical origins of Gestalt therapy (Enright, 1970a; Simkin) will not be directly considered within the confines of this review.

Two goals of Gestalt therapy make a review of its practice particularly important. One is the goal of being exclusively orientated to Here-and-Now behavior without conditioning the patient and without excluding awareness variables. The other goal is to apply the existential attitude without being excessively global and abstract.

Models of Psychotherapy

To understand Gestalt therapy, it must be located in relation to three schools of psychotherapy: the psychodynamic therapy movement, the behavior therapy movement, and the human potentials movement. This section will be devoted not to a theoretical comparison of theories of psychotherapy, but rather to the sketching of a context or backdrop against which the discussion of Gestalt therapy can meaningfully take place.

Psychodynamic psychotherapy is predicated on the assumption of a patient's having a disease or disability that the therapist will cure or eliminate. Because the patient has this disease, he is assumed to be irresponsible. The therapist discovers why the patient has become as he is (diagnosis), and the patient's cure results from discovering what the therapist has discovered (insight). This approach to psychotherapy emphasizes inferred underlying causes and relegates actual behavior to the secondary status as a symptom. Psychodynamic theorists deem changes in overt behavior as unimportant unless the real, (hidden) cause, is dealt with. By stressing their inferences (interpretations), dynamically oriented therapists neglect Here-and-Now behavior and stress the patient's cognition of the There and Then. Moreover, psychodynamic therapists seldom describe their methodology in sufficient detail to communicate exactly what behaviors take place in psychotherapy.

Behavioral therapists have replaced these mentalistic, inferential and often unscientific characteristics of the psychodynamic movement with observations of actual behavior. New and clearly specified techniques have been offered by Wolpe, Skinner, Stampfl, Bandura and others. Derived from experimental learning laboratories, these have all stressed hard data and exact specification of procedures. Vague concepts and interpretations of behavior based on unsupported constructs were eliminated from the repertoire of behaviorally trained psychologists. Among the assumptions and concepts eliminated were the importance of the irresponsibility of patients, preoccupation with etiology and the importance of awareness (consciousness).

These two schools do have in common the assumption that the therapist is responsible for making the patient change. The therapist does the work of creating change; because of his expertise, he does something to the patient, or orders mediators to do something to the patient, that produces change. The psychologist manipulates the environment of the patient so that behavior compatible with some standard of adjustment is conditioned into the patient, and undesirable behavior is deconditioned. The behavior therapist is in control of the subject, and the subject, consistent with basic S-R theory, is seen as a passive recipient of stimuli.

A third force has arisen in psychology which rejects the stress on removing either negative behavior by conditioning or psychopathology by psychoanalytically oriented psychotherapy. The humanist rebellion sees psychotherapy as a means of increasing man's potential. A discussion of the methods of this third force movement will be undertaken after discussing Gestalt therapy. Gestalt therapy is a part of this third force movement in American psychology, attempting the nonmanipulative observation of Here-and-Now *behavior* and stressing the importance of awareness. This combination of behavior and awareness in a humanistic matrix makes Gestalt therapy an attractive model.

The Theory of Gestalt Therapy

Gestalt therapy emphasizes two principles that need integrating if behavioral and experiential psychology are to be meaningfully combined into one system of psychotherapy: "*The absolute working in the here and now*"; and "*The full concern with the phenomenon of awareness*" (Perls, 1966, p. 2). The Gestalt therapist claims neither to cure nor to condition — but perceives himself as an observer of ongoing behavior and as a guide for the phenomenological learning of the patient. Although a full understanding of the theoretical support for this would entail a detailed examination of the Gestalt therapy theory of psychology, personality and psychopathology, a short detour into this subject will be necessary.

Gestalt therapy is based on gestalt theory (a discussion of which is beyond the scope of the present paper (see Perls, et al., 1951; Wallen, 1957). Gestalt therapists regard motor behavior and the perceptual qualities of the individual's experience as organized by the most relevant organismic need (Perls et al., 1951; Wallen, 1957). In the normal individual, a configuration is formed which has the qualities of a good gestalt, with the organizing figure being the dominant need (Perls, 1947; Perls et al., 1951). The individual meets this need by contacting the environment with some sensorimotor behavior. The contact is organized by the figure of interest against the ground of the organism/environment field (Perls et al., 1951). Note that in Gestalt therapy, both sensing the environment and motor movement in the environment are active, contacting functions.

When a need is met, the gestalt it organized becomes complete, and it no longer exerts an influence — the organism is free to form new gestalten. When this gestalt formation and destruction are blocked or rigidified at any stage, when needs are not recognized and expressed, the flexible harmony and flow of the organism/environment field is disturbed. Unmet needs form incomplete gestalten that clamor for attention and, therefore, interfere with the formation of new gestalten.

At the point where nourishment or toxicity (Greenwald, 1969) is possible, awareness develops. Awareness is always accompanied by gestalt formation (Perls et al., 1951). With awareness the organism can mobilize its aggression so the environmental stimulus can be contacted (tasted) and rejected or chewed and assimilated. This contact-assimilation process is operated by the natural biological force of aggression. When awareness does not develop (figure and ground do not form into a clear gestalt) in such a transaction, or when impulses are kept from expression, incomplete gestalten are formed and psychopathology develops (Enright, 1970a). This shifting figure-ground of awareness replaces the psychoanalytic concept of the unconscious; the unconscious is phenomena in the field which the organism does not contact because of a disturbance in the figure-ground formation or because it is in contact with other phenomena (Polster, 1967; Simkin).

The point at which this awareness is formed is the point of contact. "Contact, the work that results in assimilation and growth, is the forming of a figure of interest against a ground or context of the organism/environment" (Perls et al., 1951, p. 231). Gestalt therapy focuses on what and how, and not on content.

> By working on the unity and disunity of the structure of the experience here and now, it is possible to remake the dynamic relations of the figure and ground until the contact is heightened, the awareness brightened and the behavior energized, most important of all, the achievement of a strong gestalt is itself the cure, for the figure of contact is not a sign of, but is itself the creative integration of experience. (Perls et al., 1951, p. 232)

Awareness is a gestalt property that is a creative integration of the problem. Only an aware gestalt (awareness) leads to change. Mere awareness of content without awareness of structure does not relate to an energized organism/environment contact.

Gestalt therapy starts a process, like a catalyst. The exact reaction is determined by the patient and his environment. The cure is not a finished product, but a person who has learned how to develop the awareness he needs to solve his own problems (Perls et al., 1951). The criterion of success is not social acceptability or interpersonal relations but "the patient's own awareness of heightened vitality and more effective functioning" (Perls et al., 1951, p. 15). The therapist does not tell the patient what he has discovered about the patient, but teaches him how to learn.

Perls calls the system of responses or contacts of the organism with the environment at any moment the self (Perls et al., 1951). The ego is the system of identification and alienation of the organism. In neurosis the ego alienates some of the self processes, that is, fails to identify with the self as it is. Rather than allow the self to proceed with the organization of responses into new gestalten, the self is crippled. The neurotic loses awareness of (alienates) the sense of "it is I who am thinking, feeling, doing this" (Perls et al., 1951, p. 235). The neurotic is divided, unaware and self-rejecting.

This division, unawareness and self-rejection can be maintained only by restricting the organism's experiencing. The naturally functioning organism experiences by feeling, sensing and thinking. When the person rejects one of his modes of experiencing, the formation of new gestalten becomes blocked by unmet needs that form incomplete gestalten and, therefore, demand attention. Without experiencing needs and impulses, organismic self-regulation is impaired, and reliance on moralistic external regulation is necessitated (Perls, 1948).

The rejection of modes of experiencing can be traced far back in Western culture. Since Aristotle, Western man has been taught that his rational faculties are acceptable but sensory and affective faculties are not. The human organism has become split into the *I* and the *Me*. Western man identifies with his reigning sovereign (reason), and has alienated his sensory and affective modalities. However, without balanced organismic experiencing, man cannot be in full contact with nature or in support of himself and, therefore, is impaired in learning from his environmental transactions (Perls, 1966; Simkin). Western man has been alienated, split and thrown out of harmony with nature (Perls, 1948; Simkin).

Learning takes place by discovery, by the formation of new gestalten: insight. As an organism interacts with the environment gestalten are completed, awareness develops, and learning takes place (Simkin). Perls found his patients suffering from alienation of ego functions and set out to find a therapy that would integrate the split personality so that new gestalten could be formed, the patient could learn, and so forth (Perls, 1948). He noticed that patients showed their basically faulty figure-ground formation in their transactions with him. This was the clue for his founding of

Gestalt therapy. A fuller discussion of this can be found in the literature (Perls, 1947, 1948; Perls et al., 1951; Simkin; Wallen, 1957).

The basic therapeutic dilemma as Perls sees it is that the patient has lost awareness of the processes by which he alienates (remains unaware of) parts of his self-functioning. He found (Perls et al., 1951) that by using experiments with directed awareness, the patients could learn how he kept from being aware; in a sense, Perls taught patients how to learn.

The therapeutic change process in Gestalt therapy involves helping the patient rediscover the mechanism that he uses to control his awareness. The directed awareness experiments, the Gestalt therapy encounters, the group experiments which we shall discuss, all have as their goal making the patient aware of the habitual acts he engages in to control his awareness. Without this emphasis the patient might increase his awareness, but only in a limited and circumscribed way. When the patient reexperiences control of awareness control, his development can be self-directive and self-supportive.

> The ultimate goal of the treatment can be formulated thus: We have to achieve that amount of integration which facilitates its own development. (Perls, 1948, p. 12)

The therapeutic tasks the Gestalt therapist gives the patient are all reports of the patient's awareness. In therapy the patient can gain something different than he gains from experiences outside of therapy — something other than an isolated piece of knowledge, a temporary relationship or catharsis. What therapy can create is a situation wherein the very core of a person's growth problem, restricted awareness, is the focus of attention.

For therapist and patient alike, Perls' prescription is "lose your mind and come to your senses." Perls stresses the use of the external senses as well as the internal proprioceptive system of self-awareness. By resensitizing the patient, the patient can become aware once again of the mechanism by which he (ego) rejects awareness and expression of impulses. When the organism once again controls the censor, it can fight the battles of survival with its own sensorimotor behavior, learn and become integrated, that is to say, self-accepting (Simkin).

When the neurotic — with his split in personality, underuse of affective and sensory modalities and lack of self-support — attempts to have the therapist solve his life problems, the Gestalt therapist refuses; the Gestalt therapist refuses to allow the patient to thrust the responsibility for his behavior onto him (Enright, 1970a). The therapist frustrates the attempt to operate manipulatively in core areas.

In Gestalt therapy the goal is not to solve *The Problem* (Enright, 1970a), for the patient will remain a cripple as long as he manipulates others into doing his problem-solving for him — as long as he does not use his full sensorimotor equipment. Gestalt therapy is holistic and sees the human organism as potentially free of internal control hierarchies. The patient-therapist relationship in Gestalt therapy is also relatively hierarchy-free.

The patient is an active and responsible participant who learns to experiment and observe so as to be able to discover and realize his own goals through his own efforts. The responsibility for the patient's behavior, change in behavior and the work to achieve such change is left to the patient.

Thus Gestalt therapy rejects the notion that the therapist must or should assume the role of a conditioner or deconditioner.

> Every patient barks up the wrong tree by expecting that he can achieve maturation through external sources...Maturation cannot be done for him, he has to go through the painful process of growing up by himself. We therapists can do *nothing* but provide him the opportunity, by being available as a catalyst and projection screen. (Perls, 1966, p. 4)

The role of the Gestalt therapist is that of a participant-observer of Here-and-Now behavior and catalyst for the phenomenological experimentation of the patient. The patient learns by experimenting in the "*safe emergency* of the therapeutic situation" (Perls, 1966, p. 8). He continues to take the natural consequences of his behavior in and out of therapy.

The basic assumption of this therapeutic approach is that people can deal adequately with their own life problems if they know what they are, and can bring all their abilities into action to solve them.... Once in good touch with their real concerns and their real environment, they are on their own. (Enright, 1970a, p. 7)

Although the therapist in Gestalt therapy does not focus on mentalistic concepts, or on the past, or on the future, no content is excluded in advance. Past or future materials are considered acts in the present (memory, planning, etc.). Nor is Gestalt therapy static. The focus is not on finding the *whys* of behavior or *mind* nor is it manipulation of stimulus consequences to bring about a change in behavior. "Contrary to the approaches of some schools which stress `insight' or learning `why' we do as we do, Gestalt therapy stresses learning `how' and `what' we do" (Simkin, p. 4).

In Gestalt therapy the therapist is not passive, as in older Rogerian therapy, but is quite active. Attending to behavior, not mentalisms; to awareness, not speculative questions, Here and Now, and not There and Then, all necessitate action and assertiveness on the part of the therapist.

The goal in Gestalt therapy is maturity. Perls defines maturity as "the transition from environmental support to self-support" (Perls, 1965; also see Simkin). Self-support implies contact with other people. Continuous contact (confluence) or absence of contact (withdrawal) are contrary to what is implied (Perls, 1947). Self-support refers to self-support in the organism/environment field. Confluence obviously is not self-support. Withdrawal still involves the essence of non-self-support. Critical here is continuous use of the sensory-motor equipment of the organism in transaction with the environment, with awareness (Enright, 1970a). Such is self-support, and, leads to integration.

This process is achieved in the natural environment when there is struck "a viable balance of support and frustration." Gestalt therapists attempt to achieve this balance. Excessive frustration, especially in individual therapy, will result in the patient's disowning the therapist. Excessive support encourages the patient to continue to manipulate the environment for that support which the patient erroneously believes he cannot provide for himself.

While temporary improvement may result from such supportive treatment, the patient will not be aided in moving beyond the impasse point.

The impasse point is what the Russian literature calls the *sick point*. "The existential impasse is a situation in which no environmental support is forthcoming and the patient is, or believes himself to be, incapable of coping with life on his own" (Perls, 1966, p. 6). In order to achieve or maintain support from the environment the patient will engage in a number of maneuvers. Such manipulations or games are used by the patient to maintain the status quo, to keep control of his environment and to avoid coping with life on his own. When the neurotic patient avoids coping, he avoids the actual pains any organism avoids, and, in addition, "the neurotic avoids imaginary hurts, such as unpleasant emotions. He also avoids taking reasonable risks. Both interfere with any chance of maturation" (Perls, 1966, p. 7).

Therefore Gestalt therapy calls the patient's attention to his avoidance of unpleasantness and his phobic behavior is worked through in the course of the therapy.

In summary, the therapist balances frustration and support while maintaining a relationship in the I and Thou — Here and Now tradition of Martin Buber. The patient at first works hard at avoiding his actual experience and the consequences of his actual behavior. Because the patient has long since learned and practiced the manipulating of his environment to obtain support and means of avoiding becoming aware of his actual experience, he is usually quite skilled at this.

> He does this by acting helpless and stupid; he wheedles, bribes, and flatters. He *is not* infantile, but plays an infantile and dependent role expecting to control the situation by submissive behavior. (Perls, 1965, p. 5)

Gestalt Therapy Techniques

The literature of psychoanalysis is voluminous but does not describe the actual behavior that takes place in psychoanalysis with clarity sufficient to impart understanding to those who have not actually participated. The reader of *Gestalt Therapy* (Perls et al., 1951) will be aware that Perls' descriptions of Gestalt therapy are not more successful at describing his procedures than the psycho-analysts were at describing theirs.

A clearer picture of Gestalt therapy is available through numerous tape recordings, videotapes and movies. There are numerous papers by Perls and his coworkers that are available from the Esalen Institute, Big Sur; from the Gestalt Institute of Cleveland, and similar institutions. A detailed discussion of the background concepts of Gestalt therapy, including the personality theory, the theory of psychopathology and the concept of the continuum of awareness are available in Perls' books. *Gestalt Therapy*, Perls' most complete work to date, has a series of eighteen experiments which the reader can try at home and which form the crux of the work that Perls does in his psychotherapy. The experiments skillfully bridge the gap between the experience of the reader and the words of the authors.

Gestalt Therapy is not written for rapid perusal. Perls has an unusual configuration of attitudes, techniques, language and theories which need creative and persistent effort to assimilate. Communication may be particularly difficult with behaviorally trained psychologists who are accustomed to an exact, precise specification of what is done. Moreover, the idioms of Gestalt therapy and behavior therapy are different. When reading the work of a psychologist that fits in recognized categories and who uses familiar terms, the amount of time that went into acquiring essential assumptions and terminology is often forgotten. To understand even the basic terminology of Perls' theory requires time and a willingness to chew over new material beyond that which is customarily demanded when reading in one's own area of interest.

Gestalt therapy is selectively and differentially practiced according to the personality and needs of the therapist, the patients and the setting. Perls does not recommend or approve of imitation of the way he as a person applies his theory. Each therapist has to find his own way.

Perls recognizes that a corollary to the unity of the organism/environment field is that a change anywhere in the field will affect the entire field. Thus it is possible to intervene at many points and from many angles and the immediate results may generalize to the rest of the field. Some changes necessitate environmental changes, such as in the level of environmental support. Intervention with the single organism can often achieve results even when approached from a unidimensional point of view — for example sensory awareness. However, Perls himself advocates a multiple variable approach as the only way of helping patients move beyond the impasse. The Gestalt therapist uses many aspects of the Here-and-Now situation to create growth opportunities, encounter, experimentation, observation, sensory awareness and the like.

The Experimental Model of Psychotherapy

Gestalt Therapy, by emphasizing the awareness continuum of oneself and the world, is a way (Tao) of living and enhancing one's experience. It is nonanalytic. It attempts to integrate the fragmented, split personality through noninterpretive focusing in the here-and-now (Esalen Programs, Summer, 1968).

Virtually all activity in Gestalt therapy consists of experiments in directed awareness (Simkin). Perls defines an experiment as:

...a trial or special observation made to confirm or disprove something doubtful, esp. one under conditions determined by the experimenter; an act or operation undertaken in order to discover some unknown principle or effect, or to test, establish, or illustrate some suggested or known truth; practical test; proof. (Perls et al., 1951, p. 14)

The aim is for the patient to discover the mechanism by which he alienates part of his self processes and thereby avoids awareness of himself and his environment. All rules and suggestions in Gestalt therapy are designed to aid discovery and not to foster a particular attitude or behavior (Levitsky & Perls, 1969).

The prototypical experiment is to ask the subjects to make up a series of sentences beginning with the words "Here and now I am aware that..." (Enright [b]; Perls, 1948; Perls et al., 1951). The therapist continually relates back to what the patient is aware of (experiencing). The therapist encourages a continuation of the experiment by asking: "Where are you now?" "What are you experiencing now?" Questions by the patient are translated into: "Now you are aware of wondering..." When the patient begins to avoid the instructions, this is also translated into awareness reports: "Now I am aware of wishing to stop."

The variations on this basic experiment are limitless (Levitsky & Perls, 1969). The experiments are arranged in a graduated series so that each step challenges the patient, but is within the patient's grasp. In each experiment the patient can try new behaviors which can be experimented with only with great difficulty in the natural environment (Polster, 1966).

Ordinarily we think of the controller of the experiment and the observer of the data as the psychologist. In Gestalt therapy the psychologist sets up the experiments, but shares the control and observation with the patient. External behavior is directly perceived by the psychologist and the patient; internal behavior is perceived by the patient alone through his enteroceptors and proprioceptors. The relation of the two in the whole gestalt is the focus of attention. One can regard Gestalt therapy as a process of focusing on the consecutive unfolding of simultaneous internal and external behaviors. As in any experimentation, the results of the experiments indicate directions for new experiments. When the patient can experiment and experience without the therapist, the therapy is finished.

Three aspects of this Here-and-Now experimentation should be noted: the functional concept of *now*, the role of observation of the patient's total behavior, and the difference between introspection and directed awareness.

Now

Now is a functional concept referring to what the organism is doing. What the organism did five minutes ago is not part of now. An act of remembering a childhood event is now — the remembering is now. Perls states that the past exists as "precipitations of previous functions" (Perls, 1948, p. 575). The future exists as present processes: planning, hoping, fearing. The exclusive orientation with any one tense (past, present or future), the isolation of the three from each other, or the confusion of the three are all signs of disorder (Shostrom, 1966b). Gestalt therapy

experiments operate Here and Now in this functional sense
(Levitsky & Perls, 1969).

Observation and Body Language

Observation is at the heart of the Gestalt therapy experimentation. The observation concentrates on the means of avoiding
awareness of the alienated and inaccessible. When the patient
shows incongruences, often attending to one aspect of his total
communication and not another, this is reported to the patient.
Often the verbal content is incongruent with the tone of voice and
posture of the patient. This is not silently noted, but is brought to
the attention of the patient.

It has been stated that:

> This tendency to limit the discourse to the present is feasible
> only because in Gestalt therapy we are listening to the *total
> communication* rather than the strictly verbal. The relevant
> past *is* present here and now, if not in words, then in some
> bodily tension and attention that can be hopefully brought
> into awareness. It is impossible to overstress the importance
> of this point. For a purely verbal therapy to remain in the
> here and now would be irresponsible and disastrous. It is
> only the aggressive, systematic and constant effort to bring
> the patient's total communication into his awareness that
> permits a radical concentration upon the here and now.
> (Enright, 1970a, p. 15)

Listening to the total communication necessitates the active use
and trust of the senses of the therapist (Perls, 1966). Gestalt
therapy is non-interpretative; in his activity the Gestalt therapist
clearly separates his observations from his inferences and emphasizes the former. For example, Gestalt therapy starts with and
stresses the obvious (Perls, 1948; Simkin). The obvious is frequently overlooked by patients and therapists. The opening
gambit of the patient — sight, smile, handshake — are obvious
behaviors and are sometimes more laden with meaning than the
ritual verbal greeting (Enright, 1970a).

Body language is an important part of the total observation.
Physical symptoms are taken seriously and considered more

accurate communications of a patient's real feelings than his verbal communications. Simkin calls such physical symptoms truth buttons. By experimenting with taking one side and then another of a conflict, the patient "will inevitably bring on the body language — the truth signal — when he takes sides with that aspect of the conflict which is anti-self" (Simkin, p. 3).

Asking the patient to exaggerate an unwitting movement or gesture may result in important discovery by the patient (Levitsky & Perls, 1969). As an example:

> A constricted, overinhibited man is tapping his finger on the table while a woman in the group is talking on and on about something. Asked if he has anything he would like to comment about what the woman is saying, he denies much concern with it, but continues the tapping. He is asked then to intensify the tapping, to tap louder and more vigorously and to continue this until he feels more fully what he is doing. His anger mounts very quickly and within a minute or so he is pounding the table and expressing vehemently his disagreement with the woman. He goes on to say that she is "just like my wife," but in addition to this historical perspective, he has had an experiential glimpse of his excessive control of strong assertive feelings and the possibility of more immediate and hence less violent expression of them. (Enright, 1970a, pp. 3-4)

Without sensitive observation the experimental approach in psychotherapy is impossible. Perls' unique contribution to psychotherapy methodology lies in replacing interpretation with behavioral observation and experimentation. The Gestalt therapist does not interpret — he observes, sets up experiments, is a living person in the therapeutic situation as well as in other contexts.

Awareness Experiments and Introspection

The Gestalt therapy directed awareness experiments are not the same as introspection (Perls et al., 1951, p. 389; Enright, 1970a, p. 11). In introspection the organism is split into an observing and an observed segment.

When you introspect, you *peer at yourself.* This form of retroflection is so universal in our culture that much of the psychological literature simply takes it for granted that any attempt to increase self-awareness must of necessity consist of introspection. While this, definitely, is not the case, it probably is true that anyone who does these experiments will *start* by introspecting. The observer is split off from the part observed, and not until this split is healed will a person fully realize that self-awareness which is not introspected can exist. We previously likened genuine awareness to the glow produced within a burning coal by its own combustion and introspection to turning the beam of a flashlight on an object and peering at its surface by means of the reflected rays. (Perls et al., 1951, pp. 157-158)

To observe yourself in action, and eventually to observe yourself as action, introspection is inadequate. Introspection is dualistic and static. Moreover, it downplays the awareness of the body that is possible through internal sense receptors and is instead speculative. After all, there are available numerous sensory inputs from internal receptors which the organism can allow to enter into awareness or which can be kept from awareness. These form observational data available to the organism and not to the experimenter. The experimenter can only infer what he does not observe.

Perls' formulation offers an alternative to Titchnerian introspection, behavioristic mindlessness and psychoanalytic speculation. Internal self-observations are valuable even though they are somewhat unreliable. The difficulty with the reliability and validity of external observation is bad enough; the reliability and validity of inference about private events is obviously in even greater doubt.

Perls, being aware of this difficulty and of the ease with which even a trained observer can contaminate observation with inference, stresses the need to separate sensory observation and cognitive inference. He does not ask patients questions that lead to cognitive processes (inference and imagination) at the expense of sensory processes (observation, use of the senses).

In addition the general strategy of Gestalt therapy does not depend on the patient's accuracy in self reporting. We simply tell him, in effect, to sit down and start living, then note where and how he fails (Enright, p. 6).

The therapist's observations while the patient is reporting his awareness can provide some data to check internal observations, for what exists internally in an organism is usually reflected in external behavior in some manner. Since the psychotherapist and patient are observing the same organism from different angles, the simultaneous use of both observations can be expected to shed some light on basic processes.

The Gestalt therapy experiments return always to the primary sensory data of experience. For example, Gestalt therapy does not ask why, but instead focuses on what and how. What and how are amenable to exact observation; why leads to speculation (Enright, 1970a; Simkin). This will be discussed further below. The obvious, the minute and concrete, and physiological processes are all stressed in Gestalt therapy; they are often neglected in clinical psychology.

The separation of observation from inference with emphasis on the former is as applicable to internal as external processes. Gestalt therapists attempt to pin down exactly what experience is represented by a particular phenomenological report. The therapist asks about exact sensations, as in the following example:

T: What are you aware of now?
P: Now I am aware of talking to you. I see the others in the room. I'm aware of John squirming. I can feel the tension in my shoulders. I'm aware that I get anxious as I say this.
T: How do you experience the anxiety?
P: I hear my voice quiver. My mouth feels dry. I talk in a very halting way.
T: Are you aware of what your eyes are doing?
P: Well, now I realize that my eyes keep looking away.
T: Can you take responsibility for that?
P: ...that *I* keep looking away from you.
T: Can you *be* your eyes now? Write the dialogue for them.

P: I am Mary's eyes. I find it hard to gaze steadily. I keep jumping and darting about...etc.
(Levitsky & Perls, 1969, pp. 5-6)

The results of this kind of observation and experimentation have confirmed Perls' original observation of overemphasis of reason. Simkin reports:

In all cases that I have seen thus far, people seeking psychotherapy show an imbalance among their three primary modes of experiencing. Most patients that I see, and this seems to be also true of the bulk of the patients seen by my colleagues, are very dependent on and have overly stressed their development of the intellectual or the "thinking-about" mode of experience. Most of the time, these people are in touch with their thought processes and their experience is with a fantasy (memory) of the past or a fantasy (wish) (prediction) of the future. Infrequently are they able to make contact with their *feelings* and many are also *sensory* cripples — not seeing or hearing or tasting, etc. (Simkin, pp. 3-4)

The Existential Attitude

Most existential therapies place importance on the interpersonal existential encounter. Gestalt therapy is no exception, and I and Thou — Here and Now has been called a capsule description of Gestalt therapy (Simkin, p. 1; see also Polster, 1966, p. 5). In time-space Gestalt therapy locates both the experiments in directed awareness and the encounter in the Here and Now. The therapeutic relationship is seen as an I-Thou relationship as discussed by Martin Buber.

Participants in an existential encounter function on the self-actualizing model (Enright; Greenwald; Shostrom, 1967; Simkin). According to this model, there is a continuum from manipulation (Shostrom) or deadness (Perls) to actualization (Shostrom) or aliveness (Perls). The actualizer treats each human being as an end (a Thou) and not a means (an It); the manipulator controls himself and others as things, or allows himself to be controlled as a thing. The actualizer expresses his feelings directly to people as they arise; the manipulator judges, withdraws, blackmails, gossips, lives exclusively in a single time dimension. The manipulator does not trust his natural organismic self-regulatory system, and therefore depends on the moralistic regulatory system of society, not on his own support.

The neurotic patient comes to the therapist with his characteristic pattern of manipulating support. He frequently wishes to give up his self-direction and self-support or manipulate the therapist into giving up his. By design or accident, some therapists accede to these manipulations. The Gestalt therapist may refuse the assent, dissent or other support the patient seeks. Selective reinforcement via approval cues of the therapist approved behavior would be merely a form of conditioning, and therefore manipulative rather than actualizing. The patient looking to Perls for approval may find him intensely involved via eye contact and general attitude, but finds no clue to approval or disapproval. His unaverted gaze can be quite disconcerting to such patients. This is an example of the clinical use of frustration. The Gestalt therapist does not give support to a patient because he is too weak to support himself. The Gestalt therapist may indicate by his interest, behavior and words that he cares, understands and will listen. This true support is nourishing for many patients. Observers of Gestalt therapy who have not had an intimate, diadic encounter with a Gestalt therapist sometimes miss the intensity and warmth of the true support offered by most Gestalt therapists while they are simultaneously coldly refusing to direct or be responsible for the patient.

Some existential theorists discount the importance of techniques in psychotherapy (for example, Carl Rogers, 1960, p. 88), emphasizing the encounter instead. Walter Kempler, an experiential Gestalt therapist, is one spokesman for the therapist-as-person position:

> Upon these two commandments hang all the law — upon which experiential psychotherapy within families stands: attention to the current interaction as the pivotal point for all awareness and interventions; involvement of the total therapist-person bringing overtly and richly his full personal impact on the families with whom he works (not merely a

bag of tricks called therapeutic skills). While many therapists espouse such fundamentals, in actual practice there is a tendency to hedge on this biprincipled commitment. (Kempler, 1968, p. 88)

Kempler gives several long, verbatim examples of his nontechnique (1965, 1966, 1967, 1968; see Shostrom, 1967, pp. 204-205 for short illustrative examples). In the following example Kempler becomes angry at a patient who has been whimpering during the session to his wife and to Kempler.

P: What can I do? She stops me at every turn.
T: (*sarcastically to provoke him*): You poor thing, overpowered by that terrible lady over there.
P: (*ducking*): She means well.
T: You're whimpering at me and I can't stand to see a grown man whimpering.
P: (*firmer*): I tell you I don't know what to do.
T: Like hell you don't (*offering and at the same time pushing*). You know as well as I that if you want her off your back, you just have to tell her to get the hell off your back and mean it. That's one thing you could do instead of that mealy-mouthed apology, "She means well."
P: (*looks quizzical; obviously he is not sure he wants to chance it with either of us but is reluctant to retreat to the whimpering child posture again*): I'm not used to talking that way to people.
T: Then you'd better get used to it....
P: You sure paint a bad picture.
T: If I'm wrong, be man enough to disagree with me and don't wait to get outside of here to whimper to your wife about how you didn't know what to say here.
P: (*visibly bristling and speaking more forcefully*): I don't know that you're wrong about what you're saying.
T: But how do you like what I'm saying?
P: I don't. Nor do I like the way you're going about it.
T: I don't like the way you're going about things either.
P: There must be a more friendly way than this.
T: Sure, you know, whimper.

P: (*finally in anger*): I'll say what I damn please. You're not going to tell me how to talk...and how do you like that? (*he socks his hands.*)
T: I like it a helluva lot better than your whimpering. What is your hand saying?
P: I'd like to punch you right in the nose....
(Kempler, 1968, pp. 95-96)

Gestalt therapy does not exclude either a purely personal or a purely technical therapist response if it expands the awareness of the patient (Enright, 1970a).

The Gestalt therapist retains his right to be independent in the I-Thou relationship. This independence can help remove the therapist's reinforcement of dysfunctional behavior, and allows the therapist to be self-supportive, self-directive and therefore model self-actualizing. This is possible only with the careful observation and awareness discussed in the last section.

Although in Gestalt therapy the therapist is allowed to be spontaneously himself, the Gestalt therapist is self-committed to increasing the awareness of the patient, and uses the technique of experimentation. Perls goes so far as to state that he interrupts any "pure verbal encounters without any experimental substance..." (Perls, 1966, p. 9). Whatever Perls may believe philosophically about interpersonal relationship models, as a therapist he advocates discovery by the patient using his own senses while maintaining for experimental purposes an I-Thou — Here and Now relationship. The aim of such an encounter is discovery, increased awareness; such an encounter is not designed for catharsis. If expression is honest, it is usually not interfered with; it may be fostered as a learning device — but is not encouraged simply as a safe discharge of aggression.

One can question whether the therapist, by not attending to his inner response and by concentrating on setting up experiments for the patient, is not at odds with the I-Thou model of relationship. The Gestalt therapy position is that the therapist makes direct contact with the patient with his senses, attending to an agreed-on task, expanding the awareness of the patient. A competent Gestalt therapist must be able to be aware of his inner feelings as he attends to them, and express them spontaneously when he wishes. There is no preconceived injunction against expressing his feelings to a patient. In general, the moral (*should*) is to be aware — the control or expression of a feeling is up to the individual. The Gestalt therapist's human reaction is also used for its diagnostic value (Enright, 1970b).

Related to the technical versus human response question is the question of influencing the patient's choice of values in his life. There is, in Gestalt therapy, an attitude against taking a stand on moral issues of the patient. The Gestalt therapist may communicate a feeling Here and Now, or communicate something of his own values if this is in the interest of expanding the patient's awareness of alternatives. This is not accepted as a means of inculcating values. Contrast the following two views.

Bach states:
Concerning the therapist's communication to his patients of his own values by which he lives, my clinical experience shows this can be of great service, provided, however, that the patient is actively prevented from using such information to avoid finding his own identity by imitation...I stress that my ways of wrestling with value problems are to be taken only as a reference point to gain perspective, to compare, rather than to imitate. As a technical general rule, I reinforce and stress *self-differentiating* experiences in therapy...over identification processes. I consider growth through "identification with" a transitory process while self-actualization through "differentiation from" is a lifelong mode of self-assertive living. (Bach, 1962, p. 22)

Simkin states:
In my opinion, the therapist, in taking a "personal stand," uses a defensive maneuver as a result of feeling threatened by the patient at this point. I feel it is a technical mistake if the therapist forces his own values on the patient under the guise of "education". Even though in a few instances I gave in to my own needs to voice an opinion, I consider this my own weakness. And my principle is that such statements

should be generally avoided, and the patient should be left to find his own values. (Simkin, 1962, pp. 21-22)

Simkin discusses two cases (Simkin, 1962, pp. 205-209) in which he makes the judgment to share or not share his values.

In one case, a seventeen-year-boy reports that he is going to use his observation of his father with a girl friend to blackmail the father. Simkin lets the patient know that to him blackmail was immature and repugnant. It was made clear to the patient that he had a right to make his own choice. Simkin's rationale was that the boy was living in a family where there was not an adequate amount of mature behavior to sample from and the therapist's attitude could serve as a source of information about possible behavior models.

In another case he reports that a twenty-two-year-old patient was discussing behavior which Simkin regarded as unacceptable for himself (and socially). The therapist did not communicate this to the patient. This judgment was made because: (1) The behavior provided good material for analysis; (2) The therapist's objection to the behavior was neurotically motivated; (3) The patient was not unduly at the mercy of his parents as in the previous case.

The primary function of the Gestalt therapist is to help the patient learn to discriminate, and for this, direct exposure to the therapist's values may be necessary. The therapist has the function of helping the patient to perceive his behavior and the consequences and implications of his behavior. Beyond that the value choice is an individual matter.

For the I-Thou relationship the responsibility question is most crucial. The actualizing model is not imposed on or recommended to the patient; the Gestalt therapist simply refuses to give up his freedom, or accept the patient's surrender of his. The Gestalt therapist takes responsibility for behaving according to his own values, but for the patient there is only the prescription, "Try this behavior in therapy as an experiment and see what you discover." If the patient likes the Gestalt therapy model he *may* choose to adopt it. Diversity of values and behavior is highly regarded in Gestalt therapy and the patient is left with responsibility for himself. If the patient finds the therapist's behavior a model that is satisfying, he may adopt any part of it he wishes. That is his choice and the Gestalt therapist wants it no other way. The Gestalt therapist has a deep commitment to the patient's behaving on the basis of knowledge (awareness), but has an equally abiding commitment to the value in diversity of behavior. The Gestalt therapist does not try to trick or manipulate the patient out of his behavior, only out of his state of unawareness.

The importance of this last point cannot be overstated. The Gestalt therapist does not manipulate the patient into accepting the self-actualizing model. One must pick and choose from Gestalt therapy whatever is palatable for him and reject the rest (Enright, 1970a; Greenwald; Levitsky & Perls,1969; Perls, 1947; Perls et al., 1951; Simkin). Gestalt therapy insists only on the value of discovering and regaining control over the mechanism of awareness. Perls' first book, *Ego, Hunger and Aggression,* 1947, makes clear that each person must treat psychological experience as we do food — we bite, chew, digest and reject food according to our own needs. Greenwald states: "Avoiding what is toxic or nonnourishing is the critical point in enabling the person to experience adequate emotional nourishment and growth" (Greenwald, 1969, p. 6). To Perls this takes mobilization of aggression (Perls, 1947, 1953-54; Perls et al., 1951).

The freedom of the therapist is not absolute. Even Kempler, who regards any decision of his to change from catalyst to active participant as related to his own needs and not to objectivity, nevertheless goes on to say:

> For such behavior by a therapist the word "spontaneous" may be applied. However, it is incumbent upon any therapist, existential or not, to clearly distinguish within himself the difference between spontaneous and impulsive behavior. Impulsive behavior is not a thorough representation of a person but rather a fractional escape of behavior in a constricted individual. (Kempler, 1968, p. 96)

Gestalt therapy believes strongly and without qualification in the need for professional clinical training and discipline in the psychotherapist. Gestalt therapy also believes that therapists are responsible for separating reports of his emotional feelings from his hunches. The Gestalt therapist does not say, "I feel you are such and such." Hunches or inferences by a Gestalt therapist are clearly labeled "fantasy," "guess," or "hunch."

Experimental encounters have revealed that negative and positive feelings are frequently censored. Patients are encouraged to experiment with expressing any feelings that are authentic. Heated words do not necessarily mean that authentic feelings have been directly expressed (Shostrom, 1967, Chapter IV). Heat may be a means of avoiding other emotions. The exchange of heated words is frequently a circular and repetitious intellectual exercise in which each person case-builds, name calls, verbally attacks, tries to impose his *shoulds* (judgments) on the other, expresses blaming reactions, etc. Gestalt therapists have found that simple and direct statements of feeling are frequently absent from the repertoire of the beginning patient. The implications of this in terms of specific therapeutic maneuvers will be discussed below.

The encounter in Gestalt therapy does not imply forcing change by confrontation of therapist or other patients. In Gestalt therapy the therapist is open to, responds to, and expresses feelings genuinely felt. Availability, honesty and openness are the key concepts. The therapist is available and models honesty and openness — he creates an atmosphere where the patient is most likely to try out that behavior. The Gestalt therapist does not push, but does aggressively stay in the I and Thou — Here and Now framework.

Gestalt Therapy Workshops

Gestalt therapy can be illustrated by discussing the use of workshops and the specific maneuvers in Gestalt therapy workshops.

In a paper delivered at the 1966 APA convention, Perls reported that he had eliminated all individual sessions except for emergencies. He has come to the view that all individual therapy is obsolete, and now integrates individual and group work into workshops. However, he cautions that: "This works with a group only if the therapist's encounter with an individual patient, within the group, is effective and impressive" (Perls, 1966, p. 1). The advantage of workshop therapy is not a matter of economy (although that is also relevant) but therapeutic power.

Now, in the group situation something happens that is not possible in the private interview. To the whole group it is *obvious* that the person in distress does not see the *obvious*, does not see the way out of the impasse, does not see (for instance) that his whole misery is a *purely imagined* one. In the face of this collective conviction he cannot use his usual phobic way of *disowning* the therapist when he cannot *manipulate* him. Somehow the trust in the collective seems to be greater than the trust in the therapist — in spite of all so-called transference confidence. (Perls, 1966, p. 7)

Perls mentions another advantage of workshops. In workshops, the therapist can facilitate individual development by conducting collective experiments, — talking gibberish together, doing withdrawal experiments, learning to understand the atmosphere, etc. The individual can experiment and learn how he obtains the effects he does from the group. The group learns the difference between helpfulness and true support. Moreover, watching the manipulation of others in the group helps the group members in self-recognition.

Perls summarizes his approach to groups by saying:

In other words, in contrast to the usual type of group meetings, I carry the load of the session, by either doing individual therapy or conducting mass experiments. I often interfere if the group plays opinion and interpretation games or has similar pure verbal encounters *without any experimental substance*, but I will keep out of it as soon as anything genuine happens. (Perls, 1966, p. 9)

Perls states clearly, and this seems to be the case from the writer's observation of him in groups, that he is available for individual work in the group — but he does not push. The rest of the group watch and are involved in silent self-therapy when the therapist-patient dyad are at work. Perls is aggressive in his work with individuals in the group, but he does not push the individual to participate. More often the patient is seen trying to push Perls, although unaware of doing so. This is followed by one of Perls' therapeutic maneuvers.

An encounter with one or both of the parties manipulating can be used experimentally, but not for catharsis. Any genuine I-Thou encounter necessarily involves experimental substance, that is, discovery. In a genuine encounter both parties are becoming, and neither knows the outcome.

To summarize: workshops consist of one-to-one therapy, group experiments and encounter — and all three are experimentally based.

Rules

In setting up the experimental encounter, Gestalt therapists impose several rules (Kempler, 1965, 1966, 1967, 1968; Levitsky & Perls, 1969; Simkin).

From a Person to a Person

Communication in an I-Thou relationship must involve direct sending and receiving. The Gestalt therapist will frequently ask: "To whom are you saying this?" In other words, each message is made into a statement from a particular person to a particular person. Every general statement is translated into a specific encounter, as in the following example:

> An intellectualized male graduate student in group therapy announces blandly to no one in particular that "I have difficulty in relating to people." In the ensuing silence he glances briefly at the attractive nurse co-therapist.
> T: "Who *here* do you have trouble relating to?" He is able to name the nurse as the chief offender, and spend a fruitful five minutes exploring his mixed frustration, attraction and anger focused on this desirable but inaccessible woman. (Enright, 1970a, p. 3)

The counterpart of speaking directly to a person is active listening as opposed to passive hearing. Listening as an act by a person and not a passive reception of stimulation is stressed in Gestalt therapy encounter. Each person is expected to take responsibility for his statements, for directing them to another person (I-Thou), and for active listening to others.

Gossiping

A specific rule against gossiping is often made. Gossiping is "talking about an individual when he is actually present and could just as well be addressed directly" (Levitsky & Perls, 1969, p. 7; see also Kempler, 1965, pp. 65ff). Although this sounds quite simple, the use of this technique has generally had a dramatic effect. The direct confrontation mobilizes affect and vividness of experience, in contrast to a pale dissipation through gossip (Enright, 1970a). When discussing an absent person, the Gestalt therapist will attempt to bring about direct experiential dialogue by having the patient imagine and enact a direct conversation with the person and attending to his continuum of awareness.

Questions

Although questions are ostensibly requests for information, careful listening and observation have revealed that they rarely are so. Questions most often are disguised statements, or demands for support from the other person. In Gestalt therapy patients are asked to translate questions into statements starting with the word "I" (Enright, 1970a; Levitsky & Perls, 1969). This procedure is an extension of the I-Thou relationship in that communication is made directly, openly and honestly. It is actualizing in the sense that the patient is encouraged to be assertive and self-supporting.

Semantics

The rule against question-asking is one of several maneuvers designed to help the patient discover the effect his choice of language has on his thinking. Semantic clarification can be used as a vehicle for improving observation and for conveying new outlooks or attitudes. Word choice is frequently habitual and out of awareness of patients. By explaining the operations and consequences of different words, distinctions not previously attended to can come into the patient's field of focus. The Gestalt therapy encounter necessitates semantic clarification, for example distinguishing affect and cognition. To discover the benefits of expressing his or her feelings, the patient must be able to distinguish feelings from various cognitive processes. *I feel* referring to the affective realm (I feel an emotion) is distinguished from *I feel* referring to the cognitive realm (I imagine, infer, think, believe, etc.).

Work on greater awareness of the language of the patient has been a focus of Gestalt therapy since Perls' first book, in which he mentioned two tools that were helpful in his quest for an improvement in traditional psychoanalysis: "holism" (field conception) and "semantics" (the meaning of meaning) (Perls, 1947, p. 7). Perls recognized that "we still try to do the impossible: to integrate personalities with the help of nonintegrative language" (Perls, 1948, p. 567). Thus the patient is trained to discriminate and label in a way that makes concrete and clear the exact referents of any word. If a patient says "I can't," the Gestalt therapist may ask him to experiment with saying "I won't" (Levitsky & Perls, 1969, p. 5). Vague, global, dualistic concepts are made concrete, specific and unitary.

But is a good example of a word that builds a double message into a statement. In the statement "I love you but I am angry at you," the words after *but* negate the words before. *And* is a conjunction that may more accurately portray experiential reality. If the person simultaneously experiences two facts: love and anger, a more accurate communication would be: "I love you and I'm angry at you."

An especially important semantic transaction for Gestalt therapy encounters is the translation of the *it* language into the I-Thou language. *It* is a depersonalized form of expression which obscures the activity of the doer and the object of the action. It is common for us to refer to our bodies and to our acts and behaviors in this `it' language.

This deals with the semantics of responsibility (Levitsky & Perls). Neurotics frequently project their initiative and responsibility and see themselves in a passive role: thoughts occur to them, or they are struck by a thought, etc. The patient is unwilling to identify with some of his activities; he has alienated some of his ego functions (Perls, 1948, p. 583). "If his language is reorganized from an `it' language to an `I' language, considerable integration can be achieved with this single adjustment" (Perls, 1948, p. 583).

What do you feel in your eyes?
It is blinking.

What is your hand doing?
It is trembling.

What do you experience in your throat?
It is choked.

What do you hear in your voice?
It is sobbing.

Through the simple — seemingly mechanical — expedient of changing "it" language into "I" language we learn to identify more closely with the particular behavior in question and to assume responsibility for it.

> Instead of "It is trembling," "I am trembling." Rather than "It is choked," "I am choked." Going one step further, rather than "I am choked," "I am choking myself". (Levitsky & Perls, 1969, p. 4)

Another important semantic transaction that Gestalt therapy helps people discover is what Simkin calls the *why-merry-go-round* (Simkin, p. 3; see also Enright, 1970a, p. 4). The word *why*, like many questions, demands that the respondent justify himself. The respondent most frequently starts his defense (or counterattack) with the word "because." Everything after the because is a rationalization, a reason thought up to justify himself. "I did it because you made me." "I did it because I couldn't help myself." This round of case-building is contrary to the spirit of encounter in that it avoids self-responsibility, is manipulative and involves speculation on historical antecedents and causal factors.

Many patients have an internal dialogue in which they engage in the why merry-go-round. When people become aware of an aspect of their self that does not fit their intellectually chosen ideal, they look for reasons for the behavior (Simkin, p. 3). When they have found the justification they continue behaving as before, now having a reason.

In therapy, asking why leads to case-building, speculation, historicity and emphasis on causality at the expense of functional analysis. This leads away from the processes now maintaining the behavior. This avoidance of the Here and Now is frequent with psychoanalytically oriented psychotherapists and many patients and their families.

The Gestalt therapist labels *why, because, but, it,* and *can't* dirty words. Whenever they are used the therapist may call attention to them. Thus a behavior, use of certain words, which was out of awareness, is brought into awareness. This may be done through the therapist's whistling whenever these bad words are uttered (Simkin whistle). Note that no case is being made here for vocabulary change by itself apart from other procedures. Simply stated, calling attention to language is another experimental technique for patient discovery.

Gestalt Therapy Games

Principles and techniques can be made more concrete by discussing specific techniques or games used in Gestalt therapy. These games are used in individual and group work with a goal of discovery and sensitizing. Gestalt therapy does not advocate a cessation of game playing, but an awareness of games so that the individual can choose which games he shall play, and can choose companions who play games that mesh with his own (Levitsky & Perls, 1969, pp. 8-9). The following are a few Gestalt therapy experimental games. This section relies heavily on Levitsky & Perls, 1969 (pp. 9-15).

Games of Dialogue

When a split within a person is observed, the Gestalt therapist suggests that the patient experiment by taking each part of the conflict in turn and having a dialogue. This can be done with any split, e.g., aggressive versus passive, or with another person who is significant and absent. In the latter case, the patient pretends the person is present and is carrying on the dialogue. Frequently a dialogue develops between parts of the body, such as right and left hands.

An internal conflict frequently takes place between the individual as top dog (Perls, 1965; Shostrom, 1967; Simkin) and as Under Dog. The top dog is a bullying and moralizing authoritarian. Typical top dog statements are "I (you) should." "I (you) ought

77

to." "Why don't you (I)?" Most people identify with their top dogs. The under dog controls by passivity. The under dog gives nominal acquiescence, and excuses, and goes on preventing the top dog from being successful. Shostrom's (1967) therapeutic diagnostic scheme of types of manipulators is derived from Perls' original discovery of the top dog/under dog conflict.

In Gestalt therapy, this conflict can turn into an open dialogue between the varying parts of the patient. This often begins with semantic analysis of words and phrases such as: "why-because," "yes, but...," "I can't," "I'll try..."

Making the Rounds

While doing individual work in the group, a theme often arises involving others in the group. The patient may be concerned with imagining what the others are thinking, or may have a feeling about others. The therapist may suggest that the patient make rounds and communicate the theme to each person in the group. Spontaneous and authentic encounters developing during rounds are treated like any other encounter.

Unfinished Business

Any incomplete gestalt is unfinished business demanding resolution. Usually this takes the form of unresolved and incompletely expressed feelings. Patients are encouraged to experiment with finishing business which heretofore was unfinished. When the business is unexpressed feelings toward a member of the group, the patient is asked to express them directly. Gestalt therapists have found that resentments are the most frequent and meaningful unexpressed feeling, and often deal with this with a game in which communication is limited to statements beginning with the words "I resent..."

The "I Take Responsibility" Game

Gestalt therapy considers all overt behavior, sensing, feeling and thinking acts by the person. Patients frequently disown or alienate these acts by using the *it* language, passive voice, etc. One technique is to ask the patient to add after each statement "...and I take responsibility for it."

Projection Games

When the patient imagines another person has a certain feeling or trait, he is asked to see whether it is a projection by experimenting with experiencing himself with that feeling or trait. Often the patient discovers that he does indeed have the same feeling he imagines he sees in others and that he has and rejects the same trait he rejects in others. Another game is playing projection. A patient who makes a statement characterizing another is asked to play the role of a person so characterized.

The Game of Reversals

When the therapist thinks the patient's behavior may be a reversal of a latent impulse, he may ask the patient to play the role opposite that which he has been playing. An overly sweet patient might be asked to act spiteful and uncooperative.

The Rhythm of Contact and Withdrawal

Withdrawal from Here and Now contact is treated experimentally; the patient is not admonished not to withdraw, but to be aware of when he withdraws and when he stays in contact. A patient or group of patients is sometimes asked to close his (their) eyes and withdraw. Staying with the continuum of awareness, the patient(s) reports his (their) experience. The work continues as the patient comes back to Here and Now having met his need to withdraw, with and attention having been drawn to the process of attention itself.

The Rehearsal Games

The reaction of a patient to the group is itself a valuable source of therapeutic material. The patient who is afraid of exposing his feelings to the group is encouraged to report his imagination and feelings about revealing his feelings. One frequent phenomenon is internally rehearsing for a forthcoming social role. Stage fright is a fear that the role will not be conducted well. Awareness of the rehearsing for one's now role, failure to listen while another has the stage, and the interference with spontaneity can be heightened by group games of reporting awareness of rehearsing and sharing the rehearsals. Related phenomena, such as censoring, are similarly handled (Enright, 1970b, for example).

The Exaggeration Game

Small movements and gestures may substitute for and block awareness of affective processes. The Gestalt therapists observe bodily movements and report them. One game or experiment is to ask the patient to repeat and exaggerate a movement. This heightens the perception of an important means of blocking awareness (see Enright, 1970b, p. 6; Levitsky & Perls, 1969, p. 13). An example of this was cited above (the inhibited man tapping his finger).

The "May I Feed You a Sentence? Game"

When the therapist infers an unstated or unclear message, he may phrase it into a sentence and ask the patient to say the sentence aloud — repeat it, in short, to try it on for size.

"Of Course" and "It Is Obvious That" Games

Patients frequently fail to use and trust their senses. As a result they miss the obvious and search for support for their communications. The former is often dealt with by having the patient make up sentences starting with "It is obvious that..." The search for support for statements can be experimentally dealt with by having the patient add after each sentence "..., of course."

"Can You Stay With This Feeling?"

In reporting awareness, patients quickly flee from dysphoric frustrating feelings. The Gestalt therapist often asks the patient to stay with the feeling, to stay with his continuum of awareness. The endurance of this psychic pain is a necessity to pass through the impasse (Perls, 1966, p. 7; 1965, p. 4).

Dream Work

Gestalt therapy has its own method of working with dreams. In Gestalt therapy dreams are used to integrate; they are not interpreted. Perls considers a dream as an existential message, and not wish fulfillment. It is a message telling what a person's life is and how to come to one's senses — to awaken and take one's place in life. Perls does not regard the therapist as knowing more than the patient about what his dreams mean (Perls, 1965, p. 7; see also Enright, 1970a, p. 14).

Perls lets the person act out the dream. Since he regards each part of the dream as a projection, each fragment of the dream — person, prop or mood — is considered an alienated part of the individual. The person takes each part — and an encounter ensues between the divided parts of the self. Such an encounter frequently leads to integration.

> A restless, domineering, manipulative woman dreams of walking down a crooked path in a forest of tall, straight trees. As she *becomes* one of these trees, she feels more serene and deeply rooted. Taking these feelings back into her current life, she then experiences both the lack of them and the possibilities of achieving them. *Becoming* the crooked path, her eyes fill with tears as she experiences more intensely the devious crookedness of her own life, and again, the possibilities of straightening out a little if she chooses.

Couples

Gestalt therapy is most effective in family and marital therapy (Enright, 1970a; Kempler, 1965, 1966, 1967, 1968; Levitsky & Perls, 1969;). The family as a whole, as well as the individual members of the family, come to therapy with unfinished business, incomplete awareness, unexpressed resentment, and the like. The same techniques apply to families as to other Gestalt therapy groups. Workshops with couples have been quite successful. Marital partners frequently discover that they do not relate to their spouse as is, but to an idealized concept of the spouse.

Marital therapy games are an extension of the games already discussed. As an example, the partners may be asked to face each other and take turns making up sentences beginning with "I resent you for..." This may be followed with "What I appreciate in you is..." Other possibilities are: "I spite you by..." "I am compliant by..." Discovery can be emphasized by making sentences beginning with "I see..." The emphasis is Here and Now — I and Thou, and discovering the means of avoiding immediate experience. Gestalt therapy couples work emphasizes discovery of blocks to the awareness of the nature of the current marital encounter.

Walter Kempler, discussed above, achieves dramatic results working with the entire family, and stressing the therapist's communication of his own feelings as the chief therapeutic tool.

Discussion

The behavioral therapy literature tends to narrow the alternative models to behavior modification on the one hand and the medical model on the other. Gestalt therapy is certainly a third alternative and the first existential school to work out a model of psychotherapy that avoids the faults inherent in the medical model upon which the practice of psychodynamically oriented psychotherapy is based. Moreover, it is one of the few experiential psychotherapy models emphasizing behavioral observation and experimentation.

Gestalt therapy and behavioral therapy have what the average clinician lacks: emphasis on observable behavior in the Here and Now. Both approaches reject the concepts of the unconscious and inferred etiological causality notions and replace them with observation of behavior. Gestalt therapy shares with the logical positivists and the radical behaviorists a preference for functional over causal analysis. Although both emphasize experimentation and verification of inferences with behavioral observations, Gestalt therapy does not stress quantification. Both approaches also point out the undesirable consequences resulting from finding causes for an assumed inability of the patient to be responsible for his own behavior, i.e., the notion that the patient has a disease.

However, Gestalt therapy shares with most clinicians the concern with awareness, although preferring the existential-phenomeno- ogical model of awareness to the psychodynamic model of the unconscious. Gestalt therapy's concern with awareness does not sacrifice the psychologist's role as observer of behavior. The phenomenological articulations of the patient are in accord with his sensory information, while the psychologist adheres to his sensory information with his observation and experimentation. The experiments in directed awareness are an alternative to both the curing and the conditioning process. The individual discovers how to be responsible for choosing his behavior for himself — to fully use his faculties of awareness.

Both behavior therapy and Gestalt therapy are based on behavioral science. The differences can be seen by looking at how they would apply themselves in a hypothetical but not atypical example. When a behavior therapist sees a mother who has a child that has temper tantrums, he is likely to prescribe a behavior regime to decondition the mother-child interaction supporting the tantrums. A Gestalt therapist would focus on the mother's awareness of what the child does, what he feels, how she *shoulds* herself into passively allowing the child to manipulate her. The psychologist would be aware of the results of experimentation in experimental psychology bearing on the problem. The Gestalt therapy would thus help the mother to grow into a fuller and more competent person. She is likely to discontinue the behaviors she has been engaged in that have been supporting the tantrums and simultaneously gain a perspective that can generalize the rest of the mother's life (and indirectly the child's).

History

Ego, Hunger and Aggression, Perls' first published work, was written in 1941-42. Subtitled *A Revision of Freud's Theory and Method,* it represents the bridge from his earlier practice of orthodox psychoanalysis and his later systematic practice of Gestalt therapy (Perls, 1947, Introduction to the 1966 edition). Although there were changes in later works, many of Perls' basic attitudes can be seen in this early work.

When this work was written, many revisions of Freud's theory were abroad, including the ideas of Horney, Fromm and Sullivan. However, these revisions were still within the psychodynamic, medical model tradition. Experimental psychologists were then ignoring, rejecting or translating psychoanalysis, but still had offered no general clinical alternative. Behaviorism, gestaltism, phenomenology, existentialism, ideographic psychology had not yet developed a concrete clinical alternative to psychoanalysis.

Although Perls borrowed widely from psychoanalysis, phenomenology-existentialism and operationalism-behaviorism, he used an expanded version of Gestalt psychology for his framework. Perls used the holistic-semantic approach. By semantics (meaning of meaning) Perls seemed to mean the specification of the concrete behavioral referents for all terminology. He called for:

> A ruthless purge of all merely hypothetical ideas; especially of those hypotheses which have become rigid, static convictions and which, in the minds of some, have become reality rather than elastic theories....(Perls, 1947, 1966 edition, Preface)

By holism (field conception) Perls referred to the whole being greater than a sum of the parts, to the unity of the human organism, and to the unity of the entire organism/environment field. He regarded Gestalt therapy as correcting psychoanalysis' error in treating psychological events as isolated facts apart from the organism and in basing its theory on associationism rather than on holism. This is also a difference between Gestalt therapy and most behavioristic theories.

Perls regarded his theory of psychotherapy as theoretically simple, although difficult in practice (1947, p. 185). Through social learning people lost the *feel of themselves* and could learn psychotherapy to regain this. The relearning was not an intellectual process but could be likened to Yoga, although Perls noted that Yoga had as its aim the deadening of the organism and Gestalt therapy sought to "waken the organism to a fuller life" (Perls, 1947, p. 186). He included in the book a section of exercises later expanded into his system of Gestalt therapy (Perls et al., 1951).

It is ironic that many ideas now in vogue were first articulated and/or operationalized by Perls, and yet he is seldom credited in the literature. He is chronologically a pioneer of the modern existential-phenomenological model of psychotherapy (Preface to 1966 edition of *Ego, Hunger and Aggression*), and Gestalt therapy is still the only model combining this with orientation exclusively toward concrete, Here and Now behavioral realities. Many of his concepts and approaches have become popular in the last ten to fifteen years under various terminologies, showing varying degrees of direct influence by Perls. In contrast to the lack of literary recognition, Perls has had great influence where he or his students have demonstrated Gestalt therapy.

Although *Gestalt Therapy* (1951) remains Perls' most complete work, there have been developments since then. Earlier in this paper, some of these developments were discussed without identifying their recent origin. In a 1966 introduction to *Ego, Hunger and Aggression* (1947), Perls discusses some of these recent developments, e.g., "breaking through the impasse, the point of status quo at which the average therapy seems to get caught," and the view that, except for emergency cases, individual therapy is outmoded and workshop therapy a more efficacious modality.

In this same introduction Perls gauged the extent to which the ideas he had discussed have been generally accepted in the mental health field. He stated that the awareness theory — under the names sensitivity training and t-groups — has been widely accepted. The importance of spontaneous, nonverbal expression has also been increasingly recognized. And "in the therapeutic setting the emphasis begins to shift from the phobic (so-called objective) couch situation to the encounter of a human therapist with, not a case, but another human being." He also offers the opinion that there is growing acceptance of the concepts of Here-and-Now reality, organism-as-a-whole, the dominance of the most urgent need, and the treatment of psychological events in relation to the whole organism rather than as isolated facts apart from the organism.

Other ideas of Perls' have received less attention. He states that

> The significance of aggression as a biological force, the relation of aggression to assimilation, the symbolic nature of the Ego, the phobic attitude in neurosis, the organism-environment unity is far from being understood. (Perls, 1947, Introduction to 1966 edition)

He notes also that while there is a growth toward increased use of groups and workshops, these are generally regarded as more economic rather than more efficacious. In actual clinical practice the importance of the balance of support and frustration seems not to be sufficiently emphasized.

Comparison of Models

The theoretical distinction between Gestalt therapy, behavior modification and psychoanalysis is clear. In behavior modification, the patient's behavior is directly changed by the therapist's manipulation of environmental stimuli. In psychoanalytic theory, behavior is caused by unconscious motivation, which becomes manifest in the transference relationship. By analyzing the transference the repression is lifted, and the unconscious becomes conscious. In Gestalt therapy, the patient learns to fully use his internal and external sense so he can be self-responsible and self-supportive. Gestalt therapy helps the patient regain the key to this state, the awareness of the process of awareness. Behavior modification conditions using stimulus control, psychoanalysis cures by talking about and discovering the cause of the mental illness (The Problem), and Gestalt therapy brings self-realization through Here-and-Now experiments in directed awareness.

Other models of psychotherapy are also alternatives to behavior modification and psychoanalysis. In the last decade there has been a growth of third force alternatives. New models of psychotherapy have been offered by Rogers (post-1960), Bach, Berne, Schutz, Satir, Frankl, Glasser, Ellis and others. Careful analysis is needed to separate true from semantic differences between these schools and psychodynamic psychotherapy and behavior modification. Careful analysis is needed also to separate the similarities and differences between Gestalt therapy and the other third force schools.

The third force generally sees the therapeutic relationship as a direct relationship between human beings, i.e., an I-Thou relationship is preferred over a doctor-patient or manipulator-manipulated relationship. All claim to be holistic, interactional, and existential. In all the therapist is more active than in psychodynamically oriented psychotherapy. All use group modalities, such as encounter groups, family groups, sensitivity training, sensory awareness, etc. All are optimistic and stress the achievement of the potential of man.

The difference between psychodynamic and the third force therapies may be illusory. In psychodynamic psychotherapy and in most third force therapies, change is postulated to result from

talking about the patient's life with a view of increasing understanding. In both, the patient comes to greater self-acceptance as
his understanding increases. The chief differences seem to be
therapist activity, optimistic versus pessimistic attitude and the
preference for discussion of current life circumstances to discussion of the childhood.

Gestalt therapy is nominally a third force psychotherapy. When
viewing the actual behavior of therapists and patients in psychotherapy, the third force therapies seem alike and quite different
than either psychoanalysis or behavior modification. Shostrom
(1967) discusses *actualizing therapies* in a way that emphasizes
similarities. The present review will present the ways in which
Gestalt therapy is unique from other third force therapies. Gestalt
therapy's uniqueness is in the direction of increased distinctive-
ness from psychodynamically oriented psychotherapy.

1. Holism and Multidimensionality

Although many psychotherapists claim to be holistic, many are
in fact unidimensional (Perls, 1948, p. 579). Perls claims that only
a comprehensive psychotherapy can be integrative and only a
therapist with a comprehensive view can spot and tackle core
difficulties. Therapists frequently have blind spots, areas which
they will not see. They will avoid assimilating insights from schools
emphasizing such areas. Patients who are ambivalent about change
often seek therapists whose blind spot is in their area of difficulty.
The more comprehensive the biopsychosocial outlook, the more
likely is it that any difficulty is spotted in training a therapist or
helping a patient. Gestalt therapy views the entire biopsychosocial
field, including organism/environment, as important. Gestalt
therapy actively uses physiological, sociological, cognitive, motivational variables. No relevant dimension is excluded in the basic
theory.

2. "Now" and the Mechanism of Change

The modern notion of emphasizing the current life circumstances of the patient is in one sense *now*, in contrast to the
Freudian notion of *then*. However, in Gestalt therapy now is a
functional concept referring to acts done *right now*. When recounting what one did last night, now one is recounting, last night was

then. In discussing an encounter of five minutes ago, the encounter was then. Here-and-Now experience of immediate feelings and behavior is slighted at the expense of remembering the past. This emphasis on immediacy, on raw experience, has led to an explanation of the change process different from most other psychotherapeutic models.

Most therapists believe that change takes place as a function of increased knowledge, insight or awareness. They differ on how they define knowledge and what kind of knowledge is needed. In Gestalt therapy knowledge is not equivalent to what is verbalized, orally or to oneself. Psychodynamic writers discuss this distinction in terms of real insight and intellectual insight. The kind of knowledge that Gestalt therapy teaches is knowledge of how one takes attention away from the immediate raw sensory data of experience. The mechanism by which the subject substitutes for the active Here and Now on a matter of emotional concern is a particular object of Gestalt therapy experimentation. It is by the return to awareness of this mechanism, previously out of awareness, that the Gestalt therapy patient can analyze the processes by which he supports unsatisfactory behavior and acquires the tools to independently increase awareness in the future.

In therapy by Rogers, Bach, Berne, Glasser, Ellis, and Satir, the content, The Problem, the analysis of social interaction and the discussion of life circumstances, is stressed. This is different from the Gestalt therapy stress on *Now*. In Gestalt therapy talking-about as done in some third force therapies, is taboo. In its place Gestalt therapy uses experimentation.

3. Psychotherapy as Experimentation

Gestalt therapy is experimental in the true sense of the term; it is experiencing oneself, or trying a behavior on for size — "the actual living through an event or events" (Perls et al., 1951, p. 15) This emphasis can be seen by looking at the existential encounter. Gestalt therapy shares with other existential psychotherapies the belief in an I-Thou — Here and Now therapeutic relationship.

But this encounter is used in Gestalt therapy to experiment with life and to discover. Roles are played in Gestalt therapy not to practice new behavior, but for the patient to learn to discriminate which behavior meets his needs. The relationship is not curative in Gestalt therapy; learning to discover is curative. Experimentation is more than a Gestalt therapy technique — it is an attitude inherent in all Gestalt therapy. Gestalt therapy could be called a process of ideographic experimentation with awareness directed to the continuum of awareness.

This experimental focus is unique to Gestalt therapy. It is influenced by oriental religions, especially Taoism and Zen Buddhism, and by phenomenological experiments. Without this emphasis and the techniques derived therefrom, the attitudes discussed under point number four (infra) could not be maintained. The alternative to Here-and-Now experimentation is reconditioning — either openly and systematically as in behavior modification or covertly as in most psychotherapy. Although Gestalt therapy frequently discovers the same patient processes as other third force therapies, in Gestalt therapy the endpoint is the *process* of discovery, not the discovery itself.

What leads to change in Gestalt therapy is not so much increased awareness in general as increased ability to be aware. Exercises used by Schutz and at the Western Behavior Research Institute at La Jolla appear to increase awareness, but frequently without focusing on the mechanism by which people habitually avoid awareness of unpleasant experience.

Virginia Satir (1964) helps each member of a family identify feelings and identify the imaginations about self — others and what others think about self that underlies the feelings. Lines of communication are traced back to the beginning of the marriage. However, the process by which the patient now focuses on the past instead of his current concerns, the process by which the patient avoids awareness of his own feelings and attends instead to the expectations of others, is not emphasized.

Rogers believes that the encounter between a therapist with unconditional regard and the patient will result in change. This encounter and talk-about results in different psychotherapy techniques than Gestalt therapy, although there are philosophic kinships between the two systems. Both use encounter and both aim for positive growth. Gestalt therapy does not talk about; Gestalt therapy experiments to discover how *right now* one is manipulating and keeping from being aware of the manipulation.

4. *The Place of the Therapist's Value System*

The only *should* (moral) accepted by the Gestalt therapist is that the patient should be aware. Each person must contact novel elements in the environment, and decide for himself which is nourishing and to be assimilated, and which toxic and to be avoided. This discrimination changes with the constant change of dominant need. Gestalt therapy does not have a vision of what behavior is more desirable for any particular person or at any particular time. Bach (1962) indicates more of a willingness to inculcate some values.

Where the patient has a choice of behaviors, Gestalt therapy works on increasing the patient's awareness of antecedents, organismic reaction, consequences of behavior, and so forth. Myths and fears can be experienced in the safe therapeutic situation so that the patient can decide for himself what is nourishing and what is toxic. Contrary to Ellis' approach, the patient and not the therapist decides what is irrational for him. As an example, many patients subscribe to the myth that verbally reporting negative feelings is dangerous. By experimenting with direct verbal expression of negative emotions, the patient may discover that there are situations in which such behavior is quite rewarding. Further, he may become aware of the price he pays by not expressing such feelings.

In Gestalt therapy morality is based on organismic need (Perls, 1953-1954). In contrast, adjustment to the group, commitment to group harmony, and cooperation are *shoulds* implicit and/or explicit in many third force psychotherapies, such as sensitivity training groups. Pressure by therapist or group is not used to achieve this in Gestalt therapy as aggression is regarded as a natural biological force. When the patient is aware of ways he can express or restrain his aggression, the difference between aggression and annihilation, the consequences of his behavior, the Gestalt therapist believes the patient can make his own choice.

Perls is explicit in regarding people as capable of self support, and not fragile or needing protection from inner or outer reality. Nor does he regard people as needing him as a dictator who forces change. Eliminating force, he also eliminates a great deal of the need to protect patients from the therapeutic process. The patient already possesses what for him are the best mechanisms for avoiding unassimilatable information and the patient can best judge for himself what information is of use to him. When maximum use of group pressure is used, protection of some patients may be a necessary part of the therapist's activities. It is consistent that those who insist that people need pressure-type social confrontation also assume that people need the therapist's protection. Many of those using confrontation techniques tend to assume that therapy progress must await a carefully nurtured relationship. On the other hand, in Gestalt therapy the patient can learn from the first experimental encounter.

This contrasts with the approaches of Bach, Berne, Satir and Schutz. Satir regards maintenance of the system, the family system, as paramount. Both Bach and Schutz have definite norms they seek. Bach sets out rules for marital fighting; there are good and bad ways of cutting across individual differences. Both Bach and Schutz unqualifiedly exhort patients to share secrets with the group and/or with their spouses in marital therapy.

By contrast, Gestalt therapy has a different game or technique to deal with secrets: "The `I have a secret' game" (Levitsky & Perls, 1969, p. 11). The patient is asked to think of a well-guarded secret: "He is instructed *not* to share the secret itself but imagine (project) how he thinks others would react to it" (Levitsky & Perls, 1969, p. 11). The technique can be extended by having each brag about his terrible secret, thus working on the unaware attachment to a secret as an achievement. Knowledge of the guilt and shame and feelings and mechanisms for avoiding awareness of them yields different dividends than Schutz's and Bach's general advice to share secrets. A similar example is Berne's goal of the elimination of game playing. In Gestalt therapy the goal is awareness so the patient can choose.

5. *Violence and Annihilation*

Schutz allows and encourages actual violence where people have such impulses. Although Gestalt therapy encourages aggression, violence is seen as an attempt at annihilation. Gestalt therapy workshops, in contrast to Schutzian workshops, are nonviolent. Behavior which attempts to annihilate and hurt others avoids experiencing one's own dysphoric feelings. Acting out one's anger in violence is antithetical to increased experience, direct expression of feelings and the I-Thou relationship. Gestalt therapy accepts aggression and conflict as natural biopsychosocial forces and encourages experimentation with staying with negative feelings and directly expressing them in verbal reports (Enright, 1970a; Perls, 1947, 1948, 1953-4; Perls et al., 1951; Simkin).

6. Clinical Training

Although Gestalt therapy has suggestions for modification of the training of clinical psychologists (Enright, 1970b), suggestions similar to those advanced by Rogers (1956), Gestalt therapy does not advocate abandonment of professional clinical training. The clinically trained psychologist becomes aware of the range of psychopathology and of human limits. Although psychologists without clinical training have made contributions of great value to clinical psychology, they are not qualified to practice psychotherapy. Some new psychotherapies are advocated and practiced by psychologists without clinical training. Gestalt therapy deplores this development. Innovative psychotherapies have received a great deal of publicity, and there are reports of maladaptive social and psychological reactions to some workshops. The writer believes this results from the lack of professional clinical training of some human potentials therapists and the consequent lack of awareness of human limitations. Of course, professional training includes many disciplines — psychology, nursing, social work, etc. The use of nonprofessional assistants is a separate question entirely.

7. Range of Applicability

The Gestalt therapy literature has not clarified the exact range of pathology to which it is applicable, and what modifications or additional techniques are necessary with psychotics, psychopaths, children and others. But Gestalt therapy is a clinical theory, and has been developed by clinical psychologists for a wide range of patients. The details are still being worked out. This contrasts with sensitivity training, which has been developed by nonclinical psychologists for use with already functioning businessmen. The need for further work on this point is discussed below.

8. Techniques per se

In passing it should be noted that Gestalt therapy has many unique techniques, some discussed above. These techniques can be used within different frameworks, although with changed meaning. Similarly, techniques from various schools can be used within the Gestalt therapy framework. The present writer, for example, has found that when working with hospitalized psychotics, psychodrama techniques in a Gestalt therapy framework are more effective than the dialogue techniques usually used in Gestalt therapy.

Criticisms

There are need areas in Gestalt therapy which will be discussed in this section. In general, these areas point to potential in Gestalt therapy that is unexploited. Since this article has not directly reviewed Gestalt therapy personality and learning theory or views about basic research, criticisms in these areas will not be discussed here.

While we are not discussing the implication of Gestalt therapy for basic research, the area of precision of definitions and validating research is germane.

Eric Berne takes the position that operational definitions are not possible in this area (Berne, 1964). In view of the extensive research by Rogers and his coworkers, this is difficult to sustain. In Perls' writings there is no case made against more exact forms of validation; he has just chosen not to spend his time doing this type of research.

Perls offers no quantified, statistical evidence that Gestalt therapy works. He discusses this issue:

"Where is your proof?" Our standard answer will be that we present nothing that you cannot *verify for yourself in terms of your own behavior,* but if your psychological make-up is that of the experimentalist as we have portrayed him, this will not satisfy you and you will clamor for "objective evidence" of a verbal sort, *prior* to trying out a single nonverbal step of the procedure. (Perls et al., 1951, p. 7)

Perls has provided a series of graded experiments with instructions which one can use to verify the utility of Gestalt therapy, and he includes a representative sample of the comments of experimental subjects who have taken these experiments. The experiments are clear and can be replicated by any interested reader.

While there are gaps in the system (Levitsky & Perls, 1969, p. 9; Polster, 1966, p. 6), there is a stress on separating knowledge from ignorance. Gestalt therapy presents ideas within a molar framework, but with a concern for molecular details. Although Perls does not provide objective measures of his terms, his discussions stress concrete observation and concrete experience in preference to inference and speculation. In this sense, Gestalt therapy is an empirical theory.

Although Perls also makes available live demonstrations and reproductions (films, tape recordings, videotapes, and several case examples are presented in the Gestalt therapy literature: Kempler, 1965, 1966, 1967, 1968, Perls, 1948; Laura Perls, 1956; Polster, 1957; Simkin, 1962), there are an insufficient number of systematic, detailed case histories. The most detailed are by Laura Perls (1956).

If quantified and objective research and validation techniques are demanded in an area at the outset of investigation, one may be limited to a narrow and sterile subject matter. Limiting the subject matter of a science is of doubtful validity. The subject matter of Gestalt therapy appears to be important. Gestalt therapy covers new areas, explores new assumptions, but has sacrificed exact verification for the value in ideographic experimental psychotherapy. Perls does not make the mistake of assuming he has the answers, but rather readily admits the state of ignorance of the field (Perls, 1948). Moreover, Gestalt therapy does not claim that it has the only valid approach (Enright, 1970b). The burden of proof is heavier on those who define psychology so as to exclude differing approaches from the field.

Perls has presented a gold mine of insights and procedures which could be exploited in psychotherapy and by experimentally minded psychologists. But few Gestalt therapists have done much to carry out the research possibilities of Gestalt therapy (for an exception, see Shostrom 1966a, 1966b, 1967). It would be helpful if the literature were reviewed and experimental predictions and clinical expectations that could be made from Gestalt therapy were made explicit even if the research is not immediately forthcoming.

A great deal is left to the discretion of the individual clinician in Gestalt therapy. There is provision made for the style and personality of the therapist, within the bounds of professional responsibility (Polster, 1966, pp. 4-5). Even the question of the modifications in techniques and theory that need to be made for different patient diagnostic groups has not been formulated in the Gestalt therapy literature. The writer knows from informal discussions and personal experience that Gestalt therapy has been used with different patient groups, but the results are not reported in the literature. There is a particular need for a delineation of the limits of the application of Gestalt therapy.

Similarly, a great deal of responsibility is left with the patient. The basic work of psychotherapy is done by the patient with the Gestalt therapist being a guide and catalyst. The therapist's job is to present experiments and observations that dramatically and clearly portray the perceptual field being studied. Failure to do this can be a cause of clinical failure attributable to the therapist (Perls, 1948). However, the basic work of discovery and utilizing the discovery is the patient's responsibility.

Perls' validation in terms of each reader's own experience is unique. It is quite different from the demand of psychoanalysis that a critic be analyzed, and from behavior modification's strict adherence to experimental measurement criteria. The psychoanalytic argument is an ad hominem *argument which accepts validation only within the system. The length and expense needed for analysis renders this argument unacceptable. Gestalt therapy experimentation can be tried from* Gestalt therapy (Perls et al., 1951) or from weekend workshops. This outlay of time is comparable to that required to experience any approach different than the person is accustomed to. An open and critical attitude is required, but faith in the system is not required to test Gestalt therapy. It is the writer's observation that Gestalt therapy is often experienced and appreciated only after a personal encounter with a Gestalt therapist; a single encounter often makes available to a participant a perspective not available to a non-participating observer.

There is also involved here a value question that is not answerable by laboratory experiments. Objective proof of technical success cannot answer the value question: Is it desirable for the clinician to control the patient's behavior? And ultimately, this question is decided by each individual. Recognizing this, Gestalt therapists offer Gestalt therapy and leave to the individual the choice of whether it is useful *for him.*

Perls has provided a therapy that is exclusively oriented to Here-and-Now behavior without excluding awareness variables and without conditioning that behavior. It does apply existential attitudes with a unique system of psychotherapy, and validates the system in a unique way. The writer accepted Perls' offer and challenge to verify Gestalt therapy for himself and found the system personally and professionally exciting, creative and useful. To each is left the burden of deciding if the potential from Gestalt therapy for himself warrants personal experimentation, psychotherapeutic application or its use with basic research.

4

GESTALT THERAPY:
A POLEMIC

━━━━━━━━━━━━━━

Commentary

In this essay, written in 1987, I outline the history of Gestalt therapy, and the change in attitudes over the years. I discuss recent changes in clinical attitude regarding confrontation, therapist visibility and presence, continuity in relationship, understanding the overall character structure of the patient, models of Gestalt therapy in groups, importance of thinking and theory, relationship with psychoanalysis and other approaches.

When Joe Wysong asked members of the editorial board of *The Gestalt Journal* to write their reflections about the changes in Gestalt therapy in the last 10 years and I asked myself about what we know about that development, I also wondered how we can know the accuracy of what we think we know about the place of Gestalt therapy in the world. We think we are looking at Gestalt therapy as it is in the world, but how much do we actually see and to what extent do we "see" what we want to see? I believe we have fooled ourselves before. I applaud the soliciting and publishing of various perspectives for the 10th anniversary of *The Gestalt Journal,* for that at least creates the opportunity for the corrective of criticism and debate.

For the last 10 years *The Gestalt Journal* has served an important and much-needed function in creating a forum in which we can describe, remember (in print), analyze, discuss, debate Gestalt therapy's history, philosophy, methodology, sociology, etc. In this issue of *The Gestalt Journal* we have another opportunity of taking a step toward correcting the fact that, in my opinion, we in Gestalt therapy give insufficient attention to explicating empirical and philosophic perspectives. We do talk of such matters, but often merely repeat generalizations that are neither well examined theoretically or empirically nor improved by the repetition.

Glory and The Beginning of Disappointment (1965-1975)

The last 10 years were preceded by a decade in which Gestalt therapy became very popular and unlimited in its aspirations.

When I first started in Gestalt therapy in 1965 it was an era of rebellion and revolution in society and in the therapy community. Anything seemed possible if we were but willing to throw off the shackles of rigidity and risk allowing creativity to emerge. A naive faith and hope in experimentation went hand in hand with a dismissal of tradition. For Gestalt therapy it was the beginning of a decade of meteoric success.

Traditional Freudian psychoanalysis was an easy target for rebellion. It was rigid and doctrinaire, intellectualized, paid scant attention and gave little respect to the here-and-now experience of either the patient or the therapist, dictated that the therapist refrain from personal expressive presence regardless of the circumstances or personality or feelings or needs of the particular therapist or patient, could not integrate active techniques and was Newtonian in an age of field theory.

Of course, Gestalt therapy's meaning is in its relation to its background, especially in its birth and separation from psychoanalysis. The debt owed and the value of psychoanalysis was certainly appreciated by some Gestalt therapists, but in the decade of glory this was not highly visible. In those days a kind of glow emanated from and surrounded Gestalt therapy. In that particular decade there was little appreciation for traditional theories, practices and philosophies. It was as if Gestalt therapy could accomplish anything by itself, and encompass everything.

Gestalt therapy rose to heights of popularity on a wave of optimism. Although the literature was limited, the oral tradition seemed to point to great philosophic possibilities, and dramatic therapeutic work at workshops pointed to great clinical possibilities. Although it seemed clear that there were gaps in the philosophical and practice literature of Gestalt therapy, the confidence and attitude in the Gestalt therapy community was high, positive and upbeat.

Perhaps the zenith of this was the style of Gestalt therapy Perls popularized in the late 1960s (what Joel Latner calls the "California style"). The era was one of rebellion, expansion, expressiveness. Change and risk were good words; stability, caution, predictability were bad words. There was a loss of balance, loss of half of natural polarities. There was a stress on process and present moment, but not the balancing acknowledgment of structure and continuity.

This style treated excitement and ease of effort as "natural" and careful consideration as neurotic. This was true of both the "turn-on" style popular in the late 1960s and the "tune-in" style popular in the early 1970s (in which abrasive encounters, yelling, pounding, the empty chair, and the like gave way to body emphasis, meditation, etc.). In the style of many Gestalt therapists the interpersonal-intrapsychic focus of Gestalt therapy was gradually replaced by an intrapsychic attitude — without explicit commentary on the philosophic change. In this style growth started to be treated as finding salvation within rather than finding it by the awareness-contact process.

In a sense the thesis of the 1960s was rebellion, social protest, experimentation and expression of affect, the bringing of one's "I" to others. In the early 1970s there was an antithesis: the search for inner quiet. In the 1970s there was a growing recognition of narcissism as a social and clinical problem. In the 1980s I believe we are coming to a synthesis, a more balanced view.

The excitement of new possibilities covered a multitude of weaknesses. The context of rapid growth and public demonstrations of Gestalt therapy encouraged showmanship, turn-on and oversimplification. Isadore From refers to this as the theatricalization of Gestalt therapy (From, 1984; see also Resnick, 1984). Gestalt therapy was often shown as a glittering show of technique.

Technique was more publicized than craft; craft more than methodology; methodology more than philosophy. This publicity reversed the actual emphasis in Gestalt therapy.

In 1968, when I wrote a review of the theory of Gestalt therapy, I found 23 published pieces and 10 unpublished papers. To me that seemed scanty for a system that was then 20 years old, scanty but promising. By the mid-70s there had been an encouraging increase in Gestalt therapy publications with the unpublished articles and new books being published. And with the start of *The Gestalt Journal* there was a real forum for Gestalt therapy papers. Gestalt therapy seemed on its way and the optimism justified.

Of course disappointment was inevitable. As Gestalt therapists we know: "great expectations, great disappointments." The naive faith in experimentation without adequate theoretical and professional perspective needed maturing by confronting limitations and disappointments. There was need for the hard work of testing generalizations in the laboratory of Gestalt therapy practice and revising our practices, philosophy and methodology according to what insight we develop as a result of the experiment that is Gestalt therapy. Part of the glory attitude was a mistaken belief that we could accomplish great things without discipline, sacrifice, hard work at intellectual tasks.

In the first 25 years after the publication of *Gestalt Therapy*, the seminal work upon which the theory of Gestalt therapy is based, — 25 years in a rapidly changing field — there was a paucity of advanced level theoretical elaborations or advancements.

By the mid-70s psychoanalysis had become more sophisticated and its literature more useful. Writers such as Kohut, Guntrip, Kernberg, Masterson, Mahler, Salzman, Schaffer could not be easily dismissed. The passivity of the early Rogerian approach was transcended by Rogers, Gendlin and others. Behavior therapy became more sophisticated with cognitive behavior modification, behavioral counseling and other changes. Eclectic psychotherapists incorporated many of the insights of Gestalt therapy into their practice.

During this time of expansion of other therapies, many who were touting "Gestalt therapy techniques" and "Gestalt therapy" who were almost totally untrained in Gestalt therapy. Many commentators, critics and others, misunderstood Gestalt therapy theory and practice. Our literature contributed to the misunderstanding of Gestalt therapy and we did too little to correct the abuses and misunderstanding. Those who did understand Gestalt therapy did not produce a literature that could both present an accurate picture of Gestalt therapy philosophy and also become recognized by the general professional audience as representing what Gestalt therapy really was. There were excellent articles and books, but none that was a definitive sequel to *Gestalt Therapy*. Articles truly reflecting Gestalt therapy and those that did not were not distinguishable because the overall theory was not explicated enough to form a criterion against which articles could be compared.

In most of the 1965-1975 decade we were fooled by our popularity and success and did not seem to notice when our standing in the professional community declined in the middle to late 70s.

In the last 10 years we have also become aware of some sobering clinical experience. Probably the most striking fact is that a number of patients, especially the narcissistically disturbed patients, did not do well with Perls's late 1960s type of Gestalt therapy — as they did not do well with traditional Psychoanalysis. As the number of recognized narcissistic personality-disordered patients has grown and Gestalt therapists have assimilated their clinical experience, changes in Gestalt therapy practice and theory were indicated. Even the borderline patients, for whom Gestalt therapy may be the treatment of choice, demand modification and increased sophistication for good Gestalt therapy treatment. An explication of this was totally lacking in the literature of the 1965-1975 decade.

Needed improvements in our clinical and theoretical attitudes were not limited to these self disorders. Therapy systems, just like individuals, must learn and grow to live. Growing involves taking criticism seriously. Quality care and training require discovering what works and doesn't, what fits together, what can be improved and any changes have to be Gestalted, assimilated into the whole system. In the next section we will discuss some of these improvements that have begun in the 1980s.

Consider one example of a needed theoretical update with clinical implications: Many of the early Gestalt therapists were trained in psychoanalytic diagnosis, theory and treatment before becoming Gestalt therapists. Functioning as Gestalt therapists they had much background that was not acknowledged. As conventional clinical wisdom was devalued rather than integrated, and as time went on and new Gestalt therapists have been trained without this background, the treatment and training they offered has often been inadequate. The unacknowledged perspective attained in part from a psychoanalytic background was missing and nowhere in the theory was this need acknowledged before the last 10 years. Now we have begun to correct this inaccuracy of our collective self-image that had limited the quality and range of relevance of our training and therapy.

On the positive side, the awareness of holes and the feeling of disappointment that attends such awareness has led to gains that I will elaborate on in the next section. On the negative side, many have not been able to react positively to the need for further development. Many have merely devalued Gestalt therapy and/or left for other systems. Speculation on why some did not integrate newfound gems from other systems into a nexus of Gestalt therapy might be instructive. I believe that limitations of training, theoretical skills and temperament account for much of the variance.

Many clinicians, Gestalt therapists not the least of them, are naive or untutored or lazy about the amount of intellectual work it takes to build a whole system, to assimilate rather than introject, to be accountable for providing empirical evidence of effectiveness, to do competent philosophical analysis. It is unfortunate that Gestalt therapy does not have a support base in academia.

I also believe that this is greatly compounded in the Gestalt therapy scene because many just have not learned in depth either the Gestalt therapy theory or the philosophies that are the foundation of the theory. Moreover, it is possible that Gestalt therapists are less inclined toward the philosophic analysis that would be necessary to do this task. Certainly this seems true of the 1965-1975 era. This particular problem is not restricted to those who are untrained in Gestalt therapy but call themselves Gestalt therapists. This can be seen in many who write, speak, teach, and train others in Gestalt therapy.

It should be noted that I am not claiming that there is only one interpretation of Gestalt therapy or that the tenets of Gestalt therapy have been explicated in an unambiguous manner — far from it. However, some seem not to understand the philosophical foundation of Gestalt therapy and many do not know that they don't know nor show signs of caring. Some try to change Gestalt theory without understanding *Gestalt Therapy*, the most authoritative source in Gestalt therapy theory, and the philosophy behind it.

The definition of Gestalt therapy that was sometimes advanced by, or implicit in the teachings of, those who did not know the basic theory was one that reduced Gestalt therapy to technique and cliché. One can not explicate the essence of Gestalt therapy without knowing its basic theory. What they were left with was an atomistic construction of Gestalt therapy as if a therapy system could be infinitely malleable without apprehending the whole (or more accurately the relation between the parts and the whole).

The result was "Gestalt *and*...." Those who did not understand how and how much Gestalt therapy could assimilate had a concept of Gestalt therapy theory and practice that was reduced to a fraction of its potential. Then they practiced an inadequate therapy or just added new material into Gestalt therapy without integration and constructed their practice *ad hoc*. Anything that was missing, any hole, was met by appending a corrective to or into Gestalt therapy without systematic alteration/assimilation.

The "Gestalt therapy *and*..." attitude of "and-summative" combining of elements of Gestalt therapy with elements of other systems enabled each therapist to believe grandiosely that any combination of new techniques or insights he or she put together could be cogent, creative and effective. The weakness of our theoretical literature allowed this to go on.

In fact, new wildcat creations were often presented as a new wave cure-all — seeming to some to be like a snake oil sales pitch. There was no systematic way of discriminating what was to be included or excluded or how it was to be included, or what alterations needed to be made to account for the differences between Gestalt therapy and the source system of the addition. Some included everything in their definition of Gestalt therapy, some included very little and defined any additions to their practice as not being Gestalt therapy.

This lack of clear sense of Gestalt therapy's boundaries was a sign of their lack of clarity about the identity of Gestalt therapy. It is not clear how much of this relates to the ambiguities of Gestalt therapy theory, how much to the inadequacies of our written literature and how much to the inadequate theoretical training of Gestalt therapists.

I have observed a common sequence: first the theory of Gestalt therapy was not learned very well. For example, many trainees demand that they be taught techniques without theory or methodology. For most of the trainees of this type that I have seen this is a continuation of their characterological development in general. They resisted the work of acquiring a more thorough understanding of Gestalt therapy and consequently often defined Gestalt therapy in terms of techniques or clichés, and the essence of it was not appreciated. The cliché-level part of Gestalt therapy's literature supported this attitude.

The result was they were not able to discriminate what could be assimilated (and how) and what could not (and why). Their very narrow understanding of Gestalt therapy was followed by practicing their version of "Gestalt therapy *and*...." They had to do this since they did not understand that Gestalt therapy was not just a specific set of techniques, did not appreciate Gestalt therapy's ability to assimilate, and perhaps did not even know the difference between assimilation and introjection. And they often saw this not as a limitation, but rather a sign of their advanced status since they were not limited by "rigid" requirements of intellectual consistency or articulation or empirical sophistication. And when faced with a limitation or flaw they could attribute the problems to Gestalt therapy's lack of development rather than face their own inadequate development.

Clear identity requires clear boundary. Boundary means including and excluding. An overly broad and vague definition of Gestalt therapy, one that enables Gestalt therapists to believe they can include anything in any combinations, protects one against having to make discriminations, suffer loss and disappointment, describe a system in terms others can research and criticize.

We have been hurt by wildcat *ad hoc* approaches called Gestalt therapy (or "Gestalt therapy techniques" or "Gestalt therapy and....") We have been hurt by both continued naivete and by the public de-valuing of Gestalt therapy by people who discard and de-value Gestalt therapy and go on to advocate the next panacea (and the next) with the same grandiosity as had been lavished on Gestalt therapy earlier. And we have been hurt when competent Gestalt therapists talk or write and contradict Gestalt theory without knowing it.

In the last 10 years sophistication about the holes in Gestalt therapy as constituted has been growing. The last five years have been marked by positive signs, signs indicating that as a community we may be *beginning* to grapple with the issues of gestalting Gestalt therapy into a more mature system. *The Gestalt Journal* and the annual conference sponsored by the journal have provided a forum to take stock and begin dialogues (yes, Gestalt therapists can have intellectual dialogues) about our history, our theory, clinical applications and research. Although the quantity, quality and consistency of our literature as a whole has not been adequate, I see in recent years a growing attention to the need for philosophical debate, creating a forum for case studies, and at least reviewing the research literature and taking a positive attitude toward research.

The literature of the last decade has included excellent articles that have explicated aspects of Gestalt therapy and/or clarified how the most visible Gestalt therapy style of 1965-1975 has distorted or lost some of the essence of Gestalt therapy. Among these are G. Brown (1974/1977), I. From (1978 and 1984), R. Hycner (1985), J. Latner (1983), L. Perls (1978), E. Polster (1985) and R. Resnick (1984).

This beginning has been happening none too soon. For the rapidly changing therapeutic and social context of the last 10 years calls for vigilance, not complacency. There have been expansions of possibilities, a vastly improved psychoanalysis that is a clear alternative to Gestalt therapy, a convergence of therapy models, an increased demand for more sophisticated discrimination about what therapy, what therapist, what techniques, with what patients and for how long. There have been increased political pressures for verification of effectiveness, demands that third-party payments only be given for proven treatment, increased competition between professions for market shares, etc. In this context an awareness of the limitations of Gestalt therapy as constituted is vital for survival. We still have much work to do in the next 10 years to continue the work we have started. The holes are still too profound to warrant any complacency.

Crisis: Is Gestalt Therapy Rising to the Challenge? (1976-1986)

Is Gestalt therapy meeting the challenge? I believe that in the 1980s Gestalt therapy has made a slow beginning of much-needed changes in five areas (since these are not fully explicated in the literature, the extent of these changes is not clear.) (1) a more mature existential attitude; (2) a changed clinical attitude; (3) changes in approach to groups; (4) better appreciation of thinking; (5) a more eclectic attitude toward psychoanalysis and other therapies.

1. A More Mature Existential Attitude

In the past decade Gestalt therapy has been true to its existential heritage by increasing attention to human relations, an increasing respect for the phenomenology of the patient, and beginning to deal with issues of continuity. This more mature existential attitude has been the basis for a more sophisticated clinical methodology and a framework for assimilating new psychoanalytic insights.

There has been a growing realization that the importance that has been placed on momentary contact, excitement, sensory awareness and emotional expressiveness is only a building block to a more complete existential attitude, the active personal presence of the therapist without greater specification only a building block to a true dialogic presence (see, for example, Hycner, 1985). I believe we have begun to see the dialogic philosophy inherent in but not fully explicated in earlier Gestalt therapy formulations and practice.

An awareness through dialogue attitude in Gestalt therapy has recently emphasized the dialogic existential notion of inclusion, a renewed emphasis on the patient's phenomenology. The phenomenological attitude is not one of merely emphasizing the patient's subjective feelings, excitement and expressiveness, but a disciplined phenomenological relation of person and context, an integration of the "subjective" and the "objective."

A true existential attitude includes interest in the sweep of the patient's existence and appreciation of the necessity of talking about the patient's past as well as present experience outside as well as inside the therapeutic setting (see, for example, E. Polster, 1985).

The attitude in the 1980s focused not only on the awareness and expressiveness of the patient, but also on the relationship between the patient and the therapist (and other patients in groups), and with increasing attention to what kind of contact is therapeutic for particular patients. Isadore From's criticism of techniques such as the empty chair and the interpretation of dreams as exclusively projection is an example of Gestalt therapy's appreciation of the relating of therapist and patient (I. From, 1978, 1984).

Relationship is not just a summation of moments of contact, but a whole that includes continuity. Although there was always a stress in Gestalt therapy on good contact/presence, it was often episodic and did not emphasize awareness of the patient's self identity over time. The dialogic emphasis has stressed what develops between therapist and patient (Thou) as essential to the healing and the relationship of *I* to *otherness* essential to healthy functioning. Although the notion of the relation between person and otherness is part of the Gestalt therapy concepts of contact, identity and boundary (see I. From, 1978), the Gestalt therapy literature does not fully account for continuity of relationship and interdependence between people (see G. Brown, 1974,1977) and the literature as a whole exhibits an inconsistent epistemological view (see Latner, 1983).

The notion of contact is essential to dialogue, and our notion of contact leads directly into a mature concept of dialogue. The motto "I and Thou, Here and Now" has long been spoken of in Gestalt therapy. However there has been only a beginning explication of dialogue in Gestalt therapy. Nor did the style Perls popularized help — he did not share his process, only demonstrated a theatricalized Gestalt therapy. Often he treated the patient's perceptions as those of an opponent.

Although the theory stressed awareness of self and others, the connotations, especially of the clichés, stressed *I* more than *I and You*. In its degenerate form this seemed like an attitude of "turn-on" and sometimes inadvertently advanced the notion that being aware of momentary impulse and expressing and acting on it, regardless of the context in which the impulse occurred and regardless of the relation of the impulse to true organismic self regulation (including the entire range of needs and values), regardless of longer term goals and the needs of others, was somehow what maturity was all about. As the society has changed and the balance of who our patients are has changed, this lack of clarity has become even more problematic.

Now the Gestalt therapy interest in the "creative" or "creative adjustment" is balanced by an interest in "adjustment" also. In the 1960s the popular form of Gestalt therapy was geared to working with uptight neurotics, especially therapists, who needed to loosen up, and an attitude of encouraging patients to "do your own thing" made some sense. The patients were often oversocialized and needed more autonomy, creativity — more I. The importance of the needs of others, of obligations, had already been learned and overlearned.

Gestalt therapy expositions have sometimes neglected context and responsibility of the needs of the situation in general, including the needs of others, but of special importance, also neglected to make clear the responsibility of the therapist for the therapeutic atmosphere, for the results of the therapist's style of therapeutic presence and for countertransference. Sometimes this resulted in iatrogenic dysfunction, such as amplified shame, encouragement of narcissistic grandiosity and acting out.

Although the basic theory of Gestalt therapy emphasizes contact and support — self-support for interpersonal contact and withdrawal — the lack of clarity and consistency of definition often led to theoretical and practical confusion. Self-support was often discussed in a manner that confused self-support with self-sufficiency and taught an overly negative attitude toward any hint of confluence. The importance of interdependence and cooperation in normal and healthy functioning was obscured by this. This confusion may have been abetted by the denial by Perls and other Gestalt therapists of their interdependence.

Dependence and the need for empathy are now beginning to be met with a more positive and discriminating attitude. There has been more realization that the therapist's therapeutic presence includes confirming the patient's "OK-ness" and potential for growth in a context of realistic appraisal of the patient and the situation of the patient. The needed presence may also include confronting the patient and allowing the patient to be frustrated — but does not usually involve the automatically confrontive attitude of the 1960s. It is important for the therapist to note whether the dependence sought by a patient is needed at a particular stage in the patient's growth. This change has allowed our therapeutic work to be conducted with more softness, acceptance and appreciation of the patient's phenomenology and stage-appropriate need for confluence and dependence.

In group the 1-1 work is increasingly balanced by an emphasis on the relationships in the group or the group as a whole, awareness work focused on relating in the group and creating time and space for more of the therapy to be done by group members. More time and space is allowed for telling of the story of the patient. (This will be discussed below.)

I hope there is a readiness to focus on relatedness, from the dyadic to the communal and to appreciate traditional values that had been indiscriminately thrown out, such as duty, work, honor, pride in excellence.

2. Changed Clinical Attitude

Our clinical work has changed in tandem with this growth in existential maturity. The change involves a softer, more receptive and more open and direct attitude toward the patient and the patient's phenomenology, more of a sense of therapy being a cooperative venture between therapist and patient, more personal and vulnerable presence and visibility by the therapist, more emphases on continuity in the therapeutic relationship, stronger emphasis on the development of each person's whole character, interest in background variables (such as listening to the patient's story or history), and more sophistication and attention to diagnosis. We will also discuss in later sections changes in attitude about group work and changes in relation to psychoanalysis.

(a) Cooperation versus adversarial therapeutic relationship

In Perls's style of the 1960s the patient's untutored and naive awareness and the behavior that resulted from that poorly developed awareness was often regarded with disrespect and suspiciousness. When a patient did not support direct and authentic contact, Perls regarded the patient as primarily doing something to the therapist. He talked as if the patient acted primarily to fool the therapist and the therapist's primary task was to frustrate the patient.

Therapy was often viewed not as a cooperative venture of therapist and patient, but rather one of adversaries. Although the motto "I and Thou, Here and Now" was spoken of, operationally there was a lack of truly dialogic attitude of meeting and confirming the patient. Rather than talking to the patient and sharing his own process, reactions, etc. there was a distinct tendency to focus on making something happen. Perls did not share his personal process, only his excitement and creativity in creating therapeutic drama. Much of the withholding and confrontation of this brand of Gestalt therapy was shame-inducing through mystification and contempt.

In the last decade I have found kindness with clarity and directness more clinically effective in increasing awareness, self-responsibility and wholehearted experimentation by the patient than the more technique- and frustration-oriented attitude of earlier years. I have found simple interventions such as reflecting back to the patient how I perceive the patient's phenomenology and explicitly sharing my own foreground and dilemmas often more effective than using empty chairs, body work, movement enactments, dream work and so forth. All of these techniques have a place, but for me the balance and attitude in approaching the patient and the clinical work have shifted.

This newer attitude has caused some alarm. Jim Simkin, for example, was quite vigilant about any reintroduction of the concept of empathy into Gestalt therapy via the concept of inclusion. He believed that there was an inherent confusion, confluence, in "empathy," and a danger of collusion with the myth that a therapist can feel the patient's feeling. Of course, when clinicians confuse empathy with feeling and knowing another's feelings it is confluence. However, empathy (when properly defined) is not inherently a boundary confusion, it does not mean feeling someone else's feeling.

In the last decade I have found myself less afraid of the danger of this potential confluence and more trusting of a cooperative and supportive approach to awareness work. When patients feel understood and supported it has been more powerful in helping the patient develop his or her own supports and faith in his or her ability to support themselves than taking on myself the burden of disrupting the confluence-seeking attitude of the patient.

The older attitude had a paradox: while decrying rescuing the patient ("chicken soup"), the therapist took responsibility for removing barriers to growth and making something happen — thus creating another type of dependence on the therapist and inadvertently encouraging introjecting and transference and increasing the probability of the therapist feeling frustrated by the under-dog behavior of the patient.

(b) Therapist presence and visibility versus wizardry

This new dialogic attitude means showing the therapist more as a whole, flawed person, and less as a guru or wizard. The dialogic attitude has included more emphasis on the personal presence and sharing by the therapist, i.e., sharing processes of the therapist while still in progress, sharing momentary feelings (not just using them as the basis for a therapist-designed experiment or confrontation), and sharing more from the therapist's life (when clinically relevant and useful). It means being willing to work slower if the patient needs to work slower, encouraging the patient to make choices about what techniques to experiment with, and most of all taking personal responsibility for feeling frustrated, bored, stuck, angry, etc.

(c) Continuity in relationship versus here-and-now episodes

Included in this new clinical attitude has been an increased awareness of the importance of continuity in the therapeutic relationship, an emphasis not only on moment-to-moment contact, but ongoing relationship. I believe that the relationship between the patient and the therapist accounts for the biggest portion of the variance in determining the degree of success of the therapy. An attitude of looking at the ongoing therapeutic relationship as primary goes hand-in-hand with consideration of each person's character and how it develops.

(d) Development of each persons whole character over time

Recovery of background has been one aspect of the changed clinical attitude.

Classical psychoanalysis emphasized background. For example, it gathered information about the entire history of the patient, details of how the person's character developed over time. In the process the aliveness of here-and-now moments was lost. Gestalt therapy emphasized the latter, and in the process lost some of the valuable background. In recent years Gestalt therapy has been moving toward a synthesis of the background context and the figure of the moment.

My experience in ongoing Gestalt therapy treatment is that I have needed to pay more attention to the patient's story, the history the relation to which gives context and meaning to the here-and-now. I have found increased value in the patient's life script, past experiences, developmental history as well as noting that many patients need to begin sessions by relating weekly news flashes on the ongoing development of his or her life. I have given greater freedom to my curiosity about the story and been slower to insist on a return to the here and now.

This attention to the person's background is actually consistent with an accurate understanding of the Gestalt therapy meaning of the here and now. The here and now is the location in time and place of the person's awareness. One's awareness is here-and-now, but the object of the awareness is often an event out of the room, from the past or anticipated. When one is aware that the present activity is remembering, anticipating, etc. — and the awareness has the excitement and sharpness of being in contact with what is important to the organism — one can be said to be present-centered. Although this has always been the Gestalt therapy theory, here-and-now clichés in the 1965-1975 era led many to practice as if only feelings about events present at this second in this place is here-and-now and to be inattentive to history, development, life events, etc.

The newer attitude of interest in background is more consistent with Gestalt therapy theory and has resulted in deeper work, in work that captures the flow of the patient's life and gets to the heart of core issues of consciousness, development and relationship. It has also resulted in the loss of some of the here and now magic and sharpness that could be attained with more strictly here-and-now, expression-oriented interventions.

There is an increased emphasis on looking at the context of the person's current life, for example, an increased use of family and couples therapy. Of course, this corresponds directly to the increased existential concern for otherness and continuity of relationship. Hopefully, the recovery of background will also lead to a renewed emphasis on culture and community.

Increased attention to diagnosis and case discussion is a necessary part of this clinical attitude of emphasis on the development of character and emphasis on the continuity of therapeutic relationship.

In becoming more than episodic, Gestalt therapy must take responsibility for knowing what needs to be emphasized with what patient, for knowing when therapy is developing at a good speed, for knowing what the particular kind of vulnerabilities are for particular kinds of patients, for knowing the different sequences of how things need to develop with different kinds of patients, for knowing the long-term effect of immediate and intermediate interventions with patients with particular kinds of character structure.

The space *The Gestalt Journal* has created for discussion of cases can be used for such discussions. We need to do much more of this. Gestalt therapy can utilize psychoanalytic insights very well in this process.

For example, the Gestalt therapy attitude on contact, boundaries, personal responsibility, dialogue is a natural for treating borderline patients. But to do so effectively we must also deal with the knowledge of splitting, therapeutic indications, typical dynamic issues. For example, the borderline must be held tightly responsible for his or her behavior very early in treatment or else the patient's desire to be taken care of runs rampant, because the borderline splits and loses any background awareness of the limits of the actual situation the necessity of supporting himself or herself and his/her ability to do so.

If the confluent fantasy of the borderline is inadvertently fed by the therapeutic relationship, the beginning of therapy may seem to go well. This often explodes with destructive results, often in the second year, when the reality of what is possible does not at all measure up to the primitive fantasies that had been fanned early in therapy. In the meantime the lack of sufficient confrontation on issues of patient responsibility and insistence on the patients' doing their therapy work earlier in the therapy results in the patient not having developed the tools for self-support needed to deal with disappointment and feelings of abandonment. At that point the positive transference turns into a potentially psychotic negative transference.

This cannot be gleaned only from here-and-now alertness without the benefit of being psychoanalytically informed. The long-term effect of events at the very beginning of therapy can only be obtained by attention to continuity in therapy, diagnosis, knowledge of developmental patterns and shared clinical experiences. I discuss this example only to indicate the need for diagnosis and clinical discussion in Gestalt therapy — a serious discussion of the treatment of any particular kind of patient is beyond the scope of this paper.

Another example is the narcissistic personality disorders, in which the patient specifically needs careful, slow, respectful, confirming attention by the therapist to the patient's experience. Such patients do not do well with the kind of confrontation that the borderline patients need. While the borderline patients will often discuss historical, developmental information before they have developed tools to deal with the emotionally loaded material, the narcissistic personality disordered patient often needs to be encouraged to connect the present with relevant past experiences. The particular attention to the patient's experience and to the patient's awareness of developmental factors must be the backbone of the early part of the treatment. Yet the patient needs to be met with realism about actual behavior. This creates a tightrope for the therapist. It would be very helpful if there were a literature of Gestalt therapists' experiences in treating such patients so we can learn from each other.

3. Changes In Approach To Groups.

Gestalt therapy has often been erroneously equated with one particular style of group therapy and attitude about group therapy. The style Perls used in the last 10 years of his life was strictly a model of 1-1 work with the therapist in the group (hot seat model) with other participants being only observers. Groups started with "rounds," all "work" started with "I want to work," and finished with "Is there any feedback?" The relation patterns in the group were like the spokes of a wheel, with the therapist in the center and all interaction going through the therapist.

Although that was not the only style of Gestalt group therapy, nor in any theoretical way essential to or limited to Gestalt therapy, it was the one that seemed most prevalent, and certainly the most publicized one. Now one finds process/interaction style Gestalt groups and mixed models more frequently. Also group is used more discriminatingly, as one modality in a range of other modalities including individual, couple and family therapy. No longer is it thought that any willing patient could do the totality of his or her therapy in group.

As in all Gestalt therapy work the goals remain individual awareness, support for contact and withdrawal, self-responsibility, etc. But there is increased emphasis on the existential meeting of people, on the bonding of people with each other. All other interactions are used as grist for the mill of awareness work and also a chance to practice and experiment. Allowing other group members to participate during an individual's 1-1 work is another option.

Although the emphasis on continuity of relationship and attention to background variables would seem to contraindicate workshops, this dialogic emphasis can also be manifest in workshops. In workshops this would mean greater emphasis on relationships in the group as the medium for awareness, greater room for the patient to tell his or her story (even in a workshop setting), and the therapist's stance being more of a coworker than of a guru producing Gestalt therapy disciples.

Although some might think that the time taken for a patient to tell his history in a group would decrease group interaction, the opposite is often the case. The other group members often relate more easily to the patient knowing the history than to a purely here-and-now process approach. A trained Gestalt therapist can often relate to the patient on the basis of the here and now without history better than others in the group.

There are obvious dangers to the new styles, as there were to the old. There has been some loss along with this gain. There can be an increase in "talk about," and a decreased rate and sharpness of learning some traditional Gestalt tools. When others are encouaged to participate in the 1-1 work of other patients along with the therapist, there are risks, including that of fragmentation of the work, of other people being too helpful, of minor issues being raised or issues raised in poor sequence, of more aggression being pointed at a patient than the patient has support to handle, etc. There is danger of deterioration into a rap group, becoming overly interpretive or confrontive if the therapist does not work well with the group process and the individual characterological issues that emerge as well as work into the other activities the introduction of the Gestalt methodology.

The therapist must have certain skills and attitudes to minimize the probability of negative results: tact, education of the other patients, firmness by the therapist, negotiation, discrimination. On the other hand, the group can be a very powerful, supportive, humane and exciting part of a person's therapy. It can be an ongoing home base for the patient during his or her quest for both equilibrium and growth.

4. A Better Appreciation of Thinking.

During the 1960s the intellect was often treated with contempt. Thinking was considered only as a barrier between organism and environment. The amount and quality of intellectual activity was poor. Perls's weakness in theoretical discourse was balanced in the early years by the quality of the intellectual discourse of the rest of the New York City group. In the 1960s the spotlight shifted to Perls and to California. Separated from the influence of the intellectual stimulation of the New York city group, Gestalt therapy developed an antiintellectual bias quite fitting with the antiintellectual bias of the age. The intellectual dialogue was on hold. (Although the actual denotation of the theoretical statements made did not always hold the intellect in such contempt, the connotation and tone certainly did. See Polster, 1985.)

The 1965-1975 age could be called the age of the slogan and cliché. The intellectual production in Gestalt therapy was spotty and sloppy. Examples abound. "Reality is created only by the individual" was erroneously attributed to Gestalt psychology when even a cursory reading of Gestalt psychology would make clear that this was not what they were advocating. Clichés such as "lose your mind" and "use your eyes," as if one could be aware and make

116

contact without brain activity or as if the eyes could see without central brain processing.

Sometimes the Gestalt therapy interpretation of the here and now left the impression that literally nothing existed or was of importance except the here and now as opposed to the here and now being the location in time and space of one's present consciousness. Of course some wrote about it with more sophistication and accuracy and without reduction to cliché. If the strict here and now were really adhered to as stated in the clichés, it would be closer to brain damage than enlightenment. Even a cursory understanding of field theory, upon which Gestalt therapy and Gestalt psychology are built, would make clear that what the "now" is must be defined from some perspective. There is no absolute here and now.

At a clinical level we are working more on the person's thought processes. Such work helps the patient be aware of old beliefs that are unexamined and perhaps irrational and/or nonfunctional. For example, "It is a terrible thing if anyone feels hurt or angry at me." Such work also includes studying more subtle aspects of a person's thought process. For example, persons who show an hysterical style and interrupt the stream of consciousness to prevent deepened emotional experience and jump to premature closure will characteristically do so in their thought processes also — for example, being unable to work out abstract problems because of jumping prematurely from a beginning of the thought process to a conclusion.

On the theory of Gestalt therapy I see some increase in discussion of phenomenology, dialogue/existentialism and field theory. This needs to continue. I believe we still need to say more about the experimentation attitude in all clinical interventions and the explication of just what we mean by phenomenological. We have already discussed the change in therapeutic attitude from a dialogic perspective. We need to discuss the differences between the dialogic attitude and other attitudes in Gestalt therapy and the implications, dangers and limits of dialogue, and the application of the dialogic attitude to various diagnostic groups. We need more explication of field theory, e.g., of process and structure, or of fields and people as a matter of primary emphasis. How does field theory fit with systems theory?

In all of this I see an increase in concern, an increase in published articles (primarily in *The Gestalt Journal*). However, I believe we need much more over the next 10 years if we are to survive and prosper as a system of therapy.

For example, I have been very interested in the growing recognition of the importance of relationship, that is, continuous relationship, in dialogic Gestalt therapy as an alternative emphasis in Gestalt therapy. The emphasis on relationship is a needed direction in Gestalt therapy, and the emphasis on dialogue begins to define what kind of relationship is most appropriate to Gestalt therapy.

Yet many questions are raised. What is different about a dialogic approach in Gestalt therapy? What of the patients who do not have support for dialogue? What of patients who need to have their own experience tracked without taking into account the phenomenology of the therapist? Are there patients for whom Gestalt therapy in general or a dialogic approach in particular are especially indicated or contraindicated? What are the considerations in deciding when to show more presence by sharing the phenomenology of the therapist and when to show a greater emphasis on inclusion? If patients require ongoing therapy and ongoing dialogue and hearing of their story, how do we do a dialogic approach in a time-limited workshop? Is there room for technological responses, e.g., empty chair or breathing work, in a dialogic Gestalt therapy and why? Is a dialogic approach consistent with a body approach and how are they integrated? If you place importance on the early parenting of patients, how do you integrate this with the existential belief in responsibility for self?

5. *A more eclectic attitude toward psychoanalysis and other therapies*

In the last decade we have begun to informally acknowledge our borrowing from and continued dependence on other professionals, therapies, research, etc., although I read little of this in the literature. And we have had to deal with a growth of other therapeutic modalities with which we must compete, from which Gestalt therapy can learn, to which we can teach — if we differentiate and discriminate in published form. I refer to such modalities as NLP, biofeedback, short-term dynamic therapy, Ericksonianism, paradoxical therapy, etc.

We have some special affinity for Object Relations theory and for Kohutian theory. Their descriptions are more phenomenological than those of psychoanalytic writers have ever been, and their approach less dominated by drive theory and more useful to Gestalt therapists. Their detailed descriptions of how people develop, about the meanings of human interactions that are not in awareness, and about the sequence and development of treatment with different kind of patients are extremely valuable for us.

Yet they are still analysts, and many of their beliefs, attitudes, clinical methodology are quite divergent from Gestalt therapy. We have begun to take in, but the literature discussing this interaction is meager in quality and quantity.

Parallel to the development of the new psychoanalytic approaches has been the growing awareness, discussed above, of patients who do not do well in traditional therapy of any kind. The new psychoanalytic phenomenological descriptions and the new therapeutic attitudes for treating them have altered the practice of many Gestalt therapists. Certainly they have altered mine. There has been very little discussion of the absorption of the developmental and personality theory and descriptions into Gestalt therapy, and what changes and modifications need to be made to integrate this into Gestalt therapy. I hope the changes in the maturing of our existential attitude and other improvements I discussed above are part of a beginning of enlarging our framework for assimilating this new material. I believe we have begun in this past decade, and much of the work is still before us.

The differences between Gestalt therapy and the new psychoanalytic approaches that need to be explicated include the limited and nonexperimental use of phenomenology in the psychoanalytic models and the transference-based versus the dialogic mode of therapeutic relationship. Without a theoretical explication there is danger that increased empathy combined with an uncritical dialogic attitude will deteriorate into gratification of the patient's needs rather than fostering exploration and experimentation. For example, "sharing" by the therapist in a dialogic but clinically unsophisticated manner can lead to a fostered (rather than naturally developing) idealization of the therapist, increased projective identification of the therapist, and an increased feeling of lack of ability by the patient for self-support. There is also a danger that introjection of the psychoanalytic literature will result in attributing cause to the environment and increase the belief by the patient's that they are not responsible for themselves.

Discussion and Summary

It is clear in recent years that our practices need improvement, our theories need explicating, revising and building and our literature needs expanding.

The prevailing Gestalt therapy attitudes of the 1965-1975 era lost some of the virtues of the Gestalt therapy of the early New York City group. In moving forward in the current decade we may be returning to a better recognition of the Gestalt therapy philosophies at its inception. At a minimum I hope we are giving more sophisticated consideration to the basic philosophies than during the 1965-1975 era.

There are numerous social changes that must affect our work that we ignore only at great peril. Changed sociological conditions create new clinical demands. Powerful psychopharmaceuticals and changes in the political climate with respect to third-party reimbursements and HMOs have exerted pressure for discussing our work in terms of common diagnostic labels and proof of efficacy of therapy and evidence about when it works: by whom, on whom, in what way. Although work has started on a Gestalt therapy diagnostic theory, for example by Todd Burley and also by Lynne Jacobs, both of the Gestalt Therapy Institute of Los Angeles, for the present we must interface with the existing diagnostic systems.

A stiffening market for psychotherapy and an increase in the number of therapists have enhanced the competitive climate between therapists of different professions and persuasions. We use and compete with new specialists: psychopharmaceuticals for depressives, panic disorders, attention deficit disorders; sex therapy; biofeedback; etc. Patients have an extraordinarily wide range of treatment modalities to choose from, including the dramatic Ericksonian-type treatments, biofeedback, psychologically relevant work by chiropractors, self-help groups, etc. This wide range of therapeutic modalities patients now choose from make it imperative that we deal with the weakness of our literature.

We are not the rebellious new kid on the block anymore — we can survive only by living up to our promise.

I also believe that it is time that we commented more on the changing society in which we now do our psychotherapy. Some of our clinical practices were more appropriate to the 1960s than to the 1980s. For example, in the 1960s the emphasis was on working with uptight, conforming but generally functioning neurotics. Now there are more patients that are self-centered, dysfunctional, not able to function in a linear manner, interested in "creativity" without the necessary discipline, unable to establish and maintain intimate relationships. I do not know if Gestalt therapy and other therapies have been a part of this development. However, I am sure that we must take it into account in what we emphasize.

It is unclear to what degree my speculations and assertions are accurate. I began this paper by wondering about the accuracy of our self-concept, and I am concluding with the same query. The paucity of research leaves us in the position of the person combing his hair without a mirror. I believe that the trends that I indicate are real, although I have perhaps overstated how much we have done in the last 10 years and understated how much still needs to be done. I hope we are doing what needs to be done; but I do not know.

I appreciate the opportunity this issue of *The Gestalt Journal* affords us, and the opportunity the journal affords us in general. I hope we will see even more submitted articles that really deal with philosophy/theory, clinical discussions, including consideration of cases and diagnosis, and research.

II

THE THEORY

OF

GESTALT THERAPY

5

GESTALT THERAPY

Commentary

This paper, coauthored with James S. Simkin in 1981, is probably the best general introduction to Gestalt therapy that I have written. It was the Gestalt Therapy chapter in the 1989 edition of Corsini and Wedding's Current Psychotherapies *(4th Edition). It appears here with the kind permission of the publisher, F.E. Peacock, Publishers, Inc. of Itasca, Illinois. It is a slightly edited version of the 1984 chapter written jointly by Jim Simkin and myself for the third edition of* Current Psychotherapies. *The 1984 version was a complete rewriting of a version Jim did by himself for the second edition of* Current Psychotherapies. *The revisions I made in the 1989 version were minor and were made after Jim's death.*

Overview

Gestalt therapy is a phenomenological-existential therapy founded by Frederick (Fritz) and Laura Perls in the 1940s. It teaches therapists and patients the phenomenological method of awareness, in which perceiving, feeling, and acting are distinguished from interpreting and reshuffling preexisting attitudes. Explanations and interpretations are considered less reliable than what is directly perceived and felt. Patients and therapists in Gestalt therapy *dialogue,* that is, communicate their phenomenological perspectives. Differences in perspectives become the focus of experimentation and continued dialogue. The goal is for clients to become aware of what they are doing, how they are doing it, and how they can change themselves, and at the same time, to learn to accept and value themselves.

Gestalt therapy focuses more on process (what is happening) than content (what is being discussed). The emphasis is on what is being done, thought and felt at the moment rather than on what was, might be, could be, or should be.

Basic Concepts

The Phenomenological Perspective

Phenomenology is a discipline that helps people stand aside from their usual way of thinking so that they can tell the difference between what is actually being perceived and felt in the current situation and what is residue from the past (Idhe, 1977). A Gestalt exploration respects, uses and clarifies immediate, "naive" perception "undebauched by learning" (Wertheimer, 1945, p. 331). Gestalt therapy treats what is "subjectively" felt in the present, as well as what is "objectively" observed, as real and important data. This contrasts with approaches that treat what the patient experiences as "mere appearances" and uses interpretation to find "real meaning."

The goal of Gestalt phenomenological exploration is awareness, or insight. "Insight is a patterning of the perceptual field in such a way that the significant realities are apparent; it is the formation of a gestalt in which the relevant factors fall into place with respect to the whole" (Heidbreder, 1933, p. 355). In Gestalt therapy insight is clear understanding of the structure of the situation being studied.

Awareness without systematic exploration is not ordinarily sufficient to develop insight. Therefore, Gestalt therapy uses focused awareness and experimentation to achieve insight. How one becomes aware is crucial to any phenomenological investiga-

124

tion. The phenomenologist studies not only personal awareness but also the awareness process itself. The patient is to learn how to become aware of awareness. How the therapist and the patient experience their relationship is of special concern in Gestalt therapy (Yontef, 1976, 1982, 1983).

The Field Theory Perspective

The scientific world view that underlies the Gestalt phenomenological perspective is field theory. Field theory is a method of exploring that describes the whole field of which the event is currently a part rather than analyzing the event in terms of a class to which it belongs by its "nature" (e.g., Aristotelian classification) or a unilinear, historical, cause-effect sequence (e.g., Newtonian mechanics).

The field is a whole in which the parts are in immediate relationship and responsive to each other and no part is uninfluenced by what goes on elsewhere in the field. The field replaces the notion of discrete, isolated particles. The person in his or her life space constitutes a field.

In field theory no action is at a distance; that is, what has effect must touch that which is affected in time and space. Gestalt therapists work in the here and now and are sensitive to how the here and now includes residues of the past, such as body posture, habits, and beliefs.

The phenomenological field is defined by the observer and is meaningful only when one knows the frame of reference of the observer. The observer is necessary because what one sees is somewhat a function of how and when one looks.

Field approaches are descriptive rather than speculative, interpretive, or classificatory. The emphasis is on observing, describing, and explicating the exact structure of whatever is being studied. In Gestalt therapy, data unavailable to direct observation by the therapist are studied by phenomenological focusing, experimenting, reporting of participants, and dialogue (Yontef, 1982, 1983).

The Existential Perspective

Existentialism is based on the phenomenological method. Existential phenomenologists focus on people's existence, relations with each other, joys and suffering, etc., as directly experienced.

Most people operate in an unstated context of conventional thought that obscures or avoids acknowledging how the world is. This is especially true of one's relations in the world and one's choices. Self-deception is the basis of inauthenticity: living that is not based on the truth of oneself in the world leads to feelings of dread, guilt and anxiety. Gestalt therapy provides a way of being authentic and meaningfully responsible for oneself. By becoming aware, one becomes able to choose and/or organize one's own existence in a meaningful manner (Jacobs, 1978; Yontef, 1982, 1983).

The existential view holds that people are endlessly remaking or discovering themselves. There is no essence of human nature to be discovered "once and for all." There are always new horizons, new problems and new opportunities.

Dialogue

The relationship between the therapist and the client is the most important aspect of psychotherapy. Existential dialogue is an essential part of Gestalt therapy's methodology and is a manifestation of the existential perspective on relationship.

Relationship grows out of contact. Through contact people grow and form identities. Contact is the experience of boundary between "me" and "not-me." It is the experience of interacting with the not-me while maintaining a self-identity separate from the not-me. Martin Buber states that the person ("I") has meaning only in relation to others, in the I-Thou dialogue or in I-It manipulative contact. Gestalt therapists prefer experiencing the patient in dialogue to using therapeutic manipulation (I-It).

Gestalt therapy helps clients develop their own support for desired contact or withdrawal (L. Perls, 1976, 1978). Support refers to anything that makes contact or withdrawal possible: energy, body support, breathing, information, concern for others, language, and so forth. Support mobilizes resources for contact or withdrawal. For example, to support the excitement accompanying contact, a person must take in enough oxygen.

The Gestalt therapist works by engaging in dialogue rather than by manipulating the patient toward some therapeutic goal. Such contact is marked by straightforward caring, warmth, acceptance and self-responsibility. When therapists move patients toward some goal, the patients cannot be in charge of their own growth and self-support. Dialogue is based on experiencing the other person as he or she really is and showing the true self, sharing phenomenological awareness. The Gestalt therapist says what he or she means and encourages the patient to do the same. Gestalt dialogue embodies authenticity and responsibility.

The therapeutic relationship in Gestalt therapy emphasizes four characteristics of dialogue:

1. *Inclusion.* This is putting oneself as fully as possible into the experience of the other without judging, analyzing or interpreting while simultaneously retaining a sense of one's separate, autonomous presence. This is an existential and interpersonal application of the phenomenological trust in immediate experience. Inclusion provides an environment of safety for the patient's phenomenological work and, by communicating an understanding of the patient's experience, helps sharpen the patient's self-awareness.

2. *Presence.* The Gestalt therapist expresses herself to the patient. Regularly, judiciously, and with discrimination she expresses observations, preferences, feelings, personal experience and thoughts. Thus, the therapist shares her perspective by modeling phenomenological reporting, which aids the patient's learning about trust and use of immediate experience to raise awareness. If the therapist relies on theory-derived interpretation, rather than personal presence, she leads the patient into relying on phenomena not in his own immediate experience as the tool for raising awareness. In Gestalt therapy the therapist does not use presence to manipulate the patient to conform to preestablished goals, but rather encourages patients to regulate themselves autonomously.

3. *Commitment to dialogue.* Contact is more than something two people do to each other. Contact is something that happens between people, something that arises from the interaction between them. The Gestalt therapist surrenders herself to this interpersonal process. This is *allowing* contact to happen rather than manipulating, *making* contact, and controlling the outcome.

4. *Dialogue is lived.* Dialogue is something done rather than talked about. "Lived" emphasizes the excitement and immediacy

of doing. The mode of dialogue can be dancing, song, words, or any modality that expresses and moves the energy between or among the participants. An important contribution of Gestalt therapy to phenomenological experimentation is enlarging the parameters to include explication of experience by nonverbal expressions. However, the interaction is limited by ethics, appropriateness, therapeutic task, and so on.

Other Systems

Yontef notes that:

> The theoretical distinction between Gestalt therapy, behavior modification and psychoanalysis is clear. In behavior modification, the patient's behavior is directly changed by the therapist's manipulation of environmental stimuli. In psychoanalytic theory, behavior is caused by unconscious motivation which becomes manifest in the transference relationship. By analyzing the transference the repression is lifted, the unconscious becomes conscious. In Gestalt therapy the patient learns to fully use his internal and external senses so he can be self-responsible and self-supportive. Gestalt therapy helps the patient regain the key to this state, the awareness of the process of awareness. Behavior modification conditions [by] using stimulus control, psychoanalysis cures by talking about and discovering the cause of mental illness [the problem], and Gestalt therapy brings self-realization through here-and-now experiments in directed awareness. (1969, pp. 33-34)

Behavior modification and other therapies that primarily try to direct control over symptoms (for example, chemotherapy, ECT, hypnosis, etc.) contrast with both Gestalt therapy and psychodynamic therapies in that the latter systems foster change primarily by the patient's learning to understand himself or herself in the world through insight.

The methodology of Gestalt and psychodynamic therapy uses an accepting relationship and a technology to help the patient change via emotional and cognitive self-understanding. In psychoanalysis the basic patient behavior is free association; the chief tool of the analyst is interpretation. To encourage transference, the analyst withholds any direct expression of personhood (no "I" statements) and practices the "Rule of Abstinence"; that is, the therapist does not gratify any of the patient's wishes. This approach is true of all psychodynamic schools: classical, object relations, ego psychological, Kohutian, Jungian. The psychodynamic therapist isolates his or her person in order to encourage a relationship based explicitly on transference (rather than contact).

Gestalt therapy works for understanding by using the active, healing presence of the therapist *and the patient* in a relationship based on true contact. Transference, explored and worked through as it arises, is not encouraged by the Gestalt therapist (Polster, 1968). Characterological issues are *explicitly dealt with in Gestalt therapy* via the dialogic and phenomenological method.

In Gestalt therapy the immediate experience of the patient is actively used. Rather than free associate while passively awaiting the therapist's interpretation and subsequent change, the patient is seen as a collaborator who is to learn how to self-heal. The patient "works" rather than free associates. "What can I do to work on this?" is a frequent question in Gestalt therapy and frequently there is an answer. For example, a couple with sexual difficulties might be asked to practice sensate focusing.

More than any other therapy, Gestalt therapy emphasizes that whatever exists is here and now and that experience is more reliable than interpretation. The patient is taught the difference between *talking about* what occurred five minutes ago (or last night or 20 years ago) and *experiencing* what is now.

Applebaum, a psychoanalyst, observes that

In Gestalt therapy the patient quickly learns to make the discrimination between ideas and ideation, between well-worn obsessional pathways and new thoughts, between a statement of experience and a statement of a statement. The Gestalt goal of pursuing experience and insight which e-merges as the Gestalt emerges is more potent than insight given by the therapist, does help the patient and the therapist draw and maintain these important distinctions. (1976, p. 757)

Therapies such as behavior modification, reality therapy and rational emotive therapy do not work with the *patient's* experience enough to do this. In Rogerian therapy the passivity imposed on the therapist severely narrows the range or power of the therapy to teach these distinctions.

The practice of most therapy systems encourages intellectualizing: talking about the irrationality of patient beliefs, talking about the behavior changes the therapist believes that the patient should make, and so forth. The Gestalt therapy methodology utilizes active techniques that clarify experience. Gestalt therapists will often experiment by trying something new in the therapy hour. Unlike most other therapies, in Gestalt therapy the *process* of discovery through experimentation *is* the end point rather than the feeling or idea or content.

The psychoanalyst can only use interpretation. The Rogerian can only reflect and clarify. Gestalt therapists may use any techniques or methods as long as (a) they are aimed toward increasing awareness, (b) they emerge out of dialogue and phenomenologic work, and (c) they are within the parameters of ethical practice.

The power and responsibility for the present are in the hands of the patient. In the past the patient was psychologically in mutual interaction with the environment and not a passive recipient of trauma. Thus the patient may have received shaming messages from his parents, but swallowing the message and coping by self-blame were his own, as was the continuation of the shaming internally from then until now. This point of view is at variance with psychodynamic attitudes, but consonant with Adler's and Ellis's views.

This viewpoint enables patients to be more responsible for their own existence, including their therapy. When the therapist believes that the past causes the present and that patients are controlled by unconscious motivation not readily available to them, they are encouraged to rely on the therapist's interpretations rather than their own autonomy.

In therapies in which the therapist undertakes to directly modify the patient's behavior, the immediate experience of the patient and therapist are not honored. This separates Gestalt therapy from most other therapies. A resentful patient may increase awareness by expressing resentment. If the therapist suggests this as a means of catharsis, it is not the phenomenological focusing of Gestalt therapy.

In Gestalt therapy there are no "shoulds." Instead of emphasizing what should be, Gestalt therapy stresses awareness of what is. *What is, is.* This contrasts with any therapist who "knows" what the patient "should" do. For example, cognitive behavior modification, rational-emotive therapy and reality therapy all try to modify patient attitudes the therapist judges to be irrational, irresponsible or unreal.

Even though Gestalt therapy discourages interrupting the organismic assimilating process by focusing on cognitive explanatory intellectualizations, Gestalt therapists do work with belief systems. Clarifying thinking, explicating beliefs, and mutually deciding what fits for the patient are all part of Gestalt therapy. Gestalt therapy deemphasizes thinking that avoids experience (obsessing) and encourages thinking that supports experience. Gestalt therapy excludes the therapist's narcissistically teaching the patient rather than being contactful and expediting the patient's self-discovery.

Many persons claim they practice "TA [transactional analysis] and Gestalt." Usually these people use the TA *theory* and some Gestalt therapy *techniques.* Techniques are not the important aspect of Gestalt therapy. When used in an analytic, cognitive style, these techniques are not Gestalt therapy! Such a combination often aborts, prevents or neutralizes the organismic awareness work of the phenomenological-existential method. A better combination would be integrating concepts of TA into a Gestalt framework. Thus the parent, adult, and child ego states, crossed transactions, and life scripts can be translated into Gestalt process language and worked with experimentally and dialogically.

Another difference from other therapies is Gestalt therapy's genuine regard for holism and multidimensionality. People manifest their distress in how they behave, think and feel. "Gestalt therapy views the entire biopsychosocial field, including organism/environment, as important. Gestalt therapy actively uses physiological, sociological, cognitive, motivational variables. No relevant dimension is excluded in the basic theory" (Yontef, 1969, pp. 33-34).

History

Precursors

The history of Gestalt therapy starts with the professional development of Fritz Perls and the zeitgeist in which he lived. After acquiring the M.D. degree, Perls went to Frankfurt-am-Main in 1926 as an assistant to Kurt Goldstein at the Institute for Brain Damaged Soldiers. Here he was exposed to Professors Goldstein and Adhemar Gelb and he met his future wife, Laura. At that time Frankfurt-am-Main was a center of intellectual ferment and Perls was directly and indirectly exposed to leading Gestalt psychologists, existential philosophers and psychoanalysts.

Fritz Perls became a psychoanalyst. He was influenced directly by Karen Horney and Wilhelm Reich, and indirectly by Otto Rank and others. Perls was especially influenced by Wilhelm Reich, who was Perls' analyst in the early 1930s, and "who first directed my attention to a most important aspect of psychosomatic medicine — to the function of the motoric system as an armor" (F. Perls, 1947, p. 3).

Three influences on Perls' intellectual development should be noted. One was the philosopher, Sigmund Friedlander, from whose philosophy Perls incorporated the concepts of differential thinking and creative indifference, spelled out in Perls' first book, *Ego, Hunger and Aggression* (1947). Perls was also influenced by Jan Smuts, the prime minister of South Africa when Perls moved there with his family (having first escaped from Nazi Germany and then Nazi-occupied Holland). Before becoming prime minister, Smuts had written a major book on holism and evolution that, in effect, examined the broader ecological world from a Gestalt perspective. Smuts coined the word *holism*. Third, Alfred Korzybski, the semanticist, was an influence on Perls' intellectual development.

Laura Posner Perls was a cofounder of Gestalt therapy. Her influence on Perls was generally known, and she wrote a chapter in *Ego, Hunger and Aggression*. She was a psychology student at the time she met Perls, receiving the D.Sc. degree from the University of Frankfurt in 1932. She had contact with and was influenced by the existential theologians Martin Buber and Paul Tillich. Much of the Gestalt, phenomenological and existential influences in Gestalt therapy are through her, although credit and influence were limited by how little she wrote under her name (Rosenfeld, 1978).

Although Perls was a training psychoanalyst, he was among those who chafed under the dogmatism of classical Freudian psychoanalysis. The 1920s, 1930s, and 1940s were periods of great ferment and rebellion against Newtonian positivism. This was true in science (for example, Einstein's field theory*), theater and dance, philosophy, art, architecture and existentialism. Both Laura and Fritz lived in a zeitgeist permeated by a phenomenological-existential influence that later become interacted into Gestalt therapy (Kogan, 1976). Among these were acknowledgment of responsibility and choice in creating one's personal existence, the primacy of existence over essence, and the existential dialogue.

Gestalt psychology provided Perls with the organizing principle for Gestalt therapy as an integrating framework. Gestalt refers to the configuration or pattern of a set of elements. Gestalt psychologists believe that organisms instinctively perceive whole patterns and not bits and pieces. Whole patterns have characteristics that cannot be gleaned by analyzing parts. Perception is an active process and not a result of passively received stimulation of sense organs. All situations are believed to possess inherent organization. Organisms have the capacity for accurate perception when they use their native ability of immediate experience in the here and now. The task of phenomenological research and therapy is to utilize this capacity to gain insight into the structure of that which is being studied. Because people naturally perceive whole patterns as they occur, actual awareness can be trusted more than interpretation and dogma.

Beginnings

Perls' *Ego, Hunger and Aggression* was written in 1941-1942. In its first publication in South Africa in 1946 it was subtitled *A Revision of Freud's Theory and Method*. The subtitle of the book when it appeared in 1966 was changed to *The Beginning of Gestalt Therapy*. The term "Gestalt therapy" was first used as the title of a book written by Frederick Perls, Ralph Hefferline and Paul Goodman (1951). Shortly after, the New York Institute for Gestalt therapy was organized, headquartered in the apartment of Fritz and Laura

Perls in New York City. This apartment was used for seminars, workshops and groups. Among those who studied with Perls at that time were Paul Weisz, Lotte Weidenfeld, Buck Eastman, Paul Goodman, Isadore From, Elliot Shapiro, Leo Chalfen, Iris Sanguilano, James Simkin and Kenneth A. Fisher.

During the 1950s, intensive workshops and study groups were established throughout the country. Before the American Psychological Association Convention held in New York City in 1954, a special intensive workshop limited to 15 qualified psychologists was given over a three-day period. Similar workshops were held in Cleveland, Miami and Los Angeles. In 1955 the Cleveland study group formed the Gestalt Institute of Cleveland.

Fritz Perls moved to the West Coast in 1960, at which time Simkin arranged a Gestalt therapy workshop for him. Perls, Walter Kempler and James Simkin offered the first Gestalt therapy training workshops at the Esalen Institute during the summer of 1964. These training workshops continued under the leadership of Perls and Simkin through 1968. After Perls moved to Canada, Simkin, along with Irma Shepherd, Robert W. Resnick, Robert L. Martin, Jack Downing and John Enright, continued to offer Gestalt therapy training at Esalen through 1970.

During this beginning period Gestalt therapy pioneered many ideas subsequently accepted into eclectic psychotherapy practice. The excitement of direct contact between therapist and patient, the emphasis on direct experience, the use of active experimentation, the emphasis on the here and now, the responsibility of the patient for himself or herself, the awareness principle, the trust in organismic self-regulation, the ecological interdependence of person and environment, the principle of assimilation, and other such concepts were new, exciting and shocking to a conservative establishment. In this period the practice of psychotherapy was dichotomized between the older, traditional approach of psychoanalytic drive theory and the ideas pioneered largely by Gestalt therapy. This was a period of expansion, with integration of the principles with each other and the elucidation and enucleation of the principles left for the future. Thus, for example, Gestalt therapy pioneered the use of the active presence of the therapist in a contactful relationship but did not consider in detail what constituted a healing dialogic presence.

Current Status

There are at least 62 Gestalt therapy institutes throughout the world, and the list continues to grow. Virtually every major city in the United States has at least one Gestalt institute.

No national organization has been established. As a result, there are no established standards for institutes, trainers and trainees. Each institute has its own criteria for training, membership selection, and so on. Attempts in the recent past to organize a nationwide conference for establishing standards for trainers have not been successful. There are no agreed-upon standards for what constitutes good Gestalt therapy or a good Gestalt therapist. Therefore, it is incumbent on Gestalt therapy consumers to carefully evaluate the educational, clinical, and training background of people who call themselves Gestalt therapists or give training in Gestalt therapy (see Yontef, 1981a, 1981b).

The Gestalt Journal is devoted primarily to articles on Gestalt therapy. *Gestalt Theory* publishes articles on Gestalt psychology, including some on Gestalt therapy. Bibliographic information can be obtained from Kogan (1980), Rosenfeld (1981), and Wysong (1986).

As experience in doing Gestalt therapy has grown, earlier therapeutic practices have been altered. For example, earlier Gestalt therapy practice often stressed the clinical use of frustration, a confusion of self-sufficiency with self-support, and an abrasive attitude if the patient was interpreted by the therapist as manipulative. This approach tended to enhance the shame of shame-oriented patients. There has been a movement toward more softness in Gestalt therapy practice, more direct self-expression by the therapist, more of a dialogic emphasis, decreased use of stereotypic techniques, increased emphasis on description of character structure (with utilization of psychoanalytic formulations), and increased use of group process.

Thus a patient is more likely to encounter, among Gestalt therapists who are involved in the newer mode, an emphasis on self-acceptance, a softer demeanor by the therapist, more trust of the patient's phenomenology, and more explicit work with psychodynamic themes. There has also been an increase in emphasis on group process, including relation between group members, and a decrease in formal, one-to-one work in groups. There is also an increased attention to theoretical instruction, theoretical exposition, and work with cognition in general.

Personality
Theory of Personality

Ecological Interdependence: The Organism/Environment Field

A person exists by differentiating self from other and by connecting self and other. These are the two functions of a boundary. To make good contact with one's world, it is necessary to risk reaching out and discovering one's own boundaries. Effective self-regulation includes contact in which one is aware of novelty in the environment that is potentially nourishing or toxic. That which is nourishing is assimilated and all else is rejected. This kind of differentiated contact inevitably leads to growth (Polster and Polster, 1973, p. 101).

Mental Metabolism

In Gestalt therapy, metabolism is used as a metaphor for psychological functioning. People grow through biting off an appropriate-sized piece (be this food or ideas or relationships), chewing it (considering), and discovering whether it is nourishing or toxic. If nourishing, the organism assimilates it and makes it part of itself. If toxic, the organism spits it out (rejects it). This requires people to be willing to trust their taste and judgment. Discrimination requires *actively* sensing outside stimuli and processing these exteroceptive stimuli along with interoceptive data.

Regulation of the Boundary

The boundary between self and environment must be kept permeable to allow exchanges, yet firm enough for autonomy. The environment includes toxins to be screened out. Even what is nourishing needs to be discriminated according to the dominant needs. Metabolic processes are governed by the laws of homeostasis. Ideally, the most urgent need energizes the organism until it is met or is superseded by a more vital need. Living is a progression of needs, met and unmet, achieving homeostatic balance and going on to the next moment and new need.

Disturbances of the Contact Boundary

When the boundary between self and other becomes unclear, lost or impermeable, this results in a disturbance of the distinction between self and other, a disturbance of both contact and awareness (see Perls, 1973; Polster and Polster, 1973). In good boundary functioning, people alternate between connecting and separating, between being in contact with the current environment and withdrawal of attention from the environment. The contact boundary is lost in polar opposite ways in confluence and isolation. In *confluence* (fusion), the separation and distinction between self and other becomes so unclear that the boundary is lost. In *isolation*, the boundary becomes so impermeable that connectedness is lost, i.e., the importance of others for the self is lost from awareness.

Retroflection is a split within the self, a resisting of aspects of the self by the self. This substitutes self for environment, as in doing to self what one wants to do to someone else or doing for self what one wants someone else to do for self. This mechanism leads to isolation. The illusion of self-sufficiency is one example of retroflection as it substitutes self for environment. Although one can do one's own breathing and chewing, the air and food must come from the environment. Introspection is a form of retroflection that can be pathological or healthy. For example, resisting the impulse to express anger may serve to cope with a dangerous environment. In such a situation, biting one's lip may be more functional than saying something biting.

Through *introjection,* foreign material is absorbed without discriminating or assimilating. Swallowing whole creates an "as if" personality and rigid character. Introjected values and behavior are imposed on self. As in all contact boundary disturbances, swallowing whole can be healthy or pathological, depending on the circumstances and degree of awareness. For example, students taking a lecture course may, with full awareness that they are doing so, copy, memorize and regurgitate material without full "digestion."

Projection is a confusion of self and other that results from attributing to the outside something that is truly self. An example of healthy projection is art. Pathological projection results from not being aware of and accepting responsibility for that which is projected.

Deflection is the avoidance of contact or of awareness by turning aside, as when one is polite instead of direct. Deflection can be accomplished by not expressing directly or by not receiving. In the latter case, the person usually feels "untouched"; in the former case, the person is often ineffective and baffled about not getting what is wanted. Deflection can be useful where, with awareness, it meets the needs of the situation (e.g., where the situation needs cooling down). Other examples of deflection include not looking at a person, verbosity, vagueness, understating and talking *about* rather than *to* (Polster and Polster, 1973, pp. 89-92).

Organismic Self-Regulation

Human regulation is to varying degrees either (a) organismic, that is, based on a relatively full and accurate acknowledgment of *what is,* or (b) "shouldistic," based on the arbitrary imposition of what some controller thinks should or should not be. This applies to intrapsychic regulation, to the regulation of interpersonal relations and to the regulation of social groups.

"There is only one thing that should control: the *situation.* if you understand the situation you are in and let the situation you are in control our actions, then you learn to cope with life" (F. Perls, 1976, p. 33). Perls explicated the above with an example of driving a car. Instead of a preplanned program, "I want to drive 65 miles per hour," a person cognizant of the situation will drive at different speed at night or differently when in traffic, or still differently when tired, and so on. Here Perls makes it clear that "let the situation control" means regulating through awareness of the contemporary context, including one's wants, rather than through what was thought "should" happen.

In organismic self-regulation, choosing and learning happen holistically, with a natural integration of mind and body, thought and feeling, spontaneity and deliberateness. In shouldistic regulation, cognition reigns and there is no felt, holistic sense.

Obviously, everything relevant to boundary regulation cannot be in full awareness. Most transactions are handled by automatic, habitual modes, with minimal awareness. Organismic self-regulation requires that the habitual become fully aware as needed. When awareness does not emerge as needed and/or does not organize the necessary motor activity, psychotherapy is a method of increasing awareness and gaining meaningful choice and responsibility.

Awareness

Awareness and dialogue are the two primary therapeutic tools in Gestalt therapy. Awareness is a form of experience that may be loosely defined as being in touch with one's own existence, with *what is.*

Laura Perls states:

> The aim of Gestalt therapy is the *awareness continuum,* the freely ongoing Gestalt formation where what is of greatest concern and interest to the organism, the relationship, the group or society becomes Gestalt, comes into the foreground where it can be fully experienced and coped with (acknowledged, worked through, sorted out, changed, disposed of, etc.) so that then it can melt into the background (be forgotten or assimilated and integrated) and leave the foreground free for the next relevant Gestalt. (1973, p. 2)

Full awareness is the process of being in vigilant contact with the most important events in the individual/environment field with full sensorimotor, emotional, cognitive and energetic support. Insight, a form of awareness, is an immediate grasp of the obvious unity of disparate elements in the field. Aware contact creates new, meaningful wholes and thus is in itself an integration of a problem.

Effective awareness is grounded in and energized by the dominant present need of the organism. It involves not only self-knowledge, but a direct knowing of the current situation and how the self is in that situation. Any denial of the situation and its demands or of one's wants and chosen response is a disturbance of awareness. Meaningful awareness is of a self in the world, in dialogue with the world, and with awareness of Other — it is not an inwardly focused introspection. Awareness is accompanied by *owning*, that is, the process of knowing one's control over, choice of, and responsibility for one's own behavior and feelings. Without this, the person may be vigilant to experience and life space, but not to what power he or she has and does not have. Awareness is cognitive, sensory and affective. The person who verbally acknowledges his situation but does not really see it, *know* it, *react* to it and *feel* in response to it is not fully aware and is not in full contact. The person who is aware knows *what* he does, *how* he does it, that he has alternatives and that he *chooses* to be as he is.

The act of awareness is always here and now, although the content of awareness may be distant. The act of remembering is now; what is remembered is not now. When the situation calls for an awareness of the past or anticipation of the future, effective awareness takes this into account. For example:

> P: [*Looking more tense than usual*] I don't know what to work on.
>
> T: What are you aware of right now?
>
> P: I am glad to see you, but I'm tense about a meeting tonight with my boss. I have rehearsed and prepared and I've tried to support myself as I wait.
>
> T: What do you need right now?
>
> P: I thought of putting her in the empty chair and talking to her. But I am so tense I need to do something more physical. I need to move, breathe, make noise.
>
> T: [*Looking but remaining silent*]
>
> P: It's up to me, huh? [*Pause. Patient gets up, starts stretching, yawning. The movements and sounds become more vigorous. After a few minutes he sits down, looking more soft and alive.*] Now I'm ready.
>
> T: You look more alive.
>
> P: Now I am ready to explore what had me so uptight about tonight.

Self-rejection and full awareness are mutually exclusive. Rejection of self is a distortion of awareness because it is a denial of who

140

one is. Self-rejection is simultaneously a confusion of who "I am" and a self-deception, or "bad faith" attitude of being above that which is ostensibly being acknowledged (Sartre, 1966). Saying "I am" as if it were an observation of another person, or as if the "I" were not chosen, or without knowing how one creates and perpetuates that "I am" is bad faith rather than insightful awareness.

Responsibility

People, according to Gestalt therapy, are responsible (responseable); that is, they are the primary agents in determining their own behavior. When people confuse responsibility with blaming and shoulds, they pressure and manipulate themselves; they "try" and are not integrated and spontaneous. In such instances their true wants, needs and responses to the environment and choices in the situation are ignored and they overcomply or rebel against shoulds.

Gestalt therapists believe in the importance of a clear distinction between what one chooses and what is given. People are responsible for what they choose to do. For example, people are responsible for their actions on behalf of the environment. Blaming outside forces (e.g., genetics or parents) for what one chooses is self-deception. Taking responsibility for what one did not choose, a typical shame reaction, is also a deception.

People are responsible for moral choices. Gestalt therapy helps patients discover what is moral according to their own choice and values. Far from advocating "anything goes," Gestalt therapy places a most serious obligation on each person: choosing and valuing.

Variety of Concepts

Gestalt therapy personality theory has evolved primarily out of clinical experience. The focus has been a theory of personality that supports our task as psychotherapists rather than an overall theory of personality. The constructs of Gestalt therapy theory are field theoretical rather than genetic and phenomenological rather than conceptual.

Although Gestalt therapy is phenomenological, it also deals with the unconscious, that is, with what does not enter into awareness when needed. In Gestalt therapy, awareness is conceived of as being in touch and unawareness as being out of touch.

141

Unawareness can be explained by a variety of phenomena, including learning what to attend to, repression, cognitive set, character and style. Simkin (1976) compared personality to a floating ball — at any given moment only a portion is exposed while the rest is submerged. Unawareness is the result of the organism's not being in touch with its external environment due to its being mostly submerged in its own internal environment or fantasies, or not being in touch with its inner life due to fixation on the external.

Gestalt Therapy Theory of Change

Children swallow whole (introject) ideas and behavior. This results in an enforced morality rather than an organismically compatible morality. As a result, people frequently feel guilt when they behave in accordance with their wants as opposed to their shoulds. Some people invest an enormous amount of energy in maintaining the split between shoulds and wants — the resolution of which requires a recognition of their own morality as opposed to an introjected one. Shoulds sabotage such people, and the more they push to be what they are not, the more resistance is set up, and no change occurs.

Beisser advanced the theory that change does not happen through a "coercive attempt by the individual or by another person to change him," but does happen if the person puts in the time and effort to be "what he is," "to be fully in his current position" (1970, p. 70). When the therapist rejects the change agent role, change that is orderly and also meaningful is possible.

The Gestalt therapy notion is that awareness (including owning, choice, and responsibility) and contact bring natural and spontaneous change. Forced change is an attempt to actualize an image rather than to actualize the self. With awareness self-acceptance, and the right to exist *as is*, the organism can grow. Forced intervention retards this process.

The Gestalt psychology principle of *Prägnanz* states that the field will form itself into the best Gestalt that global conditions will allow. So, too, Gestalt therapists believe that people have an innate drive to health. This propensity is found in nature, and people are part of nature. Awareness of the obvious, the awareness continuum, is a tool that a person can deliberately use to channel this spontaneous drive for health.

Differentiation of the Field: Polarities versus Dichotomies

A dichotomy is a split whereby the field is considered not as a whole differentiated into different and interlocking parts, but rather as an assortment of competing (either/or) and unrelated forces. Dichotomous thinking interferes with organismic self-regulation. Dichotomous thinking tends to be intolerant of diversity among persons and of paradoxical truths about a single person.

Organismic self-regulation leads to integrating parts with each other and into a whole that encompasses the parts. The field is often differentiated into *polarities*: parts that are opposites that complement or explicate each other. The positive and negative poles of an electrical field are the prototypical mode for this differentiation in a field theoretical way. The concept of polarities treats opposites as part of one whole, as *yin* and *yang*.

With this polar view of the field, differences are accepted and integrated. Lack of genuine integration creates splits, such as body-mind, self-external, infantile-mature, biological-cultural, and unconscious-conscious. Through dialogue there can be an integration of parts, into a new whole in which there is a differentiated unity. Dichotomies such as the self-ideal and the needy self, thought and impulse, and social requirements and personal needs can be healed by integrating into a whole differentiated into natural polarities (Perls, 1947).

Definition of Health I: The Good Gestalt as Polarity

The good Gestalt describes a perceptual field organized with clarity and good form. A well-formed figure clearly stands out against a broader and less distinct background. The relation between that which stands out (figure) and the context (ground) is meaning. In the good Gestalt the meaning is clear. The good Gestalt gives a content-free definition of health.

In health, the figure changes as needed, that is, it shifts to another focus when the need is met or superseded by a more urgent need. It does not change so rapidly as to prevent satisfaction (as in hysteria) or so slowly that new figures have no room to assume organismic dominance (as in compulsivity). When figure and ground are dichotomized, one is left with a figure out of context or a context without focus (F. Perls et al., 1951). In health, awareness accurately represents the dominant need of the whole field. Need is a function of external factors (physical structure of the field, political activity, acts of nature, and so on) and internal factors (hunger, fatigue, interest, past experience, and so forth).

Definition of Health II: The Polarity of Creative Adjustment

The Gestalt therapy concept of healthy functioning includes *creative adjustment.* A psychotherapy that only helps patients adjust creates conformity and stereotypy. A psychotherapy that only led people to impose themselves on the world without considering others would engender pathological narcissism and a world-denying realization of self isolated from the world.

A person who shows creative interaction takes responsibility for the ecological balance between self and surroundings.

This is the theoretical context (F. Perls et al., 1951) within which some seemingly individualistic and even anarchistic statements of Gestalt therapy are most accurately considered. The individual and environment form a polarity. The choice is not between the individual and society, but between organismic and arbitrary regulation.

Resistance is a part of a polarity consisting of an impulse and resistance to that impulse. Seen as a dichotomy, resistance is often treated as "bad" and, in such a context, often turns out to be nothing more than the patient's following personal dictates rather than the therapist's. Seen as a polarity, resistance is as integral to health as the trait's being resisted.

Gestalt therapists attend to both the working process of consciousness and the resistance process of consciousness. Many Gestalt therapists avoid the word *resistance* because of its pejorative dichotomized connotation, which frames the process as a power battle between therapist and patient rather than as the self-conflict of the patient that needs to be integrated into a harmoniously differentiated self.

Impasse

An *impasse* is a situation in which external support is not forthcoming and the person believes he cannot support himself. The latter is due in large part to the person's strength being divided between impulse and resistance. The most frequent method of coping with this is to manipulate others.

An organismically self-regulating person takes responsibility for what is done for self, what is done by others for self, and what is done for others by self. The person exchanges with the environment, but the basic support for regulation of one's existence is by self. When the individual does not know this, external support becomes a replacement for self-support rather than a source of nourishment for the self.

In most psychotherapy the impasse is circumvented by external support by the therapist, and the patient does not find that self-support is sufficient. In Gestalt therapy, patients can get through the impasse because of the emphasis on loving contact without doing the patient's work, that is, without rescuing or infantilizing.

Psychotherapy
Theory of Psychotherapy

Goal of Therapy

In Gestalt, the only *goal* is *awareness*. This includes greater awareness in a particular area and also greater ability for the patient to bring automatic habits into awareness as needed. In the former sense awareness is a content, in the latter sense it is a process. Both awareness as content and awareness as process progress to deeper levels as the therapy proceeds. Awareness includes knowing the environment, responsibility for choices, self-knowledge, and self-acceptance, and the ability to contact.

Beginning patients are chiefly concerned with the solution of problems. The issue for the Gestalt therapist is how patients support themselves in solving problems. Gestalt therapy facilitates problem solving through increased self-regulation and self-support by the patient. As therapy goes on, the patient and the therapist turn more attention to general personality issues. By the end of successful therapy the patient directs much of the work and is able to integrate problem solving, characterological themes, relationship issues with the therapist, and means of regulating his or her own awareness.

Gestalt therapy is most useful for patients open to working on self-awareness and for those who want natural mastery of their awareness process. Although some people claim they are interested in changing their behavior, most people seeking psychotherapy mainly want relief from discomfort. Their complaint may be generalized malaise, specific discomforts, or dissatisfaction in relationships. Patients often expect that relief will result from their therapist's doing the work rather than from their own efforts.

Psychotherapy is most appropriate for persons who create anxiety, depression, and so forth by rejecting themselves, alienating aspects of themselves, and deceiving themselves. In short, people who do not know how they further their own unhappiness are prime candidates, providing they are open to awareness work, especially awareness of self-regulation. Gestalt therapy is especially appropriate for those who know intellectually about themselves and yet don't grow.

Those who want symptom relief without doing awareness work may be better candidates for behavior modification, medication, biofeedback, and so on. The direct methods of Gestalt therapy facilitate patients' making this choice early in the therapy. However, patients' difficulty in doing the contact or awareness work should not automatically be interpreted as meaning that they do not want to work. Respect for the total person enables a Gestalt therapist to help the patients become clear about the differences between "can't" and "won't" and to know how internal barriers or resistance, such as prior learning, anxiety, shame and sensitivity to narcissistic injury, inhibit awareness work.

No "Shoulds"

There are no "shoulds" in Gestalt therapy. In Gestalt therapy a higher value is placed on the autonomy and the self-determination for the patient than on other values. This is not a should, but a preference. The no-should ethic takes precedence over the therapist's goals for the patient and leaves the responsibility and sanctioning of the patient's behavior to the patient (of course, the injunctions and requirements of society are not suspended just because the patient is in Gestalt therapy).

How Is the Therapy Done?

Gestalt therapy is an exploration rather than a direct modification of behavior. The goal is growth and autonomy through an increase in consciousness. Rather than maintaining distance and interpreting, the Gestalt therapist meets patients and guides active awareness work. The therapist's active presence is alive and excited (hence warm), honest and direct. Patients can see, hear and be told how they are experienced, what is seen, how the therapist feels, what the therapist is like as a person. Growth occurs from real contact between real people. Patients learn how they are seen and how their awareness process is limited, not primarily by talking about their problems, but by how they and the therapist engage each other.

Focusing runs the range from simple inclusions or empathy to exercises arising mostly from the therapist's phenomenology while with the patient. Everything is secondary to the direct experience of both participants.

The general approach of Gestalt therapy is to facilitate exploring in ways that maximize what continues to develop after the session and without the therapist. The patient is often left unfinished but thoughtful or "opened up," or with an assignment. This is like a roast that continues to cook after being removed from the oven. This is in part how Gestalt therapy can be so intensive on fewer sessions per week. We cooperate with growth occurring without us; we initiate where needed. We give the degree of facilitation necessary to foster patient self-improvement. We facilitate growth rather than complete a cure process.

Perls believed that the ultimate goal of psychotherapy was the achievement of "that amount of integration which facilitates its own development" (1948). An example of this kind of facilitation is the analogy of a small hole cut into an accumulation of snow. Once the draining process begins, the base that began as a small hole enlarges by itself.

Successful psychotherapy achieves *integration*. Integration requires identification with *all* vital functions — not with only *some* of the patient's ideas, emotions and actions. Any rejection of one's own ideas, emotions or actions results in alienation. Reowning allows the person to be whole. The task, then, in therapy is to have the person become aware of previously alienated parts and taste them, consider them and assimilate them if they are ego-syntonic or reject them if they prove to be ego-alien. Simkin (1968) has used the simile of a cake in encouraging patients to reown the parts of themselves that they have considered noxious or otherwise unacceptable: although the oil, or flour, or baking powder by themselves can be distasteful, they are indispensable to the success of the whole cake.

The I-Thou Relation

Gestalt therapy focuses on the patient, as any therapy does. However, the relationship is horizontal, thus differing from the traditional therapy relationship. In Gestalt therapy the therapist and patient speak the same language, the language of present centeredness, emphasizing direct experience of both participants. Therapists as well as patients in Gestalt therapy show their full presence.

Since its beginning, Gestalt therapy has emphasized the patient's experience as well as the therapist's *observation* of what is not in the patient's awareness. This allows the patient to act as an equal who has full access to the data of his own experience so he can directly experience from inside what is *observed* by the therapist from outside. In an interpretive system the patient is an amateur and does not have the theoretical foundation for the interpretation. It is assumed that the important internal data are unconscious and not experienced.

An important aspect of the Gestalt therapy relationship is the question of responsibility. Gestalt therapy emphasizes that both the therapist and the patient are self-responsible. When therapists regard themselves as responsible for patients, they collude with patients' not feeling self-responsible and thereby reinforce the necessity for manipulation due to the belief that patients are unable to support and regulate themselves. However, it is *not enough for the therapist to be responsible for self and for the patient to be responsible for self*— there is also an alliance of patient and therapist that must be carefully constantly, and competently attended to.

Therapists are responsible for the quality and quantity of their presence, for knowledge about themselves and the patient, for maintaining a nondefensive posture, and for keeping their awareness and contact processes clear and matched to the patient. They are responsible for the consequences of their own behavior and for establishing and maintaining the therapeutic atmosphere.

The Awareness of What and How

In Gestalt therapy there is a constant and careful emphasis on *what* the patient does and *how* it is done. What does the patient face? How does the patient make choices? Does the patient self-support or resist? Direct experience is the tool, and it is expanded beyond what is at first experienced by continuing to focus deeper and broader. *The techniques of Gestalt therapy are experimental tasks. They are the means of expanding direct experience. These are not designed to get the patient somewhere, to change the patient's feelings, to recondition, or to foster catharsis.*

Here and Now

In a phenomenological therapy "now" starts with the present awareness of the patient. What happens first is not childhood, but what is experienced *now*. Awareness takes place *now*. Prior events may be the object of present awareness, but the awareness process (e.g., remembering) *is now*.

Now I can contact the world around me, or *now* I can contact memories or expectations. Not knowing the present, not remembering, or not anticipating are all disturbances. The present is an ever-moving transition between the past and future. Frequently patients do not know their current behavior In some cases patients live in the present as if they had no past. Most patients live in the future as if it were now. All these are disturbances of time awareness.

"Now" refers to *this moment*. In the therapy hour, when the patients refer to their lives out of the hour, or earlier in the hour, that is *not now*. In Gestalt therapy we orient more to the now than in any other form of psychotherapy. Experiences of the past few minutes, days, years or decades that are of present importance are dealt with. We attempt to move from talking about to directly experiencing. For example, talking *to* a person who is not physically present rather than talking *about* that person mobilizes more direct experience of feelings.

In Gestalt therapy this I and Thou, what and how, here and now methodology is frequently used to work on characterological and developmental psychodynamics.

For example, a 30-year-old female patient is in group therapy. She is in the middle phase of therapy. She says she is very angry at a man in the group. One legitimate and frequent Gestalt approach is "Say it to him." Instead, the therapist takes a different tack:

T: You sound not only angry but something more.
P: [*looks interested*]
T: You sound and look like you are enraged.
P: I am, I would like to kill him.
T: You seem to feel impotent.
P: I am.
T: Impotence usually accompanies rage. What are you impotent about?
P: I can't get him to acknowledge me.
T: [*the therapist's observations of her previous encounters with the man agree with that statement*] and you don't accept that.
P: No.
T: And there is an intensity to your rage that seems to be greater than the situation calls for.
P: [*nods and pauses*]
T: What are you experiencing?
P: A lot of men in my life who have been like that.
T: Like your father? [*this comes from prior work with patient and isn't a shot in the dark. The work proceeds into a reexperiencing the narcissistic injury from her father, who was never responsive to her*]

Process of Psychotherapy

Gestalt therapy probably has a greater range of styles and modalities than any other system. It is practiced in individual therapy, groups, workshops, couples, families, and with children. It is practiced in clinics, family service agencies, hospitals, private practices, growth centers, and so on. The styles in each modality vary drastically on many dimensions: degree and type of structure; quantity and quality of techniques used; frequency of sessions; abrasiveness-ease of relating; focus on body, cognition, feelings, interpersonal contact; knowledge of and work with psychodynamic themes; degree of personal encountering, and so forth.

All styles and modalities of Gestalt therapy have in common the general principles we have been discussing: emphasis on direct experience and experimenting (phenomenology), use of direct contact and personal presence (dialogic existentialism), and emphasis on the field concepts of what and how and here and now. Within these parameters, interventions are patterned according to the context and the personalities of the therapist and the patient.

At the heart of the methodology is the emphasis on the difference between "work" and other activities, especially "talking about." Work has two meanings. First, it refers to a deliberate, voluntary and disciplined commitment to use phenomenologically focused awareness to increase the scope and clarity of one's life. When one moves from talking about a problem or being with someone in a general way to studying what one is doing, especially being aware of how one is aware, one is working. Second, in a group, work means being the primary focus of the therapist's and/or the group's attention.

Differences in techniques are not important, although the quality and type of therapeutic contact and a fit between the attitude and emphasis of the therapist and the patient's needs are important. Techniques are just techniques: the overall method, relationship, and attitude are the vital aspects.

Nevertheless a discussion of some techniques or tactics might elucidate the overall methodology. These are only illustrative of what is possible.

Techniques of Patient Focusing

All techniques of patient focusing are elaborations of the question, "What are you aware of (experiencing) now?" and the instruction, "Try this experiment and see what you become aware of (experience) or learn." Many interventions are as simple as asking what the patient is aware of, or more narrowly, "What are you feeling?" or "What are you thinking?"

"*Stay with it.*" A frequent technique is to follow an awareness report with the instruction: "Stay with it" or "Feel it out."

"Stay with it" encourages the patient to continue with the feeling that is being reported, which builds the patient's capacity to deepen and work a feeling through to completion. For example:

P: [*looks sad*]
T: What are you aware of?
P: I am sad.
T: Stay with it.
P: [*tears well up. Then the patient tightens and looks away and starts to look thoughtful*]
T: I see you are tightening. What are you aware of?
P: I don't want to stay with the sadness.
T: Stay with the not wanting to. Put words to the not wanting to. [*this intervention is likely to bring awareness of the patient's resistance to melting. The patient might respond: "I won't cry here — I don't trust you," or "I am ashamed," or "I am angry and don't want to admit I miss him"*]

Enactment. Here the patient is asked to put feelings or thoughts into action. For example, the therapist may encourage the patient to "say it to the person" (if present) or use some kind of role playing (such as speaking to an empty chair if the person is not present). "Put words to it" is another example. The patient with tears in his eyes might be asked to "put words to it." Enactment is intended as a way of increasing awareness, *not* as a form of catharsis. It is not a universal remedy.

Exaggeration is a special form of enactment. A person is asked to exaggerate some feeling, thought, movement, etc., in order to feel the more intense (albeit artificial) enacted or fantasied vision. Enactment into movement, sound, art, poetry, etc., can both stimulate creativity and be therapeutic. For instance, a man who had been talking about his mother without showing any special emotion was asked to describe her. Out of his description came the suggestion to move like her. As the patient adopted her posture and movement, intense feelings came back into his awareness.

Guided fantasy. Sometimes a patient can bring an experience into the here and now more efficiently by visualizing than by enacting:

> P: I was with my girlfriend last night. I don't know how it happened but I was impotent. [*patient gives more detail and some history*]
> T: Close your eyes. Imagine it is last night and you are with your girlfriend. Say out lout what you experience at each moment.
> P: I am sitting on the couch. My friend sits next to me and I get excited. Then I go soft.
> T: Let's go through that again in slow motion, in more detail. Be sensitive to every thought or sense impression.
> P: I am sitting on the couch. She comes over and sits next to me. She touches my neck. It feels so warm and soft, I get excited — you know, hard. She strokes my arm, and I love it. [*pause, looks startled*] Then I thought, I had such a tense day, maybe I won't be able to get it up.

This patient became aware of how he created his own anxiety and impotence. This fantasy was recreating an event that happened in order to get in better touch with it. The fantasy could be of an expected event, a metaphorical event, and so forth.

In another case, a patient working on shame and self-rejection is asked to imagine a mother who says and means "I love you just the way you are." As the fantasy is given detail, the patient attends to her experience. This fantasy helps the patient become aware for the possibility of good self-mothering and can serve as a transition to integrate good self-parenting. The image can be used to work between sessions or as a meditation. It also raises feelings about experiences with abandonment, loss and bad parenting.

Loosening and integrating techniques. Often the patient is so fettered by the bonds of the usual ways of thinking that alternative possibilities are not allowed into awareness. This includes traditional mechanisms, such as denial or repression, but also cultural and learning factors affecting the patient's way of thinking. One technique is just to ask the patient to imagine the opposite of whatever is believed to be true.

Integrating techniques bring together processes the patient doesn't bring together or actively keeps apart (splitting). The patient might be asked to put words to a negative process, such as tensing, crying or twitching. Or when the patient verbally reports a feeling, that is, an emotion, she might be asked to locate it in her body. Another example is asking a patient to express positive *and* negative feelings about the same person.

Body techniques. These include any technique that brings patients' awareness to their body functioning or helps them to be aware of how they can use their bodies to support excitement, awareness and contact. For example:

P: [*is tearful and clamping jaw tight*]
T: Would you be willing to try an experiment?
P: [*patient nods*]
T: Take some deep, deep breaths and each time you exhale, let your jaw loosely move down.
P: [*breathes deeply, lets jaw drop on the exhale*]
T: Stay with it.
P: [*starts melting, crying, then sobbing*]

Therapist Disclosures

The Gestalt therapist is encouraged to make "I" statements. Such statements facilitate both the therapeutic contact and the patient's focusing and are to be made discriminatingly and judiciously. Using the "I" to facilitate therapeutic work requires technical skill, personal wisdom and self-awareness on the therapist's part. Therapists may share what they see, hear or smell. They can share how they are affected. Facts of which the therapist is aware and the patient is not are shared, especially if the information is unlikely to be spontaneously discovered in the phenomenological work during the hour, yet is believed to be important to the patient.

Mechanisms of Psychotherapy

Old Deficits, New Strengths

The child needs a parental relationship with a nurturant, organismic/environmental, ecological balance. For example, a

154

mother must see that a child's needs are met and that the development of its potentialities are facilitated. A child needs this warm, nurturing kind of mirroring. And a child also needs room to struggle, to be frustrated, and to fail. A child also needs limits to experience the consequences of behavior. When parents cannot meet these needs because they need a dependent child or lack sufficient inner resources, the child develops distorted contact boundaries, awareness and lowered self-esteem.

Unfortunately, children are often shaped to meet the approval of parents on their own needs. As a result, the spontaneous personality is superseded by an artificial one. Other children come to believe they can have their own needs met by others without consideration for the autonomy of others. This results in the formation of impulsivity rather than spontaneity.

Patients need a therapist who will relate in a healthy, contactful manner, neither losing self by indulgent the patient at the expense of exploration and working through nor creating excessive anxiety, shame and frustration by not being respectful, warm, receptive, direct and honest.

Patients who enter psychotherapy with decreased awareness of their needs and strengths, resisting rather than supporting their organismic self, are in pain. They try to get the therapist to do for them what they believe they cannot do for themselves. When therapists go along with this, patients do not reown and integrate their lost or never-developed potential. Therefore they still cannot operate with organismic self-regulation, being responsible for themselves. They do not find out if they have the strength to exist autonomously because the therapist meets their needs without strengthening their awareness and ego boundaries (see Resnick, 1970).

As Gestalt therapy proceeds and patients learn to be aware and responsible and contactful, their ego functioning improves. As a result, they gain tools for deeper exploration. The childhood experiences of the formative years can then be explored without the regression and overdependency necessary in regressive treatment and without the temporary loss of competence that a transference neurosis entails. Childhood experiences are brought into present awareness without the assumption that patients are determined by past events. Patients actively project transference material on the Gestalt therapist, thereby giving opportunities for deeper exploration.

The following two examples show patients with different defenses, needing different treatment, but with similar underlying issues.

Tom was a 45-year-old man proud of his intelligence, self-sufficiency and independence. He was not aware that he had unmet dependency needs and resentment. This affected his marriage in that his wife felt unneeded and inferior because she was in touch with needing and showed it. This man's self-sufficiency required respect — it met a need, was in part constructive and was the basis of his self-esteem.

P: [*with pride*] When I was a little kid my mom was so busy I just had to learn to rely on myself.
T: I appreciate your strength, and when I think of you as such a self-reliant kid I want to stroke you and give you some parenting.
P: [*tearing a little*] No one has been able to do that for me.
T: You seem sad.
P: I am remembering when I was a kid.... [*exploration led to awareness of a shame reaction to unavailable parents and a compensatory self-reliance*]

Bob was a 45-year-old man who felt shame and isolated himself in reaction to any interaction that was not totally positive. He was consistently reluctant to experiment with self-nourishment.

P: [*whiny voice*] I don't know what to do today.
T: [*looks and does not talk*]
P: I could talk about my week. [*looks questioningly at therapist*]
T: I feel pulled on by you right now. I imagine you want me to direct you.
P: Yes. What's wrong with that?
T: Nothing. I prefer not to direct you right now.

P: Why not?

T: You *can* direct yourself. I believe you are dir(
from your inner self right now. I don't want
with that. [*silence*]

P: I feel lost.

T: [*looks and does not talk*]

P: You are not going to direct me, are you?

T: No.

P: Well, let's work on my believing I can't take care of myself.
[*patient directs a fruitful piece of work that leads to awareness of
abandonment anxiety and feelings of shame in response to unavailable parents*

Frustration and Support

Gestalt therapy balances frustration and support. The therapist
explores rather than gratifies the patient's wishes — and this is
frustrating for the patient. Providing contact is supportive, although honest contact frustrates manipulation. The Gestalt
therapist expresses self and emphasizes exploring, including
exploring desire, frustration and indulgence. The therapist
responds to manipulations by the patient *without reinforcing
them,*without judging and without being purposely frustrating. A
balance of warmth and firmness is important.

The Paradoxical Theory of Change

The paradox is that the more one tries to be who one is not, the
more one stays the same (Beisser, 1970). Many patients focus on
what they "should be" and at the same time resist these shoulds.

The Gestalt therapist attempts to work toward integration by
asking the client to identify with each conflicting role. The client
is asked what he or she experiences at each moment. When the
client can be aware of both roles, integrating techniques are used
to transcend the dichotomy.

There are two axioms in Gestalt therapy: "What is, is," and "One
thing leads to another" (Polster and Polster, 1973). The medium
of change is a relationship with a therapist who makes contact

sed on showing who he or she truly is and who understands and accepts the patient.

Awareness of "what is" leads to spontaneous change. When the person manipulating for support finds a therapist who is contactful and accepting and who does not collude with the manipulation, he may become aware of what he is doing. This *Aha!* is a new gestalt, a new outlook, a taste of new possibility: "I can be with someone and not manipulate or be manipulated." When such a person meets "therapeutic" collusion, derision, mind games, game busting and so on, this increase in awareness is unlikely to happen.

At each and every point along the way this new *Aha!* can occur. As long as the therapist or the patient can see new possibilities and the patient wants to learn, new *Aha!'s* are possible and with them, growth. Awareness work can start anywhere the patient is willing, if the therapist is aware and connects it to the whole. The ensuing process in Gestalt therapy leads to changes everywhere in the field. The more thorough the investigation, the more intense the reorganization. Some changes can only be appreciated years later.

Patients in Gestalt therapy are in charge of their lives. The therapist facilitates attention to opening restricted awareness and areas of constricted contact boundaries; the therapist brings firmness and limits to areas with poor boundaries. As sensing increases in accuracy and vividness, as breathing becomes fuller and more relaxed and as patients make better contact, they bring the skills of therapy into their lives. Sometimes intimacy and job improvements follow Gestalt work like an act of grace, without the patient's connecting the increase to the work done in therapy. But the organism does grow with awareness and contact. One thing does lead to another.

Applications

Problems

Gestalt therapy can be used effectively with any patient population that the therapist understands and feels comfortable with. If the therapist can relate to the patient, the Gestalt therapy principles of dialogue and direct experiencing can be applied. With each patient, *general principles must be adapted to the particular clinical situation.* If the patient's treatment is made to conform to "Gestalt therapy," it can be ineffective or harmful. A schizophrenic, a sociopath, a borderline and an obsessive-compulsive neurotic may all need different approaches. *Thus, the competent practice of Gestalt therapy requires a background in more than Gestalt therapy.* A knowledge of diagnosis, personality theory and psychodynamic theory is also needed.

The individual clinician has a great deal of discretion in Gestalt therapy. Modifications are made by the individual therapist according to the therapeutic style, personality, diagnostic considerations, and so on. This encourages and requires individual responsibility by the therapist. Gestalt therapists are encouraged to have a firm grounding in personality theory, psychopathology and theories and applications of psychotherapy, as well as adequate clinical experience. Participants in the therapeutic encounter are encouraged to experiment with new behavior and then share cognitively and emotionally what the experience was like.

Gestalt therapy has traditionally been considered most effective with "overly socialized, restrained, constricted individuals" (anxious, perfectionistic, phobic and depressed clients), whose inconsistent or restricted functioning is primarily a result of "internal restrictions" (Shepherd, 1970, pp. 234-35). Such individuals usually show only a minimal enjoyment of living.

Although Shepherd's statement accurately delineates a population Gestalt therapy is effective with, current clinical practice of Gestalt therapy includes treatment of a much wider range of problems.

Gestalt therapy in the "Perlsian" workshop style is of more limited application than Gestalt therapy in general (Dolliver, 1981; Dublin, 1976). In Shepherd's discussion of limitations and cautions, she notes restrictions that apply to any therapist but should especially be noted in a workshop setting, as well as by therapists not well trained or experienced with disturbed patient populations.

Work with psychotic, disorganized, or otherwise severely disturbed people is more difficult and calls for "caution, sensitivity and patience." Shepherd advises against doing such work where it is not feasible to make a "long-term commitment" to the patient. Disturbed patients need support from the therapist and at least a minimal amount of faith in their own natural healing capacity before they can explore deeply and experience intensely the "overwhelming pain, hurt, rage and despair" that underlie the psychological processes of disturbed patients (Shepherd, 1970, pp. 234-35).

Working with more disturbed populations requires clinical knowledge of how to balance support and frustration, knowledge of character dynamics, need for auxiliary support (such as day treatment and medication) and so forth. Some statements which seem to make sense in a workshop encounter are obvious non-sense when applied in a broader context. Consider for example, "do your own thing" in the context of treatment with acting out patients!

A perusal of the Gestalt therapy literature such as *Gestalt Therapy Now* (Fagan and Shepherd, 1970), *The Growing Edge of Gestalt Therapy* (Smith, 1976) and *The Gestalt Journal*, will show that Gestalt therapy is used for crisis intervention, ghetto adults in a poverty program (Barnwell, 1968), interaction groups, psychotics and almost any group imaginable. Unfortunately the literature provides examples (and a small number at that) without sufficient explication of necessary alterations in focus and without discussing negative results.

Gestalt therapy has been successfully employed in the treatment of a wide range of "psychosomatic" disorders including migraine, ulcerative colitis and spastic neck and back. Gestalt therapists have successfully worked with couples, with individuals having difficulties coping with authority figures and with a wide range of intrapsychic conflicts. Gestalt therapy has been effectively employed with psychotics and severe character disorders.

Because of the impact of Gestalt therapy and the ease with which strong, frequently buried affective reactions can be reached, it is necessary to establish safety islands to which both the therapist and patient can comfortably return. It is also imperative for the therapist to stay with the patient until he or she is ready to return to these safety islands. For example, after an especially emotion laden experience, the patient may be encouraged to make visual, tactile or other contact with the therapist or with one or more group members and report the experience. Another safety technique is to have the patient shuttle back and forth between making contact in the *now* with the therapist or group members and with the emotionally laden unfinished situation that the patient was experiencing *then* until all of the affect has been discharged and the unfinished situation worked through.

The Gestalt therapy emphasis on personal responsibility, interpersonal contact and increased clarity of awareness of what is, could be of great value in meeting the problems of the present. One example is application of Gestalt therapy in schools (Brown, 1970; Lederman, 1970).

Evaluation

Gestalt therapists are singularly unimpressed with formal psychodiagnostic evaluation and nomothetic research methodology. No statistical approach can tell the individual patient or therapist what works for him or her. What is shown to work for most does not always work for a particular individual. This does not mean that Gestalt therapists are not in favor of research; in fact, the Gestalt Therapy Institute of Los Angeles has offered grants to subsidize research. Perls offered no quantified, statistical evidence that Gestalt therapy works. He did say, "we present nothing that you cannot verify for yourself in terms of your own behavior" (F. Perls et al., 1951, p. 7). In the publication *Gestalt Therapy*, a series of experiments are provided that can be used to test for oneself the validity of Gestalt therapy.

Each session is seen as an experiment, an existential encounter in which both the therapist and the patient engage in calculated risk taking (experiments) involving exploration of heretofore unknown or forbidden territories. The patient is aided in using phenomenological focusing skills and dialogic contact to evaluate what is and is not working. Thus, constant idiographic research takes place. Gestalt therapy has "sacrificed exact verification for the value in ideographic experimental psychotherapy" (Yontef, 1969, p. 27).

Harman (1984) reviewed Gestalt research literature and found quality research on Gestalt therapy sparse. He did find studies that showed increased self-actualization and positive self-concept following Gestalt therapy groups (Foulds and Hannigan, 1976; Giunan and Foulds, 1970).

A series of studies conducted by Leslie Greenberg and associates (Greenberg, 1986) addressed the lack of attention to context in psychotherapy research and the unfortunate separation of process and outcome studies. The Greenberg studies related specific acts and change processes in therapy with particular outcomes. Their research distinguished three types of outcome (immediate, intermediate and final) and three levels of process (speech act, episode and relationship). They studied speech in the context of the type of episodes in which it appears, and they studied the episodes in the context of the relationships in which they occur.

In one study Greenberg examined the use of the two-chair technique to resolve splits. He defined a split as "a verbal performance pattern in which a client reports a division of the self process into two partial aspects of the self or tendencies." He concludes that "two-chair operations conducted according to the principles [of his study] have been found to facilitate an increase in the Depth of Experiencing and index of productive psychotherapy...and to lead to resolutions of splits with populations seeking counseling" (1979, p. 323).

A study called the "Effects of Two-Chair Dialogues and Focusing on Conflict Resolution" by L. S. Greenberg and H. M. Higgins found that "Two-chair dialogue appeared to produce a more direct experience of conflict [split] and encouraged the client in a form of self-confrontation that helped create a resolution to the conflict" (1980, p. 224).

Harman (1984) found a number of studies that compared the behavior of Gestalt therapists with that of other therapists. Brunnink and Schroeder compared expert psychoanalysts, behavior therapists and Gestalt therapists and found the Gestalt therapists "provided more direct guidance, less verbal facilitation, less focus on the client, more self-disclosure, greater initiative and less emotional support." They also found that the "interview" content of Gestalt therapists tended to reflect a more experiential or subjective approach to therapy" (1979, p. 572).

No claim is made in the Gestalt therapy literature that Gestalt therapy is demonstrated to be the "best." There is theoretically no reason why Gestalt therapy should be more generally effective than therapies under other names that follow the principles of good psychotherapy. General outcome research may yield less useful results than process research looking at behavior, attitudes and consequences. An example of this is Simkin's assessment of the effectiveness of Gestalt therapy in workshops ("massed learning") as contrasted with "spaced" weekly therapy sessions. He found evidence for the superiority of massed learning (Simkin, 1976).

Some Gestalt therapy viewpoints on what constitutes good therapy are supported by general research. The research on experiencing within the Rogerian tradition demonstrated the effectiveness of an emphasis on direct experience by any therapist. In Gestalt therapy there is also an emphasis on personal relating, presence and experience. Unfortunately, some therapists regularly and blatantly violate the principles of good psychotherapy according to the Gestalt therapy model, but still call themselves Gestalt therapists (Lieberman, Yalom and Miles, 1973).

Treatment

Ongoing Individual Gestalt Therapy

Although Gestalt therapy has acquired a reputation for being primarily applicable to groups, its mainstay is actually individual treatment. Several examples can be found in *Gestalt Therapy Now* (Fagan and Shepherd, 1970). An annotated bibliography of case readings can be found in Simkin (1979, p. 299).

Gestalt therapy begins with the first contact. Ordinarily, assessment and screening are done as a part of the ongoing relationship rather than in a separate period of diagnostic testing and social history taking. The data for the assessment are obtained by beginning the work, for example, by therapeutic encounter. This assessment includes the patient's willingness and support for work within the Gestalt therapy framework, the match of patient and therapist, the usual professional diagnostic and characterological discriminations, decisions on frequency of sessions, the need for adjunctive treatment and the need for medical consultation.

An average frequency for sessions is once per week. Using the Gestalt methodology, an intensity equivalent to psychoanalysis can often be achieved at this frequency. Often individual therapy is combined with group therapy, workshops, conjoint or family therapy, movement therapy, meditation, or biofeedback training.

Sometimes patients can utilize more frequent sessions, but often they need the interval to digest material and more frequent sessions may result in overreliance on the therapist. Frequency of sessions depends on how long the patient can go between sessions without loss of continuity, decompensation, or lesser forms of relapse. Frequency of sessions varies from five times per week to every other week. Meeting less frequently than every week obviously diminishes intensity unless the patient attends a weekly group with the same therapist. More than twice a week is ordinarily not indicated, except with psychotics, and is definitely contraindicated with borderline personality disorders.

All through the therapy patients are encouraged and aided in doing the decision making for themselves. When to start and stop, whether to do an exercise, what adjunctive therapies to use, and the like are all discussed with the therapist, but the competence and ultimate necessity for the patient to make these choices is supported.

Group Models

Gestalt therapy groups vary from one and one-half to three hours in length, with an average length of two hours. A typical two-hour group has up to 10 participants. Gestalt therapists usually experience maximal involvement with heterogeneous groups, with a balance of men and women. Participants need to be screened. Any age is appropriate for Gestalt therapy, but an ongoing private practice group would typically range from ages 20 to 65 with the average between 30 and 50.

Some Gestalt therapists follow Perls' lead in doing one-on-one therapy in the group setting and use the "hot seat" structure. "According to this method, an individual expresses to the therapist his interest in dealing with a particular problem. The focus is then on the extended interaction between patient and group leader (I and Thou)" (Levitsky and Simkin, 1972, p. 240). One-on-one episodes average 20 minutes, but range from a couple of minutes to 45 minutes. During the one-on-one work, the other members remain silent. After the work, they give feedback on how they were affected, what they observed, and how their own experiences are similar to those the patient worked on. In recent years the one-on-

one work has been expanded to include awareness work that is not focused around a particular problem.

In the early 1960s Perls wrote a paper in which he said:

> Lately, however, I have eliminated individual sessions alto-gether except for emergency cases. As a matter of fact, I have come to consider that all individual therapy is obsolete and should be replaced by workshops in Gestalt therapy. In my workshops I now integrate individual and group work. (1967, p. 306)

This opinion was not then shared by most Gestalt therapists, and is not currently recognized Gestalt theory or practice.

Some observers have described the Gestalt therapist's style of group work as doing individual therapy in a group setting. This statement is valid for those Gestalt therapists who use the model just discussed and do not emphasize or deal with group dynamics or strive for group cohesiveness. However, this is only one style of Gestalt therapy — many Gestalt therapists do emphasize group dynamics.

Greater use of the group is certainly within the Gestalt methodology and is increasingly used in Gestalt therapy (Enright, 1975; Feder and Ronall, 1980; Zinker, 1977). This includes greater involvement of group members when an individual is doing one-on-one work, working on individual themes by everyone in the group, emphasis on interrelationships (contact) in the group, and working with group processes per se. The varied degree and type of structure provided by the leader include structured group exercises or no structured group exercises, observing the group's evolving to its own structure, encouraging one-on-one work, and so on. Often Gestalt groups begin with some exercise to help participants make the transition into working by sharing here-and-now experience.

A frequently used model is one that encourages both increased awareness through focus on contact between group members and one-on-one work in the group (with other members encouraged to participate during the work). This encourages greater fluidity and flexibility.

Workshop Style

Some Gestalt therapy and a good deal of training in Gestalt therapy is conducted in workshops, which are scheduled for a finite period, some for as short as one day. Weekend workshops may ranged from 10 to 20 or more hours. Longer workshops range from a week through several months in duration. A typical weekend workshop membership consists of one Gestalt therapist and 12 to 16 people. Given longer periods (ranging from one week up to a month or longer), as many as 20 people can be seen by one therapist. Usually if the group is larger than 16 participants, co-therapists are used.

Because workshops have a finite life and because just so many hours are available to the participants, there is usually high motivation to "work." Sometimes, rules are established so that no one can work a second time until every other participant has had an opportunity to work once. At other times, no such rules are set. Thus, depending on their willingness, audacity and drive, some people may get intense therapeutic attention several times during a workshop.

Although some workshops are arranged with established groups, most assemble people for the first time. As in ongoing groups, the ideal practice is to screen patients before the workshop. An unscreened workshop requires a clinician experienced with the range of severe pathology and careful protection for possibly vulnerable group members. Confrontive or charismatic Gestalt styles are particularly likely to exacerbate existing mental illness in some participants (Lieberman et al., 1973).

Other Treatment Modalities

The application of Gestalt therapy to working with families has been most extensively elaborated by Walter Kempler (1973, pp. 251-86). The most complete description of Kempler's work appears in his *Principles of Gestalt Family Therapy* (1974).

Gestalt therapy has also been used in short-term crisis intervention (O'Connell, 1970), as an adjunct treatment for visual problems (Rosanes-Berret, 1970), for awareness training of mental health professionals (Enright, 1970), for children with behavior problems (Lederman, 1970), to train staff for a day-care center (Ennis and Mitchell, 1970), to teach creativity to teachers and others (Brown, 1970), with a dying person (Zinker and Fink, 1966), and in organization development (Herman, 1972).

Management

Case management by a Gestalt therapist tends to be quite practical and guided by the goal of supporting the person-to-person relationship. Appointments are usually arranged over the telephone by the therapist. Office decor reflects the personality and style of the therapist and is not purposely neutral. The offices are designed and furnished to be comfortable and to avoid a desk or table between therapist and patient. Typically the physical arrangement leaves room for movement and experimentation. The therapist's dress and manner are usually quite informal.

Arrangement of fees varies with the individual, and there is no particular Gestalt style, except straightforwardness. Fees are discussed directly with the patient and usually collected by the therapist.

Clarity of boundaries is stressed, with both the patient and the therapist responsible for attending to the task at hand. The "work," or therapy, starts from the first moment. No notes are taken during the session because it interferes with contact. The therapist takes personal responsibility for note taking after the session, if needed, and for safeguarding notes, video or tape recordings and other clinical material. The therapist sets down conditions of payment, cancellation policy, and so forth. Violations or objections are directly discussed. Decisions are made together and agreements are expected to be kept by both. The therapist arranges the office to protect it from invasion, and where possible, soundproofs the office.

The evaluation process occurs as part of the therapy and is mutual. Some of the considerations involved in the evaluation process include deciding on individual and/or group therapy, estimating the therapist's capacity to establish a trusting, caring relationship, and letting the patient decide after an adequate sample if the therapist and the therapy are suitable.

Problems arising in the relationship are discussed directly, both in terms of dealing with the concrete problem and in terms of exploring any related characerological life-styles or relationship processes that would be fruitful for the patient to explore. Always

167

the needs, wishes and direct experience of both participants guide the exploration and problem solving.

Case Example

Peg was originally seen in a Gestalt training workshop, where she worked on the grief and anger she felt toward her husband, who had committed suicide. His death left her with the full responsibility for raising their children and beginning a career outside the home to support herself and her family. She was in her late 30s at the time.

With considerable courage and initiative, Peg had organized a crisis clinic sponsored by a prominent service organization in the large Southern California city in which she resided. She was one of 11 people who participated in making a Gestalt therapy training film with Simkin (1969). The following is excerpted from the film, *In the Now.*

Peg: I have a ...recurring dream. I'm standing on the ground, up by Camp Pendleton. There's an open, rolling countryside. Wide dirt roads crisscrossing all over it. A series of hills and valleys and hills and valleys....And off to my right I see a tank, like in the army — marine tanks with the big tracks...and there's a series of them and they're all closed tight and they're rumbling over these hills and valleys in a line, all closed up. And I'm standing beside this road and I'm holding a platter of Tollhouse cookies. And they're hot cookies. And they are just on the platter — I'm just standing there, and I see these tanks coming by one at a time. And as the tanks come past, I stand there and I watch the tanks. And as I look to my right I see one — and there's a pair of shiny black shoes, running along between the treads of the tank as it comes over the hill. And just as it gets in front of me...the man bends down and the tank goes on, and he comes over toward me and it's my best friend's husband. And I always wake up. I always stop my dream...and I laughed. It doesn't seem so funny anymore.
Jim: True. What are you doing?
Peg: Trying to stop my teeth from chattering.
Jim: What's your objection?

Peg: I don't like the feeling of anxiety and fear I have now.

Jim: What do you imagine?

Peg: Ridicule.

Jim: Okay. Start ridiculing.

Peg: Peg, you're ridiculous. You're fat...you're lazy. You're just comic. You're pretending to be grown up and you're not. Everybody looking knows that you're a kid inside, masquerading as a 39-year-old woman and...it's a ridiculous disguise. You haven't any business being 39. A ridiculous age. You're comic. You have a job you don't have the remotest idea how to do. You're making all kinds of grandiose plans that you haven't brains enough to carry through and people are going to be laughing at you.

Jim: Okay, now please look around and note how people are laughing at you.

Peg: I'm scared to. [*Looks around, slowly*] They appear to be taking me quite seriously.

Jim: So who is laughing at you?

Peg: I guess...only my fantasy...my...

Jim: Who creates your fantasy?

Peg: I do.

Jim: So who's laughing at you?

Peg: Yeah. That's so. I...I'm really laughing at what's not funny. I'm not so damned incompetent. [*pause*]

Jim: What are you really good at?

Peg: I'm good with people. I'm not judgmental. I'm good at keeping house. I'm a good seamstress, good baker, I...

Jim: Maybe you'll make somebody a good wife.

Peg: I did.

Jim: Maybe you'll make somebody a good wife again.

Peg: I don't know.

Jim: So say that sentence. "I don't know if I'll ever make somebody a good wife again."

Peg: I don't know if I'll ever make someone a good wife again.

Jim: Say that to every man here.

Peg: I don't know if I'll make someone a good wife again....

[*repeats the sentence five more times*]

Jim: What do you experience?

Peg: Surprise. Boy...I assumed I would never make anybody a good wife again.
Jim: Right.
Jim: What do you experience right now?
Peg: Satisfaction. Pleasure. I feel good. I feel done.

Although Peg's "ticket of admission" was a dream, what became foreground was her anxiety and fantasies of being ridiculed. The dream served as a vehicle for starting and, as is frequently the case, the work led to a most unpredictable outcome.

At the weekend workshop during which the training film was made, Peg met a man to whom she was attracted and who, in turn, was attracted to her. They began to date and within a few months they married.

A second sample of Gestalt therapy follows, selectively excerpted from a book to illustrate some techniques (Simkin, 1976, pp. 103-18). It is a condensed transcript of a workshop with six volunteers. The morning session included a lecture-demonstration and film.

Jim: I'd like to start with saying where I am and what I'm experiencing at this moment. This seems very artificial to me, all of these lights and the cameras and the people around. I feel breathless and burdened by the technical material, the equipment, etc., and I'm much more interested in getting away from the lights and the cameras and getting more in touch with you. [*inquires as to the names of participants of the group and introduces himself*]

I am assuming that all of you saw the film and the demonstration, and my preference would be to work with you as you feel ready to work. I'll reiterate our contract, or agreement. In Gestalt therapy the essence of the contract is to say where you are, what you are experiencing at any given moment, and, if you can, to stay in the continuum of awareness, to report where you are focusing, what you are aware of.

* * * * *

I'd like to start first with having you say who you are and if you have any programs or expectations.

Tom: Right now I'm a little tense, not particularly because of the technical equipment because I'm kind of used to that. I feel a little strange about being in a situation with you. This morning I was pretty upset because I didn't agree with a lot of the things you were talking about, and I felt pretty hostile to you. Now I more or less accept you as another person.

Jim: I'm paying attention to your foot now. I'm wondering if you could give your foot a voice.

Tom: My foot a voice? You mean how is my foot feeling? What's it going to say?

Jim: Just keep doing that, and see if you have something to say, as your foot.

Tom: I don't understand.

Jim: As you were telling me about feeling hostile this morning, you began to kick and I'm imagining that you still have some kick coming.

Tom: Uh, yeah. I guess maybe I do have some kick left, but I really don't get the feeling that that's appropriate.

* * * * * *

Lavonne: Right now I'm feeling tense.

Jim: Who are you talking to, Lavonne?

Lavonne: I was just thinking about this morning, I was feeling very hostile. I still think I am somewhat hostile.

Jim: I am aware that you are avoiding looking at me.

Lavonne: Yes, because I feel that you are very arrogant.

Jim: That's true.

Lavonne: And as if I might get into a struggle with you.

Jim: You might.

Lavonne: So the avoidance of eye contact is sort of a put-off of the struggle. I don't know whether they can be resolved.

Jim: Would you be willing to tell me what your objections are to my arrogance?

Lavonne: Well, it's not very comforting. If I have a problem and I talk to you about it and you're arrogant, then that only makes me arrogant.

Jim: You respond in kind is what you are saying. Your experience is you respond that way.

Lavonne: Yes. Right on. Then at this university I feel that I must be arrogant and I must be defensive at all times. Because I'm black, people react to me in different ways ... different people ... and I feel that I have to be on my toes most of the time...

* * * * * *

Mary: I want to work on my feelings for my older son and the struggle that I have with him — only, I suspect it is really a struggle I'm having with myself.

Jim: Can you say this to him? Give him a name and say this to him.

Mary: All right. His name is Paul.

Jim: Put Paul here [*empty chair*] and say this to Paul.

Mary: Paul, we have a lot of friction. Every time you go out of the drive on your own, independent, I hate you for it. But...

Jim: Just a moment. Say the same sentence to Mary. Mary, each time you go out the drive, independent, I hate you for it.

Mary: That fits. Mary, each time you go out the drive, independent, I hate you for it, because you are not being a good mother.

Jim: I don't know about your "because."

Mary: No. That's my rationale. That's the same I do to myself doing yoga.

Jim: You sound identified with Paul.

Mary: I am. I know this. I envy his freedom, even from the time he was a little kid and went to the woods. I envied his ability to go to the woods.

Jim: Tell Paul.

Mary: Paul, even when you were a little boy and you would go for all day Saturday, and not tell me where you were going but just go, I envied you for it I envied you very much, and I felt hurt because I couldn't do it too.

Jim: You couldn't, or you wouldn't?

Mary: I would not do it. I wanted to, but I would not do it.

Jim: Yeah. For me to have somebody around that keeps reminding me of what I can do and don't really pisses me off.

Mary: This is what I do to myself. I keep reminding myself of what I can do and won't do. And then I don't do anything. I'm at a standstill. Firmly planted.

Jim: I'd like you to get in touch with your spitefulness. Put your spitefulness out here and talk to Mary's saboteur.

Mary: You idiot. You've got the time to do your work. You also have the energy to do your work...which you dissipate. You get involved in umpteen dozen things so you will have an excuse not to do your work, or to do anything else... [*pause*] You just spend time making yourself miserable and complicating your life.

Jim: What's going on here? [*points to Mary's hand*]

Mary: Yes. Tight-fisted...won't do.

Jim: Are you tight-fisted?

Mary: Yes, I think I am.

Jim: OK. Can you get in touch with the other part of you — your generous self?

Mary: I don't really know my generous self very well.

Jim: Be your tight-fisted self just saying, "Generous self, I have no contact with you, I don't know you, etc."

Mary: Generous self, I don't know very much of you. I think you try every now and then when you give presents to people instead of giving yourself. You withhold an awful lot that you could give.

Jim: What just happened?

Mary: I rehearsed. I just wasn't talking to my generous self. I was talking to...you primarily. I was withholding part.

Jim: I have difficulty imagining you as a withholding person. You came on in the beginning as very vibrant and alive...to me, very giving.

Mary: I don't know whether I really am giving or not. Sometimes I feel like I do give and what I give is not accepted as a gift. And sometimes I want to give and I can't. And I feel sometimes I have given too much and I shouldn't have.

Jim: Yeah. This is what I'm beginning to sense. Some hurt. You look like you've been hurt — in the past. That you've been vulnerable and somehow hurt in the process.

Mary: To some degree I'm hurting.

Jim: To me you look like you're hurting now, especially around your eyes.

Mary: I know that, and I don't want to do that..I don't want to show that.

Jim: OK. Would you be willing to block?

Mary: [*covering her eyes*] When I do that, I can't see you.

Jim: That's true.

Mary: When I do that, I can't see anyone.

Jim: Very true. When I block my hurt, no one exists for me. This is my choice.

Mary: I made it my choice too.

Jim: I am enjoying looking at you. To me, you are very generous at this moment.

Mary: You are very generous to me. I feel that you are. I hear you respond to me and I feel that I'm responding to you...

Jim: I'm curious if you can come back to Paul for a moment now. Encounter him and explore what happens.

Mary: Paul, I want to be warm to you, and I want to be generous to you, and I think I might hurt you by being so. You're six feet tall now and sometimes I very much want to come up to you and just give you a kiss goodnight or just put my arms around you and I can't do it anymore.

Jim: You can't?

Mary: I won't. I won't, because, uh...I've been shoved away.

Jim: You've been hurt.

Mary: Yeah, I've been hurt. Paul, I think it's your own business if you want to shove me away, but that doesn't stop me from being hurt.

Jim: I like what, I believe, Nietzsche once said to the sun, "It's none of your business that you shine at me."

Mary: I keep hoping that, Paul, when you're 25 or if you go to the Army or whatever...that I can kiss you good-bye. [*pause*] I'll try to remember what Nietzsche said to the sun.

Jim: OK. I enjoyed working with you.
Mary: Thank you.

Summary

Fritz Perls prophesied three decades ago that Gestalt therapy would come into its own during the 1970s and become a significant force in psychotherapy during the 1970s. His prophecy has been more than fulfilled.

In 1952, there were perhaps a dozen people seriously involved in the movement. In 1987 there were scores of training institutes, hundreds of psychotherapists who had been trained in Gestalt therapy, and many hundreds of nontrained or poorly trained persons who called themselves "Gestaltists." Thousands of people have experienced Gestalt therapy — many with quite favorable results — others with questionable or poor outcomes.

Because of the unwillingness of Gestalt therapists to set rigid standards, there is a wide range of criteria for the selection and training of Gestalt therapists. Some people, having experienced a weekend workshop, consider themselves amply equipped to do Gestalt therapy. Other psychotherapists spend months and years in training as Gestalt therapists and have an enormous respect for the simplicity and infinite innovativeness and creativity that Gestalt therapy requires and engenders.

Despite the fact that Gestalt therapy attracts some people who are looking for shortcuts, it also has attracted a substantial number of solid, experienced clinicians who have found in Gestalt therapy not only a powerful psychotherapy but also a viable life philosophy.

Those looking for quick solutions and shortcuts will go on to greener pastures. Gestalt therapy will take its place along with other substantive psychotherapies in the next several decades. It should continue to attract creative, experimentally oriented psychotherapists for many years to come.

Gestalt therapy has pioneered many useful and creative innovations in psychotherapy theory and practice. These have been incorporated into general practice, usually without credit. Now Gestalt therapy is moving into further elaboration and refinement of these principles. Regardless of label, the principles of existential dialogue, the use of the direct phenomenological experience of patient and therapist, the trust of organismic self-regulation, the emphasis on experimentation and awareness, the "no shoulds" attitude by the therapist, and the responsibility of the patient and therapist for their own choices all form a model of good psycho-therapy that will continue to be used by Gestalt therapists and others.

To summarize, a quote from Levitsky and Simkin (1972, pp. 251-252) seems appropriate:

> If we were to choose one key idea to stand as a symbol for the Gestalt approach, it might well be the concept of authenticity, the quest for authenticity...If we regard therapy and the therapist in the pitiless light of authenticity, it becomes apparent that the therapist cannot teach what he does not know...A therapist with some experience really knows within himself that he is communicating to his patient his [*the therapist's*] own fears as well as his courage, his defensiveness as well as his openness, his confusion as well as his clarity. The therapist's awareness, acceptance, and sharing of these truths can be a highly persuasive demonstration of his own authenticity. Obviously such a position is not acquired overnight. It is to be learned and relearned ever more deeply not only throughout one's career but throughout one's entire life.

6

GESTALT THERAPY: CLINICAL PHENOMENOLOGY

━━━━━━━━━━━

Commentary

This paper was written in 1976 as an introduction to Gestalt therapy for Modern Therapies. *In it I portray Gestalt therapy primarily in terms of awareness and phenomenology. Besides its value as a readable introduction, it has been useful to Gestalt therapists and trainees as a beginning discussion of awareness and phenomenology. In 1979 it was published in* The Gestalt Journal. *It has been translated into several other languages, including French and Serbo-Croatian.*

Gestalt psychology was an experimental phenomenological approach based on a conceptual framework of holism called field theory (and a close parallel to field theory in physics). While Gestalt therapy (GT) is an outgrowth of psychoanalysis (Freud, Reich, Horney, Rank, etc.), and heavily influenced by existentialism (Buber, Tillich, Sartre), the underlying holistic and phenomenological structure of GT is a clinical derivative of Gestalt psychology. Neither Gestalt psychology nor the connection with GT is adequately understood, even by most Gestalt therapists, and has not been adequately discussed in the GT literature. Unfortunately this very important subject must be reserved for a more technical paper (see Perls, 1973).

The word *Gestalt* (plural: Gestalten) refers to the shape, configuration or whole, the structural entity, that which makes the whole a meaningful unity different from a mere sum of parts. Nature is orderly, it is organized into meaningful wholes. Out of these wholes figures emerge in relation to a ground and this relationship of figure and ground is meaning.

A good Gestalt is clear and the figure/ground relation responsive to and energized by the changing pattern of the person's immediate needs. The good Gestalt is neither too rigid and unyielding nor too quickly changing and tenuous. The awareness that cures is the awareness that forms a clear Gestalt with a figure organized and energized by the person's dominant need at each moment.

Behavior and experience are more than a summation of discrete parts. A person's behavior and experience form unities or organized wholes that optimally have the qualities of a good Gestalt. Each whole is organized around an emerging foreground or figure that is spontaneously energized and given a positive or negative valence by the person's dominant need. When a need is met, the Gestalt it organized becomes complete and no longer commands organismic energy. When the Gestalt formation and destruction is blocked or rigidified, when needs are not recognized and expressed, unmet needs form incomplete Gestalten pressing for attention and interfering with the formation of new Gestalten.

"I look up from my writings, noticing I am thirsty, and I think about getting a drink of water; going into the kitchen, I pour a full glass of water, drain it, and return to my desk. I notice it is sunny and cool in the room where I am writing; the cats are playing with each other and there is traffic passing by outside. All of these were as true a few minutes ago as they are now, but I did not notice them then. I ignored them, reaching out first to the deficit of moisture in my body and then to the water faucet, and my manipulative system organized around the water. There are many possibilities in my environment, but I organized around my thirst, in preference to the other possibilities. I was not stimulated randomly and positively by the field; rather my senses organized around my thirst" (Latner, pp. 17-18.).

Through this Gestalt process human beings regulate themselves in orderly and meaningful ways. This self regulation depends on two interrelated processes: sensory awareness and the use of aggression (NB: in GT aggression is a force, life energy, without positive or negative moral overtones).

To survive the person must exchange energy with the environment (e.g., breathe, eat, touch) and yet maintain himself as an entity somewhat separated from it. The organismically self-regulating person picks and chooses for himself what part of each thing he encounters to take in and what to reject. He takes in what is nourishing to him and rejects what is toxic to him, using his awareness to discriminate and his aggression: to destroy or de-struct the foreign, novel stimuli (lit. "de-structure"), integrate the nourishing parts into the self (assimilation), and reject or excrete the unusable. Taking in any particle whole without this assimilation process is introjection. For example, an infant who swallows a piece of corn without de-structuring it, i.e., without chewing it, has an introject, a foreign object, within his gastrointestinal tract. It shows up, unchanged, in his feces and he derives no nourishment. So too beliefs, rules, self-images, role definitions, etc., are frequently swallowed whole (introjected), and later form the basis of "character," i.e., rigid and repetitive behavior that is unresponsive to present need. Inducing patients to accept any extrinsic goal without *Awareness* and assimilation inhibits growth.

What is Awareness?

Awareness is a form of experiencing. It is the process of being in vigilant contact with the most important event in the individual/environment field with full sensorimotor, emotional, cognitive, and energetic support. A continuing and uninterrupted continuum of *Awareness* leads to an Aha!, an immediate grasp of the obvious unity of disparate elements in the field. *Awareness* is always accompanied by Gestalt formation. New, meaningful wholes are created by *Aware* contact. Thus *Awareness* is in itself an integration of a problem.

Since understanding GT depends on understanding the GT concept of *Awareness*, I suggest a careful and thoughtful second reading of the previous paragraph and the corollaries below. Each corollary refers particularly to awareness in the context of the whole person in his human life space. While all living creatures have some awareness, some means of experiencing and orienting to the world, people have a special capacity for surviving with partial awareness. For example, a neurotic may think about his current situation without sensing or knowing his feelings, or he may express emotions physically without cognitive knowing. Both of these forms of human awareness are incomplete and not the *Awareness* we seek in GT.

Corollary One: Awareness is effective only when grounded in and energized by the dominant present need of the organism. Without this the organism (person or animal) is aware but not to where the nourishment or toxicity is most acute *for him.* And without the energy, excitement, emotionality of the organism being invested in the emerging figure, the figure has no meaning, power or impact. Example: A man is on a date and worrying about a forthcoming interview. He is not *Aware* of what he needs from his date and thus reduces the excitement and meaningfulness of his contact with her.

Corollary Two: Awareness is not complete without directly knowing the reality of the situation and how one is in the situation. To the extent that the situation, external or internal, is denied, awareness is distorted. The person who acknowledges verbally his situation but does not really SEE it, KNOW it, REACT to it, is not *Aware* and is not in full contact. The person who sort-of-knows his behavior, but does not really KNOW in a feeling, physical way *what* he does, *how* he does it, that he has alternatives and CHOOSES to be as he is, is not Aware.

Awareness is accompanied by *Owning*, i.e., the process of knowing one's control over, choice of, responsibility for one's own behavior and feelings (lit. response-ability, ability to respond, to be the primary agent in determining one's own behavior). Without this the person may be vigilant to his own experience and life space, but not to what power he has and what he does not have. So, functionally full *Awareness* is equal to responsibility — when I am fully *Aware* I am at that instant response-able, and, I cannot be responsible without being Aware.

180

To say "I am" or "I know" with the belief that it was not chosen or to believe that how I am disappears by verbal incantations is self-deception or bad faith (Sartre). *Awareness* must include self-acceptance, real self-acknowledgment. The act of acknowledgment of how "I am" does not mean one transcends that which is being acknowledged. Yet people are often aware of something about themselves with a subtle attitude of being above that which is ostensibly being acknowledged. To be "aware" of how one is with an attitude of self-rejection is such a false acknowledgment. It is saying both "I am" and at the same time denying the "I am" by saying it as if it were an observation of another person, saying in effect: "I was that way, but now that I confess, I who confess am not that way." Such is not a direct knowing *of* oneself, but a way of not really knowing. It is both a knowing *about* oneself and a denial of oneself. So too merely knowing that one is dissatisfied with a problem without knowing directly, intimately and clearly what is being done to create and perpetuate the situation and how is not *Awareness*.

Corollary Three: Awareness is always Here and Now and always changing, evolving and transcending itself.

Awareness is sensory, not magical: it exists. Everything that exists does so Here and Now. The past exists NOW as memory, regret, body tension, etc. The future does not exist except NOW, as fantasy, hopes, etc. In GT we stress *Awareness* in the sense of knowing what I am DOING, NOW, in the situation that IS, and not confusing this IS with what was, could be, should be. We take our bearing from *Awareness* of what is, by energizing the figure of attention according to our present interest and lively concern.

The act of *Awareness* is always here and now, although the content of *Awareness* may be distant. To KNOW that "now I am remembering" is very different from slipping into remembering without *Awareness*. *Awareness* is experiencing and knowing what I am doing now (and how).

The now changes each moment. *Awareness* is a new coming together and excludes an unchanging way of seeing the world (fixed character). *Awareness* cannot be static, but is a process of orienting that is renewed at each new moment. The "awareness" that is static is an abstract representation of the flowing *Awareness* that is felt. We trust the evolving *Awareness* more than any pre-set, abstract idea.

Gestalt Phenomenology
and the Paradoxical Theory of Change

GT is an existential therapy (see Humanism and Technology section below). The term "phenomenology" has come to be associated with any approach emphasizing subjective variables or consciousness rather than behavior or objective variables. GT utilizes a more technical meaning of phenomenology: GT has created a therapy based on an operational existential methodology.

Phenomenology is a search for understanding based on what is obvious or revealed by the situation rather than the interpretation of the observer. Phenomenologists refer to this as "given." Phenomenology works by entering into the situation experientially and allowing sensory Awareness to discover what is obvious/given. This necessitates discipline, especially sensing what is present, what IS, excluding no data in advance.

The phenomenological attitude is recognizing and bracketing off (putting aside) preconceptions about what is relevant. A phenomenological description integrates both observed behavior and experiential, personal reports. Phenomenological exploration aims for an increasingly clear and detailed description of the IS, and for deemphasizing what would be, could be, was, might be.

People often fail to see that which is right in front of them, and do not realize it. They imagine, argue, get lost in reverie. The difference between this filtered perception and an immediate, full-bodied grasp of the current situation can best be appreciated by those who have struggled for an esoteric answer and found instead the joy of a simple and obvious Aha!

Beginning therapy patients often cannot say what they mean and mean what they say because they are not *Aware*. They have lost the sense of who they are and who it is that must live their life. They have lost the sense of: this is what *I* am thinking, feeling, doing. They ask for a cure or ask why, for an explanation, before *they* observe, describe and try to know *what* it is they are doing and *how.* Thus they try to explain, justify something whose exact existence is unclear to them. They miss the obvious.

These patients maintain this lack of clarity by two related processes: thinking without integrating the sensory and affective *and* using their aggression more against themselves than for contact and assimilation. Their behavioral Gestalten are formed more by these two rigid characterological habits than by the needs of the present (see The Neurotic section, below).

What is needed is experimentation in trying new modes of experience and new uses of psychobiological energy. The patient needs to see, to do, to cope and learn. The therapy hour provides situations that are safe enough to warrant experimentation and challenging enough to be realistic. In GT we call this the "safe emergency." If the therapist is too helpful, the patient does not have to do anything and if the therapist emphasizes verbal content (e.g., why-because), the patient can think without experimenting or feeling. If the patient only repeats in therapy the processes he already uses, e.g., obsessing (anticipating, analyzing, asking why) and being passive and uncreative ("tell me what to do"), the probability is that the patient will make little improvement.

GT is based on patients' learning to use their own senses to explore for themselves, learn and find their own solutions to their problems. We teach the patient the process of being *Aware* of what he is doing and how he is doing it rather than talk about the content of how he should be or why he is as he is. We give the patient a tool — in a sense we teach him to cook rather than feed him a meal.

Traditional psychotherapy is content-oriented in that the actual emphasis during the therapy hours is on the content of what is talked-about. GT is process-oriented in that the emphasis is on *Awareness* of how the patient is going about the search for understanding. We do more than talk-about, we "work." Work refers to phenomenological experimentation, including guided *Awareness* exercises and experiments. The exercises are not merely to make the patient aware of something, but to become *Aware* of how to be *Aware*, and as a corollary to that, to be *Aware* of how they avoid being *Aware*.

In traditional verbal therapy and behavior therapy there is an extrinsic goal; the patient is not okay as he is. Often this is agreed

patient and the therapist. In these therapies the
..nange agent and the patient gets to some ideal state.
..t) trying to be what he is not. In GT change is thought
..st by clearly knowing and accepting the given: who you
..now you are. Our only goal is learning and using this
..ss process.

..e GT theory of change (The Paradoxical Theory of Change,
Beisser, 1970) states:

> *...that change occurs when one becomes what he is, not when he tries to become what he is not.* Change does not take place through a coercive attempt by the individual or by another person to change him, but it does take place if one takes the time and effort to be what he is — to be fully invested in his current positions. By rejecting the role of change agent, we make meaningful and orderly change possible.

The Gestalt therapist rejects the role of "changer," for his strategy is to encourage, even insist, that the patient *be* where and what he *is.* He believes change does not take place by "trying," coercion, or persuasion, or by insight, interpretation or any other such means. Rather, change can occur when the patient abandons, at least for the moment, what he would like to become and attempts to be what he is. The premise is that one must stand in one place in order to have firm footing to move and that it is difficult or impossible to move without that footing.

The person seeking change by coming to therapy is in conflict with at least two warring intrapsychic factions. He is constantly moving between what he "should be" and what he thinks he "is," never fully identifying with either. The Gestalt therapist asks the person to invest himself fully in his roles, one at a time. Whichever role he begins with, the patient soon shifts to another. The Gestalt therapist asks simply that he be what he is at the moment.

The patient comes to the therapist because he wishes to be changed. Many therapies accept this as a legitimate objective and set out through various means to try to change him, establishing what Perls calls the "top-dog/under-dog" dichotomy. A therapist who seeks to help a patient has left the egalitarian position and become the knowing expert, with the patient playing the helpless person, yet his goal is that he and the patient should become equals. The Gestalt therapist believes that the top-dog/under-dog dichotomy already exists within the patient, with one part trying to change the other, and that the therapist must avoid becoming locked into one of these roles. He tries to avoid this trap by encouraging the patient to accept both of them, one at a time, as his own.

If the patient abandons trying to be what he is not, even for a moment, he can experience what he is. To *invest in* and *explore* what one *is*, to endure the reality of one's way of being in the world, gives one the centering and support for growth through Awareness and choice. Awareness develops through contact and experimentation based on: wanting to know what one needs, a willingness to stay with the confusion, conflict and doubt that accompanies the search for the given, and a willingness to take the responsibility for finding or creating new solutions. "Man transcends himself only via his true nature, not through ambition and artificial goals" (Perls, 1973, p. 49.).

Humanism and Technology

GT's phenomenological work is done through a relationship based on the existential model of Martin Buber's *I and Thou — Here and Now*. By that model a person involves himself fully and intensely with the person or task at hand, each treated as a Thou, an end in itself and not as an "It," thing or means to an end. A relationship develops when two people, each with his separate existence and personal needs, contact each other recognizing and allowing the differences between them.

Each is responsible for himself, for his part of the dialogue. This means each is responsible for whether he allows himself to affect the other and to be affected, for whether energy is exchanged. If both allow, the coming together can be like a dance, with a rhythm of contact and withdrawal. Then it is possible to have connecting and separating rather than isolation (loss of connecting) or confluence (fusion or loss of separateness).

To have this dance both must be allowed to regulate themselves without being dominated, saved or suppressed. Each regulates himself in response to the dance of the other, rather than trying to choreograph the other's dance. This requires a trust of what might happen if rigid content of the interaction is relaxed in favor of risking what is emergent between. It also requires a trust that the other can regulate and support himself in the face of an honest dialogue.

In GT we are both humanistic and technological. There is a technology, and it is embedded in a matrix in which *both people work together* to experiment in order to increase the patient's ability to experience on his own. The work may focus on a task such as sorting out a problem of the patient's, or maybe on the relationship itself. The work, structured or unfocused, unifies sensing, feeling and thinking into a continuum of *Awareness* in the Now.

We allow each person to regulate himself without substituting an extrinsic goal of ours for their mode of self regulation. We observe when the patient interrupts and rejects himself, lacks faith in himself and wants us to take over. But we trust in the orderliness and meaningfulness of the patient's behavior and his ability to cope with life. We do not use verbal or reconditioning methods to manipulate the patient into living an ideal, not even the I-Thou ideal.

However, we can do more than refuse the "change me" contract. We have a whole phenomenological technology to use. We can suggest a way in which the patient can take the risk of doing something new that might lead himself to new experience. Our goal is Awareness of the structure/function of any dysfunctional behavior and we use our phenomenological technology in the service of that goal.

Every therapeutic intervention in GT is based on seeing and feeling. Sometimes we simply share what we see (feedback) or what we feel in reaction (disclosure). Sometimes our seeing and feeling give rise to a vision of something the patient can do to be *Aware* more clearly. We value that technological creation as much as disclosing and giving feedback. Techniques arise out of the dialogue between I-Thou, and the I-Thou sometimes requires a technological intervention. Example: Patient talks without looking at the therapist. The dialogue has been interrupted in that the patient talks, but to no one in particular. A real dialogue now would require a vigorous response by the therapist. Possibilities:

(1) "You aren't looking at me," (2) "I feel left out," (3) "I suggest an experiment: Stop talking and just look at me and see what happens."

So GT combines verbal work with tasks given the patient. This is very powerful, as the new Masters and Johnson-derived therapies have recently discovered. These tasks are as varied as the creativity and imagination of the therapist and the patient. This includes work on sensing the outside world, enjoying one's body, polarity dialogues (aloud or in writing), expressive modalities (dreams, art, movement, poetry), ad infinitum. These are sometimes confused with gimmicks used for turn-on, catharsis or short-cut to cure. In GT these tasks are all embedded in the I-and Thou relation and are all used to continue the exploring by the therapist-patient dyad of each other and of the patient's problem solving and growth through *Awareness.*

The tasks give the patient something to do that is new, a new possible mode of experiencing. To repeat: The focus is not just on any kind of experiencing, or even any kind of awareness, but the *Awareness* necessary for self regulation, especially *Awareness* of the *Awareness* process itself.

Often the patient has a preconceived notion that therapy is just talking and that change comes automatically. They react to a request to try an experiment with confusion, reluctance, fright. As the work begins to produce new knowledge, charges of genuine excitement, real change, patients react in different ways: sometimes the patients really perceive the glorious possibilities and hunger for more — and, sometimes they object to the "gimmicks" when they are really frightened by a method that produces a clarity about what they are doing, their need for change, and most of all by the prospect of really changing.

Note that while this approach looks for the obvious, the surface, it is far from "superficial." In traditional therapy the real structure of the patient's life could be understood only by going linearly to the distant place (past time or very "deep") where the determinants were thought to be located (linear causality). But according to field theory all forces that have an effect are present and cannot have an effect when removed in space or time. *Awareness* training gets to the actual structure/function of the here and now forces regulating the patient's existence. This becomes more obvious as the therapy moves into later stages, as the simpler processes are grasped in *Awareness* by the patient, and other fundamental forces that are present, powerful and previously avoided by the patient become obvious too.

This is effective only by working absolutely in the here and now, with no part of the field being excluded. To start with the assumption that some part of the field is unimportant (violating phenomenological principles) may exclude access to that here-and-now residue of past experience that is available, e.g., in body language or hidden assumptions. To be purely verbal and try to be here and now would miss too much to be effective. To be purely nonverbal would suffer the same fault.

The Neurotic

The neurotic does not let himself be *Aware* of, accept and allow his true needs to organize his behavior. Instead of allowing his excitement to go fully and creatively into each need, he interrupts himself: he uses part of his energy against himself, and part to control the therapist's half of the dialogue. This he must do for he depends on the "guru" to fix him up. The neurotic cannot fully embrace the I-Thou, for his character is rigid, his self support reduced, and he usually believes he cannot grow out of his repetitive and unsatisfying pattern of behavior.

He tries to fuse with the therapist, to draw on his strength instead of allowing his own to develop. His sense of his own boundaries is weak, for he rejects *Awareness* of aspects of himself (e.g., projection) and accepts alien things as if they were himself (e.g., introjection). Thus the neurotic loses *Awareness* of the IS.

So the neurotic is split, has reduced *Awareness*, and is self rejecting. This unitary process of rejecting aspects of himself and becoming split can be maintained only by restricting *Awareness*. For with full and continued *Awareness* the rejected parts would be contacted and eventually integrated.

This self rejection and unawareness reduces the self support readily available to the neurotic. He comes to believe that he cannot be self regulating and self supporting, and therefore must manipulate others to tell him how to be or else forces himself to live by rigid rules ("character") he swallowed without assimilating.

He either tries to be self sufficient or dependent, but does not use his self support for nourishing contact and withdrawal. Thus the neurotic controls himself and others as things and allows himself to be so controlled.

So the neurotic makes the therapeutic situation into a repeat of an old one: someone telling him how to be, and he resisting or acquiescing. If the therapist believes he knows best what is good for the patient, the problem intensifies. Even if the patient changes according to prescription, he does so without learning how to regulate himself. Neither this nor the battle between an ideal of the therapist and resistance of the patient is satisfactory. It is not adopting this or that behavioral change that is sought, but the *Awareness* of the patient's behavior by the patient so he can use his strength to support himself rather than interrupt himself.

While many patients come to be changed, and do not want to be as they are, they do not want to make real changes in themselves. They want the therapist to do it for them or to make them better at playing the same game. They resist growth and invest energy in the failure of the therapist. This last motivation is almost always out of the immediate *Awareness* of beginning patients.

The problem is not that the patient manipulates, i.e., manages his environment, but that he manipulates others to help him stay a cripple more comfortably rather than manipulating based on self support in a giving/taking, contact/withdrawal relationship with his environment. The therapist must be sympathetic with the patient's true needs and give close, exclusive, non-demanding attention to the patient and at the same time frustrate the subtle neurotic manipulations and force him thereby to "direct all his manipulatory skills towards the satisfaction of his real needs" (Perls, 1973, p. 108).

> ...if the therapist withholds himself...he deprives the field of its main instrument, his intuition and sensitivity to the patient's on-going processes. He must, then, learn to work with sympathy and at the same time with frustration. These two elements may appear to be incomplete, but the therapist's art is to fuse them into an effective tool. He must be cruel in order to be kind. He must have a relational awareness of the total situation, he must have contact with the

total field — both his own needs and his reactions to the patient's manipulations and the patient's needs and reactions to the therapist. And he must feel free to express them. (Perls, 1973, p. 105)

To work with the neurotic we make contact and share our observations, our affective reactions, and our creative/artistic abilities. We give the patient needed feedback, even if the patient has decided it is not relevant (e.g., body language) or too painful to acknowledge (e.g., how he behaves). We share with the patient our experience of him, including our emotional reactions. We refuse to direct the patient's life, but do direct exercises and experiments to increase awareness.

The Gestalt therapist indicates by his interest, behavior and words that he cares, understands and will listen. This "true" support is nourishing for many patients. Observers of GT who have not had an intimate, dyadic encounter with a Gestalt therapist sometimes miss the intensity and warmth of the "true" support offered by most Gestalt therapists while they are simultaneously "coldly" refusing to direct or be responsible for the patient.

Sometimes our contact leaves the patient frustrated. For example, the patient may seek our approval or disapproval. We often refuse. Thus the patient looking for approval, or disapproval, may find the Gestalt therapist intensely involved via eye contact and general attitude, but find no clue to approval or disapproval. A therapist's unaverted gaze can be quite disconcerting to such a patient. This is an example of the clinical use of frustration. Giving subtle approval cues would be a form of conditioning that reinforces the patient's struggle to impress the therapist rather than express himself.

Consider an obsessive patient who only experiences the world in a cognitive mode and will not risk something new. He tells himself how he should be and answers "yes, but..." or "I can't," or "maybe next time." He is fearful of a suggestion that he experiment with a new mode of experience and treats the suggestion as a command. He also treats a descriptive, non-evaluative statement as a judgment or evaluation. Rather than working with the description or following the suggestion to experiment he plays the same "yes, but..." game with the therapist he plays with himself. This we must not reinforce.

We value organismic self regulation and experimentation and these values guide our interventions. The patient needs to explore so he can learn for himself how to choose which mode of experiencing fits *for him* in each situation. This *Awareness* as a tool contrasts with the awareness as a content (insight) that goes along with the analytic cure and the behavior change without *Awareness* training of behavior modification.

We have no "you should" statements for the patient. He may ask, "No shoulds? You mean I shouldn't have shoulds?" No. The patient decides whether to have shoulds, the therapist describes. "You mean I can do whatever I want and it is OK?" Again a misconception. Anything the patient does is not OK." There are legal, social, economic, moral consequences. *I do not give my sanction for "doing your own thing," nor ask you to sanction when "I do my thing."* I take responsibility for my choices, and insist that you take responsibility for yours. I aid patients to see for themselves, experiment, validate their own behaviors, evaluate for themselves. That is what is meant in GT by "doing your own thing," experiencing the world for yourself (experiment, sense, feel), making your own choices, and finding out if you have enough support.

Evaluation and Maturity

GT is successful when the patient is able to regulate himself with a process of Gestalt formation and destruction that clearly and spontaneously forms his behavior and *Awareness* into wholes/unities that are organized and energized by his dominant need. Such a person will "be Aware," — have the characteristics of Awareness discussed above — be in contact with the most important event in his life space, have excitement that flows into his behavior, be responsible and self-regulating, be able to risk new exploration, and the like.

Thus we define maturity as a continual process rather than arriving at an ideal end state. The mature person engages in this process. Saying this another way, he is engaged in the process of *Creative Adjustment. Creative Adjustment* is a relationship between person and environment in which the person (1) responsibly contacts, acknowledges and copes with his life space, and, 2. takes responsibility for creating conditions conducive to his own well being. "Adjustment" without "creative" could mean mere conformity to an extrinsic standard. "Creative" without "adjustment" could refer to dysfunctional nihilism. Individual behavior is mature only in the context of coping with the environment. And, coping or adjusting without the individual's being responsible for creating conditions conducive to the satisfaction of his most basic needs and values also fails to meet this definition. Working, loving, asserting, yielding, etc., are mature only insofar as they are part of *Creative Adjustment.*

Success in GT is measured in terms of how clearly the patient can experience and judge for himself rather than his relying on any extrinsic measure of adjustment. We expect the patient to learn how to experience for himself the extent to which any process, including GT, satisfies or frustrates his important needs. This means he must know what he needs/wants/prefers and be responsible for his own values, judgments and choices.

This maturity and Awareness validly and reliably confirm the success of GT only when they are clearly and obviously manifest to the patient and the therapist. Success is measured by both externally visible behavior and internal experiencing. The patient must feel differently: he must feel increased clarity, excitement, well-being, exploring, etc. There should be an obvious congruence between the patient's experience and the therapist's observation of overt behavior. Every internal Awareness should be accompanied by an external manifestation, that is, the patient's feeling of greater aliveness should show in observable, physiological changes. Failure of this clear evidence of success to manifest itself to the therapist or patient indicates a need for explication by further phenomenological exploration.

Comparison of Models of Psychotherapy

The foundation for traditional talk therapies is still largely psychoanalytic. Neither behavior nor the experience of the patient is trusted since both are believed to be determined by inferred, unobservable, hidden "real" causes — unconscious motivation. What the patient is left with is an unconscious that is unavailable and a consciousness that is powerless and unreliable. (Acceptance of the distant causes of one's present behavior is often referred to as "insight.") The concept of the unconscious is replaced in GT by the shifting figure/ground of *Awareness* concept, in which certain phenomena are not contacted because of a disturbance in the figure/ground formation or because the person is in contact with other phenomena (see Perls, 1973, p. 54). But the data is available and the patient can be directly and immediately taught to attend to it. It is not unavailable. Awareness in GT is seen as the powerful and creative integrator that can encompass what was previously unaware.

In traditional psychotherapy the belief in the unconscious motivation of behavior leaves the patient dependent on the therapist's interpretations rather than his own explorations in Awareness. The therapist knows and the patient either gets well by learning what the therapist already knows or he is "supported" by the therapist until the therapist believes the patient has enough ego strength to hear what the therapist knows.

What the therapist "knows" are interpretations, speculations of past events that are postulated to cause (justify?) present behavior. This linear causality model reduces the importance of here and now forces structurally supporting the behavior and available for exploration by the patient's senses. Only through the transference is the here and now entered, and then only to interpret the patient's distortions.

All of this elevates the position of the therapist at the expense of the patient; it nullifies the patient's means of orientation: his own sense of what he sees and how he feels about it. This is functionally the same as saying that the patient is not responsible for himself and cannot know himself, but rather has a disease or disability that the therapist will cure or eliminate. Even those who ostensibly reject the medical model often have the same attitude in practice. This is the very attitude that the I and Thou model of GT reacts against: the assumption that the patient is less than a Thou.

There is a split between these talking therapies and the more active models, such as behavior modification. The new "third force" claims to be a new alternative. Unfortunately many of the "new" psychotherapies are merely updates of the talking cure or the reconditioning cure. Many of the new therapies claim to be existential, but lack an existential methodology; the methods of most of the new "existential" therapies are not phenomenological. Often these "new" therapies are merely a traditional talk therapy with a different language (new content) and a slight methodological shift (e.g., more active).

In these "new" talk therapies the therapists still act as change agents believing they know better than the patient how he should be. They see the patient's task as learning what they already know (content) rather than learning a process. Thus many are weak both humanistically and technologically, and certainly do not integrate the two. They also lack the phenomenological view of *Awareness*, trusting their own analysis more. They lack a theory of causality to replace the outdated linear causality model. They lack a theory of assimilation adequate to explain an ego that has an existence apart from a sum of id impulses and external reinforcement.

The more active third force therapies are also not phenomenological. Encounter groups that use gimmicks to produce a desired emotional expression or turn-on, body therapies designed to produce the ideal body, therapies designed to produce primal screams, all have in common with behaviorism two factors that differentiate them from GT (and any phenomenology): (1) They emphasize the external behavior *and* deemphasize *the world as seen by the patient.* (2) They aim for control of that behavior at the expense of the kind of Awareness training that results in organismic self regulation. If the goal is emotional expressiveness, then the group pushes the patient to emote rather than teaching him to be Aware of and accept his impulses to express and not express his emotions. The behaviorists do this reconditioning from a scientific standpoint, with an emphasis on clear terminology, specified techniques, learning theory, objective data, etc. Encounter group leaders often do their reconditioning without as adequate a support base.

In GT we reject any split between talk and behavior. To be phenomenological we must use all the data — that of the patient's consciousness and that which we observe. We integrate behavioral and experiential psychology into one system of psychotherapy by our full concern with the phenomenon of awareness and by using a new and more cogent definition of Awareness. The elements of this new definition are included in many definitions of awareness, but most other therapists do not insist on including them all in a unified concept.

By working with here-and-now Awareness and without shoulds by the therapist, the GT patient can begin learning immediately. This immediate change is exciting and frightening. Some are misled into believing that GT promises instant growth or an easy road. Nothing can be further from the truth: GT believes that growth cannot be instantaneous. *Awareness* and growth can start immediately, but growing is a process and not an instantaneous endresult of doing just the right thing. In GT we share that road, and do not try to cheat the patient out of it by being his reconditioner or all-knowing parent/guru.

We see growth through *Awareness* arising out of a loving I-Thou relation in which the patient's independence, worthiness, and sensing ability is respected. This is very similar to Rogers' theory, but with some pointed differences. Rogers started with a client-centered approach leaving out the person of the therapist, and later advocated a completely mutual relation between therapist and patient. In GT the relationship is not completely mutual but rather focused on the patient's learning (this is Buber's concept). And, in GT the therapist is totally included: negative feelings, feedback of sensory and body language, creativity (creating ways of increasing *Awareness*), technological responses that guide *Awareness* work, and a willingness to frustrate the patient seeking help.

Most patients want the therapist to cure them. If the therapist does for the patient what the patient can do for himself, if he is too sympathetic, he reinforces the patient's own belief that he is unable to regulate and support himself. If the therapist needs to be helpful in this way, the patient goes on being dependent, neurotic and not finding out what he can do for himself. "Chicken Soup Is Poison" (Resnick, 1975). If the therapist blames or pushes the patient or gives disapproval it has the same effect.

The therapist needs to connect in a caring way with the patient as he is, and refrain from "helping." The therapist must work to restore the patient's *Awareness* of his own needs, his own strengths, his potential for creating new ways of coping with the world. In short, the therapist must support the patient's expression of his own self support.

Summary

GT is a whole different framework and not just another talk therapy, another behavior therapy or another encounter therapy. It is a new framework within which therapists have to create their own style of working. GT is more than a set of techniques. Any technique facilitating *Awareness* and learning the tools of becoming *Aware* can be used within the system — if the GT attitude is adapted by the therapist, therapist-trainee, or patient to each circumstance using their sensory/experiential tools and an understanding of the GT framework. GT has been inadequately represented by the sloganeering and naivete of advocates and critics who work without adequate understanding. People have even started "institutes" of GT, taught GT, and written books without understanding field theory, I and Thou, phenomenology, or even reading the basic GT literature.

Two aspects are always present in each GT event that other systems frequently treat as contradictory or separate: (1) The immediate personal needs of the participants in the I-Thou — Here-Now dialogue, *and*, (2) The technical requirements of the Awareness work. Each therapeutic intervention has both aspects: Each is both a technical event with implications for Awareness work (phenomenology) and a human one, expressing the therapist's need. The humanistic dialogue and *Awareness* "techniques" are integrated in GT. Those deriving their Gestalt theory from watching GT and inferring what the theory must be often confuse this. One does not have to choose between technical expertise and human concern.

GT is very powerful and can therefore be abused. This places a great demand on the Gestalt therapist. When he works he must be mature enough to be spontaneously more interested in the patient's *Awareness* than in other needs, e.g., being entertained. Blending technical work with contact and humanness takes perspective and training in how one's personal responses effect the *Awareness* and growth needs of the patient. The "I do my thing" slogan has been misused as a screen for encounters that turn-on without teaching the patient to be centered, *Aware* and responsible for his life in the world.

We use our human/technical potential to clarify the obvious through experiencing and experimenting. We value the immediate raw data of our perception of the Other and ourselves in the situation as experienced and stay in the continuum of *Awareness*, however confusing or painful, until organismic self regulation is restored. Each element is seen as meeting a need and is therefore allowed to become foreground, stayed with (coped with and communicated) until the need is met and the element becomes background. This organismic self regulation replaces rigid, artificial regulation. Fresh Awareness, I-Thou contact/exploration, and organismic self regulation are more exciting and powerful for increasing growth than analyzing, conditioning and talking-about.

Allowing patients to discover and explore is particularly suited to our modern society with its constant and rapidly changing social order. Rather than trying to be healthy by adjusting to a situation, in GT one learns how to use one's *Awareness* in whatever situation emerges. This requires going beyond placebo effect, spontaneous remission and such and learning the structure of how one can direct his own learning and change.

7

GESTALT THERAPY:
A DIALOGIC METHOD

Commentary

This densely written article was first circulated as an unpublished paper in 1981 and published in German in 1983. This is its first official publication in English. In this paper I was still using the term "I-Thou" to refer to the "I-Thou moment" (Buber's poetic "Thou"), the "I-Thou attitude," and the "I-Thou relationship." Subsequently I have adopted the linguistic style recommended by Richard Hycner (1985) of using the term "I-Thou" to refer only to the peak moment of Thou, and using the term "dialogic" to refer to the attitude and the relationship. Thus the terms "I-Thou attitude" and "I-Thou relationship" in this paper are the same as the terms "dialogic attitude" and "dialogic relationship" I refer to in later papers. There is a lot of material in this article that I do not discuss elsewhere.

Background

The theory of Gestalt therapy is a theory about what makes good psychotherapy. It integrates ideas, observations and techniques from diverse sources; hence, the reader will find much that is not unique to Gestalt therapy.

A complete system of psychotherapy explicitly or implicitly includes: (1) A theory of consciousness, including a viewpoint on what kind of Awareness or insight is being sought and a methodology for reaching that goal; (2) An attitude or prescription about the therapeutic relationship between therapist and patient; (3) A scientific theory.

Gestalt therapy can be identified by its particular integration of principles in these three areas. Many other statements by Gestalt therapists are not integral to Gestalt therapy. For example, general advice for living, often flowing from a particular zeitgeist, (such as, "do your own thing") is not important. Nor is any particular technique (e.g., beating pillows or talking to an empty chair) or style (e.g., one-to-one therapy in a group setting) important (L. Perls, 1978). What is important is: what makes good psychotherapy.

Gestalt Therapy Defined

Three principles define Gestalt therapy. Any therapy regulated by these is indistinguishable from Gestalt therapy, regardless of label, technique or style of the therapist; no therapy violating any of the three is Gestalt therapy. And, any of the three properly and fully understood encompasses the other two.

Principle One: Gestalt therapy is phenomenological; its *only* goal is Awareness and its methodology is the methodology of Awareness. (See Yontef, 1976.)

Principle Two: Gestalt therapy is based wholly on dialogic existentialism, i.e., the I-Thou contact/withdrawal process.

Principle Three: Gestalt therapy's conceptual foundation or world view is Gestalt, i.e., based on holism and field theory.

Our technology of Awareness is based on phenomenology. The Gestalt therapy scientific theory is field theory. Field theory is important for understanding several key concepts, e.g., "now," "process," "polarity." However, this topic will be addressed in a separate paper. The present paper discusses Principle Two and its relation to Principle One.

Why a Paper on Dialogue?

What is dialogue? In common usage, it is a talking together. An existential dialogue is what happens when two persons meet together *as persons*, where each person is impacted on and responsive to the other, I and Thou. It is not a sequence of prepared monologues. It is a specialized form of contact. It is in this latter sense that the term is used in Gestalt therapy. Existential Dialogue refers to the behavior that comprises the I-Thou relationship (Friedman, 1976b). Dialogue has been enlarged in Gestalt therapy to include a meeting together of two persons as persons even without words, e.g., using gestures or nonverbal sound. A pianist might dialogue with the orchestra. Two dancers can dialogue with no words.

Since its inception, Gestalt therapy has stressed treatment using the active presence of the therapist as its chief tool. This was a departure from the traditional role of the psychoanalyst who was passive, with interpretation being the sole form of therapist-to-patient contact. The I-Thou dialogue is to Gestalt therapy what the Transference Neurosis is to psychoanalysis. Thus, while the goals of traditional psychoanalysis and Gestalt therapy are similar, the methodology is different.

Although the language used in the early Gestalt therapy literature was different than in the present paper, and not precise, this was an early form of therapy by dialogue. Sometimes this was dealt with without direct reference to the word "dialogue" (Enright, 1975; Kempler, 1965, 1966, 1967, 1968, 1973; F. Perls, 1947, e.g., at pp. 82, 88, 185; F. Perls et al., 1951, pp. xi-x, 88; Polster, 1966; Polster and Polster, 1973; Shostrom, 1967; Simkin, 1962, 1976, Yontef, 1969, 1976). There was a lack of theoretical elaboration, as there was with many Gestalt therapy concepts. In practice, Gestalt therapy did show the presence of the therapist, which is the beginning of treatment by dialogue. This presence often lacked the guidance of a clear theoretical explication. Of course, without specificity there is reduced accountability.

The first part of this paper will discuss the background concepts for an understanding of dialogue in psychotherapy. The second part will discuss the characteristics of the I-Thou relation.

Phenomenology and Awareness

The Gestalt therapy literature has emphasized Principle One, the methodology for increased consciousness. Numerous articles discuss the Gestalt therapy approach in terms of the goal of Awareness and the techniques (exercises and experiments) that are utilized in the Awareness work (Hatcher and Himelstein, eds.,

1976; F. Perls, 1947, 1948, 1951, 1973; L. Perls, 1956; Polster and Polster, 1973; Zinker, 1977). This literature has long needed a more technical discussion of Awareness itself. *Gestalt Therapy: Clinical Phenomenology* (Yontef, 1976) began such a discussion. Here a brief summary is offered as background to our discussion of Principle Two.

Awareness is a form of experiencing. It is the process of being in vigilant contact with the most important event in the individual/environment field with full sensorimotor, emotional, cognitive and energetic support. A continuing and uninterrupted continuum of Awareness leads to an *Aha!*, an immediate grasp of the obvious unity of disparate elements in the field. New, meaningful wholes are created by Aware contact. Thus, Awareness is in itself an integration of a problem.

Corollary One: Awareness is effective only when grounded in and energized by the dominant present need of the organism.

Corollary Two: Awareness is not complete without directly knowing the reality of the situation and how one is in the situation. Awareness is accompanied by "owning," — the process of knowing one's control over, choice of, responsibility for one's own behavior and feelings.

Corollary Three: Awareness is always Here and Now and always changing, evolving and transcending itself. Awareness is sensory.

Individuals regulate themselves either by habit (regulation below the threshold of Awareness) or by conscious choice: Awareness is the means whereby the individual can regulate himself by choice. Phenomenology is the method Gestalt therapy utilizes to learn about the Awareness process. Our goal is to learn enough so that Awareness can develop as needed for Organismic Self-Regulation.

Phenomenology is a search for understanding based on what is obvious or revealed by the situation (which includes both the organism and the environment) rather than the interpretation of the observer. Phenomenologists refer to this as "given." Phenomenology works by entering into the situation experientially and allowing sensory Awareness to discover what is obvious/given.

This necessitates discipline, especially sensing what is present, what IS, excluding no data in advance.

The phenomenological attitude is recognizing and bracketing (putting aside) preconceptions about what is relevant. A phenomenological description integrates both observed behavior and experiential, personal reports. Phenomenological exploration aims for an increasingly clear and detailed description of the IS, and deemphasizes what would be, could be, was, might be.

People often fail to see that which is right in front of them, and do not realize it. They imagine, argue, get lost in reverie. The difference between this filtered perception and an immediate, full-bodied grasp of the current situation can best be appreciated by those who have struggled for an esoteric answer and found instead the joy of a simple and obvious *Aha!*

The phenomenology of Gestalt therapy is an experimental phenomenology inherited in part from Gestalt psychology, and utilizes experimentation to explicate.

Contacting

Contacting is the most basic aspect of Principle Two.

Contacting is the whole process of acknowledging Self and Other by moving toward connecting/merging and also toward separating/withdrawing. Contact is the basic process of relationship. It entails appreciating the difference between self and other (Polster and Polster, 1973, F. Perls, 1948; 1973; L. Perls, 1978). Contacting thus includes four aspects: (1) connecting, (2) separating, (3) moving, and (4) Awareness. Awareness is required for acknowledging/appreciating differences. To acknowledge the other requires Awareness both of self and other.

Although the term contact refers to the process of connecting and separating, it is sometimes loosely misused to refer just to the connecting aspect of the whole process. The way the term contact is used here and is usually used in Gestalt therapy would be more accurately described as the contact/withdrawal process.

The person exists in an individual/environment field. The field is differentiated by boundaries. These boundaries are not entities, but processes. A boundary is a process of separating and connecting. The boundary differentiating a person and his surroundings is called an Ego-Boundary. By differentiating oneself (Me) from what is not-Me, the individual takes in nourishment and excretes excess. The contacting process is the "organ of meeting" (Perls, et al., 1951), the engagement with the environment.

Effective boundaries are permeable and allow transactions between the organism and the environment. A closed boundary is like a wall in which the organism closes itself to the outside (isolation) and attempts to be self-sufficient, to nourish itself. A boundary that is too open threatens the autonomous existence of the organism via loss of separate identity (confluence/fusion). An effective boundary requires enough permeability to allow nourishment to enter and enough nonpermeability to maintain autonomy and keep out the toxic. Effective boundaries are flexible enough to go from one degree of openness/closedness to another. The regulation of the boundary between the polar extremes of fusion and isolation requires Awareness.

The contacting process is "the work that results in assimilation and growth"; it "is the forming of a figure of interest against a ground or context of the organism/environment field" (Perls, *et al.*, 1951, pp. 230-231). Jacobs notes: "Two essential characteristics of contact are implied by this definition. First, contact leads inevitably to living and growing. Second, contact involves behavior that establishes a *relationship* with the figure of interest; one must move either toward or away from this figure" (Jacobs, 1978, p. 28).

Isolating is the absence of contact by virtue of a lack of connecting. It is the polar opposite of confluence, which is the absence of contact by virtue of a lack of separating (syn, fusion or merging). Contacting is the moving between connecting and separating

FIGURE 1.

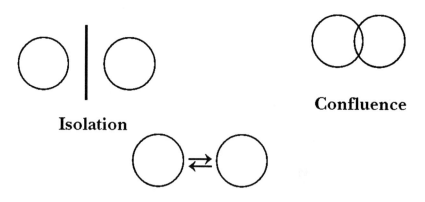

Isolation

Confluence

Contact

When a person contacts, he connects and maintains his separate existence, his autonomy. When two people contact each other they connect (even temporarily merge) and maintain their separate identities. While one person can connect and separate from a nonresponding entity (be it inanimate or a noncontactful person), fully developed human contact is a mutual process of two separate people moving in a rhythm of connecting and separating.

Dialogic relating is a specialized form of this mutual contacting. In Dialogic contacting the figure of interest for both is the interaction with the other person as a person.

With movement the person shows a part of himself as fits his need and the demand of the situation. Other aspects are background. As the situation changes, part of the background becomes relevant and is shared. Thus, with movement to and away from the other, there is a sharing over time of different aspects of self. Without movement, some aspects of the self become fixed background and are unavailable, hence isolated. The connecting is thus also fixed. This becomes habituated rather than a living process. Without movement there is no Awareness, only habituation.

The isolate chronically and habitually withdraws from the boundary and does not connect with the environment, but rather has a protective wall between himself and the outside (See Figure 1). There is phenomenologically no "other" to differentiate from. But, without some relating, some "other," a person cannot stand out or exist — be a defined person and feel alive. To accomplish this isolation and still live, a person splits himself and has relationships between parts of himself (retroflection). Introspection and talking to oneself are such isolating procedures. People who engage in this process always have a relating in fantasy to replace external contact. They are usually confluent with some introjected "them." There is a desire for and fear of confluence. Self-sufficiency is an aspect of isolation and is not a goal of Gestalt therapy. The Awareness work of Gestalt therapy does increase self-support — which includes the person acting as agent to get that nourishment from the environment which is needed for organismic maintenance and growth.

Confluence is the absence of differentiation between self and other, a surrender to sameness. Pathological compliance/subordination of one person's preferences to that of another is a form of confluence. Confluence is a loss of one's separate identity. As a temporary process it is the culmination of the connecting process and a loss of the withdrawal or isolating process. Orgasm can be seen as confluence.

When the separating aspect of mutual contact is lost, the *moment* of confluence is also lost and there is WE, fusion — a loss of egoboundary. But just as the person isolating himself fills his thoughts with confluence, the person being confluent thinks with both fear and longing of aloneness. To maintain confluence the forces that would endanger the confluence, that might impel awareness of separating or a breach (e.g., open anger) must be isolated, disowned, projected. The person clutches and relies on the Other to the exclusion of being and maintaining an independent existence. The confluent person does not experience sufficient self-support to enable an autonomous relationship.

Neither the isolate nor the confluent person appreciates differentness. The isolate allows no differentness within the wall, seeing only confluence as the alternative. The confluent person demands sameness from the Other and sees the alternative as isolation. Thus, the middle ground or polarity of contacting and withdrawing is lost and the dichotomy of confluence or isolation becomes foreground.

Two patterns illustrate this:

1. Two people are confluent with each other with a wall of isolation separating them from others (See Figure 2).

Figure 2

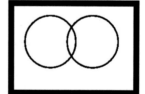

OTHERS

2. A person obliterates differences from his significant other and achieves confluence. When the confluence is threatened by

differentness, autonomy, and contact, the person withdraws totally into isolation or terminates the relationship.

I-Thou: The Existential Base

Gestalt therapy is existential in two senses. In a general sense (1966; Kaufman, 1956; Sartre, 1946), it emphasizes the present, human aspects of each patient's existence both in his current life in general and in each moment in the therapy hour (Van Dusen, 1960). Since regulating forces are considered present, the patient can, with Awareness, choose and control his existence[*]. When one believes there is an "essence" to be found, as in classical psychoanalytic drive theory and psychic determinism, existence and choice are deemphasized and the essence (e.g., unchangeable drives) are seen as causal and the organism as a whole has little potential for transcending the determining power of his essence.

The second sense in which Gestalt therapy is existential refers to a particular attitude toward relating that is a defining feature of Gestalt therapy (Simkin, 1976). At the philosophical level it is called Dialogic Existentialism. At the level of relating it is interchangeably called I-Thou Dialogue, Meeting or Existential Encounter. Martin Buber is one eloquent and persuasive proponent of Dialogic Existentialism (Friedman, 1976a, 1976b).

The Gestalt therapy literature discusses contact without making sufficiently clear that it is the particular kind of contact discussed by Buber that is needed for a successful therapeutic relationship.

---

[*]Humans do not possess an existence — they *are* their existence. They create their existence by action — by being-in-the-world. People are process — a person is "no-thing." People are their action and their experience. Sartre believed there is no absolute "human nature." A person is not determined by any prior idea or Platonic essence. Objects that exist *in* themselves (*en soi*) are produced by blueprint — their essence. People exist *for* themselves (*pour soi*) and determine their own existence. However, there is a "core" of a person which refers to the "true self." This is sometime referred to as an "essence," but need not be seen as an absolute, static, reified concept like Platonic essence. I use "core" to mean the beliefs, thoughts, feelings, behaviors, sensations, that unify the person as a person and give him a sense of "this is who I am in my heart." The "core" thus, is the most prized and vulnerable aspect of a person. "Core" refers to that which is true for the self as a whole. Self is a lived process and is not a static entity.

I-Thou as a special mutual form of interhuman meeting is perhaps the most highly developed form of contact (Jacobs, 1978). This is the relationship medium through which Awareness is increased and the patient restores his growth. This existential attitude toward relationship and the phenomenological attitude toward consciousness are but facets of a single larger whole (Van Dusen, 1960).

The I is always the I of I-Thou or I-It. The I of I-It speaks "he," "she," or "it." The other person is not directly addressed *as a person*. The I of I-Thou speaks "you," and the other person is directly addressed as a person. The attitude of Thou is that the other is worthy of respect and is not treated as a means to another end. One person can unilaterally treat another with an I-Thou attitude, but the highest form of I-Thou is *between* two persons, each speaking "you." This "Thou" is the relational event or "meeting" that enables man to become whole. In Gestalt therapy we relate with an I-Thou attitude and hope a complete and mutual Thou develops.

I-Thou is a form of contact. In isolation there is no contact, I-Thou or otherwise. In confluence there is no contact because sameness eliminates any appreciation of differences. In the I-It there is relating but to the other as an object of manipulation. The other is not directly addressed *as a person*. The particularly human and personal aspect of one person is still not allowed to connect with that of another. This is a frozen I-It contacting that does not flow from or into I-Thou.

One person with the I-Thou attitude can address another person (I-Thou) and not treat the other as an object to be manipulated (I-It), and yet the I-Thou not be complete — i.e., a mutual I and Thou not yet developed. Either the other does not trust enough, or both have the I-Thou attitude and still there is not enough support for a Thou between, i.e., mutuality does not occur. This contact can also be considered as an I-It which is a latent I-Thou.

Caring and humanistic therapists of all persuasions often relate with a mixture of I-It and I-Thou attitude, sometimes believing they are being strictly I-Thou. Sometimes therapists treat patients with an I-Thou attitude but are not clear that the relational event of "Thou" has not yet occurred.

Different attitudes about relationship in psychotherapy require a different theory of Awareness and methodology. For example, a psychoanalyst might assume that since the unanalyzed patient's motivation is unconscious and presently unavailable, the patient cannot be self-regulating, meaning able to make the best choice of what is good for him. This behavior objectifies the patient as an It. It requires that the therapist become a paternalistic and benevolent parental figure and treatment is through a fostered transference neurosis rather than I-Thou. The technology that corresponds to this attitude of relationship is extensive use of interpretation. Thus, psychic determinism corresponds to the nondialogic relating of the transference-inducing stance of the analyst.

Even the caring, empathic psychoanalyst who sees the now aspect of transference relates differently than he would if the phenomenological and/or existential attitude were paramount. In the latter situation, what the patient does know is treated with more respect. The therapist's inferences and intuitions are correctly identified as being in the therapist, and the patient and therapist work to ascertain if there is any overlap between the interpretations and what the patient becomes aware of in himself as he focuses phenomenologically in the area of the interpretation.

It relations are vertical and *Thou* relations are horizontal. A psychotherapist or body therapy practitioner who believes that he knows best how expressive or open a patient should be or how the body should look to be ideal or that there is a technique or device which must be used by the patient or that the therapist's suggestions should be treated as directives to be followed is also treating the patient as an *it*. A Gestalt therapist who uses his own charisma or Gestalt techniques for rapid change in the patient that is not grounded in dialogue and in the patient's Awareness and self-support is another example of vertical treatment and feeds the ego of the therapist more than the competence of the patient. The patient may get a temporary high but does not learn what he is doing, how he is doing it and how to support his own growth. Therapists that enter the meeting with the patient with a fixed belief that a patient cannot self-regulate without the therapist are not treating the other as a *person*.

"Shouldistic" Regulation

From the earliest moments of life, individuals face external socializing forces, e.g., demands, ideals, modeling, etc. These external standards can be automatically rejected, considered and integrated/rejected, or automatically accepted and taken in. This last possibility is introjecting or taking in without assimilating. shouldistic regulation is based on introjected shoulds and introject*ing*. Shoulds are "ought" statements which tell the individual how to regulate his behavior by external standards in isolation from organismic needs and weighing of internal priorities. Shoulds are fixed entities rather than organismic processes, and lack flexibility and responsiveness. Once the person begins shouldistic regulation he generates new shoulds which are imposed on the self by the self and not an imperative of the whole self.

On the other hand, when the individual analyzes, tastes, picks and chooses and assimilates the judgments of the others in which he believes, and rejects that which does not fit him, he is regulating via Organismic Self Regulation. Organismic Self Regulation requires the capacity to sense the external reality and its needs as well as the internal needs and feelings and beliefs and then knowing holistically what fits for the person in the environment. "Fits" requires a connection between the true inner self and the external aspect of the individual/environment field. Gestalt therapists work for an integrated regulation based on a dialectical synthesis of conflicting demands (e.g., social and impulsive) which is called Organismic Self Regulation. This transcends the person/environment dichotomy.

Regulation based on shoulds is fixed and inflexible since it is based on an unchanging entity and not the dialectical integration resulting from considering external demands and internal needs. The aspect of a person that is set rather than responsive to the current situation is his character. Sometimes Organismic Self Regulation leads people to refrain from expressing healthy impulses when it is not safe to do so in the given situation. This self-suppression often becomes habituated and results in rigid, chronic characterological conflicts.

Compliance utilizes introjection and is a functional form of coping when the person lacks the developmental maturity/support to confront the environmental press and choose to either assimilate or reject. When such compliance becomes automatic and out of Awareness, rigid character arises. Character is regulation by habit rather than fully aware response to the current environment. Obviously, character is necessary since it provides a stable basics for relating. One cannot regulate oneself by responding anew, with Awareness, to all aspects of each situation. Nor could society exist with such unpredictability. What is not governed by Awareness is governed by habitual modes of regulation. It is functional for Awareness to develop when needed.

Shouldistic regulation always creates a split within the person — it is inherently dualistic. This is because it is based on unassimilated introjects, that is, foreign processes within the person. The usual neurotic response to shoulds is either habitual, automatic rebellion or automatic rebellion disguised as conformity. More characterologically pathological responses include antisocial acting out and complete splitting of the separate forces. All dualistic intrapersonal mechanisms simultaneously constitute ego boundary problems since the person relates with one aspect and fights against relating with another.

A patient seeks change not only from a wish for health, but also from a shouldistic, self-rejecting standpoint: "I should do better." The shoulds are resisted often with "won't" disguised as "can't." (He says to himself that he can't do better, but actually won't.) His strength is disowned and the healthy power of the resistance is not acknowledged. The shoulds are not examined for what is and is not of value to the person in his *current* existence. The disowned power, the "hole" in the patient, is attributed to the therapist. The patient who will not love himself may expect the therapist to love him. Perls suggested that a good diagnostic barometer of where the holes are in the patient is to notice what the patient tries to get from the therapist (Robert Resnick, personal communication). When therapists act the role of change agent or rescuer they play one side of the internal battle of the patient and thereby lose the possibility of really aiding the patient to integrate the split.

Organismic Self-Regulation

Organismic Self Regulation is based on acknowledging the complete array of sensory, mental and emotional data concerning both one's internal needs and the needs of the environment, and also, the internal and environmental resources. Organismic Self Regulation is based on assimilating rather than either introjecting or rejecting without sufficient consciousness for Awareness to develop. Regulation based on acknowledgment and assimilation results in integrated responding. Organismic Self Regulation is based on more than conscious mental Awareness since many self regulatory processes are not in Awareness at any one moment. However, Awareness develops as needed in the Organismically Self Regulating person.

Assimilating requires biological energy ("aggression" is the Gestalt term) directed by Awareness. These processes are part of the boundary of internal/external. They are neither the imposition of external, shouldistic regulation on the person, nor imposition of the individual on the external (as in pathological narcissism or brattiness). Rather, integrated responding is a responsible synthesis of the acknowledged and integrated conflicting forces.

Note the difference between the concept of a dichotomized individual and environment and the concept of an individual/environmental field with the individual and environment as poles of a larger whole. An individual conceptualized separately from the field is usually seen with an unchangeable, innate essence that adheres only to the organism (an Aristotelian concept). In Gestalt therapy we see a potential for growth deriving from the organism/environmental field. (Field theory is the conceptual framework appropriate to understanding this distinction.) Change by Organismic Self Regulation is not the unfolding of a long-hidden essence, but rather something that develops and is known only *as it is lived in the world.* An organism only exists in a context.

Shouldistic regulation is entity-like and happens once and for all. Organismic Self Regulation is a process that is constantly renewed. It is essentially a system based on feedback and continual creative adjustment. This is a continuous biopsychosocial process requiring a continuum of Awareness and constant vigilance to new needs and changing resources in self, other and society.

Organismic Self Regulation is a natural process that functions through a process of contact/withdrawal. Since it is an acknowledgment of the entire field, different aspects come naturally to the foreground as they are needed. Shouldistic regulation is artificial and functions by dichotomizing the field; it functions through a process of confluence and isolation. Shouldistic regulation recognizes only one right way.

Polster states two principles of Gestalt therapy (Polster and Polster, 1973). Both are aspects of Organismic Self Regulation. (1) What is, is. (2) One thing flows from another. We highlight what is, and follow the development of successive foregrounds. Change flows then from acknowledgment of "is" rather than promotion of "ought." This is the core process of clinical phenomenological exploration.

Faith in Organismic Self Regulation means *accepting* the patient as he is at present (as he is "be-ing") and also *confirming* his "becoming" — his inherent potential to grow and change from the way he is presently manifesting himself to a fuller manifestation of his potential.

There is a critical distinction between attempting to change by imposing change, having shoulds, judging oneself, etc., and changing by increasing Awareness and self acceptance, i.e., by a feeling of recognition of how one is. With the latter one can know oneself and grow with Organismic Self Regulation, whereas, with the change agent approach, one splits into forces pushing for adherence to an ideal and forces resisting. Gestalt therapy Awareness and dialogue work is designed to bolster the capacity for Organismic Self Regulation and not the development of a new character conforming to a Gestalt therapy standard of mental health.

Therapy Without a Change Agent

Patients come to therapy asking for change, usually on the dualistic and shouldistic basis of trying to be what they are not. The patient is divided against himself and asks the therapist to take sides in the intrapsychic conflict. Many therapists enter into such contracts, and some positive results are reported. Much frustration is also reported. The Gestalt therapy theory of change is that the more one tries to be who he is not, the more one stays the same (Beisser, 1970). The therapist who attempts change on such a basis opts for change of some particular aspect of a patient at the cost of reinforcing the self-dividing process that inhibits Organismic Self Regulation.

Some therapists stress acceptance as the road to growth and cure. Some positive results are reported from this. Some therapists, especially existential therapists, talk acceptance but take the role of change agent. Can a therapist do more than accept the patient and still not be a change agent in the sense we have been discussing?

If the therapist defines the therapeutic task as enhancing Awareness of *what is* through an I-Thou relation utilizing phenomonenological focusing he can accept the patient and *actively* enhance growth without being a change agent. Thus, the therapist is an "agent" or facilitator for change from non-Awareness to Awareness. This is a process goal and not a goal of direction or content. Similarly, if the therapist defines his relationship task as Dialogic contacting he can actively enhance the patient's Awareness without being a change agent. For example, the therapist can neutrally observe and selectively share the observations and how he is personally affected. Contacting with Awareness results in growth.

Psychoanalysis also emphasizes the accepting relationship and insight. However, the accepting relationship in psychoanalysis works through interpretation which is not phenomenological and adopts a psychological stance on relating which is nondialogic. In Gestalt therapy we believe the phenomenological-existential method best facilitates Organismic Self Regulation by the patient and the qualities of caring, accurate empathy, etc., in the therapist. Interpretation of the transference neurosis as a chief tool decreases patient responsibility, encourages transference, makes person-to-person contact difficult and can harden cognitive defenses.

Acceptance and bracketing are the basis for any phenomenological dialogue treatment. In Gestalt therapy we aid this by using insights of the therapist (e.g., psychoanalytically informed understanding) *to guide phenomenological focusing* thus enhancing development of insight without becoming a change agent.

Example: An ambitious, hard-driving man denies any wish to be taken care of. The therapist has the belief, derived from intuition or from a theoretical analysis, that the patient has a strong wish to be taken care of and resists being aware of this. There may be very little direct observable behavior indicating the possible underlying need. Two possible interventions:

> Intervention by interpretation: "You really do wish to be taken care of and you are denying that."
> Gestalt therapy intervention: "I would like to suggest an experiment. Imagine you are a little boy and your mother says, 'I really love you. Let me give you a hug.' Now imagine that and tell me what you experience."

Both the phenomenological intervention and the interpretation are guided by the therapist's understanding of the patient's needs and dynamics. However, the Gestalt therapy intervention is not interpretive.

The choice of the phenomenological tool is guided by understanding the patient's character. The choice of an experiment rather than a more verbally confrontive statement by the therapist might be guided by knowing that this obsessive-compulsive patient would likely avoid Awareness of his wish for dependency by engaging in a stubborn power battle or by intellectualizing. If it were a hysteric patient, the therapist might emphasize calming and cognitive techniques and deemphasize techniques that are "dramatic," since the hysteric might well avoid acknowledging by acting out or by being histrionic, pseudo-hyperemotional. Example: *(In a group: the patient flits from person to person in a superficial way, getting attention and not acknowledging any taking.)* Therapist: "Try an experiment. Stay in contact with only one person." *(Patient does so.)* "Notice that you didn't acknowledge what he gave you."

On the other hand, if the patient were depressed, the therapist might choose a technique which asked him to get up and do something. Example: Therapist: "Let's stand up. Now imagine your wife is here and express yourself to her without words, using movement."

Without disciplined Awareness the techniques are only experimental explorations, the therapist becomes a change agent, the patient does not develop confidence in his own tools for focusing his Awareness, and the experiments become attempts at reconditioning. Via the phenomenological focusing the therapist can both teach and allow patients to gain insight, deal with unfinished business from the past, discover means to strengthen what is currently in the service of the organism, and reevaluate traits that were in the person and no longer are.

Psychotherapy can be more effective in terms of acceptance and insight by using direct phenomenological work on acknowledging the resistance and avoiding, e.g., training the patient to be aware of the process by which he avoids Awareness. By using phenomenological focusing and open dialogue the patient can become similarly aware of his process of relating in the present, including transference and other parataxic distortions. Process in this context refers to the patient knowing just what he is doing and how he is doing it. As in psychoanalysis, relationship is explicitly dealt with, but by using phenomenological focusing and dialogue rather than fostering a transference neurosis which is then interpreted by the therapist.

In Gestalt therapy focus is on what needs to be explored rather than what needs to be changed. The Gestalt therapist brackets and observes that which is important for the patient's regulation with faith that increased Awareness and contact lead to growth. The experiential exploration is conducted neutrally, explicating what is and highlighting what needs to be foreground for Organismic Self Regulation in dialogue with the world. This acknowledgment of what *is* includes accepting that being unhappy, stuck, unaware, frustrated, resistant, is. *Is*, period. The whole person is observed and accepted. This is the basic support for the enhancement, restoration or beginning of each patient's dialogue with the world.

Aiming directly at change, rather than acknowledging what is and growing from there, violates both the dialogic and phenomenological attitudes. Self acceptance and full Awareness give support for organismically determined growth. Patients will often move prematurely from acknowledgment of "how I am" to "what can I do about it." This is a form of disowning by dualistically trying to change oneself (Yontef, 1976).

Sometimes a patient *falsely* believes the therapist does not accept him as he is. Sometimes the therapist deludes himself into believing he accepts the patient as he is when he does not. The work of exploration must include how therapist and patient affect each other and how both are affected by each new Awareness. If Awareness work is being processed by the individual in such a way as to lead to a feeling of disconfirmation, depression, etc., the patient needs to bring this into dialogue with the therapist and the therapist must facilitate the exploration *nondefensively*.

In therapy without a change agent the therapist is a phenomenological research consultant and dialogue facilitator. The therapist takes responsibility for the milieu, behaves according to what is most vital to him, relates dialogically and the patient regulates himself according to his needs in response to the therapist and the therapeutic milieu. The therapist assists the patient in recognizing his response and his capacity for effective responding to the therapist.

Being a good Gestalt therapist depends on an overlap between the personal needs of the therapist and the requirements of the therapeutic task of the patient. The therapist who has a propensity toward expressing himself to the patient and who needs to facilitate the patient's self determination and assertive response will be more natural at Gestalt therapy than the therapist who needs shouldistic control or needs to rescue the patient.

Trusting in the process of Organismic Self Regulation means not fostering treatment through a therapeutically induced transference nor believing that a relationship can be perfect if the therapist is just accepting empathetic and congruent enough. The patient has his own regulatory system. A good relationship is worked at by both parties with and for Awareness and that is the heart of the process in Gestalt therapy. The patient's right and power to choose and regulate himself limits the therapist and means that a patient may do what will lead away from the therapist's notion of health. It is not just up to the therapist.

The therapist is responsible for the milieu, his contact, competence, caring. The life and therapeutic work of the patient is the patient's responsibility. Part of the therapist's competence is knowing and acknowledging/confirming aspects of the patient not known to the patient. To contact the core person the therapist must have his own perspective, know the patient's perspective, risk, confront, face anger, use creative technology, allow frustration. Acknowledgment of *is* in the sense of Awareness and in the sense of a real meeting, is the therapy — it is the natural process of living and learning.

Characteristics of the Dialogic Relationship

A relationship is an event that happens — it is a process. The process happens *between* two persons. Relationship is built on the process of contacting and must meet the requirements of contact discussed above: connecting, separating, moving and Awareness. In order to relate, two separate self-defining people must connect and acknowledge each other and they must also maintain their separate identities. In Gestalt therapy the relationship forms around the task of enhancing the Awareness necessary for Organismic Self Regulation. Contacting by the Gestalt therapist is modeled on the I-Thou relation. Of all the forms of contact, it is the contact of the core of one person with the core of another that has the maximum power to heal the warring factions within a person (see Footnote 1).

Both the technical task skills in therapy and the personal contacting of the therapist are indispensable. The qualities of contact required for good therapy have been commented on by many. Most agree that caring and understanding are required by the therapist, although there is little agreement on what constitutes caring or how directly the caring should be shown. For example, the caring of the classical psychoanalyst is certainly demonstrated differently than in classical Rogerian therapy.

The dialogue approach requires that the therapist approach the patient with warmth, directness, openness and caring. But as you move into more specificity, what is caring? Not just any caring is healing or dialogic. Caring is a quality that pertains to and has effectiveness only as a part of the contacting process. It is a quality of really meeting the other *as a person*. It is more than a feeling or doing something for the patient — it is a process *between* people.

We will discuss five characteristics of contacting in the Gestalt therapy I-Thou dialogic relationship.

1. Inclusion

The therapist honors the phenomenological experience of the patient, he respectfully enters the phenomenological world of the patient, experiences it as it is, and accepts the patient as he is.

The therapist makes contact with the patient and at the same time allows himself to be affected by the patient and the patient's experience. He tries to see the world through the patient's eyes. Buber refers to one of the elements of the I-Thou as inclusion, which is living at the pole of the Other in the I-Thou polarity, i.e., including oneself in the patient's world (Buber, 1965a, 1965b). By practicing inclusion the therapist simultaneously relates to the patient and gathers information on the patient.

To enter the world of another and not dishonor it, a phenomenological therapist brackets, i.e., he lays aside the perspectives he himself lives by and beliefs he has on what constitutes data, and appreciates the equal validity of another reality and a different set of data.

This is an allowing attitude in which the therapist understands and accepts the other person without judging the other's attitude or behavior positively or negatively.

2. Presence

The therapist shows his true self.

He respects his true self sufficiently to know it, maintain it, while practicing inclusion, and to prefer to show it rather than "seeming" — appearing as if he were something else. A therapist who is very concerned and wants to look neutral or who is scared and wants to look calm or who is angry and wants to look accepting and loving is seeming rather than present.

In a dialogic therapy, the therapist shows his caring by his honesty more than by his constant softness. He not only allows the patient to be who he is, he allows himself to be who he is in response. This includes more than warm acceptance. The Gestalt therapist also: shows self-doubts; expresses limits, anger and boredom; shares his observations of aspects of the patient denied by the patient but observed by the autonomous therapist; and, above all, has enough separate perspective to have a clear and accurate notion about the patient's character to guide the work.

Buber speaks of accepting the other as he is at a given moment as a necessary but not sufficient condition for successful therapy. A successful therapist also *confirms* the person in his *fullest* potential (Friedman, 1976a, 1976b). Such a therapist works beyond the present manifestation of the patient to the person he is growing into. Confirmation means acceptance not only of what the patient is aware of, but also aspects of his existence that are denied

/alienated. This necessitates the autonomy and presence of the therapist as well as his practicing inclusion. A real meeting of persons often involves giving something unwanted, e.g., accurate feedback. This confirming presence is sometimes misheard as not accepting, as a rejecting of the patient as he presently is.

3. Commitment to Dialogue

The dialogic therapist is truly committed to dialogue; he allows what is "between" to control.

Inclusion and presence are necessary foundations for dialogue. Taken together they mean the therapist makes contact in such a way that he allows himself to be affected by the patient (inclusion) and allows the patient to be affected by who the therapist is (presence). He observes how the patient is rather than analyzing and shoulding, he lives empathically in the patient's phenomenological world and expresses his inner self *as it is relevant* to the patient's task.

The therapist makes this contact with an attitude of I-Thou rather than in the spirit of control, conditioning, manipulating, exploiting the patient or other forms of I-It. Commitment to dialogue means relating based explicitly on what one experiences and respecting what the other experiences.

One cannot do good Gestalt therapy without making I-thou contact. But making contact does not establish a relationship.

A relationship develops when two people, each with his separate existence and personal needs, contact each other recognizing and allowing the differences between them. This is more than a combination of two monologues, but two people in meaningful exchange.

A commitment to dialogue not only means each expresses his inner self to the other and is also receptive to the other's self-expression, but it specifically means allowing the outcome to be determined by The Between and not controlled by either individual. Yielding solitary control means each is affected by the differentness of the other and there is an allowing of and a dedication to the dialogue process. This process of dialogue is more valued in Gestalt therapy than any particular outcome and more valued than either the therapist or the patient being in control.

We can "make" contact by will power and choice. But in a deeper sense we cannot make contact. Mutual Contact is a relational event that *sometimes* happens when two people live the I-and-Thou attitude and make contact. Mutual contact is allowed.

Contrast:
(1) "Making contact," i.e., one person "being there," being contactful and working to establish a full relationship. The therapist can be alive, sharing, reaching regardless of what the patient does.
And,
(2) "Allowing contact." This takes two and must happen by an act of grace that goes beyond making contact.

When two people show and express their true selves to each other in an attitude of I-and-Thou mutuality, a free flow of affective energy sometimes happens between them. This is possible when both give up controlling themselves and the other and allow Thou to happen. Buber says one can choose to act lovingly but cannot choose to feel love, that is something one allows to happen.

To have this relational event both parties must be available for, willing and able to support contact. In therapy the Mutual Contact usually follows preparatory work — making contact, learning phenomenological focusing, acknowledging resistance. It is unfortunate that even when two people allow themselves to be who they truly are, and their being includes honestly supporting contact, the support for Thou, for Mutual Contact, may not exist between them. An important part of responsibility, professional and otherwise, is knowing when this is so and accepting the limits. This is part of yielding to what is between.

One cannot know before the fact if Thou will happen. We live separate lives, we "make contact," we hope. We can make contact with an attitude that allows or makes probable the deepening of the dialogue. But if we try to make Thou happen, in the very process of trying, we treat ourselves and/or others as an object to be manipulated and idealized. For example, trying to be loving to make Thou happen: The therapist's anger, frustration, need to withdraw into secrecy become covert. If these processes are not allowed to be overt as well as his love and softness, the contact is between two ideals called patient and therapist rather than between two people as they are. Sometimes confrontation is necessary in the I-Thou relation (Buber, 1965a; Jacobs, 1978, p. 105). After people are present, show themselves, and risk — then and only then is it possible for Thou to develop.

Many therapists violate I and Thou by advocating overtly or covertly that the patient adopt their version of I and Thou. When a therapist adopts openness, caring, trust, etc., as the good principle for people to live up to, and uses this as a standard of health — these "humanists" have imposed an external blueprint or criterion, a new tyranny, to which to adjust people. This is what we earlier called a "should." And a humanistic should is a should nonetheless. When a group leader wants patients to share all inner secrets, or when the need for withdrawal and privacy are not respected (perhaps calling it resistance), or when the intellect is denigrated or technical responses are not allowed or when the therapist tries to prevent the patient from experiencing any frustration, or in general when he demands a mutuality that is so complete as to eliminate a differentiation of roles between the professional therapist and patient, this does violence to the allowing aspect of I and Thou.

The goal of Gestalt therapy is only Awareness and with it self-responsibility and choice. Any ideal to which the therapist adjusts people violates this: ideal relating, ideal body, ideal energy flow. That means that the patient can be a mature, good person and also choose to manipulate, be secretive, and so forth. Even full Awareness is not a should, just a tool or process a person learns and uses for his self regulation. There is no ideal Awareness process. Gestalt therapy helps people to be aware of their own Awareness process. Gestalt therapy helps people to be aware of their own Awareness process so that they can be responsible and selectively, discriminatingly choose — and even choose when and where to be aware of their own Awareness.

Dialogue and Awareness are both open-ended processes that are present centered rather than centered on a closed-ended, content-oriented criterion. A commitment to the process of Dialogue is consistent with a goal of Awareness since Dialogue naturally leads to increased Awareness and since Awareness is a necessary aspect of Dialogue. A commitment to the process of

Dialogue is not consistent with the primacy of any other goal. If modification of a particular behavior is the goal, it creates a pressure to change the patient which is contrary to both Dialogue and to phenomenological exploration. A therapist can be Dialogic and phenomenologically explore openness and expressiveness and also hope the patient will become more open and expressive; a therapist cannot be both Dialogic and also adopt openness or expressiveness as the primary goal of one's interventions.

For the psychotherapist, adhering to a commitment to dialogue and to the process goal requires a faith in the inherent worth of each person and the person's capacity to organismically regulate himself. To contact without overprotecting, neglecting, or controlling requires that value or belief in self determination. Ultimately showing one's self and allowing what is between to control is a form of surrender based at first on faith and hopefully reinforced by experiential data.

4. Nonexploitation

Gestalt therapy is a nonexploitative and nonmanipulative person-to-person relationship in which the therapist regards each person as an end in himself. Although mutuality in therapy is not complete and there is a differentiation of task/role there is no hierarchical status system encouraged or entered into by the therapist, i.e., the relationship is horizontal.

At least four forms of exploitation can be discussed: A. A person treated as a means to an end; B. Inequality of language (verticality); C. Therapist not doing his job fully; D. Failure to heed appropriate contextual limits.

A. *A person treated as a means to an end.* I-and-Thou contact not only means acknowledging and contacting the other as a person but also recognizing that the other is, like myself, a worthwhile end in himself.

The therapist as he is contacts the patient as he is in the mode of the-patient-as-an-end-in-himself and *the only goal being an increase in Awareness.* When acting according to this interhuman model a person involves himself fully and intensely with the person or task at hand, each treated as a Thou, an end in itself and not as an *it* (thing or means to an end). To do that the therapist has to care more about the process of honest contacting between self-determining people than any other outcome.*

When a person is treated as a category, as an object to be analyzed, saved, transformed, conned, that person is being treated as an *it*, as a means to the end of the ego satisfaction of the savior, or some external goal or end (e.g., mental health, social justice, etc.). The *person* is not contacted. In Gestalt therapy we treat each person, each encounter, each moment as an end in itself. Whether the person's behavior is consensually judged positive or negative or whether the encounter leads to a `cure,' is secondary to this emphasizing of *is*.

Therapists have many values, such as wishes for social improvement. If during therapy, the importance of these other goals is not considered secondary to the self determination of the patient, the patient is treated as an it. Each person has his own ability to choose, his own self regulation, his own values. Gestalt therapists respect a patient's choosing (and taking the positive and negative consequences) even when they do not agree with or admire the choice. The therapist's values are valuable to share with the patient if done in a context of dialogue and bracketing and not with an attitude of persuasion or authority. Gestalt therapy is based on the belief that individual growth, Awareness and responsibility flow from such contact and social improvement is best served if therapy is done by I-Thou dialogue and not by reforming the patient.

---

* Do we maintain our stance of no external standards (shoulds) to which the patient's existence should conform even in the face of potential violence, violations of the therapist's limits and psychoses? Yes, although our interventions are altered. In these cases it is necessary, above all, for the therapist to maintain the effort to contact the patient nonmoralistically and non-defensively. This does include the therapist expressing and insisting on his own personal limits, expressing his hopes, wishes and feelings. Sometimes it includes taking action to restrain or hospitalize the patient, arrange for community services for the patient, etc. In such actions the professional goes beyond the narrow role of therapist. Although the philosophy of Dialogue and Phenomenology is helpful background, the exact course of action in such cases is determined by the total situation, including social context and the whole of the professional's training, and not just his role as psychotherapist.

The therapist is not merely a means to an end either, since the therapist is also a person. If the therapist is merely a means to the patient's intrapsychic self-realization, the person-to-person relationship is thereby reduced, and the scope of Awareness is also reduced. The therapist and patient truly realize themselves in aware contact with each other.

B. *Inequality of language (verticality)*. Eckstein states that in psychoanalytic therapy the patient and therapist speak different languages, i.e., the patient free associates and the therapist interprets (R. Eckstein, lecture, 1978). In Gestalt therapy the patient and the therapist speak the same language of present-centered experiencing. The approach of different languages is a vertical one in which the therapist does something to or for the patient. The vertical relationship (Simkin, 1976), is one in which role goes beyond differentiation and puts the participants in a hierarchical relationship. The medical model of sick patient and intervention directed only by the therapist is an example of a vertical attitude. The consumer protection and holistic health movements are, in part, movements toward horizontal relationships.

To do something for or to the patient that leaves him without the tool of knowing how to be in charge of his growth work is always vertical and usually psychologically exploitative as well. He may feel better due to the condescending (vertical) intervention of the therapist and not know how, thus reinforcing his belief in his own weakness and not being responsible. Thus, the healer achieves power and status at the expense of the patient.

I-Thou relating is horizontal and nonexploitative and marked by dialogue and working together as equals. The therapist takes responsibility for setting the climate for dialogue and for facilitating phenomenological experimentation by the patient. The dialogue provides the context or medium of growth, the Awareness "work" provides a tool or method for intensifying the focus on that growth that the patient can use for himself. In growth by dialogue, the patient learns what *he* truly can do. I do not call any therapy lacking this horizontal dialogic emphasis Gestalt therapy.

This horizontal approach affects how techniques are used. To get the patient to a goal with "Gestalt techniques" is vertical and is not Gestalt therapy. Such a manipulation of the patient changes Gestalt Awareness *experiments* into programs, it reduces the responsibility and support of the patient (L. Perls, 1978). It is exploitative in part because the therapist is augmented at the patient's expense (for example, charismatic therapist and grateful patient).

The patient's inner, organismic self-emerging in Awareness and into the world is the healing. This occurs through meeting together in person-to-person dialogue. The meeting (not the therapist) is healing since the meeting is the sharing of inner selves. It is this meeting that explicates the intrapsychic holes of the patient.

In the vertical relationship the therapist neither voluntarily shares his own private world nor encourages the patient to enter it. The therapist's *I* remains private or hidden, and the patient is overtly or covertly led into transference rather than an I-Thou relationship. Gestalt therapists show themselves and work on Awareness of the relationship as it develops. A transference neurosis is not encouraged — the transference problems are thoroughly explored and *worked through* using the dialogic and phenomenological method.

In the vertical therapy relationship the focus is on the patient and his problems, pathology and history and this tends to be considered *apart from the actual relationship* — and the now relationship entered into *only* via concepts of transference and other patient distortions that need changing. This puts the real relationship into the background and keeps it shallow. In the horizontal relationship the focus is on fully being there with each other, fully seeing and hearing and expressing in a present-centered way. The horizontal dialogue is the matrix for getting to the center of the existence the patient is leading. In Gestalt therapy Dialogue and current existence are foreground and the transference dealt with as it arises and interferes.

"No shoulds" is an aspect of the horizontal attitude. Each party has values, likes and dislikes, needs and wants, and both are equally self determining and self responsible. A shouldistic therapist is acting vertical to the patient. A therapist who covertly believes the patient is responsible for meeting his (the therapist's) needs slips into the vertical. An example is a therapist who is bored, attributes this to the patient ("You are boring") and expects the patient to become more entertaining. A therapist can be nonexploitative and horizontal and express his wants when that is important for the therapeutic work. Such an intervention calls for caution on the part of the therapist and careful attention to the support level of the patient and his (the therapist's) responsibility for his own frustrations.

The horizontal relationship is predicated on the belief that each person is responsible for himself. This means that each is the primary agent in determining his own behavior and is responsible for his own psychotherapy — literally "response-able." With Awareness each knows what he values and what power he has and does not have. With commitment to dialogue, something between may arise from the contact of two persons exercising this autonomy. (N.B., Section C in reference to therapist responsibility.)

C. *Therapist not doing his job fully.* The therapist has an implicit contract with a patient and a violation of that contract by the therapist is a form of exploitation. For the therapist not to do his job fully exploits the patient.

Good psychotherapy requires technical competence and good relating. Different systems and styles of therapy vary on what is good relating and what technical interventions are needed. I believe a patient is exploited whenever a psychotherapist does not take responsibility for his competence both in relating and in managing the technical modality, regardless of the school of therapy. Neither authenticity nor skills at use or creation of techniques is enough without the other (Buber, 1967, p. 165; Yontef, 1969).

The therapist's job in Gestalt therapy includes at least setting the climate for dialogue, practicing inclusion, showing his presence, commitment to dialogue, being nonexploitative, living the relationship, being an experimental phenomenological experiential guide and getting an accurate and holistic clinical picture of the patient's character.

Although mutuality and a horizontal attitude are part of Gestalt therapy perspective, the mutuality is not complete. For example, the job of the therapist is his alone. Although the patient has a parallel responsibility to each of the therapist's tasks, this does not lessen the necessity for the therapist to do his job regardless of the patient's behavior.

Maurice Friedman refers to mutuality of contact, trust and inclusion (Lecture and personal communication, February 25,

1979). In psychotherapy mutuality of inclusion is not complete (Buber, 1965a, 1965b, 1967, 1970; Jacobs, 1978, pp. 114ff; Simkin, 1976, p. 79). The contract is to focus on the patient. Moreover, the patient usually comes to therapy with less support for dialogue and Awareness than the therapist. For example, the patient often cannot see the therapist accurately at the beginning of therapy (Buber, 1965a, 1970). If the therapist can see the patient accurately he has more ability to respond in the situation, i.e., response-ability. Moreover, for the patient to try as hard to see the therapist as accurately and completely as the therapist sees the patient would often make it impossible to work through transference-type distortions and other blind spots he chronically carries with him.

A Gestalt therapist is open to encounter, for the patient to observe the therapist's behavior, to talk about the therapist's life and feelings — if the patient wants to do that. But our contract is for the therapist to use all his resources for a certain time period to increase the Awareness of the patient. The therapist may grow from that as well as the patient, but the contract is to focus on the patient; although the context demands certain facets of the therapist to be foreground during psychotherapy, a "split" of therapist and person is not demanded by Gestalt therapy. A split may be maintained by the inertia or neurosis of patient or therapist.

Thus, although Gestalt therapists are horizontal in attitude, they are not completely mutual in focus on the patient and therapist. The patient's privacy is invaded with questions like: "What are you experiencing now?" The focus is on the patient since it is assumed that is what a patient wishes and needs. But the right and even desirability of the patient to say at some moments that he does not want to do that, that he wants to be unseen or focus on the therapist is respected. This is not assumed to be resistance. (The therapist too is a person and may have a need to keep private. In good Gestalt therapy this must be handled directly and openly and not by making a patient's request into a "resistance" or violation of a taboo or methodological principle.)

As a professional the therapist is responsible for bringing himself to the meeting prepared to reach out for the patient, to know and help him. He prepares to be able to do this by how he supports himself before and during the meeting. The patient usually does not prepare himself to reach out and know and help the therapist in the same way. As therapy proceeds successfully, the mutuality becomes more complete.

It is exploitative for the therapist to place responsibility (blame?) on the patient when the therapist's shortcomings are *at least* partly responsible for inadequate progress.

> In these cases (in which I can achieve little or no satisfactory integration) I either lack the ability to show them convincingly the need for change and reorientation or else I myself am insufficiently integrated to be aware of the crucial resistance (Fritz Perls, 1948, p. 578).

> As far as I am aware, I want my patient to get better. If they don't, then I have to search for what I have failed to become aware of or to make them aware of in the on-going relationship (Laura Perls, 1970, p. 126).

Would it be true that if the patient could see the therapist accurately the therapy must be over? Buber thought it was (Buber, 1967, p. 173). In Gestalt therapy, we have found that when you move from a psychoanalytic to a phenomenological orientation and from a transference base to a dialogic base for therapy, the therapy often increases potency as the patient is able to relate I and Thou. Greater growth occurs in therapy as the patient is less disturbed and can contribute more.

In Gestalt therapy we teach a tool — dialogic and phenomenological working. These can be turned to areas other than seeing the therapist accurately, e.g., seeing self accurately, increasing Awareness, making choice of life style, new disabilities that arise, etc. In psychoanalysis, under whose influence Buber was when he talked of therapy, once the content of childhood and transference is dealt with there is theoretically no task left. This is a medical model or model of pathology rather than a growth or maturational model.

Buber's attitude toward therapy has two dangers. It tends to assume the therapist's vision is accurate and the patient's is not (Buber, 1970). This is only sometimes true. It also has the danger of making I and Thou into a should, i.e., a goal of therapy. Our goal in Gestalt therapy is Awareness — including Awareness of It, of Thou, of how one does and can relate both ways, and therefore, the ability to choose. Awareness makes it possible to choose and be able to relate I and Thou. With this knowledge one can go on to deeper Awareness work.

Some claim that if the therapist would be authentically contactful without artificially adopting a vertical posture (seeming), that he would be the same when doing and not doing therapy; and, if not, the therapist is being "phony." It is true that if one does not adopt a facade as a therapist, his character structure shows through and his "therapistlike" and "nontherapistlike" traits would show in and out of therapy. But people are authentically different in different contexts. A person is different as lover, teacher, therapist, father, defendant; therapy is not the same as friendship. According to Aristotelian thought traits adhere to a person regardless of context. According to field theory, on which Gestalt therapy is built, traits are a function of the person and the field on which the person is a part. When being a therapist, a caring and also disciplined aspect comes to prominence in a way that it does not always in other contexts. A therapist takes responsibility for the growth work of another person that would be offensive and intrusive without the explicit contract of the psychotherapy session. The patient's self exploration and exposure would not be as safe without the limits of the therapy relationship. Therapy provides a challenge within limits.

Is it exploitative (inauthentic) to use gimmicks? Or perhaps: is it exploitative not to use them? I believe the therapist needs to put his whole self and his resources to the task of therapy. Refusing a technical maneuver when it would add to the work or using a "gimmick" to avoid a necessary personal encounter would be equally exploitative.

D. *Failure to heed appropriate limits.* There are other limits to the full professional therapeutic relationship of Gestalt therapist to patient. Behaviors destructive to the therapeutic relationship by the therapist are not condoned by anything written in this paper. The therapist is responsible for maintaining an atmosphere conducive to I-Thou and to be the expert on the technical requirements of the dialogue and Awareness work. Some behaviors are excluded from the full relationship because they are inconsistent with the Awareness work or dialogue, because of the sensitivities of the individuals involved (a part of any genuine relationship), the limits of one party to the dialogue, or the ethical or legal limitations of the society in which we live.

For example, shame-ridden patients cannot proceed with Awareness work when faced with teasing, humor or flipness, (which is experienced as humiliating them, showing how absurd and inadequate they are). Humor is an important aspect for relating, but the therapist who uses humor is responsible for not using it to drive a patient deeper into shame. The dialogue and the Awareness work in such a situation require discretion on the part of the therapist lest the freedom and creativity of the therapist become exploitative.

Part of the implicit contract with a professional is that certain outer limits will be adhered to. Not adhering to these is one form of exploitation. Among these are: a certain level of competence, a special knowledge base, devotion to the welfare of the patient, and also adherence to a code of ethics and certain prescribed, consensual limits.

Principle 5 of the Ethical Standards of Psychologists, states:

5. Welfare of the Consumer

Psychologists are continually cognizant of their own needs and of their inherently powerful position vis-a-vis clients, in order to avoid exploiting their trust and dependency. Psychologists make every effort to avoid dual relationships with clients and/or relationships which might impair their professional judgment or increase the risk of client exploitation. Examples of such dual relationships include treating employees, supervisees, close friends or relatives. Sexual intimacies with clients are unethical. (Ethical Standards of Psychologists, 1977 Revised, American Psychological Association)

A business relationship interferes with the therapeutic attitude of the therapist and patient and complicates the relationship to where it approaches the fullness of the world at large. Therapy is a preparation for life and not a substitute for it. When the therapist is also the outside party, how does the patient work on that relationship with the therapist?

Sexual relations between therapist and patient are, at a minimum, a dual relationship. It is against the Code of Ethics of most professional societies and in California it is also against the law. If the therapist is authentically involved in the sex he has lost his perspective as therapist and assumes a perspective as lover. The patient has a right to assume that a therapist adheres to the rules of the guild or informs the patient otherwise at the outset. Further, the patient has a right to assume that the professional will continue to do such (especially in the face of temptation) or discontinue as therapist. In the light of the authority and charisma the patient transfers to the therapist and in the social context of the sexual exploitation between men and women it is doubtful that a therapist could engage in nonexploitative sex with a patient, much less do so and also be perceived that way by the patient. The perception by the patient of the therapist as exploitative, rightfully or wrongfully, interferes with the trust necessary to conduct therapy.

On the other hand, if the therapist enters into sexual relations because "it is good for the patient" he is being inauthentic and therefore contrary to the dialogic attitude on which Gestalt therapy is built. It is my personal opinion that one cannot be a competent Gestalt therapist with a patient with whom one is having a sexual relation.

It is a paradox that the involvement of the therapist and patient outside the therapy context may make the relationship more full, real and mutual in one sense, but in another sense, the I-Thou intimacy and depth of Awareness work is less than if the full blossoming of the relationship into business, sex, etc., were truncated. The outer boundary may facilitate a deepening of the relationship within the boundary. The full growth of a plant sometimes requires pruning or cutting back.

5. Living the Relationship

Contacting is living rather than talking about living. It is doing and experiencing rather than analyzing. It is having an experience with the patient in the present. The healing is in living in dialogue. Gestalt therapists let emerge the full liveliness resulting from the meeting together.

Contacting is relating with immediacy and life — now. The relating is *living* rather than storytelling. It is dancing, acting, performing, rather than doing a chalkboard talk about dancing, acting, performing. Gestalt therapists center themselves on experience more than concept. They live in the now rather than analyzing the past. They bring the unfinished aspect of the past into the now with a variety of techniques so that we may explore it, taste it, act it, see it, rather than just talk about it.

Gestalt therapy does not have rules against self-disclosure and activism by the therapist. In the context of treatment by transference neurosis, spontaneously exposing oneself to a patient, dancing, exploding with joy, anger or tenderness is acting out, regression, a narcissistic indulgence, impulsive and disruptive of the analytic exploration. In the context of Gestalt therapy these may be a vital part of the Awareness-enhancing intimacy of the I-Thou relation. The different types of exploration indicate a different attitude or guidelines for the therapist.

It is important to distinguish hysterical behavior, regression, acting out, psychotic decompensation from the deep, lively and meaningful expressions that come from the depth of the Gestalt therapy relationship. Some critics arrogantly assume Gestalt therapists are not aware of these differences, or perhaps more accurately believe that if hysteria or narcissism show up in a Gestalt therapy patient that the Gestalt therapist is causing it or encouraging it or doesn't know the difference. I have also heard narcissism by individual Gestalt therapists attributed to Gestalt therapy. Such behavior emerges in any form of psychotherapy.

One of my students had a patient who was going through an impasse. The patient's imagery was of being drowned — the affect present and unrepressed. The patient felt "crazy" and overwhelmed because he was beyond his customary restraints. A psychoanalytic supervisor of this student saw the patient's expression as decompensation, not seeing that in this case it was a transition from repression and artificiality into the full bloom of life.

The Gestalt therapy relationship is a full one including most aspects of the human condition: feeling, thought, spontaneity, program experimentation, technology, creativity, fighting, loving, frustrating boredom, etc. Any omission is a blind spot of patient or therapist and as such, reduces the relationship. If we are not attuned to the interpersonal or intrapersonal or intentional behaviors that are out of the patient's Awareness we reduce the relationship. We work to bring Awareness where there was scotoma.

Summary

Gestalt therapy is a system of psychotherapy that combines dialogue and phenomenology into a unified clinical methodology. Understanding the methodology requires understanding certain concepts which were discussed above: phenomenology, Awareness, contacting, existential relating, organismic and shouldistic regulation and therapy without a change agent. Five essential characteristics of the dialogic relationship in Gestalt therapy were discussed. Further elaboration, especially of common errors in practice, is needed.

8

GESTALT THERAPY:
ITS INHERITANCE FROM
GESTALT PSYCHOLOGY

═══════════════

Commentary

This paper was delivered in August 1981 at a symposium sponsored by the Society for Gestalt Theory at the International Council of Psychologists Conference. At that time it was entitled "Gestalt therapy: past, present and future" and subtitled "Gestalt therapy: A legitimate descendent of Gestalt psychology?". It was published in English in the German journal Gestalt Theory *in 1982, with an abstract in German. It has also been published in Serbo-Croatian.*

Gestalt therapy started as a revision of classical psychoanalysis (Perls, 1947, 1948; Polster, 1975b). It quickly became a whole and autonomous system for integrating wisdom from diverse sources into a unified clinical methodology (Perls, Hefferline and Goodman, 1951). Clinical developmental and characterological concerns and important perspectives from psychoanalysis were utilized in a framework that was very different from psychoanalysis as it was then constituted (particularly as a treatment modality). In formulating the Gestalt therapy system, the Gestalt concept was essential.

However, doubts have been raised as to whether the Gestalt therapy system has much to do with Gestalt psychology. Some even find Gestalt therapy and Gestalt psychology contradictory in essential outlooks (Henle, 1978; Sherrill, 1947) It is the position of this writer that the basic methodology of Gestalt therapy is directly descended philosophically, if not historically, from Gestalt psychology. Emerson and Smith believe that "no one can understand Gestalt therapy well without an adequate background in Gestalt psychology" (1974, p. 8). We will discuss the basic principles so derived and also the existential philosophy Gestalt therapy uses in its clinical application of the Gestalt method.

There are conditions that have contributed to the estrangement between Gestalt psychologists and Gestalt therapy and to a general misunderstanding of Gestalt therapy. One factor has been the erroneous equating of Gestalt therapy with Fritz Perls, as if Gestalt therapy were "Perlsian." Perls' style was often unscholarly and brash. His knowledge and understanding of Gestalt psychology was limited. His popular, cliché-level statements have attracted attention and have been treated by many as representing Gestalt therapy. This style is antithetical to any good scholarship, including the careful scientific approach of the classical Gestaltists. Moreover, taken without careful definition and without adequate, overall Gestalt therapy perspective, some of these statements not only appear discrepant from Gestalt psychology, but are internally contradictory as well.

Not all Gestalt therapy is Perlsian (Dolliver, 1981; Dubin, 1976). Gestalt therapy was founded not only by Fritz Perls, but by Laura Perls (who was well founded in Gestalt psychology), Isadore From, Paul Weisz, Paul Goodman and others (L. Perls, 1976, 1978; Rosenfeld, 1978). Subsequently, many others have had a major influence e.g., Erv and Miriam Polster (1977), James Simkin (1976), Josef Zinker (1977). An excessive amount of publicity is still being given to Fritz Perls. Moreover, it is Perls' popular writings that have received attention, to the neglect of his and others' more scholarly efforts that are more satisfactory theoretically (e.g., Perls, Hefferline and Goodman, 1951).

Another factor has been the paucity of advanced texts in Gestalt therapy and the lack of a clear and well-differentiated model of Gestalt therapy. If Gestalt therapists do not clarify what Gestalt therapy is, those making comparisons between Gestalt therapy and other systems will have difficulty doing an adequate job. At present, there is an increased attention to model building in Gestalt therapy and the future of Gestalt therapy depends in large measure on the success of this effort (Yontef, 1981a, 1981c).

The present paper is intended as a synopsis of those principles of the Gestalt therapy system derived from Gestalt psychology and an indication of the relation of these to Gestalt psychology. Since this is only a synopsis, elaboration will be kept to a minimum.

It would be singularly inappropriate to compare Gestalt therapy and Gestalt psychology in a narrow-gauge, piecemeal manner. Exact details that may be similar or different between the two are less important than the structure of the whole. This is the Gestalt way. Using words in common (e.g., figure/ground) or differing on the emphasis given a particular aspect of the field (e.g., organismic variables) can show neither a basic connection nor a disconnection between the two.

Although one could take the views of the Gestaltists of the Berlin School (Koffka, Köhler, Wertheimer) as an orthodoxy, and use them to judge entitlement to the term Gestalt, it would be more useful to compare what the Berlin School Gestaltists were doing in their context with what Gestalt therapists do in their context. From that perspective it is easier to gain insight into the essential relatedness of Gestalt therapy and Gestalt psychology.

The Gestalt approach of both Gestalt movements is a form of phenomenological field theory. At its core is a mode of exploration (Wertheimer, 1983, p. 3). At this point we can foreshadow our later discussion by noting two aspects of this method: (1) It is based on trusting immediate, naive experience. This means including all data of experience, objective and subjective, internal reports and external observations; (2) It seeks insight into the functional interrelationships that form the intrinsic structure of the whole of any situation being studied (Köhler, 1969).

This method is in marked contrast to the chief modes of research to which Gestalt psychology provided an alternative (for overview see Heidbreder, 1933, and Wertheimer, 1945). The introspectionism of Wudnt and Titchener did not trust immediate ("naive") perception, but rather believed it was based on error. People had to be trained to know the "truth": that people only perceive qualities and attributes (e.g., line, color, form) and learn to infer and label and form these into meaningful objects. We do not see objects such as a chair or table but need to be taught. Subjects in introspectionist research were taught to report the qualities and attributes of "pure" perception. Thus, not only did the introspectionists not trust immediate perception, but they also had an atomistic outlook. Mind, for example, is not a whole but the sum of its contents.

The behaviorists were also atomistic with their Stimulus-Response theory and they also mistrusted or excluded what research subjects said they experienced. Subjective data of experience were especially and explicitly excluded (Köhler, 1947, e.g., p. 34).[*]

In a clinical context, Gestalt therapy faced a similar situation. Psychoanalysts of the time (1940s) strove to understand the whole patient but had a theory that distrusted the conscious experience of patients,[**] was mostly dualistic, atomistic and Aristotelian in its search for noumena, and envisioned man as motivated by forces beyond his control (Stewart, 1974). When behaviorists first entered the clinical practice scene they were still atomistic and disdainful of experience. Neither approach utilized the power of the patient's immediate experience as the tool for exploration (i.e., phenomenological focusing) and neither included all types of data (Yontef, 1969, 1976).

Gestalt therapy had the same task as Gestalt psychology, but in a different context. Wertheimer said that to do the same thing in a different context you have to do it differently (Wertheimer, 1945). Gestalt therapy differs in many aspects from Gestalt psychology not because of a difference in philosophy or method, but because of different contexts. The same figure has different meanings as a function of the ground (context). The clinical context has different demands than that of an academic psychologist doing basic research. For example, in basic research the researcher determines what to look at. In psychotherapy the patient presents the data, himself/herself and his/her phenomenology.

---

[*]Currently this is less true as some behaviorists focus on the "O" of S-O-R.

[**]This is not as true of some current psychoanalysts under the influence of Heinz Kohut.

Both Gestalt psychology and Gestalt therapy search for insight into the forces that provide the inherent structure of the situation, process or event being studied. Both include all types of data, as they are experienced and meaningfully embedded in the contemporary situation.

In the remainder of the paper we sketch the Gestalt method of Gestalt psychology and Gestalt therapy, phenomenological field theory, and then the application of this method in the Gestalt therapy mode of existential psychotherapy.

Phenomenological Field Theory

1. Immediate Experience of the Perceiver

> There seems to be a single starting point for psychology, exactly as for all the other sciences: the world as we find it naively and uncritically. (Köhler, 1947, p. 7)

What is studied in a field approach is phenomena which is given in experience, rather than noumena the forces assumed or inferred to be behind the presenting phenomena. The field method of study is descriptive, it describes what and how (structure and function). This compares to an analytic or classification approach such as the Aristotelian approach, which focuses on causation of the "why" variety (Lewin, 1935).

The Gestalt field approach is phenomenological (Yontef, 1969, 1976). It studies the "field" as experienced by a person at a moment. Phenomenology takes as its only data what is immediately and naively experienced at a moment (Idhe, 1977; Köhler, 1947; L. Perls, 1976).

In the field approach all phenomena are regarded as lawful and the proper subject of investigation. No phenomena are classified as chance, not even unique or nonrepetitive events (Köhler, 1947, 1969; Lewin, 1935).

In phenomenological terms, any event can be studied or experienced. "As experienced" does not mean only or mostly "subjective" or "feeling." It includes "objective" experience or exteroception as much as emotions and other "subjective" experience. The systematic observation of behavior is as inherent to phenomenology as is clarification of feelings*. Not only does the phenomenological therapist observe, trust and expedite the total experience of the patient, but he/she pays special attention to what aspect of the patient's experience is inhibited or neglected. Those items that are currently important and outside the patient's current awareness are brought into awareness.

Since phenomenological exploration is based on experience, it is absolutely essential that what is experienced be differentiated from elements assumed, posited, learned or inferred. Wertheimer refers to this as experience "undebauched by learning" (Wertheimer, 1945, p. 211). Husserl refers to this as bracketing (Idhe, 1977). Biases — metaphysical biases, biases about what constitutes data, personal values — are put aside or "in brackets" during the phenomenological investigation to allow the subject to experience what is "given" in the situation without contamination.

One of the most publicized and least understood aspects of Gestalt therapy is its emphasis on "now." Phenomenological field theory locates the experience of the perceiver in time and space — here and now. This means that the process of being aware always takes place in the here and now, although the object of awareness may be there or then. According to Einstein, in the field theory of modern physics there is no action at a distance — that which has effect is present contemporaneously and concretely (Einstein, 1950, 1961; Koffka, 1935; Lewin, 1935). For example, the patient who experiences feelings of abandonment by his mother discusses this in the therapist's office. Remembering and feeling happen in the here and now of the therapy hour, but the object of the experience happened in the past. The emphasis on the present in Gestalt therapy is a direct influence of Gestalt psychology (Wallen, 1970).

What is immediate or pertinent is relative to an observer and not absolute. For the field theory of Einstein in the study of motion it is relative to a reference body that is considered stationary. In phenomenological field theory, which field is being studied

---

* Thus Gestalt therapy's emphasis on observable behavior is not "behavioristic" but rather is an inherent aspect of its phenomenology.

is defined by the experience of some observer. In choosing the topic of study some individual (scientist, subject, therapist or patient) defines the subject and within that field the exploration proceeds on the basis of what is experienced.[*]

Summary. The Gestalt approach is a field phenomenological approach in that it describes rather than assumes or explains. Immediate awareness is used to gain insight into the basic structure of the field. Biases, such as the biases of introspectionism, are bracketed. In Gestalt therapy the goal is consistent with this in that awareness is our only goal (Simkin, 1974; Yontef, 1969, 1981b). For example, a patient's troublesome behavior and the patterns of reinforcement associated with it are proper subjects for a Gestalt therapist's phenomenological investigation. Suggesting a modification of that behavior or reinforcement schedule as an experiment, a means to gain insight, (i.e., awareness: for definition, see Yontef, 1976 and below) is quite in line with the phenomenological attitude. Trying to recondition the behavior as an end goal without regard for insight is not a phenomenological approach.[**]

Example: Patient believes he is unlovable unless perfect. The exploration of this thought is vital for his therapy work. Undoubtedly his therapist, Gestalt therapist or otherwise, does not hold that belief about this patient. The Gestalt phenomenological approach would explore the topic but refrain from making the choice for the patient that it is irrational thought and likewise refrain from reconditioning the patient. The exploration might include, but not be limited to, inquiry into relevant historical experiences; dialoguing with a person who rejects or has rejected

---

[*] The field may be that of the experience of a participant in an organism/environment field, e.g., one of the participants in a dialogue. It can be the field as defined by the experience of a third party observer who considers himself/herself outside the interaction being studied. That outside observer is also part of an organism/environment field that includes the interaction being studied, the "outside" observer, and the interaction between observer and observed.

[**]Such an approach may produce behavioral change and lead to a gain in awareness. However, the method is not phenomenological. It is likely to be an example of a "black-box" behavioristic theory.

him for being imperfect; disclosing contrary data (observation of an imperfection in the patient coupled with expression of the therapist's reaction to the patient); exploring the patient's feelings toward a loved but imperfect Other; describing his "perfect self"; imagining a "good parent" who loves him unconditionally; making a statement confirming or opposing the "irrational" thought and observing bodily and emotional reactions.

2a. Inherent Structure

> The basic premise of Gestalt psychology is that human nature is organized into patterns or wholes, that it is experienced by the individual in these terms, and that it can only be understood as a function of the patterns or wholes of which it is made. (Perls, 1973, p.p. 3-4)

It is a very basic and essential Gestalt belief that experience is structured rather than piecemeal (Wertheimer, 1938, 1945). This is a finding of phenomenological exploration and is a necessary support for the faith involved in experimenting, bracketing and trusting experience. This is consistent with the general field notion of the universe being orderly and determined (Einstein, 1950, 1961).

We perceive in segregated wholes. We see objects standing out (figure) or differentiated from a ground and also internally differentiated into parts. We do not see isolated stimuli as Titchener and some early behaviorists believed. Nor do we see the world as one giant whole — "a big, blooming, buzzing confusion" — as William James would have it.

Some properties of the whole are emergent and not inherent in any single part (Emerson and Smith, 1974). A whole has qualities of its own and is not merely a sum or aggregate ("and-summative") of the constituent parts (Wertheimer, 1938b). Thus: the whole is more than a sum of its parts. But more than that, the whole is a field that determines its parts (Köhler, 1969).

There are wholes, the behavior of which is not derived by that of their individual elements, but where the part processes are themselves determined by the intrinsic nature of the whole (Wertheimer, 1938, p. 2).

Moreover, meaning is an inherent part of a Gestalt, including a perceptual Gestalt. It is not added on. This Gestalt view joins the mechanistic determinism of materialism with the idealist meaning of vitalism (Koffka, 1935; Köhler, 1947). Each event has both order and meaning and is perceived as such.

Multiple forces in functional interrelationship to each other and to the whole make up the field (Lewin's Principle of Relatedness, Lewin, 1935). These forces provide structure that is not just mechanical, but dynamic and inherent in the field (Koffka, 1935; Köhler, 1947, 1969). There is an inner unity (Wertheimer, 1938). It is only when there is a "concrete mutual dependency" between the parts that a whole is a meaningful whole rather than a "purely summative" grouping of parts (Wertheimer, 1938b).

Another aspect of the field outlook is that the field is not composed of isolated parts or particles surrounded by empty space and affected at a distance by other particles.

> Empty space as mere geometrical nothingness vanished from physics, being replaced by a definitely distributed system of strains and stresses.... (Koffka 1935, p. 42. See also Einstein, 1950, 1961)

Energy is an aspect of the total field. A change in any part of such a field affects the rest of the field since the particles are a part of a field of continuous energy. Any change "ripples" through the field. The order is not mechanically imposed as a concrete channel directs water. The order is in the dynamic of the field forces.

An example of the utility of this approach can be seen with the application of the principle of Prägnanz to problem solving. The principle of Prägnanzs hold that the field forms itself in as orderly a way as is possible — with as much cleanness and definiteness — directedness and economy, stability and strength, as the global conditions allow. A situation that contains a problem also contains its solution (Wertheimer, 1945). Thus in psychotherapy the description of a situation via phenomenological focusing and dialogue yields a solution inherent in the situation.

This notion of the structure of the whole is a key to the goal of Gestalt therapy. Gestalt investigations seek an understanding of the structural features of the field. The goal is insight, structural clarity (Köhler, 1947; Wertheimer, 1945). In Husserlian phenomenology there is a similar emphasis (Idhe, 1977).

This writer previously defined Awareness and discussed it as the goal of Gestalt therapy (Yontef, 1976). I would now add that the Awareness which is sought in psychotherapy aims for insight as defined by Gestalt psychology:

Insight is a patterning of the perceptual field in such a way that the significant relations are apparent; it is the formation of a Gestalt in which the relevant factors fall into place with respect to the whole (Köhler, cited in Heidbreder, 1933, p. 355).

2b. Structure of the Field and "Organismic" Factors

Some have discussed the relation of Gestalt psychology and Gestalt therapy as if Gestalt psychology believes that the structure of the field is a function of external factors while Gestalt therapy believes that the important factors are internal, that is, "organismic" (Sherrill, 1974).

Both Gestalt groups conceive of whole situations including external and internal forces (Köhler, 1938; Perls et al., 1951). The whole is bipolar rather than dichotomous or undifferentiated. In Gestalt therapy language, we study the organism/environment field. The field as a whole has multiple determining forces. Which ones are emphasized depends on the actual situation being studied. What is figural depends on the task at hand.

The situation includes individual and external (other people, society, inanimate forces) factors. When studying the process of basic perceptions, e.g., the perception of objects as objects, the situation is largely determined by an immediate connection between the perceiver as a whole and what is "out there." Perception at this level is not primarily learned or determined by organismic factors. A table is readily perceived as a table regardless of organismic interest, feelings, etc. However, if one studies ambiguous stimuli in subjects whose motivation level is raised, e.g., hungry subjects, perception is likely to be influenced by their motivation state. This is a function of the whole situation. Experimentally, if one studies the interruption of tasks and the unfinished Gestalt

244

one will see results vary depending on such "organismic" factors as how ego-involved the subject is in the task.

In psychotherapy we are constantly dealing with situations more complex than the ideal situation for basic research. Organization in that situation and other situations at a similar level of complexity means that some stimuli will command more organismic energy than others and the individual organizes his perception. The situation is controlled by organismic and external variables. The difference between Gestalt psychology and Gestalt therapy on this matter is only in the context in which they operate. For example, Köhler, a Gestalt psychologist, discusses the organization of his own awareness process just as a Gestalt therapist would.[*]

It is universally known that therapists in general and Gestalt therapists in particular work to increase patients' sensitivity to what they feel. It is not as widely known that the Gestalt theory of Gestalt therapy calls for an equal emphasis on sensitizing patients to the external situation. Self awareness without world awareness deals with only part of the organism/environment field.

Wertheimer (1945) discusses a woman who has a problem at work. At first he is unable to understand the situation since her discussion is so self-preoccupied that she focuses on her feelings and she does not describe the whole situation. Some people

---

[*] "...the whole development must begin with a naive picture of the world. This origin is necessary because there is no other basis from which a science can arise. In my case, which may be taken as representative of many others, that naive picture consists, at this moment, of a blue lake with dark forests around it, a big, gray rock, hard and cool, which I have chosen as a seat, a paper on which I write, a faint noise of the wind which hardly moves the trees, and a strong odor characteristic of boats and fishing. But there is more in this world: somehow I now behold, though it does not become fused with the blue lake of the present, another lake of a milder blue, at which I found myself, some years ago, looking from its shore in Illinois. I am perfectly accustomed to beholding thousands of views of this kind which arise when I am alone. And there is still more in this world: for instance, my hand and fingers as they lightly move across the paper. Now, when I stop writing and look around again, there also is a feeling of health and vigor. But in the next moment I feel something like a dark pressure somewhere in my interior which tends to develop into a feeling of being hunted — I have promised to have this manuscript ready within a few months" (Köhler, 1947, p. 7).

mistakenly think that Gestalt therapy would duplicate this woman's neurosis. Self-preoccupation is not insight producing.

On the other hand, there are clinical situations in which the client adequately describes the external situation and does not know his or her own emotions, wants, needs or thoughts. A contribution of Gestalt therapy is its application of the insights of Gestalt psychology to the awareness of bodily, emotional, and motivational processes (Wallen, 1970). The Gestalt exploration aims for structural clarity (insight) and lets the actual deficit determine which variables are focused on.

3. Systematic Experimentation

The phenomenological field approach utilizes systematic experimentation to find a description that is true to the structure of the phenomena being studied. Idhe calls this the "variational method" (Idhe, 1977). The phenomenological approach uses experimentation rather than interpretation as the chief tool for research or therapy. Experimentation enables one to sense for oneself what is fitting or true (Simkin, 1974).

This writer believes that all Gestalt therapy techniques are a means of experimentation. This contrasts experimenting with a behavior modification program. For example, asking someone to repeat and say louder something said in therapy is, by this notion, not aimed at catharsis (although that might happen) but to aid in increasing awareness. In repeating and shouting the patient might, for example, discover what he feels and how intensely and how he subdues his feeling. The particular intervention is only a part of an overall phenomenological exploration whose goal is to raise the level of awareness.

Systematic experimentation can be used to study any phenomenon that is experienced. The field is a unit of study that is defined by an observer. In Gestalt therapy the field is chosen by clinical relevance. The utility of the Gestalt method so applied is limited by the clinical acumen of the Gestalt therapist.

The phenomenological field method makes special note that the observer is part of the situation. This involves three aspects.

(1) How one sees is in part a function of how one looks. To look "naively" as the Gestaltists advocate yields a very different

experience than introspecting. To look without bias, that is, with bracketing, takes discipline.

(2) The observer affects the object of his study. In modern physics they have found that measuring or observing changes the physical event being studied. The patient or subject who is being observed is somehow affected by being observed. He/she is not exactly the same as before the observation. In Gestalt therapy this is dealt with by utilizing dialogue between patient and therapist. The human subject can report his experience of the effect of being observed.

(3) No one can see it all. One can only be clear about what vantage point is being used to describe what aspect of the phenomena.

4. Awareness of the Awareness Process

The Gestalt approach has a special emphasis on understanding the process of gaining awareness or insight (Perls et al., 1951, 1973; Wertheimer, 1945).

Insightful awareness is always a new Gestalt and is in itself curative (Perls, et al. 1951; Yontef, 1976). The formation of the new Gestalt, in which "the significant relations are apparent" and the "relevant factors fall into place with respect to the whole," is a process that happens naturally without Gestalt training. When it does not, when habit patterns and unself-conscious efforts do not yield insight, Gestalt training can use phenomenological exploration to gain an understanding of the insight/awareness process.

The ability to form this insightful new Gestalt is essential to successful organismic self regulation. To be aware in a structure-clear, rather than a structure-blind, manner is most important. This means to be aware of self and situation with respect to that task or issue that most needs the attention of consciousness (Yontef, 1969, 1976).

Ideally the awareness process has the quality of a good Gestalt. The figure is sharp and is perceived in clear relation to the ground. The figure shifts in a manner appropriate to the situation, reflecting the dominant need or salient feature of the situation. The figure is neither too fixed or rigid nor does it shift too rapidly.

As the sophistication of the phenomenological subject or patient grows, the emphasis shifts from straightforward awareness (e.g., emphasis on some social problem) to more reflexive awareness, i.e., awareness of straightforward awareness (Idhe, 1977). Reflexive awareness leads to awareness of one's overall awareness process. In Gestalt therapy this sophisticated phenomenological attitude leads to insight into character structure and into the pattern of avoidance of awareness.[*]

In the discussion of the existential applications of the Gestalt method we will see how this phenomenological emphasis in Gestalt therapy shifts from the awareness process to a more comprehensive focus on the existence of the perceiving person as a person.

In superior quality Gestalt therapy a piece or segment of work is a figure that is related to a larger background picture that minimally includes straightforward awareness, awareness of the awareness process itself, the character structure of the patient, a comprehensive picture of the patient's existence and the nature, strength and development of the patient-therapist relationship. Piecemeal work tends to be structure-blind, hence, not productive of insight. Again the acumen of the therapist is essential.

5. Intentionality

The phenomenological approach is based on intentionality. Awareness is always awareness of something. There is a correlation ("intentional correlation") between the perceiving and the perceived. The split of subject and object is joined into a unified polarity of perceiving and perceived. The thought that the person creates perception mostly from his own need is contrary to intentionality. On the other hand, there is no external world

---

[*]Idhe discusses the incorporation of the phenomenological attitude into ordinary perceiving as "phenomenological ascent." (Idhe, 1977, p. 128). The person who has incorporated the phenomenological attitude perceives with increased clarity, is open to and expects to find a variety of facets to any situation, and is sensitive to when one is clear or not clear about the structure of a situation. With phenomenological ascent one tends not to limit the experience of a situation to a single, narrow vantage point.

humanly experienced without a perceiving person. Without the world I would not know, without I, there is no world humanly conceived.

The Existential Application of the Gestalt Method

Gestalt therapy took from psychoanalysis a sensitivity to certain developmental and characterological themes. It took the phenomenological field method largely from Gestalt psychology. The application of the Gestalt method in Gestalt therapy is given philosophical direction by existentialism. This phenomenological existential approach supplies the theory of relationship in Gestalt therapy and gives direction to the awareness work.

Gestalt therapy is an existential psychotherapy (Edwards, 1977; Van Dusen, 1968, 1975a, 1975b, 1975c). Like most existential approaches, it is based on the phenomenological method. Gestalt therapy moved the Gestalt method into the existential direction for much the same reason as Heidegger, Sartre and others moved the Husserlian phenomenological approach in an existential direction (Idhe, 1977).

Gestalt psychology, as Husserl's phenomenology, is largely a content psychology. Gestalt therapy transforms the Gestalt method into a psychology system that is both act and content oriented. In an act psychology attention shifts to the person who perceives and experiences. The interest shifts in the existential manner to the structure of the person's opening to the intentional correlation, i.e., to the person and how he meets the world.

Gestalt therapy differs from Gestalt psychology in that in Gestalt therapy the emphasis shifts from essence to existence, especially the existence of individual persons. The reality that is of most importance in Gestalt therapy is being — people as they live. Gestalt psychology views people as unique and whole, hence, the special inappropriateness of studying people with a reductionistic attitude. However, the emphasis has been on aspects such as perception or cognition rather than the person *qua* person and the whole of his/her experience.

The application of the phenomenological method to the study of individual persons *as persons* and their existence resulted in the discovery that only by dialogue with other persons as persons do humans *truly* define themselves. People exist only in constant relation to each other.

To *truly* define oneself is one more important key to understanding the existential attitude. Phenomenological-existential explorations reveal that people live in an unstated context of belief. This learned habit of conventional thought forms a sediment that muddies the immediate experience of the world as it is and the self as it is (Idhe, 1977). The definition of self based on a clear and accurate immediate experience enables one to know what one is responsible for and to know what choices one is making. This is what is referred to as authenticity. Clouding one's perception of self based on sediment is self-deceptive (Sartre, 1966).

Gestalt therapy utilizes the Gestalt phenomenological field method of exploration to increase the patient's support in putting sediment aside and sharpening awareness so that choices will be made based on responsibility and authenticity. Full awareness and self-deception are antagonistic concepts (Yontef, 1976). The Gestalt view of perception provides additional support for personal responsibility. Since the ground contains many possible figures, it is the individual who organizes a complex experiential field for himself/herself. For example, when an unfinished situation clamors for attention and competes for attention with other aspects of the field, the individual regulates which will be foreground. "Only I can feel my feelings, think my thoughts, sense my sensations, and act my actions. Only I can live me" (Emerson and Smith, 1974, p. 9).

The Dialogic Relationship

Dialogue is the particular form of contact most appropriate to a phenomenological-existential psychotherapeutic relationship. Contact is thoroughly discussed in the Gestalt therapy literature (F. Perls, 1947, 1973; L. Perls, 1976, 1978; Polster and Polster, 1973). Here we will just note that contact entails an acknowledgement of another person. Dialogue, i.e., the I-Thou form of contact, is a form of contact based on authenticity as discussed above. Interpersonally, I-Thou contact means treating the other as a person equally capable of authenticity and worthy of being treated as an end rather than a means to an end. Doing that usually entails saying what one means and meaning what one says.

All psychotherapeutic relations are built on caring. The underlying warmth and acceptance of the psychoanalytic relationship are expressed through the medium of a relationship marked by the rule of abstinence. In Gestalt therapy the caring, warmth and acceptance are manifest through a dialogic relationship (Jacobs, 1978; L. Perls, 1976, 1978; Rosenfield, 1978; Simkin, 1974; Yontef, 1969, 1976, 1981a, 1981b, 1981c).

Five characteristics mark this dialogic relationship (see Yontef, 1981b).

(1) *Inclusion.* This is putting oneself as fully as possible into the experience of the other without judging, analyzing or interpreting while simultaneously retaining a sense of one's separate, autonomous presence. This is an existential and interpersonal application of the trust in immediate experience that is the heart of phenomenology. Kohut's alteration of psychoanalysis to emphasize empathy moves psychoanalysis in this direction. The practice of inclusion provides an environment of safety for the patient's phenomenological work and, by communicating an understanding of the patient's experience, helps sharpen the patient's self awareness.

(2) *Presence.* The therapist expresses the therapist rather than abstaining from expressing his self. He regularly, judiciously and with discrimination expresses his observations, preferences, feelings, personal experience, thoughts, etc., as a part of the therapeutic relationship. Thus, the therapist can share his perspective by modeling phenomenological reporting thereby aiding the patient's learning about the trust and use of immediate experience to raise awareness. If the therapist relies on theory-derived interpretation, rather than personal presence, he leads the patient into using phenomena not in his immediate experience as the tool for raising awareness.

(3) *Commitment to Dialogue.* The contacting process is a whole that is more than a sum of the people involved and even more than a sum of inclusion and presence. Beyond contacting the other and expressing one's self is a commitment to and ultimately a surrender to an interpersonal process. This is allowing contact to happen between rather than controlling the contact and the outcome. Wertheimer (1945) states that finding the solution that is inherent in the situation requires wholehearted desire for and

commitment to the truth in the situation rather than any previously held belief or attitude.

(4) *No Exploitation.* Any form of exploitation is at variance with the dialogic relationship (Yontef, 1981b). Exploitation influences the patient's experience to adjust to a goal of the therapist rather than protecting the integrity of the patient's actual experience.

(5) *Dialogue Is Lived.* Dialogue is something that is done rather than talked about. "Lived" emphasizes the excitement and immediacy of doing. The mode of dialogue can be dancing, song, words or any modality that expresses and moves the energy between the participants. An important contribution of Gestalt therapy to phenomenological experimentation is enlarging the parameters to include explication of experience by nonverbal expression of it. For example, directly expressing love to a loved one rather than reporting about it, may lead to feeling and showing the love with a wholeness unmatched by words alone.

Summary

When adequately elaborated the basic method of Gestalt therapy can be traced directly to the phenomenological field theory of Gestalt psychology. The chief characteristics of this method are: (1) reliance on the total immediate experience, here-and-now with biases put in brackets; (2) a search for insight into the inherent structure of the segregated whole which is the experiential field of perception; (3) systematic experimentation to obtain a description true to the structure of the phenomena being studied; (4) seeking insight into the awareness process itself; (5) intentionality. The relation of "organismic" factors to the total field was discussed.

The existential application of the Gestalt method was discussed. The method changed emphasis from the content to the act of consciousness, from the search for essence to the existence of the perceiver.

The paper delineated the development of an existential attitude which regards people as both inextricably bound to other people and also inevitably confronted with the phenomenological existential task of discriminating between the immediate and authentic on the one hand and self-deception, confusion and bias on the other.

Also discussed was the dialogic relationship as the type of psychotherapeutic relationship appropriate to a phenomeno-logical-existential therapy and its characteristics of inclusion, presence, commitment to dialogue, non-exploitiveness and a full living dialogue.

These philosophic principles form an integrating framework that is the primary identity of Gestalt therapy. Particular therapeu-tic techniques, therapeutic style and the usual clichés are of so little importance that they could be eliminated without diminish-ing the essential nature of Gestalt therapy. One of the beautiful features of Gestalt therapy is that it is a framework that can be applied in a rich variety of styles. (Melnick, 1980; L. Perls, 1976, 1978; Polster, 1975a; Simkin, 1974; Yontef, 1976, 1981a, 1981b, 1981c; Zinker, 1977). The principles can be applied in any modal-ity (individual, group, workshop, conjoint, family) and, with appropriate professional precautions and modifications, can be applied in any diagnostic group. It can be applied to group process as well as individual-oriented therapy. Moreover, this list in no way exhausts the possibilities. What is important is the overall integrity of the existential phenomenological field method.

9

ASSIMILATING DIAGNOSTIC AND PSYCHOANALYTIC PERSPECTIVES INTO GESTALT THERAPY

━━━━━━━━━━━━━━━━━

Commentary

This essay is a transcript, edited by me, of my opening address at The Gestalt Journal's *Ninth Annual Conference on the Theory and Practice of Gestalt Therapy in May 1987 on Cape Cod. It was published in* The Gestalt Journal, *Spring 1988.*

Good evening. I am pleased and honored to be here, at what has become one of the premiere conferences for exchange of ideas about Gestalt therapy theory and practice, a conference where I can talk about my current perspectives in Gestalt therapy rather than just repeat basics.

I want to talk about a methodology for assimilating diagnostic and psychoanalytic perspectives into Gestalt therapy theory and practice. Gestalt therapists do take psychoanalytic perspectives into their practice. I am interested in how to do it and still preserve the integrity of the system. My topic: "Principles By Which We Transform Psychoanalysis and Other Perspectives Into Gestalt Therapy Theory and Practice, and How Gestalt Therapy Theory and Practice Is Altered By This Process."

Why Are Gestalt Therapists Borrowing From Psychoanalysis?

We have always been an integrating framework. That's one of the things I love about Gestalt therapy. We don't have to re-create the wheel. We take what we need from the total field. In Gestalt therapy we emphasize the importance of people knowing what they need and finding sources to meet the need — support from anywhere, excluding nothing of value. This freedom from dogma is characteristic of Gestalt therapy.

Effective state-of-the-art treatment requires the kind of characterological and developmental descriptions that some new psychoanalytic approaches provide. They are extremely valuable for knowing patients better.

Ongoing psychotherapy requires a different kind of knowing than workshops or demonstrations. We need a compass and map for long term journeys. Wandering and trusting organismic self-regulation is not enough, especially with the personality disorders. We need to know the long term effect of immediate interventions. We need to know if therapy is working. Are the right structure building processes being addressed? Is it reasonable for the therapy to take as long as it is taking with a particular patient? What are the central issues for a particular patient?

Object relations and self psychology have valuable insights into people's phenomenology, development, human relationships and the course of therapy.

I think we need this new insight, especially for working with the severe personality disorders. Classic styles of Gestalt therapy and psychoanalysis have resulted in negative or minimal effect with patients with serious character disorders, especially the narcissistic personality disorders and the borderline patients. And we are seeing many more of them. Much of what we need to treat these patients has not been developed within Gestalt therapy. Therefore many of us have borrowed insights from object relations therapists who have a good perspective on these patients.

I think a denial of the limits of what has been developed in Gestalt therapy would be defensive and counterproductive. Merely restating the ideas of Perls, Hefferline and Goodman does not fill the holes. Nor do references to the oral tradition or implicit theory help. It is time we hold ourselves responsible for our literature. For example, I've heard reference to the fact that narcissism can be explained with the concept of confluence, but I have yet to see a complete explication of the narcissistic personality in the Gestalt literature.

I think there have been great improvements in Gestalt therapy practice. I think we're doing better therapy now than ever before, especially with the personality disorders. I think we have observed and acknowledged, learned and improved, and now have a clearer perception of character pathology. We differentiate in a clearer way between serious character pathologies and neurosis and psychosis, and between the different types of character pathologies.

I think we have improved in part because of greater experience in doing therapy, and in part because of exchange between therapy systems. Much of Gestalt therapy has been incorporated into other systems, and Gestalt therapists have borrowed much from other systems also. Of course, doing that is not new to Gestalt therapy.

Recently many Gestalt therapy practitioners have been borrowing from object relations. But this is insufficiently noted in the literature. That alone warrants my topic tonight. What are we borrowing and how are we using it? Because these improvements are not discussed in our literature, many have just associated the changes and improvements in Gestalt therapy practice with practicing something other than Gestalt therapy.

We need to consider how to utilize and integrate this new knowledge and preserve the integrity of the system. We need to address what to borrow and how to do it. Many have accomplished this task piecemeal, introjecting, creating "Gestalt therapy *and...*" The problem with "Gestalt therapy and ..." is that there is often a violation of those principles that make Gestalt therapy unique and effective, for example, by reifying structure, losing the sense of the individuals being responsible for themselves.

My Exact Topic: How To Assimilate

My exact topic tonight is how to assimilate: things to keep in mind in transposing psychoanalytic concepts so that they do not become "Gestalt therapy and...."

257

As Gestalt therapists we know that growth is by assimilation. It is by assimilation that Gestalt therapy changes and grows. The second part of my topic is to indicate some changes I see in Gestalt therapy.

Although I'll be speaking indirectly of the treatment of the personality disorders, my topic is not how to define or treat personality disorders, nor is my topic what principles of psychoanalysis to borrow. There is a clear psychoanalytic literature that I encourage Gestalt therapists to explore. The ideas that I will discuss are mostly a continuation and explication of Gestalt therapy as I know it, with some changes in emphasis.

Using Psychoanalysis to Know
Our Gestalt Therapy Patients Better

Gestalt therapy supports us in doing great therapy. It supports us in integrating diverse material. And our system is not self-sufficient.

Perls, Hefferline and Goodman brilliantly discussed and explicated the here-and-now moment of experienced contact as a key to therapy. But do we stop with this? Is this enough? Is that the upper limit on how we can know the patient in Gestalt therapy? And what does it mean to really know the patient?

We center on here-and-now moments of experienced contact, but that is not the end of our horizons. We need to be aware of larger Gestalten.

Phenomenological experiences are a rich tapestry referring to four time-space zones. I think our practice has improved by increasing explicit attention to the four time-space zones.

First, of course, is the most familiar to Gestalt therapists: the whole person environment field at a particular moment. This includes the concrete and immediately observable; the meaning to the person; unfinished business that is represented concretely here and now; wishes and fears about the future expressed here and now.

The second zone is the "there and now," the person's life space. The "now" does not end with this very second. It includes what the patient is presently living through out of the therapy office as well as within, the whole of a person's current existence.

Thirdly, the "here and then," the therapeutic context — that which happened here in the therapy room, but not right at this very moment. I think there is a new emphasis in Gestalt therapy on the importance of the therapeutic relationship, including recognition of patterns of transference and increasing dialogue about the therapeutic relationship within therapy.

And there are other factors of the here-and-then context. For example, working for agencies introduces other contingencies. I remember working as an intern for the Veterans Administration, and all of the therapy that we did was very heavily influenced by something we didn't talk about, which was the V.A. paid the patients to be sick, and withdrew financial support if they got well. That was a very active part of the therapeutic context.

I once consulted with a trainee who was quite frustrated with the difficulty she was having in handling demands by her patients to be taken care of in a way she thought was inappropriate in Gestalt therapy. In exploring a little further, it turned out that part of the therapeutic context was that most of her patients came to her through a brochure that she wrote and distributed. In the brochure she made implicit promises which implied providing the very dependencies she was trying to frustrate.

The fourth time-space zone is the "there and then," the patient's life story. For example, Erv Polster discussed this in his new book, *Every Person's Life Is Worth a Novel.* Is any real dialogue possible if we are not interested in this — in the developmental history — how a person developed over time? The background that allows meaning to emerge includes history and development, the sequence of prior experiential moments.

Knowing the patient better means making diagnostic discriminations: at the beginning of therapy and all through therapy; between each unique person and patterns of individuals. Is the patient psychotic, suicidal, dangerous to others? Does the patient need referral to a physician for medical problems or for psychotropic medication? Is the person neurotic or have a personality disorder? Is the person borderline or a narcissistic personality disorder? Operationally, not all of what we need to make these discriminations is observable immediately in the here and now. It is observable over a long period of time, and clinically we need to start making these discriminations from the very beginning.

It is vitally important for the therapist to accurately and adequately understand a patient's phenomenology and current behavior from the beginning of therapy.

For illustration let's discuss borderline patients who engage in splitting — that is, being in touch with one part of the field, being out of touch with another part, perhaps a polar opposite, and then on other occasions reversing that. For example, being in touch with dependency wishes, being out of touch with adult competent, autonomous abilities. And then on another day being in touch with their adult competence, their ability to be autonomous, and not acknowledging the difficulties of their regressive urges. Such patients have regressive urges such that when they are met they tend to keep regressing more and more instead of reconstituting and pulling together. They often come in early in therapy talking about their history with very strong primitive affects, but not able to integrate, not able to utilize the discussion to gain perspective. They are very impulsive, lacking object constancy — meaning they have trouble keeping the therapist or other people in mind when they are out of sight. And, of course, they have very intense issues of abandonment.

This kind of patient needs very early limit setting, for example on transference. They need to be taught contact and boundary skills, sensory contact. I had one patient who had made multiple suicide attempts, very serious suicide attempts, before I started therapy with her, and had attacked her last therapist with a weapon. She was unable to remember me between sessions. I mean, she remembered my name, but that's about all. I gave her a picture of me to carry.

I tend to make very compulsive, here-and-now person-to-person contact before and after each piece of work with a borderline in a way that's different than I would do with most patients. Two examples, both from when I first set up in private practice many years ago and didn't know what a borderline was — a successful and an unsuccessful example.

One patient we can call Bundini. I call him Bundini because at the beginning that's what he called me. For those of you who don't know, Bundini was Mohammed Ali's manager. This patient saw himself as very, very sick, and indeed acted that way. And by my magic, he was going to become a champ — in life, not in boxing. Now this patient seemed so unbelievable to me, his sickness seemed so put on, that I was very firm with him and used a lot of confrontation. Even though I didn't know what a borderline was at the time, this approach worked very well. Over time Bundini began behaving in a much healthier way and began serious and effective psychotherapy work.

I had another borderline patient at the same time that we could call the Gatekeeper's Daughter. She was an Oriental woman who saw herself as a peasant's child, sitting at the gate of the big house, getting none of the goodies. Now I believed at that time that the patient had an underlying thought disorder and I treated this patient with a kind of patience or tolerance or gentleness that would have been quite appropriate if indeed she had a thought disorder but was not appropriate for this patient. Along about the second year, when the transference turned negative, which is inevitable, it took on psychotic proportions. I've since found out this is very common. What she needed was more confrontation, more firmness, more limit setting. That's the kind of insight I think we need from the beginning of therapy and we don't have this sufficiently worked out within Gestalt therapy.

Contrast this kind of borderline patient with the narcissistic kind of patient who has object constancy, does not feel understood or respected, has intense and very primitive feelings of hurt, fright, rage that he/she is not able to neutralize. Such a patient primarily needs his or her phenomenology to be heard, acknowledged, respected and stayed with. If you try to teach contact skills, for example, to this kind of narcissistic patient early in therapy, you are very likely to have big problems. They will resist, you will be frustrated and they will feel narcissistically injured. Usually the idealization that sometimes happens at the beginning of therapy is very useful for this kind of patient. And in contrast to the borderline, they need to be encouraged to tell their history.

It is important to be able to discriminate these kind of differences when the patient is angry with the therapy or the therapist. With the narcissistic patient, if you acknowledge their point of view and acknowledge your own part in the interaction without defensiveness, the chances are that the narcissistic patient will be able to settle down and resume his or her therapy work. However, it is not that simple with the borderline — who needs more firmness, more dialogue, more ego building work initiated by the therapist.

This is the kind of discrimination that we need, for example, when patients report being discouraged with psychotherapy. Is it a schizoid patient for whom the discouragement may actually be a good sign, a sign of finally getting in touch with a kind of life-long despair that has been lived with and not in awareness? Or is it a narcissistic patient who is reflecting a kind of empathic failure in the previous session? Or perhaps a borderline patient for whom the therapist has to be kind of a guardian for the polar nature of psychological processes?

An example: The patient I mentioned that I gave my picture to. I went on vacation. Before I left she was feeling quite a bit of despair, not particularly connected with my going on vacation. A very fine therapist was taking calls for me, had a session with her, sat beautifully with her while the patient expressed her despair, did the kind of reflecting and empathic listening that usually is very helpful. And the patient went home and almost killed herself. What she reported was she looked at my picture and said, "I will wait until Gary comes back." What was wrong with that session was that for the borderline patient sitting with the feeling of despair excluded any sense in the background that there might be any hope. And the therapist's empathic attunement with that feeling seemed to be a confirmation that there was no hope. She needed some simple statement of "I want to sit with you with your feelings although I don't feel hopeless about you."

Another time in therapy where you need these kinds of insights is knowing what the next characterological step or phase is. Sometime later in therapy the borderline will often feel better and want to stop therapy. Though I think mostly in Gestalt therapy we feel quite respectful of patients making their own decisions, taking the responsibility for when to start and stop therapy — the border-line patient who is feeling better and wants to stop therapy is often still splitting. Now they feel autonomous, and they want to leave therapy to protect that autonomy, but they are thinking of that as being self-sufficient. They do not yet conceive of autonomy and interdependence. This is equivalent to emotional starvation. That is not sustainable, and a discussion of this needs to be initiated by the therapist whether or not the patient does stop therapy at that point. That needs to be talked about.

We have been discussing my views on why we should utilize these psychological insights. Next I want to talk about how to convert the psychoanalytic ways of thinking about patients into field theoretical terms that can be truly integrated with Gestalt therapy theory and practice, and after that how to use these concepts in the Gestalt therapy dialogic and experimental phenomenological methodology.

Concept Transposition: Action By The Whole Person

How do we transpose the Newtonian and pre-Newtonian language of psychoanalytic personality theory into field theoretical, process terms? This is a lot of what Perls, Hefferline and Goodman did.

In psychoanalytic drive theory, people are seen as entities moved by separate forces or drives. Very Newtonian: there are things and there are forces and they are dichotomized. Psychoanalysis reifies human process into mechanistic, thing-like concepts. Ego, id, superego — again Newtonian. Even the newer psychoanalytic schools, which I find quite useful, treat the self as thing-like structure. One of the chief aims of Perls, Hefferline and Goodman was to eliminate Self (capital S) and only have self (no reification). Masterson, whom I find very, very useful in treating the borderline, has concepts like the Withdrawing Object Relations Unit (WORU), and the Rewarding Object Relations Unit (RORU). Very thing-like, but translatable into process terms.

The first transposition: *Each psychological process, behavior, structure is to be treated as an "action," and designated by an active verb and/or adverb rather than a noun, thing or thing-like description.*

I have borrowed from Roy Shafer, a Freudian analyst, who wrote a book called *A New Language for Psychoanalysis*. He took the entire Freudian metapsychology and translated it into process terms very consistent with Gestalt therapy — in fact in some ways more radical than our process language.

In this way of thinking mind is not a thing. It is something we do or the way we do something. In this way of thinking I don't "have anxiety about speaking." I do give this speech very anxiously. What is it that a psychoanalytic thing-like concept claims that a person does? What is the process? What is the person experiencing and doing? These are the transposing kinds of questions. The person doesn't have guilt. There is an act, usually an act of condemnation.

Action is by the whole person, not by "part of me." In this action or process orientation the person is treated as the finder, assigner and creator of action and meaning. Otherwise we have things that collaborate and oppose each other rather than a relationship between persons. For example the libidinal ego fighting with the harsh superego or an alliance between the therapist's ego and the patient's ego. There is a danger that if we introject the psychoanalytic concepts we also take in such reification.

This reification and treatment of part of the person as if it were a separate person is not restricted to psychoanalysis. Terms like top dog, under dog, inner child are used in the same way. This happens subtly when human processes are described in a way that leaves out the whole person as the agent, e.g., referring to contact boundaries or figure as if they were the agents of action. I think some descriptions in Gestalt therapy lose the sense of whole persons acting as the chief agent, at least as the chief focus. When patients use part or thing language — the Gestalt therapy language of integrated semantics, for example, translating "it" into "I" and "but" into "and" is very useful. The spirit of this therapeutic semantic attitude could serve us well in our professional literature as well.

My preferred focus is on the person who is experiencing and not just on experiential moments. It is a person that experiences, that is in conflict or harmony, that feels whole or fragmented — not parts.

Action is chosen. This is a crucial aspect to the action principle: People are self-determining, choice-making, responsible and active. Although events are jointly determined by the individual and circumstances, the action of the individual is chosen. In our sympathy for our patients, I think we need to watch, to guard against treating patients according to the psychoanalytic tendency of regarding people as being determined by (a function of) their environment.

People choose what they do. In both safe and
people may feel unsafe. But they do have a ch〈

Say that Mom is unloving and the person res
him or herself, denying attachment, and belie
to be unlovable. This common set of respo
possible response to that situation. The action ⌐┐

The beliefs that result from the situation, including the coping
responses of the person as part of the situation, might well become
introjects. But these are not things either. They are actively maintained by the person and carried forward.

Introjecting is an action, that of taking into the organism
without contact, discrimination and assimilation so that the person
is not able to integrate or reject. Introjecting is an action, hence
chosen, although usually not owned. Later the result of the
introjecting, for example, shoulds can be used to interrupt spontaneous behavior. This too is chosen action. Although we say that
"we have an introject," from beginning to end the introject is
actually mental behavior by the person.

How we frame things is very important in our work. We all know
that in the beginning of any therapy or training group, there are
a lot of issues of fear and trust and confluence. One of our trainers, under the influence of self psychology, taking a first trimester
group, focused on these issues of fear, trust and confluence. He
framed it as "Since you feel unsafe, of course you cannot be
contactful and take risk." I want to tell you, the course of that
group did not go well. It was difficult for those trainers who
followed and thought the individual therapist-trainee in the
training group could, with awareness, take responsibility even
when feeling afraid.

I had a borderline patient that I was working with on taking
responsibility for some marital issues. I had previously talked with
this patient about her being "responsible for this, and not responsible for that. Your husband is responsible for that." During one
particular session I automatically talked about responsibility
without being pedantic. She went away convinced I was telling her
she was one hundred percent responsible for everything in the
family. How we frame things does matter.

I want to make very clear that when I talk about these attitudes
I am assuming that we show clinical discrimination and good

265

gment about what is said to the patient and how it is said. I'm not advocating automatically saying anything like "you are responsible," "you are not responsible," "you are safe," or "you can risk," or "you can't risk." Everything must be done with clinical discrimination.

Disclaimed action refers to when the patient keeps him or herself unaware, for example, does not know that his or her action is chosen, hence disowns or avoids. All actions may be either acknowledged and claimed or not acknowledged — including disclaiming, which is also a behavior and can be claimed or not claimed. I think our work in therapy is to help patients to be attentive as needed to actions and to work as much as possible on owning these kind of choices.

Shafer has a very serviceable definition of insight in these terms, defining *insight* as *"claimed action"* and defining *resistance* as *"disclaimed action."* Resistance is treated as the act of resisting; the action is the person engaged in two paradoxical and contradictory actions at once. For example, wanting something from other people and being afraid and keeping unaware of wanting and/or the fear. The disclaiming of the wanting or the fear is "resistance."

In Gestalt therapy we want to avoid reductions of the whole person. We want to avoid reducing them in space to "part of me," and reducing them in time to isolated moment. I think this assimilating perspective enlarges Gestalt therapy, focuses on the sense of the whole person, and gives attention to processes previously not sufficiently attended to in Gestalt therapy.

The Concept of The Self

One example of how to make this transformation is in the concept of self. As it is usually used it is one of those reified part-self concepts. We use the term and think we are communicating some meaning. Actually it is a very confusing term with multiple and undifferentiated usages. There are at least fifteen different, contradictory meanings to the word. Self is that about a person that continues over time; self is nothing fixed but rather is here-and-now interrelations. Self referring to the whole person; self referring to the core part of the person; self as the sense a person has of himself. And there are also different types of selves: ideal self, false self, grandiose self, and so on.

Perls, Hefferline and Goodman assimilated, digested and transposed the self concept into field terms. However, I'm not sure that their definition is semantically useful anymore. I think the denotations of our usage of the term "self" are clear, but the connotations have become so contaminated that I would like to propose a change.

Some of us, wanting to move closer to the subjective experience of patients, have been giving greater attention to the person's sense of identity over time and have been importing into Gestalt therapy object relations and self psychological perspectives on the whole unified person. Unfortunately this has often been done without aggressive assimilation and without acknowledging and reconciling contradictions. As a result the connotations of the word *self* have become too confused and contaminated, even when the denotations are clear (as they are in the Perls, Hefferline and Goodman usage).

I think it's ironic that in searching for wholeness the person has been reduced to a part — you know, self as a core. This is not only a loss of wholeness, it reduces the person to an *it*, a structural entity. "*It*" gets cohesive or "*it*" gets fragmented. And that is a disowning of responsibility, a loss of agency.

I propose that we maintain the perspective that action is always by the whole person and not by "the self" and we use the term self only as a reflexive pronoun, a pronoun referring to the whole person where the subject and the object are the same person. For example, when I refer to me.

In this usage the word *self* would be used as a marker for persons pointing at themselves and processes that were considered aspects of the self now would be discussed as functions of the whole person. The whole person would be thought of as the system of interactions; the self-concept would be the sense people have of who they are; the ideal self the picture of who the person wants to be; the false self would refer to inauthentic behavior and a distorted sense of self constructed in order to gain acceptance; the grandiose self a person's inflated sense of self that excludes or minimizes past or present flawed aspects. Then when we distinguish people on qualities such as stability, groundedness, confidence, flexibility, values, a cohesive versus a fragmented sense of self, it would be in terms of whole persons and not in terms of qualities of selves. To talk about a fragmented self in these process terms we would ask what the whole person does. It may be something like "the person keeps awarenesses separately and does not integrate into a cohesive picture. The person does not maintain object constancy about himself/herself across situations, for example remembering successes during times of failure."

One of the clinical phenomena I frequently observe is of people who have an idea that self is a thing and they start doing awareness work and they get in touch with the experience of void. They come to believe "Oh, I don't have a self. Other people do; I don't have a self." When they learn the process viewpoint, that self is not a thing, it is often a very useful part of the clinical work.

We have discussed the concept of splitting, which is absolutely vital for treatment of the borderline patient. This is a phenomenon we have to be sensitized to look for, as the patient will not get clear about it spontaneously. However, we don't have to use this concept in the Newtonian psychoanalytic language, e.g., Masterson's Withdrawing Object Relations Unit and the Rewarding Object Relations Unit. In action language we can say that the patient regards other persons as either totally nurturing and loving or totally abandoning. Or we could say: the patient alternates between thinking of himself as either competent and therefore needing and receiving no nurturance and on other occasions thinking of himself as dependent, incompetent and clinging and in each mode of thinking has no awareness of the other mode.

And I think we can treat other functions of the person in the same way: the id as the person's aggressive and libidinal feelings, the ego as the person's thinking, object constancy, orienting in time and space, etc.

Concept Transposition: Here-and-now Matrix of Intersecting Forces

A second transposition is to put the concept into a field theoretical vantage point by taking into account the Gestalt notion of the here-and-now matrix of multiple intersecting forces.

In Gestalt therapy a person is always part of a person-environment field. There is no dichotomy between inner and outer. Even if we do look at the same event from different perspectives (e.g., inner and outer), and even if some events are kept private and uncommunicated, there are no separate inner and outer in the field theory of Gestalt therapy.

Everything that exists does so only in relationships, in webs of relating. There are always multiple forces concretely present — interrelating, creating multiple ripples and graduations in the field. We transform psychoanalytic unilinear, unidirectional causality statements to account for the multiplicity of forces that are always interacting and simultaneously present.

In field theory, any change in the field affects the entire field. It creates ripples through the field. An implication of this is that there are always multiple valid and useful starting points in doing therapy. You read in the analytic literature statements starting with words such as "the correct analytic response is" such and such. Since there are always a multiplicity of valid and useful starting perspectives from a field perspective, there obviously cannot be only one correct response. With our field emphasis the focus is more pragmatic, variable, open to considerations of individual style and creativity

One other aspect of this matrix notion is that there is no action at a distance. What has effect must exist concretely in the here-and-now field, in the matrix of forces. It must be simultaneously present.

Developmental Theory as an Example

Psychological development involves the interaction of multiple forces developing over time. The Gestalt therapy concept of human psychological development is that it is always a function of biological maturation, environmental influences, interaction of the individual and the environment, and creative adjustment by the unique individual.

In Freud's drive theory, the emphasis was only on the biological factors and there was a very negative viewpoint on the human potential for growing. Perls, Hefferline and Goodman, and other writers of the time, such as Karen Horney, added an awareness of environmental influences, interaction between individual and environment, and maintained an optimism about individual creativity and growth — the innate potential to grow and mature.

Kohut and object relations theorists, who have given us great patient descriptions, especially on the sequence of development, have indeed recognized environmental and interactional influences. However, they have tended not to recognize biological forces. Moreover, although sympathetic and empathic with the patient, they see the individual more pessimistically as caused by past historical influences. There is a loss of the perspective of the patient being unique, creative, and having positive potential. Or, putting it another way, there's a loss of optimism about each person's innate potential to grow and mature.

My integration of this is consistent with the Gestalt therapy model in that I use the psychoanalytic concept to sensitize me to background and developmental factors, but I maintain an awareness of biological factors as well as the other factors in the field, I maintain a sense of optimism about each person's potential to create and ability to choose and grow, and I maintain an emphasis on interaction among these multiple factors over time. I trust that the person's awareness of the complexity of who he/she is leads to organismic self-regulation (the paradoxical theory of change).

Concept Transposition: Movement Over Time

Continuing our discussion of the transposition of the Newtonian and Pre-Newtonian concepts into field theoretical terms, we come to the concept of movement over time. Our dialectic adds a time dimension. We are a process theory and process refers to development over time. Even structure is slowly changing process.

Everything is moving in space and changing in time, becoming, moving, developing. In this way of thinking people are in an unending series of these matrices that we have been discussing.

Of course we know that meaning refers to the relation between figure and ground. And the historical sequence of a person's experience is a very important part of the background. It is only one aspect, not the whole. But I believe that knowledge of past experience is necessary for meaning and for understanding a person's identity.

Therefore we explore, and I believe increasingly so, the person's past. But we need to do so remembering that we explore phenomenologically in order to understand, not believing that the past caused the present. There is no action at a distance. History happened, now it is a given, and the person processes the given and can choose action by doing something different. This contrasts with the Newtonian notion that A precedes B in time and causes it.

I believe that one past matrix does not cause or control later events, and one past childhood event does not, in itself, determine a future event.

An example of the importance of the time perspective is in distinguishing between the concepts of repression and splitting. In repression the person keeps something unaware. He or she may say Dad is wonderful, be unaware of any anger at Dad. And that is maintained consistently over a period of time.

Splitting at one moment may look very much like repression. The person may be unaware of any anger at Dad. However, what happens over time distinguishes the two processes. The person whose act of splitting appears at one moment to be very similar to repression, at another moment will reverse what is out of awareness and what is in awareness. The person who was not aware of any anger against Dad will then, perhaps, not perceive anything wonderful about Dad at all and only be aware of anger and rage. So from moment to moment there is a reversal, a seeing of only one half of a polarity and then the other half only. A balanced picture, reasonably accurate perception, good judgment are all impossible without undoing the system of splitting.

So for effective treatment we must maintain an awareness of how the processes we work with develop over time — whether they remain the same, whether they change, how they change.

In sum, so far I've been talking about how to integrate psychoanalytic concepts into the Gestalt therapy model of the whole person embedded in the person-environmental field, as the agent of action — and that develops over time — retaining the capacity to choose and experiment in the present.

The Therapeutic Relationship

I want to talk now about how to use this psychoanalytic perspective and work with patients in the Gestalt therapy way. How do we use these descriptions for the Gestalt therapy type of relationship?

Of course, the Gestalt therapy emphasis is on a relationship based on contact and phenomonological focusing as opposed to a relationship based on transference and interpretation. In the model of all of the psychoanalytic theorists that I know, the transference is encouraged and the therapist is required to remain neutral and practice the rule of abstinence. This means one does not gratify any wishes of the patient, there is no "I" statement by the analyst and the chief tool is still interpretation.

Now of course we know that relating is always a mixture of contact and transference, but we deal phenomenologically and dialogically with transference. We recognize it, neither forbid it nor encourage it. We know and use alternatives to interpretation of the transference.

Contact is the first reality. In the Gestalt therapy field theory everything is seen through the lens of relating. In working with a patient in Gestalt therapy contact is the first reality. Perls, Hefferline and Goodman is in the existential tradition with an emphasis on human person-to-person relations. In fact, in the lens of our dialogic and field emphasis, the person can't even be defined except in relation to other persons. Relations are inherent and not added on. This belief is not found in psychoanalytic theory, although perhaps the object relations people share that emphasis on inherent relationship.

Relationship is the heart of our practice of Gestalt therapy. But the episodic Gestalt therapy of the late sixties lost that emphasis. It was very freeing and exciting, but the technique orientation lost the primary existential emphasis on relationship. I also believe that talking about process without emphasizing the person, and without talking about the person as the person sees him or herself, also loses the existential emphasis on relationship and fails to develop clarity about patterns of relating. Therefore to do so is fragmenting.

Relationship is contact over time. Carl Rogers has said that contact is the basic unit of relationship. I think in Gestalt therapy we're clearest about moments of contact and not always as clear that relationship is more than a series of moments, is more than a summation of isolated moments. I'm not referring to relationship as a thing. I'm referring to it as contact over time, as a Gestalt that extends over time.

The Nature of the Gestalt Therapy Relationship

Contact: People Effecting Each Other as People.
I think good therapy requires a particular kind of contacting by the therapist, contacting marked by understanding and accepting the patient, showing the personhood of the therapist, and guarding the between, i.e., surrendering to that which happens between the therapist and the patient. It is not enough to have "I" and "you" and to recognize the difference, but in a dialogic approach there is also a surrender to what develops and emerges out of the interaction. This means the therapist is affected as well as the patient.

Understanding the patient refers to *inclusion* (Buber's concept) or empathy (the more generally used word) to project oneself into the phenomenological view of the patient. This means as much as one can to see the world as the patient does, while simultaneously keeping aware of one's own separateness and remembering that it is projection — one cannot truly experience another person's experience.

Inclusion and confirmation: accepting persons as they are and also confirming their potential to grow. And as patients interrupt their actual experience we accept their naive experience as experience, plus we interrupt or try to interrupt their interruption. We not only honor and accept the patients' awareness, but we confirm their potential for more refined awareness.

It is new in Gestalt therapy to put an emphasis on doing this interruption of their interruption in a way that the patient feels understood. The test of the accuracy of the therapist's empathy or any other intervention, is the patient's phenomenology. The goal, of course, is still to increase the patient's awareness of self and other.

When I was first in Gestalt therapy with Jim Simkin he interrupted my self-interruptions and I felt understood by him and as a result of this process I understood myself more. I saw a lot of other people engaged in this process in groups with Jim get paranoid, get into power battles, increasing their sense of shame and narcissistic injury. This was especially frequent among those with pronounced narcissistic issues. Often they did not feel understood or accepted. Frankly, I see now that often they were not understood. As was true with many Gestalt therapists of that time, Jim did not vary his approach to the relating with an object relations type of understanding. This, I think, is a new emphasis that has been coming into Gestalt therapy.

Emphasis on the *presence of the whole person of the therapist* is, together with inclusion, the hallmark of any existential therapy. This emphasis on the manifest presence of the therapist as a person in therapy is one of the most important of the differences between Gestalt therapy and psychoanalytic approaches with their analytic stance. The Gestalt therapist shares observations, affective responses, prior experience, creativity, intuition, etc.

However, I think we need to develop more specification of what type of presence has what effect with what type of patient or situation: when to share personal reactions, when to share observations, when to emphasize, clarify and underline the patient's phenomenology, when to emphasize experimentation. I think we need a presence that takes into account the strengths, weaknesses, needs, wishes, values, and circumstances of the patient. Just sharing the "I" of the therapist is not enough.

In this clarification object relations can be useful to guide, to help us focus on central issues in useful sequence and with good timing. Object relations in the background can sharpen the therapist's focus and broaden his or her perspective.

For example, patients with a narcissistic personality disorder who really do need to talk about their hurts and heal in the gentle glow of idealization and mirroring need a different presence than does a borderline patient who needs firmness with caring, being taught responsibility and emphasis on awareness of polarity. The Gestalt therapist who truly understands the Gestalt therapy methodology and truly understands his or her patients will be spontaneously and authentically different with the different patients.

When we're talking about presence we also need to talk about countertransference and self responsibility. For me, there is nothing more important in therapy than self responsibility by the therapist and the ability of the therapist to relate dialogically and therapeutically regardless of the personality style of the patient. The therapist needs an awareness clear of remnants of old business to be able to respond to the patient as the patient is, to have a real relationship and not one that's contaminated by elements being transferred and projected onto the patient. Effective therapy requires that the therapist be able to accurately reflect the patient's awareness, make uncontaminated observations, have a clear perspective on the next step for the patient's therapeutic work — without imposing biases, points of view or needing dramatic change for the therapist's need. This puts strong demands on the therapist's self-support.

For example, I believe it is parataxic distortion and not authentic presence when the therapist is impatient and needs a quick fix. The quick fix is for the therapist's own narcissistic gratification and not in the patient's best interest. When the therapist is impatient and frustrated, this is action by the therapist. This action (of impatience and frustration) is the responsibility of the therapist and not the patient. "I am frustrated" is a clearer existential statement than "you are frustrating."

I believe the most dangerous therapist is one who is able to be effectively and powerfully present but in a narcissistic constellation. Such a therapist can be very charismatic and it takes sophistication and good self support for a patient to realize the need to stand clear of such a powerful influence.

This self-protection is often missing in beginning therapy patients. Often the patient's psychological difficulties are such as to make him or her blind to the therapist's countertransference and other parataxic difficulties and may even cause him/her to like or positively value that counter-transference of the therapist that makes effective therapy unlikely or impossible. Thus for example, for the patient whose fantasy desire for dependency excludes autonomous self-responsibility and who is in therapy with a therapist who needs a patient to be dependent on him or her, the results may be a very long, unproductive and even harmful therapy.

I believe the effective therapist needs the relational skills I've been talking about plus the traditional Gestalt therapy technical skills at the phenomenological awareness work. I think it's important that we don't lose that, i.e., the ability to make sensory observation and contact in the here and now, to clarify process, to gauge the right amount of risk, knowing how to facilitate aliveness, be able to facilitate forward movement, knowing how to design experiments, and so forth. One of the risks of assimilating psychoanalytic material is that some of the strength of the Gestalt therapy methodology may be weakened.

I think that integrating psychoanalytic perspectives has resulted in an increase in emphasis in Gestalt therapy theory and practice on the quality of relationships in individual and group therapy. And I think it's changed a lot how we've conducted group therapy, especially increasing the emphasis on relating between group members, increasing emphasis on the factors of the whole group, an increasing emphasis on relationships over time in groups (as opposed to the workshop model). I also believe that, because of our increasing recognition of and sophistication in doing more intense characterological work, Gestalt therapists are using more individual or individual and group therapy and less the group therapy alone as the main modality for serious psychotherapy.

I believe quite strongly that using psychoanalytic insights within the framework of a Gestalt therapy relationship has a lot of advantages over doing psychoanalysis or psychoanalytic psychotherapy, in part because we have a wider range of allowable and developed interventions (since techniques are not forbidden because of interference with the development of the transference neurosis). And we can deal with the transference with a greater variety of interventions more openly and more experimentally. The emphasis on the therapist showing him or herself personally gives the patient stronger evidence of the healthful and the harmful responses by the therapist. And the emphasis on the phenomenology and self-direction of the patient and therapist makes maximum use of the wisdom of both and gives maximum support for the development of skills based on how each person actually is.

Relationship Based on Immediate Experience of Both Patient and Therapist

A key factor to keep in mind in working with concepts which come from outside of the Gestalt therapy tradition is that the therapeutic relationship in Gestalt therapy is based on the immediate phenomenological experience of both the patient and the therapist. In psychoanalysis more of the interventions are guided primarily by psychoanalytic theory and the actual experience of the analyst and the analysand are less emphasized and are treated less positively than in Gestalt therapy. While theory is vital to Gestalt therapy, when conducting Gestalt therapy we focus on the immediate awareness of the patient and of the therapist. Gestalt therapy interventions are professionally guided, but they are always based on this immediate experience.

Dialogue is shared phenomenology. Other interventions are also shared phenomenology. For example, reflections, shared observations, experiments, and the like can be seen as shared phenomenology.

The Gestalt therapy methodology emphasizes moving from a naive awareness to a more disciplined awareness. I want to state emphatically that in Gestalt therapy one should always begin the exploration by finding out the actual naive awareness of the patient. First get clear what this particular patient deems important at the moment — understand and accept that experience as the patient's experience.

Take, for example, the patient who acts helpless. Our first job is not to frustrate the patient's manipulative behavior. Our first job is to find out what that feels like to the patient. What is it like? How does the patient understand it? I think in the 1960's style of Gestalt therapy not enough of this kind of understanding was done, and sometimes the therapist had a pejorative or sarcastic or contemptuous attitude that was equivalent to laying "shoulds" on the patient. I think the therapist's job is to explore. The job is not to gratify. It is not to confront. It is not to frustrate. Our prime directive is to explore.

I would like to share with you an example of two different pieces of work that may illustrate this issue of finding out what the patient's awareness is. When I first started out in Gestalt therapy I did two different pieces of work on my confusion, one with Fritz and one with Jim. (I was confused a lot then.) When I was working with Fritz, he seemed to see me as manipulating for support — he may have been right. And I remember following his directions and wandering about the group confused, until I finally figured out that the thing I wanted the most was to be off the stage. So I sat down. But I didn't learn very much except I learned to sit down.

During the same time period, somewhat later in the same year, I was working with Jim Simkin with the same kind of confusion. Jim first carefully found out what my experience of the confusion was. For me it was like a fog. And when Jim asked me to be the fog, it was the beginning of the most important piece of work I did in therapy. So I'm making the suggestion to always emphasize first getting the patient's awareness, and then later you can refine and experiment and set up action programs based on the patient's experience of him or herself. First find out what the patient experiences, and clarify that. Make sure that what you come to believe is the patient's experience is actually what the patient confirms that he or she experiences.

Stages in Awareness

Awareness and Awareness Work Has a Developmental Sequence.

(1) Simple awareness. The patients come and talk about the problems they have in their life. They are not aware of process, they are not aware of being aware, are not aware of relationship with the therapist.

(2) Awareness of awareness. At this level of awareness the person becomes aware of being aware. It is in this process work that Gestalt therapy is most indebted to phenomenology. Often training groups operate at this level of awareness. This includes awareness of avoidance and resistance, bracketing, here-and-now

contact work, development and refinement of the tools of awareness and contact.

(3) Awareness of the character of the experiencing person. Awareness of awareness leads to awareness of the character of the experiencing person. As one is aware of the pattern of awareness and avoidance, conditions that lead to awareness and avoidance, patterns of awareness and unawareness, etc., one becomes aware of the overall character structure of the experiencing person.

(4) Phenomenological ascent. This is the stage at which the phenomenological attitude permeates the person's ordinary life. The attitude of knowing that there are always multiple realities, bracketing, using repeated observations to achieve insight into the actual workings of a situation become ordinary rather than something restricted to moments of being in therapy or doing therapy.

Example: Working with Resistance

Understanding and working with resistance is one of the most important and indispensable aspects of doing effective psychotherapy. In the perspective we are talking about resistance is treated as an action to be explored and shared phenomonologically. In working with it we find out what the patient is experiencing when he/she is "resisting." We also pay attention to the therapist's immediate phenomenological experience. We start by bracketing and do not start with a belief that what is being resisted is therapy or the therapist. As a result of the phenomenological focusing we have available the patient's experience (or several experiences) and our own experience and using both experiential perspectives we can dialogue, focus and experiment. In this process the therapist can also grow by gaining an understanding of his or her part in the interactions.

"Insight" Develops from "Between," from Dialogue

I believe that insight develops from this kind of dialogue.

Insight. Aha! A simultaneous grasp of the relationship between the parts and the whole.

I believe that the goal of Gestalt therapy awareness work is insight, although I've seen other statements in the Gestalt therapy literature. The insight goal in Gestalt therapy awareness work is not the same as psychoanalytic insight. If you define insight as I have, using this Gestalt psychology definition, then insight is what we are aiming for. Even if you restrict the psychoanalytic word to "emotional insight," the historical, interpretive "why" orientation in much of the psychoanalytic usage is different than the consistently holistic, sensory, phenomenological, existential usage in Gestalt psychology and Gestalt therapy.

I believe insight emerges from the dialectic between the patient (patient's awareness) and the therapist (therapist's awareness). In my Gestalt therapy model it does not come from technique or frustrating or from the "Gestalt therapy" style of behavior modification. It does not come from the therapist's power and charisma. It is not controlled by the therapist. It emerges out of the work together of patient and therapist.

There is a Gestalt of the sequence of the therapist's experience, the patient's experience, the therapist's experience, the patient's experience, and so on — Aha!

If enactment and stage dramas are needed, I think we need to ask: needed for whom? for what? at whose pace? Overuse of technique may lead to mystification and oversimplification. An example is not listening enough to the patient's story and overuse of the empty chair technique.

Therapy as Art and Love

I want to close with something in Gestalt therapy that is very important to me and absolutely crucial to our theory and practice. *Gestalt therapy is art.* Joe Zinker said that Gestalt therapy is permission to be creative. I agree and beyond that I think that *creativity and love is a necessary and essential part of effective Gestalt therapy.*

Without professional knowledge and discipline therapy may be ineffective and harmful. Some therapy does cause negative results.

But there is no Gestalt therapy cookbook. Cookbooks are for craft, and therapy is an art. And I think that doing therapy is an art that requires all of the therapist's creativity and love.

Thank you.

III

FIELD THEORY

10

INTRODUCTION TO FIELD THEORY

═══════════════════

Commentary

1991. This essay is meant to be a readable introduction to and overview of the entire field theory section. Much of what is discussed here is elaborated in the two other papers in this section [#12, Modes of Thinking in Gestalt Therapy (1984) and #11, The Self in Gestalt Therapy: Reply to Tobin (1983)].

Gestalt therapy theory is based on field theory. This is not just historical accident. Field theory is the kind of scientific thinking that works best with the rest of the Gestalt therapy theoretical system. There is a close fit between field theory and Gestalt therapy's phenomenology, dialogic existentialism, eclecticism, flexible attitude toward clinical options, and so forth. Moreover, field theory is the theoretical approach that can best encompass the broad intellectual, social, cultural, political and psychological issues that Gestalt therapy theory addresses (especially Perls, Hefferline and Goodman, 1951).

Considering the importance of field theory in Gestalt therapy theory, there has been surprisingly little elaboration of field theory in the Gestalt therapy literature. I know of no discussion of field theory in the Gestalt therapy literature that I consider clear, cogent, consistent, systematic and comprehensive. In my paper on

"Modes of Thinking in Gestalt Therapy" (1984a and below) I discuss some aspects of field theory, but it was written in response to an article by Joel Latner (1983) and is incomplete even in those aspects that were discussed without the text of Latner's article. It is my opinion that Latner's article is excellent and cogent on some aspects of field theory but inadequate and misleading in other aspects. In this essay I will not repeat the arguments I put forth in my response to his article. I recommend the reader to Latner's excellent and readable discussion of the difference between classical scientific theory (Newtonian mechanistic) and post-modern theory (field theory) (Latner, 1983) and to my dialogue with him (cited earlier in paragraph).

Talking and reading about field theory and understanding it is very difficult, perhaps the most difficult aspect of Gestalt therapy theory to discuss. It is a very different way of thinking and it is very abstract. Its relationship to clinical concerns is less clear than other aspects of Gestalt therapy theory.

I wrote this introduction to field theory hoping to provide a clear overview, especially for those who find field theory discussions too far from sense experience and clinical relevance or who have a visceral fear of and aversion to the abstract nature of most discussions on the topic.

Why Do We Need Field Theory?

Why do therapists need to study something as abstract as field theory? Gestalt therapy tends to attract therapists who find a home in our emphasis on actual concrete experience, direct expression of emotions, and so forth. Why not just focus on here-and-now sense experience, add a little clinical experience, and leave it at that?

The practice and theory of Gestalt therapy is built on the importance of being aware of our awareness process. The process of our thinking is an important aspect of this. We address it in therapy and we need to address this in our theorizing and teaching as well. Perls, Hefferline and Goodman (1951) discuss the necessary interplay between how one thinks and how one is in the world. How one thinks about the world, including one's philosophic orientation, is in part a function of character; conversely, character is in part a function of how one thinks. Field theory points to the process of how we think.

It seems clear to me that Kelly was right in his belief that all people have implicit scientific theories (Kelly, 1955). Without aggressive intellectual examination, individual functioning is colored by unexamined biases, beliefs, metaphysical assumptions, linguistic usages, introjected modes of thinking, and so forth. We stand on these assumptions, they permeate our contact and awareness processes, they determine and shape our thinking, feeling, perceptions and actions. Being clear about these is one of the functions of phenomenology and central to the Gestalt therapy methodology. It would be inconsistent for a system that finds awareness and assimilation so important to allow a topic as important as how we think to be left at the level of confluence and unexamined introjects.

But examining these unaware intellectual processes is not only a difficult and arduous task, but often raises anxiety and avoidance mechanisms. I always have to fight this in writing on field theory, including writing this paper. It has been said that an "uncritical assumption of a metaphysical posture provides welcome escape from our anxieties" (Bevan, 1991, 477).

Unfortunately, not examining these processes leaves in place inconsistencies and theoretical biases and limitations that have unexamined consequences. For example, I believe that the dichotomy of the biological and social in Perls, Hefferline and Goodman is at variance with their central holistic (field theory) theme and not theoretically examining this has had the consequence of limiting, or at least slowing up, the full blooming of the potential of Gestalt therapy.

Not examining Perls' individualistic, confrontive and drama oriented theoretical stances of the 1960s, had an extremely harmful effect on the development of Gestalt therapy. A field analysis would look at the total context of the work, especially the interpersonal relations. A field analysis would bring familial, group and other social processes to the fore, moderating the individualism. A field analysis would look at how the processes develop over time, moderating the confrontational and drama orientation with awareness of the negative effects that result and also show more appreciation for the long-term positive effects of softer and more subtle interventions.

I think that field theory illustrates Lewin's view that there is nothing so practical as good theory. Field theory can help focus on what is important and essential about what we do and what is peripheral. It can help identify commonalities undergirding various forms of what we do and what we study. I believe that field theory can provide guidance and orientation, e.g., in evaluating and assimilating new ideas, methodologies and technologies. Not only can field theory provide intellectual guidance for our research and therapy, but also a framework for communicating.

Moreover, I would also argue that since field theory is a vital part of the Gestalt therapy theory upon which the Gestalt therapy methodology is built, a Gestalt therapist who wants a comprehensive understanding of his or her chosen approach must study field theory. Some of the central concepts in Gestalt therapy are difficult or impossible to understand without a field theoretical attitude. Perhaps one can get by with only a superficial study of field theory to do Gestalt therapy, but certainly a deeper understanding is needed for theoretical work, teaching or doing training. I think anyone teaching or writing Gestalt theory needs a thorough understanding of field theory.

I think the Gestalt therapy field theoretical viewpoint could help resolve many issues in psychology that are unresolved because they are based on logical dichotomies, mechanistic thinking, and simplistic causality models. While such models work for certain kinds of explorations and within certain parameters, such as the Newtonian physics model working accurately within the parameters of its operation, they do not account for the full range of situations and data either in physics or psychology.

Field theory is touted in physics as a theory that can encompass the Newtonian mechanistic theory and also account for phenomena that the earlier theory cannot adequately deal with. That makes the field theory more comprehensive. Although the mechanistic theories in psychology and the field theoretical theories both adequately explain some phenomena, and field theory can explain all of the phenomena of the mechanistic theories, the reverse is not true.

Field theory language is able to describe phenomena that can also be described in mechanistic language. My response to Tobin (#11, The Self in Gestalt Therapy: Reply to Tobin, 1983) deals exactly with this point. And the field theory approach avoids some dilemmas that are created by the dualistic thinking of the mechanistic mode of understanding. For example, does the individual create his environment or does the environment create the individual? In the mechanistic mode experiments can be devised to study this question in linear fashion. But the question as posed creates a false dichotomy that is more easily dealt with in field theory. The individual/environment field creates itself, with the individual part influencing the rest of the field and the rest of the field influencing the individual. Circular causality is somewhere between the linear causality of the mechanistic model and the true field theory.

The debate over Freudian drive theory is another example. Many object to it as mechanistic, reductionistic and dualistic. Those reacting against it who are without a field theory foundation, often reject all physical energy concepts as mechanistic, reductionistic and dualistic without realizing that physical energy is a necessary aspect to a holistic theory and can be well accounted for in field theory without mechanistic, reductionistic or dualistic thinking. In fact, excluding all energy concepts from a psychological theory is itself dualistic and reductionistic. A field theory perspective can provide theoretical support for integrating a psychological theory that includes the body, mind, emotions, social interactions and spiritual and transpersonal aspects.

The Gestalt therapy concept of self is another example. I think it a more elegant and useful concept than it is given credit for, but it can be adequately understood only in the context of field theory. Without a sophisticated understanding of field theory one is usually left with one of two common attitudes toward self. If one treats self as a concrete existent, as an inner homunculus, then there is an inner "core" that does things, but the person ("I") is not the active agent. Some people then are seen as "having a cohesive self" and others having a "fractured self." This attributes physical concrete existence to an abstraction.

On the other hand if one defines the self in process terms, then one has a self-concept and no overall self, no tangible existent.

The reader interested in an erudite discussion of this general topic is recommended to Harré (1991) and Robinson (1991). For example, in 1971 Kohut's defined the self as a "low level abstraction" (Kohut, 1971). "By 'low level abstraction,' he meant that people form ideas about themselves that are generalizations based on particular experiences" (Wolfe, 1989). Concept, but no existent. The Gestalt therapy definition of self has been misinterpreted in this way (for example, Tobin, 1982).

Perls, Hefferline and Goodman define self as "the system of contacts at any moment....The self is the contact-boundary at work; its activity is forming figures and grounds (Perls, Hefferline and Goodman, 1951, p. 235)." This emphasizes the emerging self, the self that is continual interaction in the organism/environment field and that integrates the field. However, if one thinks in Newtonian mechanistic terms this would mean there is no continuity of self from past through present and no difference in functioning of the self between someone with little overall self-cohesion and someone with self-cohesion since there is no "real self" (Tobin, 1982).

In field theory all events and things are constructed according to the conditions of the field and the interests of the perceiver. Everything real is constructed in this way, no matter how materially concrete or abstract. Some now believe all concepts, memory, etc., are not stored and then remembered as much as reconstructed (see discussion in Gergen, 1991, especially at p. 26). "Things" are phenomenologically constructed according to the situation as well as needs, memory of past understandings, etc. Without understanding field theory, the Gestalt therapy notion that the self does not exist "as a fixed institution" apart from the current organism/environment field (Perls, Hefferline and Goodman, 1951, p. 5) is misinterpreted. The self is a process, it is as real as any tangible existent, and it is constructed in the current organism/environment field.

The Gestalt therapy concept of self can account both for a concept of self that has cohesion, wholeness and continuity over time and for the self that at any moment is always constructed in a particular context. Field theory enables Gestalt therapy to keep the focus on the person as active agent, keep mindful of the complexity of field relations in the present and the changes that inevitably occur over time and in different contexts, and the differences in how people construct their selves. This Gestalt therapy concept of self does need further elaboration and development, more than appropriate for this article.

Some people construct a self that has harmony and continuity while flexibly adapting to the current field. People with self disorders frequently cannot do so, and their self-constructions do not harmoniously integrate previous constructions, do not maintain a sense of cohesion, continuity, safety and self-esteem, especially when the current field is stressful. Instead their self-processes and self-experience are often fragmented, based on rigidly fixed negative introjects and pictures of themselves, their sense of self-esteem and cohesion easily disrupted by the forces in the current field, without clear and flexible union of who they are and what the situation is. Other people construct a fixed sense of self that is not affected by the environment, that is always the same, regardless of context. This fixed Gestalt has no flexibility and only a limited capacity to grow by being transformed by the interaction in the field.

There are many dynamic concepts in Gestalt therapy that can be adequately understood only in field theoretical terms. A few of these concepts are: organism/environment field; boundary; support; figure/ground; dialogic relation; phenomenological construction of perception; and so forth.

Limitations on the Use of Field Theory

Sometimes field theory is discussed in a manner that deters interest.

What is heard often is such a simplified aspect of field theory, perhaps a vague reference to Kurt Lewin, and then a change of subject, that people don't see it as worth all the hoopla. But field theory is more than a semantic device or just anything referring to the whole of a system. It is more than Lewin's topology.

Some of the best field theory discussions occur indirectly when other theoretical perspectives are discussed. For example, phenomenology, dialogue and the entire theoretical structure of *Gestalt Therapy* is based on field theory and field theory interweaves with many of the most important but most difficult aspects of those perspectives. When phenomenology is fully understood, aspects of field theory must be understood also.

Frankly I think I am clearer when I discuss phenomenology or Gestalt psychology, even about aspects of field theory, than when I discuss field theory directly. So, out of a good sense of tactics, cowardice, laziness or ignorance, I often teach phenomenology and dialogue and less often directly discuss field theory. This does not give people a fighting chance at understanding field theory so they can decide if it is worth the effort. In part that is what has motivated me to write this essay.

Sometimes field theory seems to be used as if it could give validity and prestige to some point of view. It is as if saying that something is in accord with field theory principles makes it true. This associates whatever one is advocating with the prestige of physics — and may indeed confer a modicum of prestige. I don't like the use of field theory to confer status and prestige.

Field theory does not give validation. For example, I think field theory can provide a decent post hoc rationale for how mystical or transpersonal ideas might be possible, but no more than that. Yet I have heard people use field theory as if it could actually validate transpersonal experience or mystical ideas. What I am saying here is not a commentary on mystical or transpersonal experience, but rather a comment on limitations in using field theory as validation.

Sometimes field theory seems to be treated in Gestalt therapy as if it were a religious icon, one that can be invoked to get a positive and revered response. "Field" is a "good word." Sometimes the discussions about field theory strike me as two children saying "Na na na na! I am more field theoretical than you." I have heard some react that way to Latner's field theory analysis of the Polsters' work (Latner, 1983; Polster and Polster, 1973) and dismiss his analysis as "picky," asking "so what?" This is unfortunate.

Theories can provide guidance and cogency but cannot prove the truth or falsity of a proposition. A theory is merely a theory, a systematic integration of ideas. As such it may be useful, comforting, stimulating, provocative, of heuristic value, and so forth. But in postmodern science, theories are not regarded as any kind of absolute truth. Putting something into field theory terms does not make it true.

Joel Latner states: "Rather than believing that some [theories] are more true than other, it seems to me that some speak more to me than to others" (Latner, 1983, p. 85). Field theory is a point of view that "speaks to me," one I find useful — but it is not a truth.

Perls, Hefferline and Goodman (1951) go beyond this when they claim that field theory is the "original, undistorted, natural approach to life." This implies that field theory is true and the other ways of thinking inherently erroneous. Latner disputes this claim (1983, pp. 86, 87), and I agree with him. I believe it is more consistent to say that no theory is inherently true or best for all purposes. Field theory is the theory upon which Gestalt therapy theory is based, and it has many advantages. Some of us find it more natural. This is our preference.

In physics, field theories are essentially mathematical formulations, and capable of mathematical manipulation and mathematical proofs and ultimately subjected to empirical verification or falsification. The verbal formulations coming out of physics are only approximations. The metaphysics and world view of physicists (verbal formulations) do not change as a result of their mathematical work with field theory. In another essay in this collection (#12, Modes of Thinking in Gestalt Therapy, 1984a) I cite a physicist (Sachs, pp. 92-93) who gives a striking illustration of two physicists opposing each other in orientation and philosophy, and not altering their opposition to each other at all when they discover that their mathematics formulations were actually equivalent step by step.

Field theory indicates "truth" even less in psychology. For without the mathematical base for field theory, without direct empirical tests that distinguish between field theoretical statements and others (or between various field theoretical presentations) there is no empirical way of deciding between formulations.

Some enthusiasts make field theory into a political issue, pointing to any common use of language as Newtonian, hence a violation of Gestalt therapy theory, regardless of context or degree of clarity, and the entire discussion therefore invalid. I do not find this knee-jerk reaction useful. Often simpler Newtonian language communicates more clearly. I think discrimination is called for.

In a clinical context one must use whatever language communicates with the patient and also furthers the development of a therapeutic relationship based on empathy, respect, understanding and caring. For example, "You have no ears" is not a good Gestalt therapy theoretical formulation. It implies that hearing is a possession of the person rather than an integral process of the organism/environment field. Although it does communicate clearly, and therefore might be useful, it also sounds accusatory and insulting. "You have no ears" shows the therapist is not thinking in either field theory or dialogic terms. This interpretation is Newtonian and non-dialogic in the assumption that the difficulty rests only within the patient and not between therapist and patient. The "You have no ears" formulation reflects a perspective that is narrow in the range of variables that is expressed and one-sided in its attribution of causality. Might the therapist's attitude not have something to do with the patient's not listening?

Sometimes a statement in Newtonian language communicates quite clearly and does further the therapeutic relationship. One attempt to do that, one that I have been finding increasingly irritating, is the reference to the "inner child." This makes a thing out of a process, definitely not field theoretical. Yet sometimes it is useful terminology and can facilitate an empathic bond between the therapist and the patient.

Sometimes when I hear "My inner child did it," it sounds like a bad joke, as if saying: "I am not responsible, my inner child did it." When someone even leaves out the word "inner" and says "my child" felt such and such, and for a moment I think the patient is talking about one of his or her actual children, it seems like a bad joke indeed. The attitude is sometimes that "It is not I who has this feeling — and I am not responsible for and have no choice about the inner child, it was created in the past by my abusive parents." There are very important subjective experiences such a patient is expressing that need to be heard, honored and made clear. But this can be done through field language: "I was scared, lonely, despairing and didn't believe I had any choice, as I felt when I was a child — when I really had no good options."

A former patient wrote to me of her therapy experience with me, reminding me of metaphoric imagery in Newtonian language that had been extremely useful to her that had emerged in therapy.

To describe my static, unrelenting, unyielding sense of desolate isolation, I pictured a blanched fetus tucked inside a popcorn kernel. (After I discovered Guntrip [she refers to Guntrip, 1969], the fetus was wearing glasses and reading Guntrip.)

The fetus was turned away from the world, and could not hear or feel anything beyond the kernel.

A major change, resulting from the long periods of intense and sustained focus on contacting, and especially on our relationship, was the emergence of the experience of *loneliness*, as opposed to simple isolation.

As I was able to bring my loneliness into the contact with you, eventually a green shoot grew out of the top of the kernel. A pathway of connection between my isolated sense of myself, and our contacting. I knew that green shoot meant I would never feel utterly and totally isolated again.

Later, with my analyst, after going through the worst depression of my life, the world inside my kernel moved from being by definition private and unshareable, to being *in principle* (and in experience with her) shareable (knowable to another).

But the connection between the two worlds (my lived-in world and my kernel world) came with the green shoot.

Language must be fitted to the context and is not in and of itself true or false. The clinical test is what works with the individual patient. Ease of presentation and articulation predominates over theoretical accuracy in many contexts. Shafer (1976) constructs a thoroughgoing process language for psychoanalysis, one even more radical than ours. Yet he makes clear that this is very important in theoretical discussion and formulations and not binding in the clinical situation. The field theoretical physicist talks Newtonian language when referring to instruments, desks, lunch, promotions, etc.

The mechanistic, Newtonian theoretical system works well enough within the parameters of its purview. As long as we are dealing with moderate-sized bodies moving slowly through space, Newtonian theoretical predictions work fine. For some of our work as therapists the simple mechanical language may even be superior for simple communication to patients.

Unfortunately, many Gestalt therapists who do not use field theory language do not realize what they are doing. This means that they are not merely being pragmatic about their language usage, but that they are not aware of the theoretical conflict between their language in practicing or talking about Gestalt therapy and the Gestalt therapy theory itself. When this sloppy language is also used in lecturing or writing about Gestalt therapy theory, it is most unfortunate.

Understanding Field Theory

Field theory is an approach to studying something and "field" is a basic tool in that approach. Anything can be studied from a field perspective — events, objects, organisms or systems. What makes an approach field theoretical is that its philosophy and methodology adhere to certain principles.

This does not mean there is a "correct" or true field theory. There are many differing and equally valid field theories and I know of no valid claim for any particular version of field theory being *the* way.

The field is phenomenologically defined. The scope and exact nature of the field and the methods used varies depending on the investigator and what is being studied. The field may be as small and fast as subatomic particles, or as large as the universe. The forces in some fields can be observed with the five human senses, in others they cannot. The field may be tangible and physical or may be intangible. In Gestalt therapy we study people in their organism/environment fields. The environment of the organism/environment field may be a school, business, family, couple, training group, an individual in his or her life space, and so forth.

In the following sections nine general characteristics of field theories will be discussed. Following this discussion the article will end with a formal definition of field theory and a summary of the discussion. [Many of the topics in this article are discussed in more detail in other articles in this volume, especially #12, "Modes of Thinking in Gestalt Therapy" (1984), but also #6, "Clinical Phenomenology" (1976) and #8, "Gestalt Therapy: Its Inheritance from Gestalt Psychology" (1982) and #11, "The Self in Gestalt Therapy: Reply to Tobin" (1983)].

The characteristics are listed here to orient the reader:

Characteristics of Fields
1. A field is a systematic web of relationships.
2. A field is continuous in space and time.
3. Everything is of-a-field.
4. Phenomena are determined by the whole field.
5. The field is a unitary whole: everything affects everything else in the field.

Additional Field Theory Attitudes
6. Perceived reality is configured by the relationship between the observer and the observed.
7. The Principle of Contemporaneity.
8. Process: everything is becoming.
9. Insight into genotypic invariants.

Characteristics of Fields

A Field is a Systematic Web of Relationships
I define field as: "A totality of mutually influencing forces that together form a unified interactive whole."

The field approach is a holistic one. Lewin's Principle of Relatedness states that an event is always the results of an interaction between two or more facts. Each phenomenon studied is studied in the context of a complex web of interrelated forces that come together in a time and place, form a unified whole that we call the field and dynamically change over time. Or as English and English put it: "In psychology, field is used to emphasize the complex totality of interdependent influences within which an organism functions, the constellation of interdependent factors that account for a psychological event" (p. 206).

The field is interactive, determined by the forces concurrently present. This preference for interaction includes a reluctance or suspiciousness of simple one-way linear causality, since these linear explanations do not account very well for the complexity of multiple factors and mutual influences that occur in interaction.

Simple linear explanations involve additional difficulties that will be discussed below, e.g., they do not emphasize contemporaneity, and often posit "action-at-a-distance."

Recently a health care provider told me that things always seem to go wrong when a particular orderly is on duty. How do we explain that? There are a number of variables, each of which could be formulated into a simple linear explanation. The health care provider is a woman and the orderly is a man. Is gender a determining factor? Is the woman dominating, or perhaps repetitively allows herself to be a victim? One could formulate a number of psychodynamic interpretations. An additional fact is that the woman is a physician. Is there a problem relating to the male orderly's difficulty with physicians? With authority? Or with women? The physician's difficulty with men? Furthermore, the physician is black and the orderly is Hispanic. Factors of cultural and race relations seem to be involved. And a closer examination of the structure of the institution might well reveal structural factors making such conflicts more likely. For example, the physician is a recent addition to the staff. How does this structure and this staff welcome new physicians? How does the poorly paid orderly who supports a family feel toward the better paid single physician?

An adequate understanding of this situation requires relating multiple factors: individual psychodynamics of two individuals, political and structural factors of staff relations, cultural and race relations, and so forth. Were I to simply use a cognitive map involving simple causality between this woman's childhood and her present difficulty, it would be inadequate and simplistic. Were I to reduce this to a simple interpretation of how women or blacks or black women are treated, it would leave out the factors of the characterological functioning of the individuals involved. Were I to reduce this to a problem of the structure of the institution, it would not be adequate. Yet all of these factors were very much involved in this situation.

Relationship is Ubiquitous

Relationship is inherent in existence as we know it. From a field theory standpoint, everything that exists consists of a web of relationships. A field is a web of relationships and exists in a

296

context of even larger webs of relationship. Knowing is also a relationship, i.e., between perceiver and perceived — as we will discuss in Section 6. We perceive things in relationship, e.g., to what we want to know, what we believe, background of the event being observed, history, our needs, linguistic influences, and so forth.

Perls, Hefferline and Goodman set forth the basic Gestalt therapy notion that contact — relationship, is the first reality (phenomenologically) and the organism has no meaning apart from its environment (and the phenomenological environment has meaning only as perceived by a perceiver).

"Existence precedes essence." Existence is relationship in the world. This contrasts with both Platonic idealism and Aristotelian logical categorization in which an inherent essence precedes existence. Existentially there is no absolute nature. There can be no human traits without human existence and consciousness, and there cannot be consciousness except as a relationship in the organism/environment field. Language and concepts are learned or created as a social process; they are not absolute essences.

When I was in high school we learned a model of how the physical world is organized at a subatomic level that was mechanistic and did not emphasize relationship. The model was like a miniature solar system, with electrons circling around the nucleus, as planets circle around the sun. The nucleus and the electrons were pictured as solid, each thing isolated in its own position — with space between them. Through the empty space between these discontinuous particles, somehow was created an order. Of course, the particles were moved by some kind of energy (electromagnetic, analogous to the force of gravity in the astronomical level) that were of different stuff than the particles. A very Newtonian model.

However, now physicists who study the subatomic world do not see it in this way. The electrons and the energy are not separate stuff, the "solid" particles are intense energy concentrations (which are waves or particles depending on how they are observed), the entire structure works by the relationships among the energy concentrations. The effects are caused by ripples through the space of the field and through the time of the field.

Relationship is Inherent, Dynamic and Organized

The web of any natural phenomenon is an organized, integrated whole. There is differentiation between a relationship web and that which is outside it, and there is differentiation within the relationship web. There is an inherent dynamic organization in the web of relationship. Stars are in gravitational relationship, and the system is organized and integrated. The state of organization of the web changes over time, sometimes disintegrating (entropy), sometimes forming into better Gestalten (prägnanz).

The Gestalt psychologists made much of the fact that organization in the field was inherent in the relationships of the field and not by "special arrangement." The natural organization of the field is like a river finding its natural course by interacting with the other forces of nature, as opposed to concrete pathways being added to force the water into rigid and predetermined pathways. When there are problems or dysfunctions in the organization of the field, the solutions are also present in the dynamics of the field (Wertheimer, 1945).

Good theory clarifies the inherent structure of the field (see Section 9 on insight). Theory is itself a field, and good theory is developed by searching for natural factors that are inherent in the theory and that reveal insight into the inherent structure of the field of study, rather than arbitrarily adding on explanatory factors or utilizing data that has no inherent relationship to the theory.

Fields are always made up of multiple factors with complex, multiple and differentiated interrelationships. In field theory a web of relationships is always determined by a multiplicity of determining variables, with an inherent systemic organization of the whole that is vital toward understanding the phenomenon being studied. Inevitably there are crucial contextual factors that are an inherent part of the field way of thinking, as they are not in Aristotelian logic or Newtonian thinking.

Perhaps the import of this can be understood by contrast with the attitude of structuralists such as Wundt. He saw psychology as analyzing mental contents into elements, and then finding the laws of their connection. This was a mental chemistry approach that emphasized elements and associations and did not emphasize the dynamic whole (Mesiak and Sexton, 1966, p. 80). This mental chemistry approach was like the Newtonian mechanistically

298

determined universe in which the whole can be taken apart like a clock, and put together again. To the structuralist the whole exactly equals the sum of the parts and the observer could know absolutely, without affecting that which is studied.

A Field is Continuous in Space and Time

"Field" and "forces" carry the connotation of dynamic, of movement and energy (Mesiak and Sexton, 1966, p. 354). This usage derives literally (in physics) and by analogy (in psychology) from the study of electromagnetic fields and treatment of time in relativity theory (English and English, 1958, p. 207). Using the field approach one thinks of living, moving, changing, energetic interacting over time. The forces of the field are of a whole and develop over time.

"Field: Something that exists throughout space and time, as opposed to a particle that exists at only one point at a time" (Hawking, 1988, p. 184). The field takes the place that was occupied by material points in Newton's mechanics (Einstein, 1950, p. 74).

Lewin points out that in psychology, "As in physics, the grouping of events and objects into ... logical dichotomies is being replaced by grouping with the aid of serial concepts which permit of continuous variation, partly owing simply to wider experience and the recognition that transition stages are always present" (1938, p. 22). In a sense the field view is of the world as a continuum (Einstein, 1961, p. 55) rather than either/or dichotomies.

Until the introduction of the field concept in the nineteenth century, the description of nature was in terms of things,

> ...separate, perceivable, distinguishable bits of matter, each at a particular location at a particular time, and moving under its own `self energy' or under the influence that each exerts on the other. The field concept, on the other hand, asserted that the most fundamental description of the material world should rather be in terms of continuity — just as one envisions the distribution of waves on the surface of turbulent water. (Sachs, 1973, p. 5)

In the lens of field theory, movement replaces static, events replace things, continuity replaces discontinuity.

Everything Is Of-a-Field

> ... objects are not independent physical forces but gain their
> object quality from the organism that reacts to them....
> (English and English, p. 207)

Objects, organisms, etc., only exist phenomenologically as a part of a phenomenologically determined field and have meaning only in interaction in such a field. Lewin states that any "manifestation of energy by a person ... must be defined in terms of the whole field" (English and English, p. 206). This includes both the influences of the person on the rest of the field and the influences of the rest of the field on the person. This is a crucial aspect of field theory, and identical with aspects of phenomenology (especially, that reality is a phenomenological construction of the observer and the observed) and the dialogic view that "I" is only of the "I-Thou" or the "I-it."

Being *of a field* is not just being *in* a field. "In a field" defines the organism or object in absolute terms, i.e., outside the field, and then adds the field for context. A person has an existence (form, essence) irrespective of the field, and is conceptually placed in a field. The of-a-field view does not consider anything to be not of-a-field.

A person and an environment are of a field, the organismic/environmental field. People are of that field and are of the organizing and determining force of the field. The psychological field does not exist apart from the people; people do not exist apart from a field. It is not a case of simple relationship between a separate individual and an external environment. The individual is only defined at a time by the field of which he or she is a part, and the field can only be defined via someone's experience or viewpoint.

The distinction between of-a-field and in-a-field is often missed. Even English and English's definition of field and field theory did not clearly distinguish "in a field" from "of a field." They define field as

1. An area having boundaries. As used in psychology, both field (area) and boundary may be used metaphorically. E.g., when we speak of rules setting boundaries to action, we refer not merely to a physical place but to the kind of action permitted (English and English, 1958, p. 206). "Field" also refers to "2. the entire space within which a set of forces operates." (English and English, p. 206)

It is as if English and English consider the field to be merely an empty receptacle for events and things.

Not of-a-Field

The idea that an organism can only exist in a field is a viewpoint of field theory and not objective fact. There are alternatives to the of-a-field viewpoint. In order to clarify this I will critique two other viewpoints, both of which can still be seen in psychology.

Galilean Versus Aristotelian Modes of Thought

Lewin contrasts the field (Galilean) view with Aristotelian classification logic (Lewin, 1938). In the Aristotelian system, each thing has an essence or virtue, and that essence is the first cause and teleological end goal of the existence of that thing. The thing is determined by its essence (form), not by the field of forces of which it is part. Platonic systems also have this characteristic. Most psychological classification systems have this same logic.

Example. Patient is rageful at the therapist who confronted the patient with an interpretation that the patient is partly responsible for an unfortunate interaction in the patient's life. The therapist thinks: this patient is upset because of his narcissistic personality disorder. A more field theoretical description might be that in the field of interaction between the therapist and patient, the patient experienced the therapist as not understanding or caring about the patient's subjective experience, and that with the patient's experience of a lack of understanding the patient's sense of self-cohesion was disrupted and rageful feelings emerged. The propensity toward this disruption of self-cohesion is what the narcissistic personality disorder terminology refers to.

Both characterizations may be true, and not necessarily contradictory, but the point of view is very different and has different consequences. The field view looks at the current relationship forces, and the classificatory approach looks at the essence of the patient apart from the current interaction. In the classificatory approach contextual factors are considered neither inherent nor necessary for understanding.

Since the Aristotelian system was a classification approach, that which could be studied was only the frequent and invariant. Moreover, only the invariant and frequent were considered lawful. You know the essence of something by the class to which it belongs. When you knew the essence of an object, you knew the class to which it belonged, and that was the explanation of the object. How did you know the class? You knew the class by the objects that comprised it. Of course, this was circular.

In the "of-a-field" approach every event is unique, and is also orderly and can be studied. Malcolm Parlett call this The Principle of Singularity (1990). In field theory any event can be studied, since it can be observed, measured, etc., without having a large number of repetitions in order to classify.

The Aristotelian classification system tended toward "classification in terms of values" especially absolute, value-laden dichotomies: good and bad, heaven and earth, and so forth (Lewin, 1938, pp.3-4). To Aristotle the orbit of planets must be circular, since circular motion is a better motion. This seemed deductively true to him, as it did seem deductively true to him that the earth revolved around the sun.

These value classifications and dichotomies can be compared with dialectical polarities that are "of the field," unified and differentiated wholes such as yin/yang. The positive and negative poles of an electrical field are not value-laden dichotomies, but belong to a unifying whole. Knowledge of these dialectical polarities arise from descriptive interaction in the field, not primarily from deduction.

Mechanistic Natural Science

The classic ("modern") natural science approach, e.g., Newtonian physics, also does not look at events as being of-a-field. In Newtonian physics objects and events are in empty space. "In the framework of classical physics, the concept of field appeared as an auxiliary concept, in cases in which matter was treated as a continuum" (Einstein, 1960, p. 144). In this dualistic system space and objects are polar opposites, one being empty and the other being solid.

Events "in the field" in mechanistic science are discontinuous, not of a whole. A star could be said to influence the movement of a planet, when no intervening media conducting a force are shown. Influences or effects can happen at a distance in classic physics. Time, the time it takes light to transmit information from one thing to another and create an effect, time to move through a continuous medium, did not have to be taken into account in the Newtonian system (Sachs, 1973).

One could try to expand this natural science viewpoint and look at multiple factors interacting and say that the object is in a field. But this concept of an object and space being of different stuff, this dichotomy of empty space and filled mass, is not field theory. Of-a-field refers to everything being of the field, of the dynamic organizing of the field. In field theory everything is made up of these forces. In physics since Einstein, mass and energy are of the same stuff, they do not constitute a dichotomy. They can be converted one to the other. Mass when looked at in subatomic physics can be understood as organized patterns of energy.

In psychology there is a strong history of following this Newtonian viewpoint. The mental chemistry approach of structuralists such as Wundt and Titchener were prime examples, and to some extent all positivistic, linear, causality statements and controversies in psychology are of the same paradigm. The paradigm that goes beyond Newtonian mechanics in physics and psychology is strikingly parallel in attitude, e.g., between Einstein's field theory and Gestalt psychology (for example, Latner, 1983).

Phenomena Are Determined by the Whole Field

Lewin: Behavior is a function of the field of which it is a part; a field analysis begins with situations as a whole. Experiencing is also a function of the field of which it is a part; an experiential field analysis emphasizes the situation as a whole.

Every event, experience, object or organism is determined by the field of which it is part. All movements of any part are determined by the whole field. "...the properties of related phenomena are derived from, or dependent on, the total field of which they are at that time a part" (English and English, p.206). The organism/environment field determines the person. Of course, this is but one way of expressing the Gestalt psychology principle that the whole determines the parts. Parlett calls this The Principle of Organization: "Meaning derives from looking at the total situation, the totality of co-existing facts" (1990).

A patient's progress is a function of the whole field. It is not only determined by the patient's motivation and strength, but by the skill of the therapist, the relationship between the therapist and patient, the factors of organization of the delivery system (clinic, hospital, insurance company, etc.), the family and friends who are part of the patient's life space and so forth. I am thinking now of a patient who stayed in group beyond the first two weeks primarily because her field included a prior patient of mine who was a therapist and told her to stick it out a while longer. She did and the therapy has been quite successful. I am also thinking about a borderline patient who went into the hospital against my advice only because he wanted to come multiple times per week, and his insurance would only pay for this if he were in the hospital. I feared that the regressive pull of the hospital environment would be too seductive for this patient. And indeed it was and he succumbed to it and subsequently spent many years in hospitals. Patients are part of and determined by complex whole fields and we ignore such forces only at our peril.

This principle applies to Gestalt therapy training workshops. Quality of training depends on a multiplicity of factors, including group processes. Sometimes Gestalt therapy workshop leaders emphasize 1-1 work early in the workshop and put little attention on how the individuals in the group are coping with being in the group. This ignores much of the field and teaches trainees to also ignore much of what is actually happening in the field.

When factors of safety are given empathic attention early in the group, the subsequent 1-1 work is different than when the group leader prematurely does intensive one-to-one work in the group and doesn't show attention and sensitivity to and caring about the group as a whole. The whole field determines the parts. Some trainees show difficulties later in the group stemming from not taking the time early to deal with their place in the group. Premature focus on individual work puts a premium on those prepared for that risk, and devalues those who are not so prepared. If the group focuses on the sharp figure of the work of trainees who are ready to work early, those who need to observe, stay back, who are anxious, who fear shame and humiliation, who need help in finding their role in the group, and so forth, do not build the internal or interpersonal support to do their work later in the group. The result can be intensive individual work with those who are able to rapidly focus on work with the trainer, work that enhances the charismatic quality of the group leader at the expense of individual and group needs, and damages the overall development of the group and the training and personal development of many of the group members. Such an approach meets the narcissistic needs of the therapist rather than the needs of the group.

When the group leader respects and helps the group explicate the anxiety, fright, shame, guilt, and so forth that participants often feel at the beginning of the workshop, it is more likely that the individuals will feel met, accepted, understood and safe in the group. This also serves as a better model for therapists in training in their work with regular patients in their practice. When this does not happen early in the workshop, when there is differential value on openness and risk taking and not on self-protective processes, the group becomes unsafe for many. In such circumstances, some will increase their defensiveness, often becoming the target of negative evaluations by the leader and/or the rest of the group. In my experience, group leaders who rush into individual work and do not respect the safety needs at the beginning of workshops, often do not at all recognize a problem let alone their contribution to the problem. Unfortunately the participants who suffer from this group attitude are often also not aware of the extent to which their suffering is due to the way the group leader structures the group rather than to their own inadequacy.

When I do a workshop of five - nine days, the time spent dealing with feelings about being in the group in the first two - three days pays great dividends in terms of group cohesion, therapy in the training context and training itself. When this does not happen, in the end the group cohesion is not as great, the active participation of all group members suffers, the depth of individual work and theoretical understanding by the end of the workshop is more shallow, the level of warmth, satisfaction and excitement is less and problems of divisiveness and structural difficulties increase. When I have been part of a team of trainers serving in a series with a group, I have noticed that if the first trainer takes the time and shows respect for the variety of personalities, feelings, fears, roles in the group, that the work with later trainers goes better. Conversely, when the first trainer does not do this, there are more problems later with defensive group members, with development of group cohesion and safety, and other group difficulties.

The Field is a Unitary Whole: Everything Affects Everything Else

The essential property of a field is its dynamic aspect. In a dynamic field there is interaction between all of its parts so that, as Kurt Lewin puts it,"the state of any part of this field depends on every other part of the field" (Misiak and Sexton, 1966, p. 355). In a field of energy all parts interrelate and any alteration in any part of the field ripples through the field. This is one of the necessary aspects to our use of the word "field." In fact: "At a very superficial level, the reader may take field theory to mean an emphasis upon the interrelatedness of a present event, upon the totality of influences that determine behavior" (English and English, 1958, p. 207).

The unified whole can and must be differentiated into parts in order to get a dynamic understanding. But the whole is a systemic unity, and not one composed by addition of elements.

Perhaps the clearest example of this in psychology is a family. When something happens to one member of a family, everyone is affected in some way. When one person in a family changes, everyone in the family is affected in some way. Often the family as a whole has a need that is embodied in one person, e.g., the identified patient. Everyone in the family is affected by this. If that identified patient should change and not carry the family pathology, the system changes, e.g., some other family member may begin to carry the pathology.

Another example is the area of organizational policy and structure. Often small changes have huge effects, because everything in the field is affected in unpredictable ways. In recent years chaos theory, one kind of field theory, has talked about this kind of unpredictable result of small changes. When people in charge of planning make changes without adequately considering the effects on every aspect of the field, there are often unfortunate, negative and perhaps preventable disruptions in functioning.

Other Characteristics of Field Theory

Perceived Reality is Configured by the Relationship Between Observer and Observed

From a field theory point of view, no field can be defined apart from specifying the time, space and awareness (including modes of observation and measurement) of the observer. Nothing is absolute and there is no such thing as "objective."

In a prior paper (#8, Gestalt Therapy: Its Inheritance from Gestalt Psychology, 1982) I observed that: (1) "How one sees is in part a function of how one looks" (p. 31); (2) "The observer affects the object of his study" (p.31); Lynne Jacobs adds: "Also, the observed affects the observer, because there is the observed's observations of the observer's observing!!" (Personal communication, August, 1991); (3) "No one can see it all. One can only be clear about what vantage point is being used to describe what aspects of the phenomena"(p.32). This is a postmodern viewpoint that denies the simple Newtonian assumptions about being separate from nature and able to measure it objectively.

What we look at, how we look, the context of our looking all determine what we observe. In early modern physics it was thought that some phenomena occurred in waves, some in particles. In postmodern physics it was discovered that the same phenomena can be seen as a wave or a particle — depending on the mode of observation. This was quite upsetting to some of the greatest minds in physics. It seems that reality is not objective and absolute.

Looking from the astronomic distances of relativity theory, we can see that even the "simple" question of contemporaneity and of what comes first in time is relative to someone's position. You know two things happen at the same time when the light waves from the two events strike some arbitrary point (the observer's eyes) at the same time. Change the angle of the observation, and the events are not exactly contemporaneous.

An interesting consequence of this unification of space and time was that it no longer became possible to talk of absolute simultaneity. For it now had to be concluded that if a pair of events should appear to happen simultaneously to one observer, they would not generally appear to be simultaneous to other observers who would be in motion relative to the first observer. This, of course, is because time became a subjective entity, a measure that depended on the condition of motion of whoever was referring to it (Sachs, 1973, p. 50).

One knows which of two events comes first by the light waves of one reaching an observer earlier. Imagine event 1 comes before event 2 from the vantage point of an observer at one end of the universe. The time/space position of event 1 is closer or earlier to this observer. But if there is an observer on the exact opposite end of the universe, the light waves from event 2 might seem earlier or closer to that second observer. Which is correct? It is relative to the observer. There is no absolute time, no absolute reality.

Not only does how we look determine what we see, but often-times the act of active observation actually changes what we observe. This can be seen most clearly in subatomic physics in which the light of the measuring instrument affects the phenomena being studied so that there is a limit to the simultaneous measurement of position and movement of the phenomenon. As you put energy into measuring one, you affect the other.

In psychology it is clear that the observer affects the observation. There is a vast amount of evidence of "experimenter bias," in which slight changes in wording of the instructions or demeanor of the instructor changes the effects one gets. But more amazing, even rats seem to behave differently according to the expectations of the experimenter. People who are tested perform differently on tests depending on characteristics of the tester. For example, minority group members usually perform better if the tester is of the same minority group. Yet test scores are too often reported as if they are objective measurements with an existence unaffected by the observer or tester.

The Principle of Contemporaneity

The time center of ourselves as conscious human time-space events is the present. There is no other reality than the present. (Perls, 1947, p. 81)

Lewin's Principle of Contemporaneity stated that anything that has an effect is present in the here and now, or in other words, only present facts can produce present behavior and experience. The emphasis on the here and now has been such a highlighted part of Gestalt therapy that it is familiar to all Gestalt therapists.

Contemporaneity is defined in Gestalt therapy theory in terms of the phenomenology of a person in the experienced here and now. From the beginning Gestalt therapy theory emphasized the here and now as the central point in a flow of time from past to future. The "now" has not been considered either static or absolute. Awareness is a sensory event occurring in the here and now, but includes remembering and anticipating. Getting lost in any time zone, losing the flow of time, losing awareness of the present function of awareness, was always considered a distortion in awareness and often plays a part in psychological dysfunction. It is good Gestalt therapy method to talk about the past when doing so is the figure of interest in the present and part of lively current functioning. Not talking about the past when it is currently needed is as dysfunctional as talking about the past in order to avoid some aspect of the present. The Gestalt therapy theory of contemporaneity has been largely unchanged since the beginning.

Sometimes the here-and-now concept of Gestalt therapy theory was and is distorted in practice or in talking about the theory. In the theoretical formulation, the past and the future, that which happened and that which is predicted, that which is presently unfinished from the past and that which is wanted in the future, are all part of the here and now. This was often distorted into a hedonistic concept that nothing was important except momentary excitement. Although neither the hedonism nor the static conception of here and now were ever good Gestalt therapy theory, it was often talked about in this way and this distortion supported the "boom-boom-boom" style of Gestalt therapy. I discussed this in my first paper about Gestalt therapy in 1969 (#3, A Review of the Practice of Gestalt Therapy, written in 1969). Recently I have been discussing the necessity for an enlarged sense of contemporaneity (#1, Recent Trends in Gestalt Therapy in the United States And What We Need To Learn From Them (1991), and Essay #9, Assimilating Diagnostic and Psychoanalytic Perspectives into Gestalt Therapy, 1988).

Contemporaneity is one of the themes running through field theories in general. In physics since Einstein, there can be no meaningful statement of a physical phenomenon without specification of both time and place. In order to study an event, either the subatomic events of quantum mechanics or the celestial movement of relativity theory, the event must be placed in time and space. It is the measurement of an event in a succession of time and place events that defines movement (see next section).

One of the hallmarks of relativity theory, and most twentieth century physics, is the idea that there can be no action-at-a-distance, that is, that the connection between cause and effect must be some connection in time and space. The simple linear causality in which something in a current field is determined without a force present in the current field by something in the past is no longer acceptable in post-modern field theory. When an element exerts force on another, it is now thought that instead of the Newtonian concept of action-at-a-distance, there is a "potential field of forces that fills all of space in a continuous fashion" (Sachs, 1973, p.7).

The forces of energy that make up the field interact in the present; they are simultaneously present. There is no action-at-a-distance, just as there is no energy moving things apart from the energy of the field. This is virtually the same as Lewin's Principle of Contemporaneity. In psychology: if the past, genetics, society have an influence, then the forces have to be present in the contemporary field. Effects happen when phenomena touch each other, when they interact in the same time and place. When one becomes aware of forces outside a defined field affecting the processes being studied, then the boundary or definition of the particular field is enlarged to encompass a greater territory. The new enlarged field has all of the properties of any field, i.e., being of a whole, everything in the field affecting everything else, development over time, etc.

Example. Consider borderline patients who blame their parents for their current state, creating an air of bitterness, believing themselves victims, wanting revenge. Developmental explorations reveal abusive childhoods. But how does the past cause the present? It is carried forward by the patient in the form of beliefs, unresolved emotional processes that are constantly renewed, body posture, intense affective states that are kept hot rather than completed, images of self that are in the form of fixed Gestalten, etc. These are all processes that the patient does. To the degree that the patient does differently in the present, to that degree the past will no longer create the dysfunction. The power for health and pathology is in the current field, although the forces started in some prior field.

Process: Everything Is Becoming

It is often said that Gestalt therapy is a process therapy. Indeed process is a necessary and central aspect of field theory. But what is process?

Everything and everyone moves and becomes. In a process orientation everything is energy (movement, action), is structured by the dynamic forces of the field, and moves through time and space. Just as field treats phenomena as a continuous whole rather treating discrete particles, it treats the field as in motion rather than static.

Parlett: "The Principle of Changing Process refers to the fact that experience is provisional rather than permanent. Nothing is fixed and static in an absolute way" (Parlett, 1990). It is interesting that the universe is now considered expanding or contracting, when before the twentieth-century no one thought the universe expanded or contracted. Everything changes. Even that which appears static is in fact changing over time.

Process from a Physics Viewpoint

Perhaps it would be useful to start our discussion of the concept of process with the relatively simple area of physics.

Physics studies physical phenomena as they change location in time and space. What is happening in physics is process, i.e., movement through space and time. Movement is merely being at a point in space at time one, at another space at time two, another at time three and so forth. Movement is defined in terms of time and space; time and space have meaning in reference to movement through it.

The post-modern viewpoint in physics accepts that all physical process is located in both time and space, and is in movement relative to the frame of reference of the observer. Measurement itself requires movement, e.g., the movement of light waves to measure a physical phenomenon and back to the observer for recording.

Physics deals with mass and energy. In Newtonian physics these were considered of different stuff, i.e., mass was inert and moved by energy. Since Einstein this is no longer the case. Solid matter is composed subatomically of energy, can be converted into energy, and asserts energetic influences on other bodies.

Mass is a quantity of matter. The word comes from the Latin word *massa* "that which adheres together like dough" and the Greek word *maza* "a barley cake." In physics it is "the quantity of matter in a body as measured in its relation to inertia; mass is determined for a given body by dividing the weight of the body by the acceleration due to gravity." Thus the meaning of mass involves energy and movement (Webster, p. 1107).

Energy refers to potential force or capacity for action, or a force-producing effect. It comes from Latin and Greek roots referring to action, operation, active, at work. In physics it refers to "the capacity for doing work and overcoming resistance" (Webster, p. 601).

Webster also says this of energy: "With energy is connected the idea of activity; with force that of capability; with vigor that of health" (p. 601). When energy and force are defined in this way, the psychological notion of force (Lewin, for example) and energy

are demystified and stripped of experience-distant metapsychology
(Lynne Jacobs, personal communication, August, 1991).

Process in Gestalt Therapy Theory

In Gestalt therapy field theory everything is considered the
energy and movement of a field (our area: the organismic /envi-
ronment field). Everything is action and is in the process of
becoming, in the process of evolving and changing. This is what is
involved in our translating nouns into verbs. Any phenomenon
can be considered from a process standpoint. Even the reified
concepts of Freudian psychoanalysis can be put into a radical
process language (e.g., Shafer, 1976). There is a preference in
Gestalt therapy for process language in theory, describing clinical
phenomenon in process terms, and using interventions that
emphasize development through time and space (expressing
emotions rather than just talking about them, use of movement
interventions, experimenting with doing something different, faith
in the development that is a part of the paradoxical theory of
change, and so forth).

The process orientation trusts what emerges, the emerging
Gestalt, rather than relying on fixed, static concepts.

Webster's Dictionary (1960, p. 1434) lists several definitions of
process. The first five are of interest to us. I have emphasized one
definition — the one most applicable to our discussion.

1. a proceeding or moving forward; progressive course;
tendency; progress; procedure.
2. the course of being done: chiefly in process.
3. course, as of time.
4. *a continuing development involving many changes; as, the
process of digestion.*
5. a particular method of doing something, generally involving a number of steps or operations.

All of these have in common the sequential moving through
time and space. A process orientation contrasts with an orientation
that emphasizes unchanging structure, i.e., looking at one point
in time and not taking into account the march of events through
time. In the static orientation one looks at fixed Gestalten instead

of examining the emergence of Gestalten at this time, in this sequence of interactions, and its subsequent surrender to the next Gestalt.

Process focuses on the time dimension. Dialectic, another aspect of Gestalt therapy theory, is a process variable — it describes development over time.

> Process is:
> a change or a changing in an object or organism in which a consistent quality or direction can be discerned. A process is always in some sense active; something is happening. It contrasts with the *structure* or form of organization of what changes, which structure is conceived to be relatively static despite process change. (English and English, 1958, p. 410).

As in other areas of our discussion, here again we find some commonality between the Gestalt field theory and other field theories, e.g., physics. Not only do things change, but there is an order to the change. Process is a continuing development, and not random. One of the exciting recent developments in physics is chaos theory. But even in the chaotic and unpredictable field of chaos theory, they are finding an underlying order.

This belief in inevitable change, and the related belief in an underlying order, is important to our therapeutic methodology. We know that things change with or without our intervention. Sometimes things will change for the worst if we do not intervene or if the patient does not experiment with new action. While new action involves risk, so do the changes that come with repetitive functioning. We can clarify present awareness, knowing that things change — that one thing leads to another — and that clear awareness can be a useful part of that change.

The paradoxical theory of change and our process orientation support action that is experimental, hence leading to changes that cannot be precisely predicted. Of course, any competent and experienced therapist (or scientist) has some idea guiding the experiment, so there is order not only in the ultimate sense, but also in guiding the original intervention. Obviously, all therapists intervene without knowing precisely the ultimate outcome of the

314

intervention, but we have our process theory to make clear the fact that we do not know the future and to guide us in the present.

Gestalt Therapy as an Act Psychology: A Short History

Going backward in time, many of the pathways leading to Gestalt therapy theory converge on Franz Brentano (*Psychology from an Empirical Standpoint*, 1874). Phenomenology, existentialism, Gestalt psychology and field theory were all heavily influenced by Brentano's act psychology.

Part of a process orientation is distinguishing act from content and emphasizing act rather than content. The phenomenological approach defines reality according to the act of the perceiver perceiving the perceived. Focusing on perceiving, measuring, responding, taking responsibility (c.f., being responsible) are all act oriented.

Distinguishing act and content, and the beginning of act psychology, goes back to Brentano. Psychology for Brentano was a study of psychological acts. He made a distinction between the act of hearing and the thing heard (content). Brentano talked of ideating acts, judging acts and loving-hating acts, all of these acts being "intentionally" directed to some object. This was the origin of the phenomenological construction of reality by the perceiver and the perceived. It is the philosophical background for the Gestalt therapy principle that awareness was always of something. And it was an important influence on the process thinking of field theory in psychology.

Brentano brought to psychology an Aristotelian influence that has been very important in the formation of the process, act psychology of Gestalt therapy. Brentano's act psychology and his moving away from Cartesian dualism, away from the general Platonic influences of Descartes, was partially from the heavily Aristotelian influence of his background in Scholastic thought (Misiak and Sexton, 1966, p. 89). While, as Lewin pointed out, field theory is in part a movement away from Aristotelian classification (Lewin, 1938), field theory is also heavily influenced by Aristotelian thought. The concept of the unity of the organism/environment field, and other Gestalt therapy concepts,

depends on this Brentano-mediated Aristotelian influence. Therefore, we will take a short excursion into an aspect of Aristotelian
thought.

Aristotle's philosophy was a synthesis of materialism (Democrit-
us) and idealism (Plato). His philosophy was more rationally and
empirically based than the idealism of his mentor (Plato). Although more empirically based, still "The Aristotelian tradition ...
held that one could work out all the laws that govern the universe
by pure thought: it was not necessary to check by observation"
(Hawking, 1988, p. 15).

Important for Gestalt therapy, Aristotle's hylomorphism took
the unity of man, the unity of spirit and matter, as a starting point
— unlike Plato (Misiak and Sexton, 1966, p. 7). Aristotle distinguished two principles that together formed one whole or one
substance. Potency and act, matter and form, combined together
to form a single substance.

If the reader will substitute "Gestalt" for "form," it may be
clearer how this Brentano-mediated Aristotelian influence came
to Gestalt therapy. To Aristotle, form (Gestalt) is the source of all
properties and determines characteristics. The highest form is the
human form, since only humans can think (see Shapiro, 1990, on
speciesism). Applying this to the human being: the human soul is
the form of man, the body is the matter.

Perls, Hefferline and Goodman (1951) discuss the Aristotelian
concept of act and how it is important in unifying the organ-
ism/environment field (e.g., p. 229). To Perls, Hefferline and
Goodman it is act that unites the object and the biology of perception. "Aristotle's saving and accurate insight that `in act,' in
sensing, the object and the organ are identical" (Perls, Hefferline
and Goodman, 1951, p.229). The absence of water and the desir-
ing of water are the same act (Perls et al., 1951, p. 260).

> Every contact act is a whole of awareness, motor response,
> and feeling — a cooperation of the sensory, muscular, and
> vegetative systems — and contacting occurs at the sur-
> face-boundary *in* the field of the organism/environment.
>
> We say it in this odd way, rather than `at the boundary
> between the organism and the environment,' because... the
> definition of an animal involves its environment: it is mean-

ingless to define a breather without air ....The definition of an organism is the definition of an organism/environment field; and the contact-boundary is ... the specific organ of awareness of the novel situation of the field....

All this is, ultimately, to simplify the organization of the organism/environment field, to complete its unfinished situations....

As a boundary of interaction, its sensitivity, motor response, and feeling are turned both toward the environment-part and organism-part. Neurologically, it has receptors and proprioceptors. But in act, in contact, there is given a single whole of perception-initiating movement tinged with feeling. It is not that the self-feeling, for instance of being thirsty, serves as a signal that is noted, referred to the water-perception department, etc.; but that in the same act the water is given as bright-desirable-moved toward, or the absence of water is absent-irksome-problematic. (Perls, Hefferline and Goodman, 1951, pp. 258-260)

Insight into Genotypic Invariants

Most field theories assume phenomena are ordered (as discussed above) and have a methodology for discovering more about this order. We will discuss this under the two topics of (1) insight and methodology and (2) the nature of lawfulness.

Nature of Knowing and Definition of Insight

I have heard many in Gestalt therapy talk about insight as if it were foreign to Gestalt therapy, a psychoanalytic term and synonymous with an orientation of an intellectualized and interpretive search for the causality of the present in the past. This is a straw man, since most psychoanalytic theorists would say that the insight they are talking about is an emotional or feeling insight that is based on the current relationship between analyst and patient. Not only is this strawman an oversimplified, inaccurate and unproductive characterization of psychoanalytic thought, but it is also not a good understanding of Gestalt theory.

Insight is a necessary concept to understand Gestalt psychology and Gestalt therapy. When insight is defined as it is in Gestalt psychology, it is the goal in Gestalt therapy. This is the Aha!, the simultaneous integrative awareness of the parts and the whole. This is implicit in Perls, Hefferline and Goodman, although not explicit. I discuss this Aha! in "Clinical Phenomenology" (#6, 1976), although I don't use the word insight in that earlier article, and explicitly in "Gestalt Therapy: Its Inheritance from Gestalt Psychology" (#8, 1982).

"Insight is a patterning of the perceptual field in such a way that the significant relations are apparent; it is the formation of a Gestalt in which the relevant factors fall into place with respect to the whole." (Heidbreder, p. 355, from Kohler).

Insight is a form of awareness, awareness in which there is a grasp of the structure of the whole. The point of the discussion of the organization of the field is that this is the goal of the awareness work — to be aware of how the field is organized. Field has structure. Insight is fully connecting with, knowing that structure.

Psychological insight is also feeling the meaning, the emotional significance, of the organization of the organism/environment field. It includes knowing one's own emotions, needs, motivations, behavior, but is not primarily inward looking; it is knowing self and other, including the entire field. It includes being aware of one's awareness process, and one's character structure. It includes identifying fixed Gestalten transferred from fields that were in other times or places rather than newly perceived in the current field.

Insight in the psychological realm includes knowing what one is responsible for, owning one's own part of the field and knowing it is chosen. It is knowing the effects of one's choices. It is also knowing what one is not responsible for, disowning what is not one's own and knowing what was not chosen. Insight in psychotherapy is not just random awareness, but accurate, felt understanding of the organization of the field that is relevant to the characterological and interpersonal themes of the patient.

The phenomenological method provides guidelines for getting insight into the organization of the field (see Idhe, 1977; Spinelli, 1989). I discuss the phenomenological method in several other papers in this volume (#5, #6, #8, #9). Here I will just list five characteristics of the phenomenological method:

1. Put customary modes of thought in *brackets.*
2. Search for structural features of the field (insight)
3. Use systematic experimentation (variational method).
4. Make straightforward awareness the subject of reflexive awareness.
5. Pay attention to the intentional correlation of the experiencer experiencing the experienced.

Nature of Lawfulness

Insight requires that first, context-specific or phenotypic manifestations be phenomenologically clarified and genotypic invariants identified. This means relating what first appears in one's awareness to a more general understanding, to that which is invariant in the situation. Further, it means that what appears to be an invariant in a particular context is related to invariants across situations and contexts.

Lewin states that the field approach, the approach of what we call postmodern science, is a concrete constructive method. It places a rigid requirement on understanding each individual case. No manifestation can be dismissed because it is not regular or frequent, because it is an "illusion," and so forth. Nor is it sufficient just to name the class to which it belongs. An auditory hallucination is not adequately explained by labeling it and putting it in the category of symptoms of schizophrenia.

It is this attitude that allows experimental data to be valid. Finding out what happens in the pure case is valid data, regardless of whether the pure case occurs in nature. Science in the field approach is not a matter of frequency count, but understanding exactly how the forces of the field form together.

When possible, coordinates are used that apply to all cases, regardless of which object was being studied. Of course, this is easier in physics where the object of study has to do mostly with the motion of physical objects. In physics this means that if you can measure an object (height, width, depth) and its movement through space and time, you can discover natural laws. The generalizations have to be true to all observers, i.e., the generalizations have to account for the position of the observer. In Newtonian physics it was only space that was relative to the observer, but in postmodern physics the time perspective of the observer must also be part of the equation. The laws must apply all over, taking into account the time/space perspective of all observers.

In physics, field theory goes beyond description. Description is necessary and important. But simple data is not enough to indicate what the genotypic laws are, as opposed to the phenotypic manifestations. If one wants laws that are both faithful to their context, e.g., cultural context, and also of more general validity, something beyond mere description is necessary. Genotypic laws are true in multiple context and explain the differences between the various phenotypic manifestations.

In physics, sensing is extended through instrumentation and mathematics. Many of the phenomena studied are not in the domain of common experience or directly available to the human senses. Human experience unextended by instrumentation may be insufficient for a postmodern physics study, yet it is just this human experience that is the object of psychological studies. In a field theoretical psychology the description is extended with phenomenology and dialogue. Unlike physics, in psychology we can talk to the objects of study and find out what they experience. Psychological studies that use questionnaires and experiments but do not ask about the experience of the subjects do not take advantage of this phenomenological extension.

Another way to get this genotypic validity is to study the phenotypic manifestation in one cultural context and then study it cross-culturally. A truly insightful understanding would have the rich descriptive detail of the phenomenon in one culture, including the place of the phenomenon in the overall culture, and insight into what is cross-culturally variant and what is cross-culturally invariant. Does the phenomenon occur in all cultures, and if so does it play the same role in each culture?

The fullest understanding from a field theoretical scientific view must not only explain the individual case, but it must also search for insight into exactly *how* the law operates, not just that it operates, so that laws can be made that have general applicability. The phenotype, i.e., the specific appearance of a phenomenon, is not fully understood until its principles can be seen from the vantage point of the genotype, the more general laws of which it is a specific illustration.

In the recent psychology literature there are those who are now advocating laws that are limited to the concrete historical and cultural context. Others advocate or advance general findings in the form of general laws. The fullest understanding of field theory finds a way out of this debate. Understanding the specific cultural manifestation is only complete when it is seen as part of a larger field; the general laws are only valid to the extent that they are specifically related to the multiple concrete realities of time, place, person, culture, etc.

This same sophistication is useful in understanding the difference sometimes noted between acceptance and confirmation. Acceptance is sometimes defined as accepting the person as he or she is. Confirmation accepts the person as he/she is and also confirms the living and growth potential of the person's existence. This is an exact parallel to the genotype/phenotype situation. The person manifests a "phenotype" (the exact way the patient is in one here-and-now context), but this is not the only possible manifestation of the "genotype" (the variety of authentic ways the person is capable of being). In short, confirmation means accepting a person, but not just a single manifestation of the person.

Definition of Field Theory

Now we may be ready for my formal definition of field theory. The following is my rather dense definition of field theory. In a way it could also serve as a synopsis of the whole paper.

Field theory is a framework or point of view for examining and elucidating events, experiencing, objects, organisms and systems as meaningful parts of a knowable totality of mutually influencing forces that together form a unified interactive continuous whole (field), rather than classifying them according to innate nature or analyzing into discrete aspects and forming and-summative wholes. The identity and quality of any such event, object or organism is only in-a-field, contemporaneous and can only be known through a config-

uration formed by a mutually influencing interaction between perceiver and perceived.

In different ways and to different degrees, field theories tend to
make the following five assumptions about fields:

1. A field is a systematic web of relationships.
2. A field is continuous in space and time.
3. Everything is of-a-field.
4. Phenomena are determined by the whole field.
5. The field is a unitary whole: everything affects
   everything else in the field.

In different ways and to different degrees field theories tend to
have the following four additional attitudes:

6. Perceived reality is configured by the relationship
   between the observer and the observed.
7. The Principle of Contemporaneity.
8. Process: everything is becoming.
9. Insight into genotypic invariants.

Summary

Field theory is an attitude that permeates Gestalt therapy. It is
the lodestone that guides the compass of Gestalt therapy. Field
theory is the scientific world view that integrates the fruits of the
diverse sources of Gestalt therapy. Field theory makes possible
dynamic organizing concepts, such as contact boundary, self as
process, etc. It is the cognitive glue that holds the Gestalt therapy
system together.

There are numerous field theories, and there is no absolute way
of saying any are more right than others. Everything in field theory
is relative to the time, space and phenomenological awareness of
the observer.

Field theory is a framework for studying any event, experience,
object, organism or system. It emphasizes the totality of forces that
together form an integrated whole and determine the parts of the

field. People and events exist only through being of-a-field and meaning is achieved only through relations in the field. Only the facts present in the field have influence in the field.

In the Gestalt therapy field approach everything is seen as moving and becoming. Nothing is static, only some things, e.g., structure, move and change slowly relative to other processes that move and change more quickly.

Field theories attempt to gain insight into how the field operates, into exactly how the forces in the field fit together into a whole structure.

Reality is neither objective nor arbitrary, but rather is jointly and contemporaneously configured by "what's out there" and the perceiving organism.

Field theory is a way of thinking that is a necessary and central part of the general theory and methodology of Gestalt therapy and that has great potential for contributing to the further development of Gestalt therapy theory and practice.

11

THE SELF IN GESTALT THERAPY

Commentary

This paper was written in 1983 as a response to a 1982 article by Stephan Tobin in The Gestalt Journal. *In his paper Tobin advocates many changes in Gestalt therapy that I have also advocated, both in this reply and elsewhere. I summarize his position in my paper and I believe the reader who is not familiar with Tobin's article will be able to follow the issues without difficulty.*

In spite of the areas of agreement between us, I felt compelled to write my reply because Tobin's discussion of self, self-disorders, "boundary" and "core," etc. theorized about these issues in Gestalt therapy theory while showing no understanding of the field theory base of Gestalt theory. I think this discussion may illustrate the issue of field theory. It is best read in conjunction with #10 "Introduction to Field Theory."

It was with mixed feelings that I read Stephan Tobin's article "Self-Disorders, Gestalt Therapy and Self Psychology" (*The Gestalt Journal*, Fall, 1982). I was pleased that my colleague at the Los Angeles Institute wrote such a timely article. I wholeheartedly concur with the need to consider the Object Relations and Kohutian psychoanalytic approaches, to discuss Gestalt therapy treatment of character disorders (and other diagnostic groups), to discuss more frankly failures (both personal and systematic), to discuss the concept of self, and the need to relate the patient's current interaction to the historical-experiential background that gave rise to the present.

On the other hand I disagree with several theoretical statements in the article. Some of these seem important to me, and some of these statements recapitulate themselves in Tobin's treatment approach.

A Needed Shift in Attitude

Tobin advocates a shift toward more realistically taking the patient's character structure and experience into account, listening with respect to the patient's experience, increasing the sophistication of when the therapist shares his or her own experience or reflects the patient's experience or brings in genetic material. Toward that end Tobin advocates assimilation of information from recent psychoanalytic writers such as Heinz Kohut and the Object Relations theorists. He advocates more attention to the relation between therapist and patient and more attention to the needs of the patient as experienced by the patient. Concomitantly he discusses the importance of the therapist being aware of his own feelings and needs so that they will not unconsciously contaminate the therapeutic work. Tobin chronicles and advocates a shift from reliance on abrasive, confrontational techniques to a more empathic approach and from a confluence-phobic attitude to a more open-hearted attitude. In his honest self disclosure of the changes that his treatment failures have necessitated and in his attempt to connect this acknowledgement with basic theory Tobin sets an example I hope we all emulate.

Where I have a problem with Tobin's article is in how he theorizes about the needed shift in attitude. I disagree both with how he characterizes the existing theory of Gestalt therapy, and with how he theorizes about the changes he advocates. His clinical warning is well taken, but I take issue with how he uses this as a criticism of Gestalt therapy. I will discuss Tobin's general description of Gestalt therapy theory and how I regard it as inaccurate. Then I will discuss the following theoretical problems: self as process, self as a boundary phenomenon (not as "core"), sequencing in psychotherapy, the role of the past, and clinical issues relating to the I-Thou model.

Tobin's Description of Gestalt Therapy Theory

Tobin implies that there are agreed-upon definitions of self and ego that Gestalt therapy disregards. He characterizes the Gestalt therapy theory of self as being one of a boundary phenomenon that neglects the "core" of the person. Thus he sees Gestalt therapy treatment as interpersonal and not dealing with core conflicts.

He states that the theory of Gestalt therapy "...fails to touch some of the important self-functions of stability, groundedness, confidence and flexibility..." (p. 5). Moreover, it is Tobin's opinion that Gestalt therapy does not account for the continuity of self as a structure, does not acknowledge that the person brings an existent self of the immediate situation. Rather Tobin describes Gestalt therapy theory as conceptualizing the immediate situation without reference to any existing self.

Of greater importance, Tobin goes on to state that since there is no portrayal of the core existence of the self, Gestalt therapy does not make needed alterations in treatment for patients of various diagnostic groups (e.g., borderline and narcissistic). Further, he draws the implication from *Gestalt Therapy* that "each person has an equally effective, well functioning self" (Tobin, p. 5).

Tobin characterizes the I-Thou mode of Gestalt therapy as an abrasive confrontation that is imposed regardless of the clinical situation. He makes the damning indictment that Gestalt therapy does not provide a framework for therapists to distinguish their feelings and needs as they arise in the course of treatment and that Gestalt therapists are therefore unable to consistently dedicate themselves to the welfare of the patient (since Gestalt therapy does not discuss countertransference, p. 14). Thus, a patient with a self disorder who experiences fragmentation under stress would receive the abrasive treatment Tobin states he introjected from Perls (resulting in wounding rather than curing).

Further it is Tobin's view that Gestalt therapy deals with conscious intention and self awareness and does not deal with the unconscious and with resistance. Tobin advocates more intense therapy and believes that most Gestalt therapists do not see the benefits of more frequent sessions (to increase transference) and a lengthier treatment process.

General Representation of Gestalt Theory

The psychology literature on "self" and "ego" shows no agreement on the meaning of these terms, and in various sources they are used in exactly reversed manner. The seminal works in Gestalt therapy, Perls' *Ego, Hunger and Aggression* (1947), and *Gestalt Therapy* by Perls, Hefferline and Goodman (1951) were devoted to explicating a theory of the self as process.

In *Gestalt Therapy*, Perls et al. explicate a theory of personality of the normal and the neurotic, and they mention more severe pathology only in passing. Although I agree with Tobin that Gestalt therapy needs to publish more reports of clinical experience with various diagnostic groups, to my knowledge it is not and never has been Gestalt therapy theory that all people have equally sound selves. To believe that all people have equally sound selves would be tantamount to believing there are no such phenomena as psychopathology and significant individual differences in level of functioning. Personally I have found neither Gestalt therapy theory nor my mentors in Gestalt therapy that naive.

In my reading of the Gestalt therapy literature I do not find any denial of the phenomenological reality of the self. Yet Tobin goes out of his way to state that "I believe the self as a *phenomenological reality*" (p. 8). Although some might prefer to conceptualize this differently than "[I am] the same person I was at age nine (p. 8)," I do not believe any reputable Gestalt therapist or theorist would dispute Tobin's assertion of the phenomenological reality of a "self."

As I understand Gestalt therapy it has neglected neither the "core" processes nor the structural aspects of self. The Gestalt therapy process theory of self is far from being a product of "intellectual laziness" or "lingering anti-intellectualism" (though, to be sure, these traits are found in the Gestalt community) (Tobin, p. 9). Process thinking is still unconventional in psychology and not fully developed and requires very rigorous thought. This requires more rigor than the conventional Newtonian mechanistic ideas which Gestalt thinking replaces. On the other hand I believe that when Tobin separates structure from process he oversimplifies and misinterprets the theory.

Of course Tobin has been selective in choosing discussions from the Gestalt therapy literature that support his view of Gestalt therapy, but I also believe that he has not adequately represented Gestalt therapy works that discuss the I-Thou therapeutic relationship (e.g., Polster and Polster, 1973; Yontef, 1981a, 1981b, 1982, etc.). Although Perls was often abrasive, confrontational, narcissistic, etc., and many Gestalt therapists introjected this (as Tobin acknowledges he did), I never thought that Gestalt therapy *theory* advocated this. Gestalt therapy made the transition from a transference based relationship to a dialogic based relationship and the early literature did not specify exactly enough the nature of the desired relationship. There has been much attention to this since, and the attitude changes discussed by Tobin are still timely and needed, but in my opinion the theorizing about the characteristics that delineate the dialogic relationship needs to be more sophisticated than the discussion in Tobin's article if I-Thou is to be a useful concept in our theorizing and in our practice.

Tobin makes several other statements about Gestalt therapy theory that I disagree with. He states: "Gestalt therapy, along with other existential-humanistic therapies, has placed almost total reliance on conscious intention and self awareness" (p. 34). Gestalt therapy uses phenomenological awareness to explore the total awareness process, including unawareness (unconscious), resistance, and transference. I disagree with Tobin's claim that Gestalt therapy does not deal with resistance (p. 31). I was trained in Gestalt therapy to focus on what is kept from awareness and how, trained in dealing with resistance and the unconscious, but doing so with the phenomenological approach. That certainly has also been a major part of the training of the Gestalt Therapy Institute of Los Angeles for the past decade. Tobin states that *he* threw the baby out with the bathwater, but I take exception to his attributing this to Gestalt therapy.

Tobin implies (p. 33) that awareness work is expressive as opposed to insight-oriented. I think of insight as the form of awareness that Gestalt therapy is working toward, although we define insight in Gestalt psychology terms (awareness of the structure of the whole current situation) rather than being mostly historical insight (see Yontef, 1982). Expressiveness is merely one aspect of our insight-seeking phenomenological work.

Self: Process and Structure

Gestalt therapy is built on the field theory idea that structure and function are inseparable and that human structures are process. That stable structures exist is not doubted, but they are conceptualized as processes. Process is rhythmic, continual, has internal consistency, i.e., it is structural. In *Ego, Hunger and Aggression* (1947) Perls elaborates on this process interpretation of such concepts as ego and self. In *Gestalt Therapy*, Perls et al. explicate the self as process. On the other hand, Tobin takes the position that Gestalt therapy doubts the reality of the self, that it has continuity and that it is brought into every situation.

Self: Core and Boundary

The self in Gestalt therapy theory is the person's system of contacts. There is no "core" or "self" apart from an organism/environment field, and no human environment without the processes that we usually characterize as "internal." Whether the self is healthy, neurotic, psychotic or in the range of a self disorder, Gestalt therapy notion is that this is a process that occurs at the boundary. That there is severe pathology, and that some patients deteriorate under certain kinds of stress is obvious. However, Perls was addressing how we conceptualize that phenomena and it is on this point that I take issue with Tobin.

The greater the complexity and organismic interest in the interaction (not just conflict) the more self that is activated. Some people obviously fragment in the face of stress, conflict, etc. A way of conceptualizing this that is consistent with the Gestalt therapy process theory is that conflict, e.g., in the self disorders, does not reduce the amount of self of the fragmented person as stated by

Tobin (p. 6), the *self processes are fragmented*, ineffective, etc. The self is less cohesive, but the self is still the system of contact. This includes internal and interpersonal aspects of the contact boundary functions (self).

Tobin states: "One of the major limitations in Gestalt therapy is that the primary focus has been on the functional boundary disturbances between the person and his/her environment, and almost no recognition of structural disturbances in the core of the person" (p. 5). Later he states: "...Gestalt therapists have devoted most of their attention to the boundary disturbances between the self and no-self, no attention to disturbances within the self" (p. 9). Tobin's claim that Gestalt therapy only deals with disorder between self and other (p. 9) rests on his separating process and structure and separating boundary and core. The problem is that if you create a structure core that is conceived of as separate from boundary and separate from process, one would not recognize the discussion of internal conflict and fragmentation since in Gestalt therapy discussion of process includes the notion of structure (and vice versa) and any discussion of boundary phenomenon in the organism/environment field includes those functions Tobin labels as core.

Tobin seems to believe that there is a core separated from the boundary and that if the core is fragmented treatment must be of this core before work can be done at the boundary between therapist and patient. This will be specifically discussed in the next section. Theoretically and clinically it is one of the most important of the theoretical disagreements I have with Tobin.

Sequencing in Psychotherapy

It has been acknowledged that Tobin's article clearly delineates some needed shifts in clinical attitude. With this shift Tobin has experienced a great deal more success with narcissistic patients. Although my early style was different than Tobin's, I have made a similar shift toward softer, more empathetic, more relationship-oriented treatment, utilizing more understanding of the character structure of the patients. I too have benefited from studying Kohut and Object Relations theorists. And I can confirm that this has led to more success with self disorders, the narcissistic disorders being only one variety.

However, Tobin attributes this success to a particular sequence of long-term treatment. First he establishes rapport and understanding, then works on the self (working on the "core" and thus not seen as doing Gestalt therapy), then doing Gestalt therapy (boundary work), then termination. I think the label of the self work as not Gestalt therapy is unfortunate on theoretical and practical grounds. It limits one's conception of Gestalt therapy and splits off the strength of Gestalt therapy from this very important self work (Tobin, p. 40).

Although Tobin and I have made similar shifts in attitude and have experienced similar improvements in therapeutic effectiveness, I conceptualize the sequence very differently. Therefore, it may be that Tobin's success is related to the improvement in his attitude and knowledge, as was true with me, and not necessarily to the sequence that derives from his definition of self as structural "core." Although Tobin discusses only the narcissistic personality disorder, I have also found a greater success with borderline and schizoid patients. And my experience is that many patients, especially the borderline patients, do not do well in the particular sequence that Tobin is outlining. I believe that this relates to the theoretical problem of self and "core."

Tobin states that ..."I think it is more likely that a cohesive self is a *prerequisite* for contact with the field, rather than *vice versa*" (p. 11). This is difficult to understand if the self is the system of contacts. And, even if there were a "self" that is a core, how does one nourish this self except through some form of contact? We can debate the form and manner of the desirable contact, but I do not see how nourishment gets in except through some boundary.

The belief in self developing before contact rather than with contact or after contact logically results in a particular treatment choice: first Tobin builds support, then he works on the self through discussion of childhood, then he does Gestalt therapy work on awareness of process, then termination.

Tobin seems to believe that one can treat the person to develop this core self until it is strong and then work at the boundary phenomenon. I do not see how one reaches this core *except through a boundary*. This boundary phenomenon may be made salient or it may be done without drawing attention to it, but to get to the "core" one goes through a boundary. At a practical level, treatment that builds the boundary functions also builds that patient's strength to do his own awareness (insight) work on the relationships between present functioning and the experiential-historical background of the past. Tobin discusses the first two phases of treatment as not being Gestalt therapy because Gestalt therapy is confrontational and interactional and does not deal with the internal self. However, I regard Gestalt therapy as a more comprehensive and flexible system than Tobin accounts for in his article. For me Gestalt therapy includes emphatic listening, building mutual understanding, utilizing genetic material, using confrontation, and more.

I have found that the picture of Gestalt therapy as primarily or necessarily utilizing a dissonant and abrasive style is one that is frequently held. However, I believe this to be just one style of Gestalt therapy. If one gives up the idea that this one style is Gestalt therapy, one can more easily understand the conceptualization that the beginning work with a narcissistic or borderline patient is boundary work. This leaves unanswered many questions, including the issue of to what degree the therapist should introduce at the earliest stages of therapy genetic material not raised by the patient and whether this must be done by interpretation. Tobin and I disagree about this.

I believe that all work in intensive psychotherapy is both boundary work and work on what Tobin refers to as the core, and that the exact focus varies as a function of the clinical requirements of each patient and diagnostic group and is best derived out of the dialogic and phenomenological work rather than derived primarily from theory. Even within the self disorders there are contradictory needs. For example, the narcissistic personality-disordered patients and the borderline patients frequently need very different clinical attitudes and sequencing. The therapist who has as available background a good grasp of personality theory and psychodiagnostics (including psychodynamics) is in a position to give the best treatment.

My clinical experience certainly corroborates Tobin's view that the narcissistic patient is likely to dialogue only after he or she feels understood and that it is ineffective to confront such a patient prematurely with what the therapist experiences. I would note that in terms of dialogue in Gestalt therapy, I regard the narcissistic injury as not done to the patient by the therapist, nor created by the patient in response to the therapist, but rather that it happens as an interaction between the therapist and patient. The hurt can be acknowledged and *the present processes explored,* thus exploring and building self. Then the therapist can bring in transferential material as advocated by Tobin, can share the therapist's perspective (as a sharing, not as an encounter-group style encounter), or can go even further into the current, here-and-now process. For example, after acknowledging that when the therapist looked tired the patient felt hurt as if the therapist was not interested, the therapist has many choices. He or she could point out the similarity with a parent figure, could share what the therapist actually was experiencing, or could inquire into the process by which the patient got hurt. For example, after the patient hears the therapist's reflection of his/her hurt, and feels understood, the therapist could say: "What did you say to yourself when you saw that I looked tired?" ... "And when *you* said to yourself `He's not interested in me,' what else did you say?" Perhaps the answer is something like: "If my therapist isn't inter-ested in me, I must not be interesting." Therapist: "Wow, that is really much worse than if I was bored with you. That really wipes you out. Not only are you boring to me then, but to everyone in the world. That really wipes you out."

If the sequence that Tobin advocates for the narcissistic person-ality disorder (of working with core self and later working on contact) is extended to other self disorders, e.g., borderline patients, it is my experience that it is often disastrous. For if the therapist with such a patient introduces too early in treatment material about childhood, or even explores thoroughly the childhood material raised spontaneously by the patient, the borderline patient will often experience very intense, primitive affect, but not have the self functions developed sufficiently to contain, assimilate and work through. At the beginning of therapy the borderline patient typically can discuss without affect in the split-off coping mode, or explode with primitive rage or demands to be taken care of without much observing ego, but is not able to bring together the primitive and the adult functioning. Even if the rage does not explode out of control, the regressive pull of the borderline is easily reinforced and results in an exaggerated positive transference, and a year or two later the therapy blows up when the almost psychotic positive transference turns into a psychotic negative transference. If the early treatment of the borderline encourages the degree of positive transference advocated by Tobin, and the genetic material is introduced early, primitive and regressive wishes are reinforced, and my experience is that later in the therapy the patient develops a negative transference that the patient has not developed sufficient self support to handle and the feelings of betrayal are too great for the patient's as yet underdeveloped interactional skills.

By dealing with genetic material only by going through the self, i.e., the contact functions, the patient is able to develop more self to be able to relate to and finish with the past. For example, the borderline patient who learns that one can say "No" without being abandoned, starved or beaten down, and has developed a contactful relationship with the therapist based on that knowledge, is in a position to confront childhood demands for conformity, abandonment by parents upon asserting self, etc. I believe that the boundary work clarifying such issues as distinguishing blame and awareness, contact/fusion/isolation, splitting, etc., should precede any significant attempt to work through genetic material.

Summary: Tobin's theorizing has implications for his choice of therapeutic sequencing that in my experience can be unfortunate. To me the self in Gestalt therapy is not a core that is treated without going through a self boundary, but rather the person is treated through the self boundary. This is quite consistent with the notion that the I-Thou meeting is the Gestalt therapy path to empathic understanding and is an illustration of the existential premise that the self becomes present through contact.

Role of the Past

It is clear that the past is a background of the present. Perls clearly stated that the past leads to the present (1947, p. 93 and p. 95). Since meaning is the relation between figure and ground, with figure being the present and ground being the past, it is clear that past experience is an important part of Gestalt psychotherapy.

It is also clear that for intensive, long-term therapy to be meaning-ful the patient must develop a sense of past, present and future (Yontef, 1969). That requires the therapist, Gestalt or otherwise, to provide guidance in that process. I doubt that many Gestalt therapists would disagree with this.

Although it is true that the narcissistically injured, defensive patient who experiences no connection with the past gains from understanding how the past led to the present and how he/she maintains the status quo, Tobin makes several statements in his discussion that I disagree with (pp. 26-27). First, because the patient's present is related to his past experience, it does not mean that in the past he was a victim of his environment. Rather, the patient and environment are and were in constant interaction, and the patient brought something into the interaction and also had some role in maintaining into the future the negative effects of past interactions with the environment. However, Tobin utilizes the Newtonian, mechanistic, linear model of causality found in psychoanalytic thought when he believes that the past causes the present, that the patient is a victim of his past, and that the patient had and has no choice (Tobin, p. 9 and p. 26). Second, even though the therapist might hold the patient responsible for his behavior, it does not mean that this is immediately interpreted to the patient as stated by Tobin (p. 27). The therapist can hold a more accurate viewpoint of causality than the patient without prematurely disclosing it to the patient. Thirdly, there is some reason to believe that when you say that the patient could not help how he/she is, the shame may be increased. If the parenting was so bad that the patient had no choice, the patient is then seen as so damaged and crippled as to be beyond hope. Winnicott's idea of the "good-enough mother" takes into account that given a certain minimum of parenting the child is not beyond hope and does have choice.

Dialogue, Countertransference and Therapist Responsibility

Tobin and I agree on the importance of patient autonomy and independence from the therapist. It was precisely this point that attracted me to Gestalt therapy. Although I had previously been in psychoanalytically oriented psychotherapy and had been trained in a traditional psychodynamic manner, I had never experienced acceptance or self acceptance or autonomy until Gestalt therapy. I was attracted to Simkin's "No shoulds" idea.

I think it is unfortunate that Tobin discusses the Gestalt therapy I-Thou approach as if it is something imposed on the patient. His discussion of wanting patients to be independent rather than acting independent because of the therapist's wish for the patient to be independent *as if this desire for authenticity and autonomy is something new in Gestalt therapy* (p. 30) misses the essence of what attracts me to the Gestalt therapy dialogic approach. Telling a patient he or she is responsible for current misery relating to childhood abuse without clinical judgment, tact, or timing is not good Gestalt therapy practice. For me dialogue is not equivalent to abrasive confrontation.

Similarly, Tobin goes out of his way to make the case for withholding some of himself when the clinical situation calls for it, and implies that this is contrary to my writings on I and Thou (pp. 27-28). I disagree with his characterization of the I-Thou concept, but agree that the withholding out of a good sense of what is needed is necessary and desirable and not burdensome unless the therapist's own needs get in the way of the therapeutic task (rather than the therapist's needs being satisfied elsewhere and the therapist being fully available as a therapist). I have always practiced and believed in withholding or expressing myself to patients *as clinically indicated.* Tobin's presentation does not represent my view accurately.

In 1969 I wrote: "For the I-Thou relationship the responsibility question is most crucial. The actualizing model is not imposed on or recommended to the patient; the Gestalt therapist simply refuses to give up his freedom or accept the patient's surrender of his. The Gestalt therapist takes responsibility for behaving according to his own values, but for the patient there is only the prescription: 'try this behavior in therapy as an experiment and see what you discover'" (Yontef, 1969, p. 13). If the patient is not aided to develop an autonomous awareness, I do not consider it good therapy, Gestalt or otherwise.

In 1976, I expressed my point of view even more cleaner: "Beginning therapy patients often cannot say what they mean and mean what they say because they are not *Aware*" (Yontef, 1976, p. 4). In that same paper I refer to recognizing the differences between the patient and the therapist, and to the therapist surrendering to what really is happening between them rather than trying to make something else happen (p. 6). I also refer there to the need for the therapist to be mature enough to be authentically interested in the patient's work rather than being entertained, etc. Tobin misrepresents my previous discussion of I-Thou in a manner that supports his view of Gestalt therapy, but takes the quotation out of context. My writing is just one example of a point of view within the Gestalt therapy literature that already advocates some of what Tobin presents as contrary to our theory.

Tobin models a key element in the dialogic approach when he acknowledges his own past errors and expresses them as a means of improving the field. For me this exciting and useful discussion was marred when he sometimes went on to blame the theory for his previous personal practices, often by presenting a picture of the theory that disagreed with my understanding, and made of Gestalt therapy theory something much less adequate than the Gestalt therapy theory I had always used. For example Tobin acknowledges that in the past his sarcasm toward patients came from his own self and that the responsibility for his attitude and for his introjecting was his own (pp. 25-25). But then he goes on to state: "I think, however, that, as long as anyone works strictly within the framework of Gestalt therapy, in which there is little mention or consideration on countertransference phenomena, it is difficult to create the framework to examine one's own behavior and feelings as possibly due to one's own problems" (pp. 25-26).

Gestalt therapy has stressed since its inception the importance of the therapist's awareness of and responsibility for himself or herself. It is my experience that most good Gestalt therapy training takes this quite seriously. I believe that the boundary approach used in Gestalt therapy practice and training requires that the therapist be routinely open to considering his or her responsibility and role in what is happening and being experienced. This self awareness is not labeled as countertransference since the reality of the relationship, the reality of the therapist's reactions, and the transferential aspects of the therapist's reaction are treated with equal respect. The different label does not detract from the fact that the therapist in Gestalt therapy theory are held responsible for being aware of and responsible for his or her own reactions.

I have found that the existential, dialogic, I-Thou relationship and the phenomenological, awareness approach provide an excellent framework for this training. I learned about my own problems impinging on my professional performance mainly from my Gestalt therapy training. It grieves me that Tobin's fine article and suggestions for the directions in which he wants Gestalt therapy to move is not coupled with a picture of Gestalt therapy theory that I would deem accurate.

I am in agreement with Tobin that there is a lot of bad treatment being done, some by Gestalt therapists, and that many therapists use Gestalt therapy clichés and jargon to justify irresponsible projecting responsibility for self onto the patient. Many Gestalt therapists hold the patient responsible for their frustration, boredom, etc. Many charismatic therapists add to their narcissistic glorification at the patient's expense. Where I disagree with Tobin is in whether this is because of Gestalt therapy's lack of focus on therapist self-awareness and self-responsibility, or because of abuse of the system.

Tobin discusses making Gestalt therapy more intensive than is usually done, an undertaking that I also encourage. For some patients that means more than one time per week. I believe that this is consistent with Gestalt therapy theory, and that many therapists, Gestalt and others, err in not making therapy sufficiently intense or sufficiently lengthy. I differ with Tobin in his rationale that the increased sessions are to increase the transference. There are numerous clinical reasons for increasing the frequency of sessions. This is also true within the I-Thou framework. I prefer more frequent sessions to develop the total *relationship*, rather than to increase transference. More frequent sessions are sometimes useful to decrease risk of decompensation and to increase the intensity of the awareness work. It is important to note that Gestalt therapy can be increased in intensity without trying to develop a transference neurosis.

I was and am excited about Tobin's much-needed paper. His discussion of shifting the attitude in Gestalt therapy toward more recognition of the self and more sophistication in consideration of needed treatment alterations and sequencing with patients with different character structures is a step in the direction I would like to see Gestalt therapy move. His shift toward more respectful attention to the patient's experience and making explicit the therapist's responsibility for knowing the structure of his own emotional response to the patient is similarly a step in this same direction. In the process of the paper he makes a major contribution in setting an example by discussing his own errors as a therapist. Perhaps he will give the rest of us the courage to do the same.

However, I disagree with much of his discussion of Gestalt therapy theory. In this paper I have discussed my disagreement with his presentation of several Gestalt therapy concepts and with several aspects of his own theorizing. I believe his elaboration of Gestalt therapy theory makes it appear more impoverished, simplistic and less adequate than I understand Gestalt therapy theory to be. Although Tobin and I agree on some needed changes, I regard these changes as an elaboration and improvement on Gestalt therapy theory. Tobin's interpretation of Gestalt therapy theory makes it inadequate to deal with what is needed clinically and his conceptualizing of the improvements puts them unnecessarily in conflict with Gestalt therapy theory. The changes he discusses are consistent with my interpretation of Gestalt therapy theory (an interpretation that I do not regard as novel, but rather in Gestalt therapy theory as I have known it since I was first exposed to Gestalt therapy). However, Gestalt therapy theory as Tobin interprets it is inadequate to encompass these new clinical directions.

Among the key concepts that I would have liked to see treated differently are the equivalence of process and structure and the nature of the self as a process that includes continuity. We also disagree on the relation between self as "core" and self as a boundary phenomenon. I dissent very strongly wherever Tobin's discussion is built on a dichotomy between internal and interpersonal. I believe that such a discussion undoes the beautiful integration of that false dichotomy accomplished by Perls, Hefferline and Goodman. In addition I disagree with Tobin's abandonment of the field idea of the present being the connection between past and future when he assumes a more psychoanalytic, Newtonian stance in which the past not only leads to the present but causes it (with the patient having no choice).

Following from this theoretical approach he advances the idea that one should treat the core of the person and then work on contact. An approach that I have found to be more powerful, flexible and effective builds on the Gestalt therapy notion that the self is the system of contacts and that the core must be reached through the contact boundary. To me all treatment in Gestalt therapy is both boundary and core. From the notion of first treating the core Tobin discusses a treatment sequence to which is attributed an increased effectiveness that may come not from that sequence but from an increased responsiveness to patient needs and increased sophistication about the nature of self disorders. Moreover, the sequence may actually be harmful for some self disorders, especially borderline patients.

Finally Tobin equates dialogue (I-Thou) with abrasive confrontation and compulsive self disclosure and does not see the sensitivity, power and flexibility I see in the Gestalt therapy dialogic approach. Gestalt therapy as pictured in Tobin's model is not adequate to the clinical tasks it faces and necessitates utilizing psychoanalytic concepts to fill clinical needs that could also be filled with Gestalt concepts more favorably treated, such as more intense relationship rather than just increased transference.

12

MODES OF THINKING IN GESTALT THERAPY

Commentary

This article was written in 1984 in response to Joel Latner's article "This is the Speed of Light" (Latner, 1983). The first part of the article is actually a commentary on the politics of the Gestalt therapy movement as discussed by Latner. The second part responds to his discussion of field theory. My discussion of field theory puts field theory in a general historical perspective. I put this article in this section rather than under "The History and Politics of Gestalt Therapy" because I believe the discussion of field theory in the article is more important than the discussion of the political situation.

This article has been stimulated by Joel Latner's article "This is the Speed of Light" (Latner, 1983). I want to make alterations and add suggestions to the theoretical discussion he started.

Latner looks at two strains of theoretical assumptions in Gestalt therapy, the Newtonian (especially systems theory) and field theory. He describes each of these modes of thought, and shows the presence of Newtonian thinking in writings in Gestalt therapy and how this is different from field thinking. Although he clearly prefers the field view, he recognizes that other strains of thought, including Newtonian thinking and a piecemeal ("West Coast") strain, do exist. He labels these strains "schools" of Gestalt therapy and gives them geographic designations (New York, Cleveland, West Coast).

This article is composed of two very distinct halves. In the first half I discuss themes raised by Latner that detract from a theoretical dialogue in Gestalt therapy. In the first section I do an extended analysis of the issue of sectionalism in Gestalt therapy in support of my thesis that this is an unfortunate distraction from more important issues. In the second section I do a shorter analysis on another barrier to clarity, the confusion between what I call "Slogans and Techniques" approaches and those approaches I call "Concrete and Episodic."

In the second half of the article I discuss some of the issues I believe are fundamental in a theoretical dialogue in Gestalt therapy — especially the need to be clearer about the variety of different post-Newtonian modes of thinking. I conclude with a discussion of the need for an integration of field process conceptualizing and humanistic concerns as phenomenologically experienced.

East Coast - West Coast: Dialogue or Polemics?

In this section I want to discuss the troublesome New York - West Coast cleavage and the difficulty with using these U.S. geographic labels for the models of conceptualizing in Gestalt therapy. In the course of the paper I will suggest labels that I believe more adequately correspond to the theoretical issues and that may incite less antagonism.

The effects of semantics on awareness and behavior have been an aspect of Gestalt therapy theory from the beginning (Perls, 1948). In my first training workshop in Gestalt therapy (1965) Perls discussed the importance of using language that accurately differentiates and represents the phenomenon being explored.[*]

---

[*]Parenthetically I might note that this helped attract me to Gestalt therapy since he attributed this to the "Confucian" idea of rectification of names. Oriental philosophy was a major study of mine before coming to the mental health field and I was attracted to a therapeutic orientation that might integrate some of the Oriental philosophy. It also attracted me because I knew that modern scholars generally believe that the rectification-of-names

(Continued...)

Recently Miriam Polster has called attention to the importance of accurate use of language (M. Polster, 1981; and in Wysong and Rosenfeld, 1982, p.67). The labels of the "schools" of Gestalt therapy will make useful discriminations only if the descriptions are accurate and the labels adequately represent the material being classified. For me the labels Latner chooses are not adequate to that task.

My first reaction to Latner's article was an emotional one: I was excited finding an author doing the kind of useful and exciting theoretical analysis that I want more of in Gestalt therapy. I enjoyed identifying similarities in the backgrounds we brought to the discourse: I too studied in political philosophy before coming into the mental health field and also studied Oriental philosophy. I also studied field theory in physics and Gestalt psychology in order to better understand the theory of Gestalt therapy, and also was limited in the former by lack of training in physics and mathematics.

As I read the article I felt exhilarated with the quality of the theorizing, with the acknowledgment of differences, with the advocacy of discoursing on theory rather than personal, *ad hominem* grounds. I sharpened my thinking on topics that have long interested me and on which I have intended to do more writing. I recognized ideas I teach as Gestalt therapy theory but have never found described in the literature. I read his account and learned from his analysis. I read points I could add to or clarify. I read issues I have debated with colleagues in California, sometimes feeling quite alone in wanting more abstract discussion. I particularly found helpful the detailed and lucid description of the Newtonian, mechanistic thinking present in Gestalt therapy.

For example, his discussion of the difference between "of the field" and "in the field" is theoretically important and often missed (Latner, 1983, p.78). Showing that "having a feeling" is a Newto-

---

(Continued...)
philosophy was done in the name of the Confucian school but was actually a concept of a very different school called Legalism. The implications of the Legalistic philosophy was quite at odds with Gestalt therapy. I gave that a personal meaning: that I might have a place in improving the conceptualizing in Gestalt therapy theory.

nian mode of thinking and that the oneness of us and our feeling is a field theoretical mode of conceptualizing is helpful in making the connection between the more abstract and concrete levels of theorizing (p.p. 78-79).

Another example: pointing out that Perls, et al.'s belief in fragmentation coming from living in a world of splits itself points to a dualistic split makes explicit an obvious theoretical contradiction that has bothered me for years (p.p. 85-86).

But I also started to feel uneasy and troubled. The labels he uses for the strains of theory in Gestalt therapy not only strike me as inadequate to the conceptual task, but also misleading, and leave me personally feeling dismissed because of geographical identification (rather than because of the content, style, or quality of what I write or teach).

Unfortunately, lately I have heard and read articles, talks, letters, personal communications from people on both the East Coast and the West Coast that have been discussing the East Coast - West Coast issues in very disrespectful, contemptuous, arrogant terms that close rather than open lines of communication. In part I am taking this opportunity to discuss this general issue in public and not just replying to Latner. But I also regret that his exciting theoretical discussion is unnecessarily contaminated by this issue. I want to see the issues he raises responded to as theoretical issues on a theoretical level. This is made much less likely because of the slippage out of the theoretical analysis and into a more polemic and pejorative style.

In places he contemptuously dismisses the entire West Coast and detracts from the topic of his paper (subtitled: Field and Systems Theories in Gestalt Therapy). Latner clearly intended to discuss the issues *qua* issues and not in *ad hominem* terms. He states that "...the differences amongst us are rooted not in geographical differences and differences in personality and temperament but in opposing and unintegrated elements of our theory and practice and unresolved conflicts between them. (Latner, 1983, pp.71-72). Later in the article he says in reference to physics "it is impressive that these differences are dealt with entirely as problems of explanation" (p.86). He adheres to this attitude when he states that contrary to *Gestalt Therapy*, Newtonian thinking is not neurotic per se, but only when used in unhealthy avoidance (p.87).

However, elsewhere in the article (pp. 84-85) he discusses consistency and the crucial problem of technique-oriented, turn-on-oriented Gestalt therapists and the difficulty with their piecemeal or sloganizing mode of conceptualizing without regard for integration or wholeness of theory. A vital point! But he discusses this as if the problem were geographical and dismisses the entire West Coast as if that really deals with the issue. At such points the analysis of theory gives way to polemics.

What of the West Coast in Gestalt therapy? There has been a definite style of Gestalt therapy (not *the* West Coast style) practiced by Perls in the last decade of his life and by others. This style, usually practiced in workshop settings, has some distinctive features that are unfortunate: group therapy limited to one-to-one therapy in a group setting, a very confrontive and sometimes abrasive attitude, a phobic attitude about confluence and abstract theory, inflexibility, a discounting of the need for external nurturance during the therapy process, low emphasis on ongoing individual psychotherapy, and a discounting of the contribution of others besides Perls in the founding of Gestalt therapy. I disagree with this style on each of these counts.

Laura Perls discusses this in accurate and less inflammatory terms when she states:

> Gestalt therapy was conceived as a comprehensive, organismic approach. But later on, particularly in the West, *but in the East, too*, it became identified mostly with what Perls did at the time. It became very well known in the last five years of his life when he was predominantly using his hot-seat method. That method is fine for demonstration workshops, but you can't carry on a whole therapy that way; yet people do. I think they are limiting themselves and doing a lot of harm. (Wysong and Rosenfeld, 1982, p.16) [Emphasis mine]

She goes on to discuss Gestalt therapy today:

> Oh, it is in many ways blossoming. In many ways I have a lot of reservations because what's been done with it is the same thing that has been done with psychoanalysis and other approaches which have become more well known and

popular. It has been simplified and falsified and distorted and misrepresented. (Wysong and Rosenfeld, 1982, p.17; see also L. Perls, 1976, 1978)

Elsewhere in this volume Isadore From uses the term "neo Gestalt" to characterize the product of Perls' later days. He discusses the problems of this style with clarity and incisiveness — and some contempt — but at least he attributes Perls' behavior to Perls. He considers neo-Gestalt technique-oriented and having more of an eye to good theater than good therapy. He sees other flaws in this style: by using the empty chair the therapist is once again "behind the couch," so to speak, the body-mind split is reintroduced, the iceberg of psychoanalysis is brought in again with the theory of layers, that work to break down armor does not deal with the importance of the yes/no function of boundary processes, and that dream work around the "existential message" reintroduces psychoanalytic-type interpretation (From, 1978, 1984; see also interview in Wysong and Rosenfeld, 1982, pp. 26-46). He also discusses Perls' emphasis on showmanship, which he calls Perls' "demonstration style" (Wysong and Rosenfeld, p.37), and that his episodic attitude toward therapy in the last decade of his life has encouraged an association of Gestalt therapy with technique and slogans.

It is true in California as elsewhere that "For many of us these latter works of Perls are an embarrassment, despite their immediacy and spontaneity" (Rosenblatt, 1980, p. 12). The low theoretical quality of Perls' writing during this phase makes Gestalt therapy less credible and very vulnerable to criticism.

The criticism of Perls' later work and the results of the narcissism and "easy answer" philosophy of the 1960s has been discussed by *many*. In his 1982 keynote address to the Fourth Annual Gestalt Conference, Robert Resnick, a founder of the Gestalt Therapy Institute of Los Angeles, discussed the heightened profile techniques achieved as Perls moved west and demonstrated Gestalt therapy to wider audiences. Rosenblatt refers to Perls' "California phase" and then goes on to discuss the seductive influence of LSD and the hippie movement (Rosenblatt, 1980, pp. 11ff). I believe their criticism of Perls' practice is more useful than a discussion of the West Coast on which he lived. Questions arise if one is going to discuss the latter. For example, one would need to discuss not only the central tendencies, but variations from that trend. A good sociological analysis would define the terms, time and place.

It should be noted that California of 1965-1970 is not the California of 1984. California has moved from the excesses of the late 1960s and early 1970s just as the rest of the nation has. A good field theoretical statement always states space and time (as Latner knows). In this case Latner is discussing Gestalt therapy on the West Coast in 1970 not 1980.

I also find the use of United States geographic names to label the theorizing in Gestalt therapy quite ethnocentric. I believe that Gestalt therapists in the rest of the country *and the rest of the world* are too easily dismissed by discussing Gestalt theory in terms of New York City, Cleveland or the West Coast of the United States.

If the term West Coast was used as a title only to indicate the location of Perls during his "neo-Gestalt" days, the term would be inadequate, but I would have no great objection. In that usage it would be like the geographical usage of the "Berlin School of Gestalt Psychology." To my knowledge that usage is not a disguised political/sociological statement about Berlin. In Latner's usage the term West Coast is used not to designate a kind of approach Perls used from 1965 to 1970, but also to caricature a large part of the country.

Latner discusses individuals in a class at the Gestalt Therapy Institute of San Francisco and finding the introduction of basic Gestalt therapy terms being "met with blank, uncomprehending faces and, then, mocking smiles — as if to say, `What is this weird stuff, anyway?'" He implies this is the general attitude on the West Coast (Latner, 1983, p.83)[*]. He states:

---

[*] This group seems very different than groups I have had. I don't know if that particular group was different or if there is some general population difference than in L.A. I also don't know if Latner's inferences about their looks ("as if to say, `What is this weird stuff, anyway?'" (Latner, 1983, p.83) accurately represents their mood or the target of their negativity. Even if he is right about their mood, I don't know from what he wrote if their attitude was indeed directed at theory or perhaps something about Latner's person or style elicited that reaction. I am *not* saying that the latter possibility is the one I believe, just that I don't want to be personally dismissed nor have the L.A. Institute, nor the other fine trainers of Gestalt therapy on the West Coast dismissed on the basis of his experience in San Francisco.

I find myself tending towards writing them off....Without a concern for consistency, the next new thing down the pike becomes attractive simply for its novelty. There is no standard for judging whether it is related to what is in place and what has gone before. (It's like a skirt-chasing husband; any new thing gets him going, and his experience with his wife doesn't make a difference to him.) (Latner, 1984, p. 84)

We all know of individuals and institutes on the West Coast that are antitheory, take on each new technique without any integration, who do not understand Gestalt psychology, Gestalt therapy, phenomenology, etc. I also know of Gestalt therapists throughout the world practicing and thinking in this way. *Our* fight is with this ignorance, wherever residing. Throughout the world there are Gestalt therapists who are not direct descendants of the so-called "New York School" (unless one considers everybody in Gestalt therapy as such) but who are interested in quality intellectual work on Gestalt therapy theory. They need the discourse resulting from intellectually aggressive articles such as Latner's, but they are not adequately taken into account in Latner's categorization.

The East-West issue is not new and not restricted to Gestalt therapy. Evidence of the rivalry between the East, especially New York City, and the West, especially Los Angeles, are ubiquitous. Is there any real theater in California? Californians are all laid back, "flaky," unreliable, incapable of abstract thought, tolerant of variations in life-style (to a fault) and excessively pluralistic. On the other hand, New Yorkers are sophisticated, condescending, intolerant, doctrinaire, arrogant and abrasive. California joke: The country is on a tilt, and all the nuts roll to California. New York joke: Tourist stops a New Yorker and asks: "Can you tell me the way to the Empire State building, or should I just go fuck myself?" There seems to be some truth to both stereotypes, but I don't know how much. There is also a great deal of distortion in the stereotypes. I distrust stereotype as a basis for serious analysis.

The East-West designation issue is not new in Gestalt therapy either. In 1978 Miriam and Erv Polster were asked their view of this geographic categorizing. Both expressed difficulty with this division, pointing to the great individual differences that exist from person to person. In my words: *more of the variance is accounted for by the differences between individuals than is accounted for by the geographical division.* Erv pointed out the great variation within the New York group and within the Cleveland group. He also pointed out that work in Gestalt therapy in California would be different because the California context was different (in Wysong and Rosenfeld, 1982, pp. 59-60).

No one I know on the West Coast considers that there is a school or unitary viewpoint on the West Coast. Referring to the phenomena as a "school" not only mechanistically dichtomizes the field, but it also elevates the practices Latner is discussing into a school. I would rather discuss issues as issues with openness than harden into schools and debate between schools. I believe the West Coast school was created by fiat.

Latner uses a weakness in theory of Jim Simkin and Claudio Naranjo to support his dismissal of the West Coast. Simkin is quoted as stating that he has read and is not able to comprehend Perls, Hefferline and Goodman's *Gestalt Therapy* and regards it as "tangentially related to Gestalt therapy." Latner also cites Claudio Naranjo's failure to see any relation between Gestalt therapy and Gestalt psychology (Latner, 1983, pp. 83, 89-90). My personal view is quite different than that of Simkin or Naranjo. I am just one of many on the West Coast who do not follow the piecemeal or anti-theory line that Latner designates as "West Coast." My personal viewpoint and experience with others on the West Coast are different than Latner's. To round out the discussion in Latner's article I would like to discuss this briefly in personal terms.

Unlike Naranjo I do find the roots of Gestalt therapy in Gestalt psychology (Yontef, 1982). Unlike Simkin I regard the book *Gestalt Therapy* as indispensable for understanding Gestalt therapy. Many on the West Coast agree with me. I learned from California's pluralistic tolerance of differences in temperament, style, theoretical persuasion, life-style. I learned from Simkin that there is "enough room" and to live more with *is* than *shoulds* (Simkin, 1974). It is a lesson I keep learning and perhaps others in Gestalt therapy could also learn from. When I was first trained in Gestalt therapy by Perls and Simkin, I took what I could from them and rejected what was not useful to me. I rejected their antitheory bias and looked elsewhere for help with needs they did not meet.

Learning that I could and must do this self-regulation was the most important thing I learned from Gestalt therapy in general and Jim Simkin in particular.

Some very fine Gestalt therapy and training is being done on the West Coast. We also do have our share of quacks, turn-on artists, know-nothings. Many of those who demonstrate and conduct workshops throughout the country from the West Coast do mostly experiential work in the traveling workshops. Some of these do not know or care about basic theory, some do know and care about theory and that does not manifest itself in that context.

Latner's description of the training situation at the San Francisco institute in which basic concepts (e.g., confluence) are not known and even disparaged is appalling. My experience in Los Angeles has been quite different. I have offered didactic courses in Gestalt therapy theory at UCLA and at GTILA since 1971 and have not found the kind of mocking and incredulity that Latner did. I not only taught at the concrete level of "introjection," "confluence," etc., but also talked of field theory, phenomenology, existentialism and Gestalt therapy in context of the history of Western and Eastern thought. I found the classes generally receptive, even when my teaching style and the difficulty of the material got the class lost on subjects such as existentialism and field theory.

I cannot imagine any first-year trainee, much less any member of GTILA, giving Latner the reception he describes having received in San Francisco. I did not receive such a reception when I assumed the head of the GTILA training program in 1974. Although I found the theory instruction at that time quite limited and haphazard, I also found the faculty and trainees supportive and respectful of efforts to improve the situation. By 1974 the anti-theory and antithinking bias of the 1960s had largely changed. Since then in order for our trainees to go on to the second year of training they have been required to take a theory exam in which they not only have to define such terms as "confluence," but also show some understanding of abstract issues.

Latner states that Perls was: "...actively averse to serious thinking and intellectual activities, a bias which pervaded the West Coast during the last ten years of his life and largely continued since his death" (Latner, 1983, p.83). Although I no longer hear the antitheoretical rhetoric, there has long been a paucity of serious intellectual dialogue *in Gestalt therapy in general*, perhaps more so on the West Coast. *The Gestalt Journal* has done a good job of changing this by providing a forum that encourages dialogue. However, even from the "New York School" there has been very little new produced since Perls, Hefferline and Goodman. I have tasted the intellectual fruits of Laura Perls and Isadore From. I agree with Latner about the high ("sophisticated") quality. But I did have to remain hungry for more and there has been very little forthcoming. *The problem of our theoretical literature is not restricted to the West Coast.*

In the Los Angeles Institute I have not found the faculty contemptuous of theory and I have found them generally knowledgeable at the level of basic terms. However, I do find many trainers that are weak on theory at the philosophic level and actively averse to personal participation in intellectual debate. Some that do speak of theory do so without a real appreciation of the kind of issues Latner refers to and avoid active engagement with peers at this level. Thus there seems to be some truth to Latner's characterization. I believe this would be more effectively covered by description of the behaviors and ideas rather than by creating a school of theory avoiders.

One of the unfortunate consequences of the West Coast label is that it tends to banish the intellectual "sin" to the West Coast. Labeling the "know-nothing" adherents as West Coast not only fails to adequately label the problem and ignores those on the West Coast with a good understanding of Gestalt therapy theory, but it allows Gestalt therapists elsewhere a dangerous complacency by atributing the sin to the West: "Oh, that's only in West Coast Gestalt therapy." Moreover, it also gives a kind of sanction to the knownothings by such a title, as if it is a school and within normal expectations to be a "know-nothing" if you are in that school.

The problem of inadequate theorizing and inconsistent understanding of field theory and of the Gestalt psychology framework can be found everywhere (even within the "New York School" of Gestalt therapy?). Contempt for the know-nothings can be a defense against critics. When Gestalt psychologists criticize Gestalt therapy as not even knowing Gestalt psychology, let alone being related to it (e.g., Henle, 1978), I have heard people respond: it is only because of those who demonstrate and discuss Gestalt therapy without knowing the theory (especially the West Coast?). In my opinion, no one has fully explicated the consistencies and inconsistencies between Gestalt therapy and Gestalt psychology.

We would do better to focus on the inadequacy and incompleteness of Gestalt therapy theory than to continue the East-West controversy and the related rivalries revolving around Perls and the other founders. In my opinion, these controversies and rivalries are impeding closer attention to the theory and greater contact among those really interested in the intellectual dialogue.

I don't like the West Coast in Gestalt therapy being dismissed as if we all were a form of breakfast cereal (nuts, flakes and fruits) — as a vast wasteland. By the same token I also don't like it that some contemptuously dismiss Gestalt therapy in New York City in the same sarcastic manner. The caricature of New York City shows a smug, doctrinaire, dogmatic, hostile attitude in which people are dismissed when there is disagreement[*]. The content changes, but the dismissing attitude is the same.

In our dialogues I would like to see a greater respect for the person, i.e., an acknowledgment of the difference between criticizing the person and criticizing the theoretical point made by the person. Latner exposes an example of the attitude I find objectionable when he discusses Perls, Hefferline and Goodman's idea that Newtonian thinking is "neurotic" and an "erroneous conception of reality based on an erroneous psychology of consciousness" (Latner, 1983, pp. 85-86). Latner makes clear his objection to calling the Newtonian thinking neurotic.

However, when Latner begins his discussion of the schools he does dismiss Perls as if he were not connected with founding Gestalt therapy. He states: "There is the Gestalt therapy of Perls et al. It is the one described in *Gestalt Therapy*....Then, there is the Gestalt therapy of Perls" (Latner, 1983, p.82). Although I agree

---

[*] I have heard of individuals in the New York area that avoid the Gestalt therapy scene altogether because trainers reportedly will not even talk with members or trainees from other institutes. Since this is mere gossip I consider this only as illustration of what people say about Gestalt therapy in New York and do *not* treat this as true.

with the criticism of Perls' later works, the attitude here seems not to give him any credit for founding Gestalt therapy. I believe that it is due founders and mentors to acknowledge the debt and also to confront with differences. Latner confronts Perls and dismisses him without an acknowledgment.

In this article I have disagreed with a mentor of mine, Jim Simkin. Some seem to assume an identity of mentor and mentee, as if everyone on the West Coast agreed with Simkin. We are not all clones of Perls and Simkin.

I would like to see Latner's lead followed in improving clarity about our conceptual framework, but with the change that geographic labels and *ad hominem* arguments be avoided and schools not be prematurely created. I would rather focus on the quality and content of theoretical presentations.

"Slogans and Techniques" and "Concrete and Episodic"

Many have commented on those who discuss Gestalt therapy without demonstrating or imparting an understanding of the whole of the Gestalt therapy system and who practice without an apparent appreciation of the whole of a therapeutic system. In the latter regard incremental work and long-term therapy frequently give way to an episodic attitude that does not provide the continuity or the sophistication about psychodynamics and relationships that would support long-term, intensive psychotherapy (I. From, 1978, 1984; Latner, 1983; F. Perls, 1969; L. Perls, 1973, 1976, 1978, in Wysong and Rosenfeld, 1982; Rosenblatt, 1980.)

Although there is a large variety of such therapists, I would like to distinguish two modal types. I do this with full appreciation of the existence of other types and that the two I discuss are but two poles along a continuum.

One type talks in slogans and practices in techniques. The second type does more than sloganize, but does talk concretely without explicit integration with the theoretical whole. This fits the classic Gestalt psychology definition of piecemeal (Koffka, 1931, 1935; Köhler, 1938, 1947, 1969; Wertheimer, 1938, 1945). The therapeutic practice of the second type does not necessarily overemphasize techniques, but does not explicitly appreciate the importance of continuity, of long-term, incremental therapy. Perls' declaration that individual therapy was obsolete would be an example of this.

It would be prudent to acknowledge and take seriously the fact that in particular contexts, episodic therapeutic encounters and talking at the level of concrete bits are quite responsible and good professional practice of Gestalt therapy. When such practices are done with awareness and choice I have no objection. When done from rigidity of personality, inadequacy of training, without developed ability to do otherwise, without discrimination, without informing participants of the fuller picture, I see great difficulty. With awareness the therapist can talk in concrete terms, e.g., "mini-lectures," and practice in a style that emphasizes workshops, and still make very clear the limits of this approach, the alternative Gestalt therapy modes and resources available, and that this is but one style of Gestalt therapy and not its essence.

It would be very useful to differentiate these two very different types of approaches to all aspects of Gestalt therapy. Unfortunately, in dismissing the West Coast "school" Latner dismisses experienced therapist/trainers with both impeccable credentials and their own styles of Gestalt therapy. He confuses and fuses them with virtually untrained persons who lack clinical background and adequate Gestalt therapy training and demonstrate no talent for conceptualizing in a holistic manner. It is polemical to dismiss Perls, for example, as equivalent to Latner's students who neither knew nor wanted to know what confluence was.

Operating in the slogans-and-techniques mode means minimal conceptualizing. In that mode people repeat slogans, practice by techniques, and are not concerned about integration into wholes. Such people often talk of "Gestalt therapy techniques." A lot of the practices that are called West Coast Gestalt therapy or neo-Gestalt therapy are properly categorized here.

It is difficult for me to envision anyone practicing or teaching from this mode who are also competent. They do not understand the wholeness of Gestalt therapy theory or the importance of wholeness in Gestalt theory. They talk of techniques — which are the least important aspect of Gestalt therapy. My experience is that they often do not even know what a whole theory is, not having ever done the abstract work necessary to appreciate a theory as a differentiated whole. Sometimes such persons make criticisms of Gestalt therapy that would not be made if they appreciated the wholeness of the theory. Many of the "Gestalt-and" presentations fall into this category (L. Perls, 1973, 1976, 1978, and in Wysong and Rosenfeld, 1982).

Although I have seen and heard this all over the world, I have never heard any of my mentors consider this to be good Gestalt therapy. To the contrary, although Perls may have inadvertently fostered this approach in his later days, both he and Jim Simkin were in principle against oversimplification, quickie-training, and quickie-therapy (F. Perls, 1969).

Many Gestalt therapists and trainers who are competent in their practice conceptualize piecemeal. Many are not aware of the difference between piecemeal theorizing and integrated theorizing. Some address general issues, but are not aware that they do so piecemeal nor that their integrative thinking is sparse. Some of these practice-competent but piecemeal-theorizing persons understand Gestalt therapy theory in general (perhaps on a less well-articulated or intuitive basis), but only talk about concrete concepts or oversimplified generalizations. The mini-rap approach to theory, delivered in experiential workshops, often substitutes for more general theory discussions. Those who put on the workshops have some power over the agenda, and of course the trainer in such circumstances can make the importance of general theory known and be explicit about the limitations of the particular workshop.

Yet it seems obvious that there is a weakness in theoretical discourse and in attitude about theory in many who otherwise are excellent Gestalt therapists and trainers but who teach and discuss theory piecemeal. In this mode there is some concrete level conceptualizing that may include some abstract theorizing, but the theorizing does not tie the pieces to the whole. Ideas taken from other contexts (e.g., Kohutian psychoanalysis) are not considered in their original whole context and this taken into account in utilizing the concept in Gestalt therapy. Aspects of Gestalt theory are not considered in terms of consistency with each other. I am not discussing whether anyone is or is not a piecemeal conceptualizor — rather I am interested in piecemeal conceptualizing versus holistic conceptualizing.

Piecemeal theorizing that addresses general issues have either roughly Newtonian or field theoretical overtones (mostly the former), although not consistently (by definition since it is piecemeal). Although it would seem that the piecemeal approach is more consistent with the mechanistic approach, one does hear a lot of globalized, piecemeal, fuzzy statements of field theory that are on a par with piecemeal, fragmented, Newtonian presentations. In the next section I discuss the confusion of the Gestalt approach with universal interactionism; much of the field theory-oriented piecemeal conceptualizing confuses the two (talking glibly of the world as one big Gestalt).

I believe that both the Slogans-and-Technique approach and the Concrete-and-Episodic approach are somewhat problematic. However they are not the same problem. The former is a problem that might be called quackery. The latter is a problem of quality and adequacy in people that are above the quackery level.

Post-Classical Modes: Neo-Newtonian, Universal Interactionism and Gestalt Psychology

Latner dichotomizes the Newtonian-mechanistic and the field theoretical systems of thought in black and white fashion; in my opinion he made the division between Newtonian and post-Newtonian psychological thought too absolute and created a confluence between distinguishable post-Newtonian and Eastern systems. Moreover, he failed to distinguish between the human systems we study in Gestalt therapy and the physical systems studied in physics. Some of the postclassical field theory attitudes in physics are at variance with Gestalt psychology. While in Gestalt therapy we do not have to agree entirely with Gestalt psychology, I think that intellectual honesty requires that we articulate this.

A. Background

Gestalt field theory is one of several autonomous twentieth-century reactions to the classical, Newtonian world view[*]. Psychoanalysis was founded upon a Newtonian world view while Gestalt field theory is a cornerstone of Gestalt therapy.

Although Latner discusses field theory as if there is one kind of field and field theory, there are various kinds of fields and field theories, including the physical force fields of Faraday, Maxwell and Mach, metric/geometric fields (Einstein), statistical/probability fields (quantum theory) and environmental/behavioral fields and phenomenological fields (Gestalt theory). In the section following this background section I intend to

---

[*]In psychology that includes functionalism, phenomenology, existentialism, humanistic psychology, etc. The field approach in Gestalt psychology is indebted to field theory in physics, but had begun autonomously before the early Gestaltists knew of the parallel work in physics. Köhler states:

> Clearly, therefore, the early Gestalt psychologists were not wrong when they trusted their observations which appeared so mysterious to other psychologists. For now the Gestalt psychologists discovered that this procedure made them neighbors of the most advanced natural scientists, the physicists.
> But this was not all. Several years later I discovered that some eminent physicists agreed with the Gestalt psychologists' scientific procedure in a much more general sense....
> My quotations, I hope, have made it clear that, far from proceeding in a fantastic fashion, the early Gestalt psychologists (at the time not yet acquainted with these remarkable statements of great scientists) almost naively worked in a direction which entirely agreed with tendencies that had emerged in natural science. (Köhler, 1969, pp. 59-62) (Emphasis mine).

Parenthetically, there is an interesting discussion of Einstein's thinking process in developing his theory in Wertheimer (1945) based on extended contact made in 1916. (Wertheimer's basic research and publications founding Gestalt psychology were from 1910 to 1912.)

distinguish two kinds of field theory particularly relevant to Gestalt therapy, Gestalt field theory and universal interactionism.[*]

There are commonalities in all field theories, e.g., space, events and things are treated only as part of fields from which they derive definition and meaning. People are not born with a separate essence that later interacts with an environment, but the individual and environment are a whole out of which the external and the personal aspects are differentiated.

In a field theory analysis the concept of field replaces discrete material points (Newtonian physics) and dichotomous categories (Aristotelian classification) (Lewin, 1935) as the unit of study. Everything is considered an integral part of a matrix of multiple interrelated forces and not caused by single, linear causes. In this view relations are inherent (Lewin's Principle of Relatedness) and one starts with the whole rather than the parts. Zukav discusses this as new for physics (pp. 308-309), although it has always been the essence of the Gestalt psychology approach.

In Einstein's relativity field theory the universe was orderly and comprehensible. Time and space were always considered relative to the framework of an observer and inseparable from each other. He discovered that mass (structure) and energy (process or function) are equivalent and not made up of "different stuff."

Since Galileo physics has sought dynamic explanations that hold across situations (genotypic laws) rather than observations of superficial correlations (Lewin, p.11). This is more of a constructive activity and progressively less based on simple sensory (phenotypic) observation (Lewin, 1935, p. 13; Einstein, 1950).

An attitude of strict and complete lawfulness without excluding any data led to Einstein's revision of Newtonian physics and to Gestalt psychology's criticism of much of experimental psychology. Exceptions from generalizations on such grounds as "optical illusions" was not considered acceptable in Gestalt psychology: a

---

[*] For background in field theory in physics I recommend: Bentov, 1977; *Capra*, 1975; Capra, 1976; Davies, 1983; Einstein, 1950; Einstein, 1961; Keutzer, 1984; King, 1976; *Sachs*, 1973; Wolf, 1981; *Zukav*, 1979 (see especially those in italics).

complete functional analysis had to account for all of the data and do so on more than a mere statistical basis.

This demand for exact functional understanding combined with the need to take the speed of light into account and the new notion of relativized time/space also meant that the idea of causality (action) at a distance without a specific intervening medium was no longer acceptable (Sachs, p. 69). This also was a part of the Gestalt psychology field theory.[*]

Much of Latner's discussion of field theory was influenced by quantum theory. Quantum field theory arose from the study of unbelievably small and rapidly moving atomic and subatomic particles that cannot be seen at all or located with certainty. One can only make statements of the probability of finding them. In this subatomic area there is an inherent indeterminancy: one cannot simultaneously measure to an arbitrary accuracy level the position and momentum of a particle.[**] In principle the more precise one's knowledge of one measure becomes, the more indefinite becomes the knowledge of the other (J. King, 1976). Thus the quantum field theory involves fields that are waves of statistic probabilities of finding a certain event. This is more than merely accounting for the position of the observer, it is a statement that observing inevitably disturbs the observed. Further, the quantum theory is often interpreted as proving that the observed does not even exist except by the conceptualizing and measurement of the observer. This calls into question the very basic belief in classical physics and in relativity theory that the universe is orderly and comprehensible (Sachs, p. 110).

In addition quantum theorists believed the nature of the object being studied depended on the observer rather than on its own nature. For example, it had been thought that physical events took the form either of a wave (energy) or a particle (mass), but not

---

[*] However, the contemporaneity notion in Gestalt psychology did not have to take into account the speed of light and the resultant complications in what constituted "now."

[**]It should be noted that the indeterminancy is in relation to arbitrary accuracy levels in measurement that are more exact than anything we are even close to in psychology.

both. The mathematics of each was different and well worked out. But it has been discovered that, depending on the manipulation of the experimenter, the same subatomic particles sometimes act like a wave and sometimes like a particle (wave-particle duality).

What does this all mean? There is clarity at the level of mathematics and experimentation. The philosophic implications are neither clear nor static. Commentators seem to agree that the present state of theoretical physics is pregnant with change (Sachs, 1973; Zukav, 1979). Is there any external reality? Is the universe "intrinsically random" (Heisenberg) and particles inherently imprecise (Born) (Sachs, p. 84). Is the universe comprehensible?

Some say the universe itself is inherently imprecise (Sachs, p. 84). The most accepted interpretation of quantum theory (The Copenhagen Interpretation) holds that a "complete understanding of reality lies beyond the capabilities of rational thought" (Zukav, p. 38). Einstein fought both these views until his death, insisting that the universe was both orderly and ultimately comprehensible. Some believe that human consciousness is a "hidden variable" behind vagaries of experimental results in subatomic research.

What is found in quantum physics are not solid particle building blocks, but interconnections (Capra, 1975, p. 68). "Particles" were found, but not isolated particles — they have no meaning outside their activity of interconnecting. In subatomic physics one cannot separate the existence of a phenomenon from its activities (Capra, 1976).

If everything is process, energy and interconnections and flux, does this mean that there is really no structure or stability? (See discussion in Keutzer, 1984; Sachs, 1973). Clearly our view of thingness, language and structure is fundamentally changed as a result of modern physics, but is all structure and thingness an illusion?

In fact, physicists seem to agree that it is the presence of structure that creates movement; without resistance there is no life (J. King, 1976). But the structure is a web of interconnections that is defined only in terms of the probability of the experimenter finding it on experimental manipulation and measurement.

How does one deal with the apparent duality, i.e., the physical world can be shown to be thing (particle) and process (wave)? Bohr introduced the concept of *complementarity*: when two experiments give different views of the same phenomena, both are necessary to a comprehensive understanding and cannot be reduced to each other. For example, a thing itself cannot be adequately and fully accounted for with either a wave (continuity) or particle (distinguishable thing) theory alone. This complementarity can be contrasted with a reductionistic interpretation.

The complementarity principle, which I see as consistent with the polar differentiation of the field discussed in Gestalt therapy theory (*Ego, Hunger and Aggression*), treats the object (thingness) or mass aspect of a phenomenon as the space aspect (apart from the time aspect) and the process or energy view as the time aspect (apart from the space aspect). A reductionist view would lose one or the other of these vital perspectives. I believe Latner's analysis becomes reductionistic in this way.

Clearly modern physics is not monolithic. Some, like Einstein, adhere to the belief that nature is complete, ordered and everything we describe is a manifestation of universal law (Sachs, p.87). At the same time the Copenhagen Interpretation of quantum theory holds that the fundamental features of nature are only consequences of the way in which they are viewed (Sachs, p.88). Some adhere to something like the latter interpretation of physics, but also refer to a universal cosmic law borrowed from Far Eastern mysticism when discussing the spiritual significance.

What is clear is that experimental evidence and mathematic formalisms do not determine the metaphysical orientations of the physicists. Sachs cites one controversy that illustrates this. Schroedinger, whose continuous field approach is allied with Einstein, and Heisenberg, whose algebraic approach is opposing, found that their mathematics were equivalent, step by step. Yet they both disliked the other's orientation and philosophy and neither changed (Sachs, pp. 92-93).

Complementarity means that no concept can accurately and fully represent all aspects of any thing or process (J. King, 1976) and no language is effective in all contexts. The mechanistic language of the everyday macroscopic world does not work in the subatomic world (Capra, 1975, p.159). Although at first glance this might point to the inadequacy of our ordinary language, note that even subatomic physicists use classical, mechanistic language in their experimental work. For the truth is that the pure process, no-thing language of subatomic physics does not work in the macroscopic world (Capra, 1975, pp. 132-133).

> It is further maintained in the quantum theory that the laws of physics that must be obeyed by the large measuring apparatus are those of classical physics, while those obeyed by the microscopic observed matter are those of quantum physics. (Sachs, p. 89)

In psychology we have great need for both languages. Even in a field approach, much of our language must remain mechanistic and macroscopic.*

What has emerged in physics is agreement on some fundamental ideas: space-time relativity, equivalence of mass and energy, that phenomena (particles or waves) have meaning only in fields of interconnections (no meaning to isolated particles), that the structure and function (activities) of events cannot be meaningfully separated, that the observer is a participant that must be taken into account, that attributes and labels are man-made abstractions and that the world is inherently dynamic, not static.

However there is as yet no agreement on a unified field theory even at the mathematical level. There is less disagreement in merely verbal approximations. There is no consensus on epistomology or metaphysics from either quantum mechanics or relativity theory, let alone a unified theory of physics (Capra, 1975, p. 132). The two major theories in modern physics retain their axiomatic basis. The field theory in the Theory of Relativity is deterministic, its fundamental existent is continuous fields and it is non-linear. The field theory in quantum theory is nondeterministic, its fundamental existent is discreteness (al-

---

* No-thing language in the macroscopic world is too cumbersome to use clinically, e.g., many phenomenological research reports. Physicists do not have this problem since their basic work is done in the language of mathematics and the verbal language is secondary.

though not in the Newtonian sense), and linear superposition (Sachs, p.105).[*]

The last word is not in. Physics is in a state of rapid change, with constant efforts to reconcile the conflicts amidst predictions of experimental breakthroughs and new theories integrating the disparate schools and interpretations.[**] Einstein cautions that the kind of field explanation he wants may not be possible. He acknowledges that many physicists believe it is not and that a quantum type field theory is the best that is possible. He disagrees concluding:

> I think that such a far-reaching theoretical renunciation is not for the present justified by our actual knowledge, and that one should not desist from pursuing to the end the path of the relativistic field theory. (Einstein, 1961, p. 157).

In light of all this I believe it behooves us all to show some caution about introjecting theories from physics.

Capra discusses the fact that we do not have a direct experience of four dimensional time-space. However he has noted that the dynamic universe now seen by physicists is "similar" to that of Eastern mystics (Taoism, Hinduism, Buddhism) whose epistomology can accommodate the findings of modern physics (Bentov, 1977; Capra, 1975, p.17, 81; Capra, 1976; Zukav, 1979).

Latner goes further: "The perspective of modern physics is identical in its outlines to Buddhist, Taoist and Hindu thought" (Latner, 1983, p. 76). This seems to assume not only that modern

---

[*]Efforts to create a field theory accounting for relativity and quantum mechanics continues and is essential for the study of particles approaching the speed of light. It seems clear that the current state of quantum theory and relativity theory is unstable (Sachs, pp. 111 -112; Zukav, 1979). This is especially so since nonrelativistic quantum theory is considered only an approximation to a relativistic quantum theory, just as Newtonian physics was an approximation to relativistic physics (Sachs, p. 94).

[**]This is supported by recent indications that there may be effects that are caused "at a distance" mediated by information being passed at speeds faster than light (Zukav, 1979).

physics is identical in outline with these Eastern philosophies, but also that modern physics theories are identical in outline to each other and that the Eastern philosophies are also identical to each other.

Although both modern physics theories do agree in going beyond the Newtonian, mechanistic system, there are significant differences between relativity theory and quantum mechanics. They study different phenomena and their different mathematical formulations yield different predictions. Between the Eastern philosophies and physics there is a difference of method (Capra, 1976). There is a difference between philosophic religious systems based on metaphyscial positions and scientific systems based mainly on empirical investigation and mathematical calculation. In my opinion the similarity between all these theories is remarkable and fascinating but they are not identical. The Eastern philosophies are not the same, the physics theories are not the same, and the two groups of theories are not the same (Zukav, 1979). I would like these ideas to be distinguished and not fused.

Capra, although obviously enthralled with the similarities, states: "I am not saying these dimensions are exactly the same as those we deal with in physics. However, it is striking that it has led the mystics to notions about space and time that are very similar to the notions we have in relativity theory" (Capra, 1976). Capra uses the concept of complementarity to make clear that to him the "scientific world of abstraction" and the world of the mystic cannot be reduced one to the other or brought into unity (Capra, 1976).

The heart of Gestalt therapy is not in either physics or metaphysics, but in phenomenological clinical work. We strive for insight into the structure of existential situations based on phenomenological explorations of the phenomenological field, including not just physical connections (as in physics) but inherently including psychological meaning for each event for each person.[*]

The consideration of models from physics is intellectually stimulating and useful, as long as we do not oversimplify or

---

[*] Lewin refers to the importance of explicating the "actualizing energy" and essential (genotypical) dynamics (Lewin, 1935).

introject them and limit ourselves to these models. There are several field theories and multiple interpretations of the meaning of each. The possibilities for change are presently great. At a minimum it is clear that there is not just a Newtonian and a field theory model to deal with.

B. Post-Newtonian Theories in Gestalt Therapy

1.Central Principles

According to Einstein, field theory in physics increases the distance between what we study and what we can sense, i.e., we cannot see much of what is studied in the field approach in physics. In physics this problem is solved with instrumentation, thinking and mathematics, and experimentation. In Gestalt therapy there is little systematic, detailed, controlled, empirical investigation, use of mathematics or measurement or extension of observation through instrumentation. Nor do we do very much rigorous and systematic logical-philosophic analysis. How do we deal with what we cannot directly observe with our own senses?

We study human systems using a phenomenological philosophy and methodology and the system being studied can report its internal experience. We put this together with phenomenological experimentation and external observation in order to discover what we need to know. This makes our existential phenomenology critical in theory building in Gestalt therapy.

I am reminded of Sartre's summary of existentialism: existence preceeds essence. In my estimation we do best in Gestalt therapy when we constantly center ourselves on our existence as experienced and judge theories of our essence against that experience. The phenomenological method of utilizing direct experience and bracketing metaphysical bias is coupled with this existential focus. I hope that we do not become so enamored of physics and receptive to Eastern mysticism that we are seduced into losing our center in direct and immediate phenomenological experiencing in favor of metaphysical speculation.

2. Three Alternatives (in brief)

Below I discuss three alternative emphases in Gestalt therapy theorizing: linear (neo-Newtonian), nonlinear (universal interactionism) and integrated (Gestalt psychology). Linear and nonlinear theorizing are dichotomized and reductionistic in that each reduces the whole to a half of a polarity; integrated theorizing combines the two.

Linear theorizing emphasizes what has been called "left brain." It shows significant remnants of classical, Newtonian, mechanistic, thing-like thinking. The brand of systems theory described by Latner as "The Cleveland School" fits here.

I make a distinction between nonlinear, "right brain" thinking such as Eastern mysticism and integrated thinking such as in Gestalt psychology. This section is being written largely to clarify this distinction, I believe is not sufficiently clarified in the Gestalt therapy literature.

Joseph Zinker provides us with a concrete example of an integrated attitude when he states that the creative therapist is able to integrate two modes of consciousness, e.g., "naming things" and "experiencing spatial imagery," also "being intellectual" and "attending to intuitions" (Zinker, 1977, pp.59-60).

3. Linear Theorizing in Gestalt Therapy

In his article Latner makes clear that the transition away from the atomistic and mechanistic language and attitude of Newtonian thinking is incomplete in Gestalt therapy. Although he focused on the systems theory utilized in the Cleveland Institute, clearly the Newtonian fragments are not limited to the systems approach and certainly not limited to Cleveland. Also it should be noted that not all systems approaches are Newtonian or mechanistic. But there are myriad remarks in Gestalt therapy practice showing mechanistic influences, e.g., "Use your eyes!" This is Newtonian in its dichotomizing between the actor ("I") and the eyes and inconsistent with the Gestalt psychology view of perception in that it treats perception as an activity of the peripheral sense organs rather than simultaneously involving the central nervous system.

Mechanistic language is still used extensively because of the linguistic difficulty of process language and because the ordinary, Newtonian, mechanistic concepts work pretty well, and it is a "good approximation to say that things consist of constituent parts" (Capra, 1975, p. 81). Also we study different systems than in classical or postclassical physics. One example: in psychology we do not need to take the speed of light into account and therefore do not need as sophisticated a model of simultaneity ("now") as in modern physics (although our "now" model is also unlike the absolute and linear notion of Newton).

In modern physics sense observation unextended by machinery is inadequate given the parameters of their topic and the degree to which observation disturbs many of the events being studied. In Newtonian physics it was assumed one could observe and do so without affecting the systems studied. In Gestalt therapy we do not make the Newtonian assumption since we are aware of being a participant and not an objective observer, but we do assume that observation without measurement and mathematical calculation can lead to insight. Observations of the observers are integrated with awareness reports by the patient. *We need to evolve to a new model, rather than adopting classical or postclassical models from physics. Any analysis of Gestalt thinking solely in terms of models of physics is likely to come up short.*

Linear Gestalt therapy theorizing varies from very mechanistic in language and attitude to those who have much of the spirit of field theory but write in ordinary language with its mechanistic, Newtonian taint. Those who discuss "self" as a "core" recreate the inner homunculus that creates artificial structure, divides the person, aids the avoidance of responsibility (by projecting it onto the homunculus). (See Yontef, 1983 for debate between myself and Stephan Tobin, *The Gestalt Journal,* Spring, 1983.) On the other hand, I find no such distortions in the writings of the Polsters, although I do find the nonprocess language issues that Latner refers to.

Unfortunately Latner groups these all together, and if evidence of Newtonian language is present he labels the theory as entirely Newtonian. He carefully delineates small, important detail, but than leaps with abandon to overgeneralization. While it is useful to point to the remnants of classical theory in a theory that aspires to be holistic, this sharp dichotomizing and loose overgeneralization is premature and arbitrary. This either/or mentality is mechanistic in its spirit and to that extent not entirely congenial with his analysis.

The Polsters show remnants of Newtonian language, but it is misleading to label their work as merely Newtonian. They are certainly more field oriented than psychoanalysis with its central attitude of linear causality, absolute treatment of time and space, assumption that the phenomena they study are "out there" to be objectively studied without affecting the subject of the study, their attitude of analyzing and synthesizing by "add-summative" processes (Wertheimer, 1938, pp.12-16; 1945), use of static, reified, homunculus-type concepts, etc.

Koffka states that we must do what the facts demand (Koffka, 1935, p. 9). I believe that the whole person descriptions described in the Polsters' book are demanded by the facts and have not been adequately accounted for in process language. I will discuss below my view that doing this would be more useful than dichotomizing between the humanistic and field theory approaches as Latner does. Field theory has to account for these phenomena to be complete, and the humanistic concerns would be better served if integrated with process thinking.

4. Distinguishing Universal Interactionism and Gestalt Psychology

In discussing the Eastern mystics' view Capra states they are "aware of the unity and mutual interrelation of all things and events, the experience of all phenomena in the world as manifestations of a basic oneness" (Capra, 1975, p.130). This much also fits Einstein's view of the field approach.

Latner describes the universe in the field theory model with terms such as "seemless" universe (Latner, 1983, p.87) and "undulating field" (p.75). His lyrical description imparts a feeling, but it is not clear what these concepts exactly refer to. Latner's undifferentiated field seems to be a *homogeneous* field. In a homogeneous continuous energy field entities (including structures and concepts) are seen as an artificial product of abstraction. Moreover, in this mode of thought there is a tendency to treat *the world as one big Gestalt.*

In his book (1973) Latner states:

Growth consists of being able to form gestalts of greater and greater complexity....

Making gestalts is making wholes....

In our terms, this direction is toward the *last gestalt*. The momentum of our development is toward wholes that encompass more and more of the potential of the organism/environment field. In the more advanced stages of this process, we are embracing ourself and the cosmos. The gestalt is: I and the universe are one. All of me and all of the infinity of activities and energy around me, people and things, *all of them all together are one figure.* Nothing is excluded.

Sitting here, this volume is related to me, I to my chair, my chair to the floor, the floor to the house, and on and on to all the human beings, *all the objects in the world* — and to the sky, the stars, and the rest of everything. The last gestalt is beginning to know the immensity of the extent of our *interaction with everything else.* As we read, *we move our eyes — and the whole interconnected universe moves.* The last gestalt is apprehending this viscerally, body, mind, and soul, to the depth of our being, leaving nothing out. (Latner, 1973, pp. 193-195) [Emphasis mine].

This nonlinear viewpoint of universal interactionism was discussed explicitly by the Gestalt psychologists and they raised strenuous objections (discussed below). Whereas the linear theorizing does not take into account the oneness of nature, the nonlinear theorizing does not take into account the linear, differentiated aspect of nature. Both lose one part of a basic complementarity and force a choice between a field without boundaries or a dichotomized field.

This is an old issue in psychology. William James was one of the early influential thinkers in psychology who protested against elementarism. James considered consciousness as a continuous stream. Not only did he emphasize that continuity is primary, but he regarded all distinctions as secondary. `Things' are extricated, for partial and practical purposes, from the flux of experience, which is originally `a big, blooming, buzzing confusion'.... With ... these interpretations *Gestalt* psychology emphatically disagrees" (Heidbreder, 1933, p.337).

How do we account for the phenomenological experience of thingness, structure, there being discrete particles, discontinuities? In classical physics this does not pose a problem. Perls, Hefferline and Goodman give some support for two interpretations. (1) Things and structure are creations of abstraction and therefore artificial impositions of the mind. I think this is the interpretation subscribed to by Latner. This is an idealist view in which the immediate experience of thingness and self is not given primacy. (2) In the integrated view both the process and the structural aspect are considered natural. Of course the labels and personal meanings are man-made, but *the field is a differentiated one.* This is the view of complementarity and Gestalt psychology.

Let us look for a moment at Latner's statement: "The assumption of the existence of an objective reality is out of synch with field theory, which ... affirms that what is real depends on the point of view of the person — in more formal terms, the position of the observer" (Latner, 1983, p. 77). If the objective world is rejected because he rejects absolutism and the subject-object split, I have no quarrel. If the objective world is questioned by Latner because the world is subjective and the individual creates not only the idea and name of the thing, but the thing itself, then I do object.

The formal term "the position of the observer" is accurate in that it is now clear that this must be specified for accurate measurement. At a philosophical level the question is whether one is asserting no world except as subjectively created and therefore no objective world, a dichotomized view, or asserting the phenomenological position that there is a world out there but our knowing is part of our relation to the world and therefore the world we know is always *in part* determined by us. *

The existental-phenomenological perspective assumes a polarity — one intends toward otherness (noetic pole).** Awareness is of something — there is a world apart from the person. Knowing is

---

*This is analogous to the interaction aspect of Bohr's complementarity.

** A very readable account of intentionality can be found in Idhe, 1977.

a connecting of self and other, a combination of subject-ive/objective. This existential phenomenological view rejects the concept of a dichotomized subjective or objective. Rejecting the objective world is a split or reductionism as much as the Newto-nian objectivity.

Although Korzybski's statement "The map is not the territory" is undoubtedly true, nonetheless naming and labeling is vital to human functioning and not an artifact (J. King, 1976). In this naming we simultaneously create the opposite of the concept and thereby take a part in the differentiation of the field into polari-ties. Latner gives us the choice only of the Newtonian dichoto-mous field or the undifferentiated field being primary. The Gestalt psychology approach is a third alternative — the differentiated field. Either we ignore or reduce phenomena or else we acknowl-edge the natural existence of polarities and create usable concepts that do not oversimplify.

Concepts such as self, personality and boundary depend on how this issue is handled. In the linear viewpoint the self is not only accepted as a phenomenological reality, but described as a thing, an homunculus. It is abstracted from the field — "in the field" not "of the field." In the nonlinear view the self is process without structure, regularity or temporal continuity. From this latter viewpoint only the interactions of the organism/environment field at the moment are real and this means that the only regularity is character (seen only as neurotic, rigid and not natural). This is "of the field" but without recognition of the natural emergence of entities and people from the field.

The concept of boundary involves the same issues. Do we treat boundary as thing, as *nothing but flux*, or as process and structure? Because the electron has been shown not to be a discrete particle building block consisting of mass without force does not mean the electron only exists as an abstraction or is equivalent to all other subatomic particles. Its name and attributes are abstractions, but its existence is not. This is even more clear at the macroscopic level where we can directly experience the existence of persons, self, etc.

Although I disagree with much of his analysis and solution, I believe Tobin is correct in pointing out that, if the field view is interpreted as excluding a whole, continuously existing self, it contradicts our phenomenological experience and therefore is at variance with our phenomenological orientation (Tobin, 1982; Yontef, 1983). In the integrated view the self refers to the whole person and this includes organismic regularities or repetitions. Of the field but with differentiation. Is there any nonneurotic character? Are there not repetitions not based on thing-like structure, and not based on repeatedly trying to adhere to a mental (self concept) picture, but rather an acknowledgment of who I am as I repeatedly and naturally experience myself?

Clearly Perls, et al. were in agreement with Gestalt psychologists in reacting against the Newtonian approach of abstracting the individual from the environment and then recombining them by addition (Latner, 1983, p.78). But what does it mean to state that persons "are meaningful only when referred back to the interactions of the field"? (Latner, 1983, p.78). It certainly means that people exist with meaning only as part "of a field." The pulsating contact boundaries between person and environment are "of the field." The first reality is contact between. This is consistent with the existential dialogic belief that there is no "I" except of the "I-You" or the "I-it," i.e., there is no "I" except of an interpersonal field.

But what of the sense that each person has of personal boundedness? Here Latner dichotomizes (Latner, 1983, p. 80). The Polsters elaborate by acknowledging that the person, although a part of an organism/environment field, phenomenologically feels a sense of self concept and of boundedness. This awareness of self boundedness also constitutes a field — a phenomenological field. There is both the contact boundary between persons and also the I-boundaries each experiences. The Polsters deal with this and Latner eliminates it from field theory (Latner, 1983, p.80). "This ambiguity signals a subtle shift from what appeared to be a holistic approach to a systems approach, for the Polsters are now describing defined entities which meet at their boundaries and make contact — like billiard balls" (Latner, 1983, p. 80).

Latner goes on: "Perls, et al., are saying that we can *think* of ourselves as whole beings: We can accomplish the feat of abstracting our experiences of ourself into an idea of the person we think we are. We can also conceive of ourselves as billiard balls in empty space" (Latner, 1983, p.81). The reality of thinking of ourselves as whole beings does not necessarily mean we are not experiencing ourselves "of the field" nor that we are engaging in Latner's billiard ball thinking.

Latner states that "Insistence on boundaries suggests a fear of healthy confluence" (Latner, 1983, p.87). The insistence on separation can indeed be an avoidance of healthy confluence, but note: insistence on no personal boundaries can be an avoidance of healthy withdrawal. *Healthy awareness includes the separating and connecting function of the boundary process operating between self (the whole person) and the environment.*

The self concept the Polsters elaborate on is an existing phenomenon and as such is part of a field. Social psychological research on the "looking glass self" indicates that self concept may be largely a product "of the field." When Perls, Hefferline and Goodman state that in health there is very little personality, they are addressing the process of attachment to an old image rather than the current field reality. That is quite consistent with the Polsters' emphasis on the importance of expanded I-boundaries. This outlook is not Newtonian, but the macroscopic world uses Newtonian language. Perls, Hefferline, and Goodman's stand is against attachment to an idea instead of to what is. I do not believe it is a stand against awareness of personal wholeness.

Latner dichotomizes so we have to choose between dealing with personal boundedness and self concept as real phenomena or a field without objects. I believe this is an example of Latner's dichotomizing Newtonian and post-Newtonian attitudes and oversimplifying post-Newtonian attitudes. He uses linguistic detail to support overgeneralization.

In his treatment of personality Latner also tends toward treating each moment of self/environment as discretely existing without natural regularities (for example, Latner, 1983, p.81) and thereby does with the temporal aspect what Newtonians do with space. This interpretation acknowledges the spatial unity of person and environment, but not the temporal aspect. An isolated moment is no more meaningful than an isolated particle. One interpretation (not one I agree with) of the "now" of Perls, Hefferline and Goodman actually treats the now as such an isolated moment and life (and therapy) as episodic. Many have made clear that now as an isolated moment is not what is usually meant in Gestalt therapy by now (L. Perls, 1973, 1978).

There is a parallel issue in Gestalt therapy in the social/political arena. In his book[*] Latner refers to social structure as limiting free functioning and discusses anarchism in a laudatory way (Latner, 1973, pp.62-63, 107). He does not discuss the polar opposite: that this limit is essential to free functioning. Although he does not say so explicitly, he leaves the impression that social/political structure is unnatural and that we would be better off without it. This overreaction to authoritarianism does not distinguish artificial, arbitrary, capricious governing structure from necessary, rational, socially organismic governing structures. It does not acknowledge the negative effect of too little structure and the Gestalt psychology idea that nature always involves structure.

In his book Latner states that "Social norms and events are not dealt with in therapy, for they are not available to the process of therapeutic change. Nor are natural processes available for alteration" (Latner, 1973, p.131). Here he sets up a dichotomy that is more Newtonian than field theoretical. He separates social norms from therapy when we certainly do deal with social norms in therapy with or without our awareness) and help change them (not necessarily in a constructive direction). More important, Latner dichotomizes natural processes from unnatural processes. Biofeedback has shown that, with awareness, many natural processes can be controlled and changed.

Between the extremes of Newtonian and Aristotelian dichotomies and the undifferentiated whole is the differentiated field with its unified polarities. Although total flux, change, absence of structural limitations may sound like freedom, it is more equivalent to nonexistence. Life and action come from the inhomogeneous field (Koffka, 1935, p. 43); from resistance comes life and without resistance there is no energy (J.King, 1976). Individual things do exist as part of fields, although this particularity happens

---

[*] This paper is not a critique of his 1973 book. Obviously Latner 1973 is not exactly the same as Latner 1983. However on the themes discussed here I do find some consistency between the earlier work and the later work.

376

in the context of an all-embracing unity (Capra, 1975, p. 145; Einstein makes the same point).

5. *Gestalt Psychology: Integrated Theorizing*

Köhler gives a succinct summary of the issues:

Summary. One point of view would be that nature is composed of independent elements whose purely additive total constitutes reality. *Another,* that there are no such elements in nature, that all states and processes are real in a vast universal whole, and hence that all parts are but products of abstraction. The first proposition is completely wrong; the second hinders comprehension of the Gestalt principle more than it helps. ... The hypothesis of universal interaction, however, far from helping us in this, gives instead a picture of nature that is completely misleading.

If natural science has never been greatly concerned with the doctrine of universal interactionism, philosophy, unhampered by concrete examples of physical phenomena, has suffered all the more. The doctrine appears to be a complete acceptance of the Gestalt principle; in point of fact, it only corrupts that principle.

.... The outcome is a confused misdirection of emphasis leading eventually to a position diametrically opposite to Gestalt principles. The *important* point is missed: viz., the existence of self-enclosed, finitely extended Gestalten with their scientifically determinable, natural laws...

.... The Gestalt principle, in harmony with its own empirical objects, involves a *finite* application and leads therefore to direct results (Köhler, 1938, pp.30-31).

Köhler discusses dynamic distributions of energy in which no part is self-sufficient and in which the local flow of energy depends on the process of the whole.

If a similar conception is to be applied to the processes which underlie sensory experience, we must avoid a mistake. In his protest against psychological atomism William James once said that in the sensory field local experience are interwoven with their neighbors in a manner which is beyond the grasp of purely intellectual theory. He also thought that original sensory experience is uniformly continuous, and that all cuts and boundaries are later introduced into the field for pragmatic reasons.

From the point of view of Gestalt Psychology, such a statement does not correspond to the facts. Notwithstanding the general dynamic interdependence throughout the field, there are boundaries in it at which dynamic factors operate toward a measure of segregation rather than uniform continuity (Köhler, 1947, p.80).

Talk of the similarity of Buddhism or modern physics to Gestalt therapy often either adopts the James viewpoint or at least fails to distinguish it from the Gestalt perspective. The relativity and quantum field theories are mathematical and do not have this problem. The problem enters when the mathematical models are translated into words and their philosophic significance is assessed. In this mode of inquiry some interpretations are similar to James', i.e., that the world is one big Gestalt in which there is no inherent structure and that everything is related to everything else ("seamless").

Koffka discussed the issue of the world as one big Gestalt:

Do we then claim that all facts are contained in such interconnected groups or units that each quantification is a description of true quality, each complex and sequence of events orderly and meaningful? *In short, do we claim that the universe and all events in it form one big gestalt?*

If we did we should be as dogmatic as the positivists who claim that no event is orderly or meaningful, and as those who assert that quality is essentially different from quantity. But just as the category of causality does not mean that any event is causally connected with any other, so the gestalt category does not mean that any two states or events belong together in one gestalt. `To apply the category of cause and effect means to find out which parts of nature stand in this relation. Similarly, to apply the gestalt category means to find out which parts of nature belong as parts to functional wholes, to discover their position in these wholes, their degree of relative independence, and the articulation of larger wholes into sub-wholes. (Koffka, 1931, 1935, p.22) [Emphasis mine]

Is any differentiation not humanly imposed? Any structure not created by the observer? The view that the healthy person exists only here and now without stable self structure is a form of this view of the world as one great big, undifferentiated Gestalt with the moving process held static by human concepts. This is a form of philosophic idealism.

Wertheimer did not interpret Gestalt field theory in this manner:

The given is itself in varying degrees 'structured' ('gestalten'), it consists of more or less definitely structured wholes and whole-processes with their whole-properties and laws, characteristic whole-tendencies and whole-determinations of parts. 'Pieces' almost always appear 'as parts' in whole processes. (Wertheimer, 1938, p.14)

He went on to say that naturally given articulation and inclusiveness vary. This discrimination of what does and does not fit together contrasts with universal interactionism and is quite consistent with the Gestalt therapy notion that not all opposites form a true polarity, only those that arise from a common context.

Kurt Lewin warns: "It is particularly necessary that one who proposes to study whole-phenomena should guard against the tendency to make wholes as all-embrasive as possible....It is no more true in psychology than in physics that "everything depends upon everything else" (Lewin, 1935, p. 289).

The Gestalt psychologists were clear that the relation between figure and ground was largely determined by the nature of the situation, and that not all order comes from the observer. There is structure in the situation. This is part of what Perls referred to when he said of "Let the situation determine."

The Gestalt psychology viewpoint avoids dichotomous philosophical choices in favor of differentiated wholes, especially structure (mass, entity, static) and function (energy, process, change). Structure and function cannot be united if structure is eliminated or treated as some kind of illusion or epiphenomenon. *The disparate views of self as pure interpersonal boundary process without core and as reified core (homunculus) need integration for a whole view.* The idea of self concept as a present process does not suffice to account for the phenomenological experience of self (Tobin, 1982), although it must be part of an overall explication.

There is organismic continuity or spontaneous repetition that can be called self in a way that is more than memory or snapshot. I believe the phenomenological reality of self and other entities is not illusion and should not be dismissed as such.

I believe that greater sophistication about the Gestalt psychology attitude would be of great help in Gestalt therapy. One example of the kind of help we can get is in the area of a simple contradiction in Gestalt therapy: some say we do not interpret, but we do. (It is sometimes easier to see in others than in oneself.) Isadore From points out the interpreting involved in the kind of popularized Gestalt therapy dream work looking for the "existential message." Latner's seamless universe is also an interpretation, one in which all knowing is reduced to a subjective interpretation.

Although some say that Gestalt therapists do not interpret, the word interpret is usually not defined. Sometimes it has been defined as "adding to the data, to the obvious." That definition is quite Newtonian. Clearly what we see is always partly a function of ourself and not only of what is out there. In a field theory the statement that we do not interpret makes little sense, unless the term is defined to exclude some kinds of interpreting.

This does not mean that there is no truth to the statement, since *the Gestalt approach emphasizes immediate experience rather than piecemeal, mechanistic analysis.* In Gestalt psychology they describe in detail the difference between mechanistic, atomistic interpretation and analysis and Gestalt interpretation and analysis. In the former all of the assumptions of the Newtonian approach are adhered to, and in the latter the parts are differentiated from the whole and always related to the whole in an organic way. The latter is consistent with the experiential approach in Gestalt therapy; the former is consistent with psychoanalytic interpretation and analysis.

C. Summary

The discussion of theories in physics is useful for stimulating thought in psychology. However, in spite of the prestige of physics, these similarities prove nothing in our realm of discourse. Even in physics a unified field theory is not yet possible. Therefore, we have no reason to expect physics theory to adequately cover our area. It can stimulate but not replace our own thinking.

I believe we need to distinguish true Newtonian mechanism from field theories with some Newtonian language or concepts, and to distinguish between universal interactionism and Gestalt field theory. It is my understanding that the goal of a Gestalt research or therapeutic exploration is to gain insight into the structure of the situation being studied. Our goal is not to be at one with the universe nor to follow any metaphysical system, but rather to explore situations in accordance with the phenomenological existential methodology with metaphysical beliefs "put in brackets" (Idhe, 1977).

I believe that a Gestalt field conception somewhat consistent with relativity theory would describe the field in terms of a closed unit of study that is differentiated internally and differentiated from a larger universe of which it is a part. The differentiation often takes a polar nature so that opposites have to be combined to get the whole picture. When Gestalt therapy is discussed as a "right brain" therapy I believe this idea of polarity is contradicted and the linear pole is not accounted for (or at least minimized).

We need further explication of the field approach in Gestalt therapy, including: relationship as the fundamental process in any field theory; comparison of this with innate self, the modern equivalent of the Aristotelian notion of essence, whose essential nature is discovered rather than chosen and is not dependent on the social situation (seen in that viewpoint as an evil corrupter of our essentially good nature); relationship between field theory, phenomenology and existentialism and how that is manifest in our literature; greater explication of the nature of structure in a process theory; relationship between these issues and the definition of the self; what the here and now means in terms of field theory; recommendations on research methodology in psychotherapy as derived from our field theory point of view; explication of diagnostic, personality, human development, family systems, organizational development from the field viewpoint, etc.

People and Process Orientation

Latner does a great service in pointing out that humanistic theorizing such as that of the Polsters is often not well integrated with the process-oriented Gestalt field view. It is also true that the explication was not finished in *Gestalt Therapy*. For example, it did not account clearly enough for the phenomenological experience of continuity. The whole person and the experience of self and boundedness needs explicating. The extension of contact into an account of the relationship of therapist and patient, i.e., the continuing and committed dialogue, is not accounted for. Nor is the relation between ego and self accounted for.

I think we need to stretch field theory to explicate humanistic level concerns and phenomenological realities. I believe we need to re-work the humanistic writings into field process terms without sacrificing the holistic conception of people. It is possible to be people oriented and still use field theory. If not we confirm Tobin's criticism that Gestalt therapy has not dealt with the phenomenological reality of the whole person (Tobin, 1982).

Latner discusses the humanistic orientation of the Polsters and the field orientation and describes them as competing and antithetical. He shows Newtonian or mechanistic notes in the Polsters' writing and states: "The differences in the meanings of these terms is huge. (*They come from different universes.*)" (Latner, 1983, p.81). Although I believe he did show that the Polsters' theorizing was done with some strong Newtonian language, Latner concludes with a dichotomous view that there is the humanistic discussion of people as objects in space and the different universe of the field conception of process: "different universes." He concludes the section with this paragraph:

I mentioned that this shift permits the Polsters to focus on object in space, rather than the field and the convergence of energy. Abstractly, formally, that is true. But in fact, the entities the Polsters concentrate on are people. Where Perls et al. specialize in the functioning of the self — itself a process — the Polsters' way of seeing emphasizes people, their selfconcepts, and the way their self-concepts form their meetings with others. It is a humanistic perspective, lucidly presented. I am not spending all this time to deride it. I want to emphasize its roots and its assumptions, and to distinguish it from another way of thinking about Gestalt therapy. (Latner, 1983, p.83)

Here Latner falls into a mechanistic view. How is it that the world is one big Gestalt, and yet humanism and field theory are from different universes? I believe that there is one universe, and that we are not discussing which universe but rather what kind of lens to use in looking at the universe. In discussing his general theory of relativity Einstein did not treat the world as one big gestalt, nor did he assume that there were several universes. He just held that natural laws apply in all realms of the one universe. We need a one universe language that applies to people as objects and the polar complementarity view of people as processes. Latner describes a single rider on two horses. Rather than hitching these horses so they can pull in tandem he dichotomizes (Latner, 1983, p.72).

The field is a concept that can apply to any level or area of work. It can describe the present and the sweep of time from past to present to future.

The phenomena that are represented by the concepts of objects in space can be restated as "of the field." I do not want to reduce our theoretical work to choosing between Newtonian humanism or field language that does not deal with the phenomenological reality of people as people.

Let us address the issue of describing the person/environment field with concepts that represent the whole person and that are also field theoretical. The related belief that there is little personality in health (Latner, 1983, p. 81) needs reformulating to take into account the primacy of the organism/environment relationship while accounting both for the repetitions the organism manifests (self) and the pictures the individual maintains of these repetitions (self-image).

What is is. We exist as part of fields, and we do experience ourselves as objects in space; both facts need accounting for. We may have to stretch and create to do so, but to end with choosing between our process theory and our humanism is intolerable to me.

Gestalt psychology and Husserlian phenomenology both had the same shortcomings that Perls et al. had in dealing with human process in holistic terms but not describing whole persons. This was solved when existential phenomenology diverged from transcendent phenomenology. I believe being cognizant of the existential-phenomenological ground from which we have emerged would be very useful. For me our essence is not in metaphysics or physics but in our direct existential experience. We can increase our effectiveness with bracketing and experimenting. We reduce our effectiveness by centering on sophisticated idea from other fields without full assimilation and integration.

Some Final Words

I would like to see Latner's lead followed in increasing our sophistication in improving our conceptual framework, but I would prefer that we use names and labels that refer to the conceptualizations and not to geography. Further I would prefer we focus on the quality of theoretical presentations and the content of these presentations rather than *ad hominem* arguments. To do this we would need to put aside sectional and personal rivalries.

I have advocated that we recognize that the use of Newtonian concepts in Gestalt therapy does not always make the approach Newtonian, and I have urged greater sophistication in distinguishing between postclassical viewpoints, especially in distinguishing between the Gestalt psychology and universal interactionist approaches.

I have also argued that the humanistic concepts of the whole person should be our focus, rather than the focus only on particular processes as did the Gestalt psychologists, but that we do so in field theoretical language. I believe that this is one of the more important theoretical tasks presently in front of us.

384

IV

THE PRACTICE
OF
GESTALT THERAPY

13

THE DIFFERENTIAL APPLICATION OF
GESTALT THERAPY

Commentary

1990. This essay and essay # 14 (Treating People with Character Disorders) were written as one unit especially for this book. In this first essay I discuss the general topic of diagnosis in Gestalt therapy, why it is necessary, the dangers, and how to do it. I illustrate the utility in #14 when I discuss treatment of character disorders in general, and treatment of the Narcissistic and Borderline Personality Disorders in particular.

Some people have the impression that Gestalt therapy is practiced in isolated, fragmentary episodic encounters without regard to any broader context in time (history), space (family, community, culture), personal identity of the patient (sense of self, developmental history) or nature of the individual's characterological personality organization. If this were true, Gestalt therapy would be practiced without differentiation according to who is being treated or the context in which the treatment is taking place. Critics who believe this of Gestalt therapy justifiably regard it as an almost fatal flaw in a system; some Gestalt therapists also have this view of Gestalt therapy, and to a few of these it may seem like an advantage in flexibility, spontaneity and humanistic attitude.

To the reader who has read the earlier sections of this book, it must be clear that I most vehemently disagree with this characterization of Gestalt therapy and even more vehemently with the notion that such a limitation would be an advantage. I believe such a limited methodology would severely limit the competence of a therapist and the effectiveness and safety of the therapy. For me, state of the art practice of Gestalt therapy requires differential application.

The above stated issues are vital to understanding the range of Gestalt therapy and how to work in Gestalt therapy with a variety of patients, in a number of settings. I will discuss the diagnostic process from my Gestalt therapy perspective and following that I will illustrate by discussing the differential treatment of the borderline and narcissistic personality disorders.

Diagnosis

I want to make a case for a humanistic diagnosis and assessment. Some people regard diagnosis and a humanistic dialogic relationship with patients as diametrically opposed to each other. My personal experience has been different — my experience is that accurate diagnosis aids humanistic therapy. When I have not been clear about diagnostic issues with a patient, my understanding of the patient and the patient's self-experience has been reduced, hence the effectiveness of my therapy has been severely reduced.

However, the humanistic concern about the potential negative effects of diagnosis is valid and needs to be understood in order to derive a diagnostic and assessment theory and practice that is effective and also takes into account the dangers. A short historical view of the progression from classical psychoanalysis will be our starting point.

The Case Against Diagnosis
The Classical Psychoanalytic Establishment
At the time of my initial training in psychotherapy (1962- 1964), psychiatric clinics, under the influence of classical psychoanalysis,

had an unfortunate tendency to emphasize and debate theory-driven and experience-far interpretations and medical-type diagnoses not based on behavioral descriptions and which contributed very little to the efficacy of differential treatment.

Treatment often started with a lengthy diagnostic phase (e.g., testing and detailed psychosocial history), and then staff debate about diagnosis (e.g., schizophrenia, paranoid type versus paranoia). The diagnosis made little difference in the treatment approach, although it did give a lot of content that became the focal point of the therapist's attention and a chief source for the therapist's interpretations. It seemed that more attention was being paid to categorization and diagnostic debates than to contact with the patient.

The lengthy diagnostic phase together with the Basic Rule of psychoanalysis gave patients the message that they were supposed to passively talk about "the problem" or about the past while waiting for the therapist to tell them what this all "really means." The therapist was the authority who worked out in advance what was the problem, the causes, the treatment and the desired outcome, and then told the patient.

In this traditional model, the therapist was in a hierarchically authoritative position, having the wisdom and imparting it to the patient. Making a diagnosis was part of the support for keeping the therapist in that role. The therapist was the expert who could diagnose and interpret. The analysis of problems, strengths, goals, etc. and choice of treatment was treated as the sole province of the professional. There was a decided lack of belief in the capacity of the individual to choose and grow, to recognize his or her personal situation for him or herself.

The immediate experience of the patient was not respected since it was assumed that patients keep meaning unconscious and do not have immediate access to that unconscious meaning. The therapist had access to the theory that made sense out of the material that emerged in the social history and the sessions of free association. Thus the lengthy diagnostic stage was part of the vertical, hierarchical system in which dialogue and the actual immediate experience of the patient were subordinate to theory, diagnosis and authority.

If the interpretations did not create understanding, the patient was said to be resisting. After all, the interpretations had been worked out carefully through the diagnosis and assessment process by the therapist. Resistance was to be overcome by the therapist. There was little room for spontaneity, diversity, choice, dialogue or emergence.

In this traditional relationship the therapist kept a professional distance and demeanor, did not gratify patient wishes, and was supposed to be several steps ahead of the patient, carefully considering each utterance before making it, and not feeling (and certainly not showing) any emotion (since that would be countertransference). The therapist's role in that model was to diagnose and interpret rather than contact. The actual immediate experience of the therapist, like the patient's, was not emphasized, unless it were labeled as countertransference and then emphasized as something to be analyzed out of existence.

The theory proscribed the therapist or patient from being active or the therapist from showing emotion. The therapist showed no feelings and made no "I" statements, etc. If either the therapist or patient were active or overtly interactive it was labeled as "acting out" and "acting in" — not considered one of the good things to do. Thus the creative and vital potential of the therapist, the patient and the relationship were severely limited rather than encouraged by the theory and rules of practice of that time.

There was also a tendency to treat the disease rather than the person (let alone relate to the person). The patient was categorized and put into a cubbyhole. In existential terms the patient was treated as an "it," a thing to be modified.

Theory-driven interpretations, categorization and the therapeutic mask were part of a methodological outlook. This therapeutic methodology was consistent with the Freudian view of human nature in which the patient was seen as dominated by dangerous innate drives and rigid social injunctions. This whole system was based on a lack of trust in the capacity of human growth and the human encounter. This was not consistent with the emerging zeitgeist and therapy movements that followed.

Reform Within Psychoanalysis

Gestalt therapy has been influenced by those within the psychoanalytic movement who introduced a social emphasis into psychoanalytic personality theory, instead of the Freudian emphasis on innate drives and preset maturational developments, and a more active model of therapist involvement than the classical model. This stream of development includes Rank, Reich, Horney and, in fact, most of the neo-Freudian theorists. They wrote of the human potential for growth and the importance of relationship in growth (both in developmental character formation and in treatment).

However, in general they still remained within the psychoanalytic ken and kept four of the objectionable aspects of the psychoanalytic system in place. First, they kept the psychoanalytic theory of consciousness in which thought and behavior were believed to be determined by unconscious drives that were neither chosen nor readily available to awareness except through lengthy psychoanalytic procedures.

> Freud is clearly explicit that the unconscious is absolutely inaccessible to consciousness without psychoanalytic method. This view is to pervade the entire fabric of Freud's completed writings, and become a cornerstone emphasis within much of the later refinements of Freudian psychoanalysis. (Masek, 1989, p. 275)

It is interesting that pre-Freudian concepts of the unconscious did not treat the unconscious as totally or absolutely inaccessible to the person's perception, but rather conceptualized it as that which was implicit but not immediately reflected in the person's experience (Masek, 1989, p.274). In this regard, the pre-Freudian concepts are closer to post-Freudian, phenomenological concepts, including those of Gestalt therapy. But the socially minded psychoanalytic reformers did not make the revolutionary switch to a phenomenological theory of awareness in which that which is out of awareness is thought to be directly available to sensory awareness.

Second, they also kept the psychoanalytic relationship theory which emphasized the establishment, management and analysis of transference as the central technique in treatment. Third, they kept the emphasis on interpretation as the chief intervention. This connected the prior two points since it was largely the unconscious aspects of the transference that was interpreted.

Psychoanalytic debate has tended to question the content of the interpretation, but leave in place the emphasis on interpretation itself. Thus the latest psychoanalytic theories challenge drive theory as the basis of interpretation, but still maintain a transference-based, interpretative focus as the essence of psychoanalytic treatment. Even Heinz Kohut states that empathy must be followed by a stage of interpretation if the psychoanalysis is to be finished (Kohut, 1984).

Fourth, they still largely maintained the mechanistic, linear causality model in which the present was thought to be determined in a linear fashion by past events (especially childhood events).

The Humanistic-Existential Response

The humanistic and existential movement remonstrated against these trends. A phenomenological theory of consciousness, a dialogical theory of relationship and a nonlinear process theory of causality formed the core of the alternative theories. In the vanguard of this movement were Carl Rogers; the group process movement out of the NTL labs in Bethel, Maine; and, of course, Gestalt therapy.

In treatment the emphasis was on the uniqueness of the individual, the relationship between the therapist as a person and the person who was the patient, the here and now, faith in the vigor and power of the human spirit and consciousness, and encouragement of zesty personal interactions, creativity and spontaneity. Carl Rogers was perhaps the clearest in explicating the nature of the relationship (the empathic bond with a therapist who is emotionally present as a person and showing unconditional positive regard, warmth and congruence).

In the humanistic movement there was a marked antipathy to the medical and classical psychoanalytic models, an antipathy to putting people in categories and reducing people to disease entities. The humanistic and existential attitude was that we treat whole people and that the wholeness of people emerges in the context of the person-to-person encounter.

In the humanistic existential movement the relationship was horizontal rather than vertical, the patient and therapist working together as equals (although the focus was more on the patient since that was the therapeutic task). Authority did not rest with the professional, or with the theory, but rather with the actual experience of both parties to the therapeutic dialogue.

The new humanistic attitude went along nicely with Gestalt therapy's strong political and philosophic commitment and passion against tyranny, arbitrary imposed or authoritarian limitations, rigid adherence to static arrangements that did not meet current need, and "fixed Gestalten." Gestalt therapy rejected the diagnostic emphasis of classical psychoanalysis along with the theory of the unconscious, the relationship theory and the mechanistic theory of causality. The view of the therapist as the authority that worked everything out in advance, necessitating a lengthy diagnostic process, and then told the patient what was true was discarded in favor of a belief that growth, clarity, truth, values for the individual emerged from social interaction — the dialogic relationship between patient and therapist.

I was excited when I discovered Gestalt therapy and its view of human nature and how to treat people. The Gestalt therapy rebellion against the categorizing, analyzing and putting patients into cubbyholes according to theory-driven, a priori beliefs and concepts was liberating for me. The rebellion against interpretation as the mainstay of treatment was relieving for me. And the rebellion against the professional relationship theory that dictated that the presence of the therapist be kept distant and indirect and that proscribed showing compassion for or other emotions to the patient was growth producing for me.

Of all of the systems that were part of the movement toward a new view of people and therapy, Gestalt therapy attracted me by its integrating foundation which provided a new theoretical framework that accommodated the power of both the therapist's and patient's vitality and creativity and an accepting attitude of assimilating a diverse array of technical and personal interventions.

The phenomenological treatment of Gestalt therapy, Rogerian and others was a radical departure from the classical formula that treatment equaled interpretation, and interpretation was a function of diagnosis and theory. The older system was far from the phenomenological experience of patient (or therapist). Interventions (content, sequence, timing) were all prescribed by theory.

Spontaneity, creativity and art in psychotherapy were not well supported.

The new attitude was called the human potential movement, for good reason. Gestalt therapy was a prominent part of that movement. It affirmed that growth happened when people were in contact with those around them. Growth was what emerged from phenomenological focusing (which was contact between observer and that which was observed) and dialogical contact. The human potential movement put psychotherapy into the truth-and-understanding business rather than the disease-curing business. In this heady atmosphere, diagnosis was thrown out along with drive theory, the unavailable unconscious, therapist-induced transference and mechanistic causality.

The Case for Diagnosis
Did the Antidiagnosis Bias Go Too Far?

Sometimes forward progress moves from one extreme to its opposite before finding a middle ground. I believe the total rejection of diagnosis was a case of going to the antithesis, and this section is a brief for a synthesis, for a middle ground between categorization and assessment displacing contact and awareness work on the one hand and throwing out all categorization and assessment on the other. I wrote this section, "The Case for Diagnosis," for those in Gestalt therapy who believe that diagnosis is antithetical to the Gestalt therapy attitude. In this section I will discuss the advantages. For those who already know that diagnosis is a necessary and important aspect of Gestalt therapy, the current section may be dispensable. After this section I will define diagnosis and discuss its nature.

I do not regard the stance against diagnosis as integral to Gestalt theory. On the contrary, I think that good diagnosis is an integral and indispensable part of Gestalt therapy.

One of the unfortunate aspects to attributing the antidiagnostic bias to Gestalt therapy is that when clinicians have become clear about the need for diagnosis and sharing information about character structure and treatment indications, they have often moved from Gestalt therapy into other frameworks. Antidiagnostic bias, especially at a cliché or naive level, makes Gestalt therapy a haven for students who want their learning to be a therapist to be easy and it makes Gestalt therapy an easy target for disrespect, disregard, polemics and criticism.

This has been a problem throughout the humanistic psychotherapy movement. It has been noted that the lack of clinical literature about differential application of Rogerian therapy might be a contributor to the relatively greater success of self psychology in the 1980s in spite of the fact that the self psychology empathic approach is not only similar to the Rogerian approach, but may have stemmed from the early work of Carl Rogers at Chicago (see discussion in Kahn, 1989). The Rogerian movement has produced research of great quality and quantity, but its theoretical bias has limited its development of a discussion of differential application according to diagnosis. Parenthetically, one might note that Rogers tried to show that the client-centered approach unmodified would be successful in treating hospitalized schizophrenics. Of course, the evidence, courageously and clearly published by Rogers, showed the opposite and supports my thesis (Rogers, 1967).

Therapists Do Categorize, Assess and Diagnose

Diagnosis can be a process of respectfully paying attention to who the person is both as a unique individual and in respect to those characteristics shared with other individuals. Categorization, assessment and diagnosis is an indispensable part of assessment and competent therapists all do it. We make discriminations about general patterns, about what kind of person the patient is, what the central problems and strengths are, what the probable course of treatment will be, what approaches are likely to work, danger signs. Since all patients are not alike, we take notice and are affected by the differences that do exist between patients.

We cannot avoid diagnosing: our choice is whether to do so in a sloppy or inadvertent way or else in a well-considered way with full awareness. The danger of imposing a belief or judgment system on the patient is made worse by diagnosing without awareness. We can make these discriminations with the latest research evidence in mind, or we can try to discover by ourselves without regard to what has been learned by the profession.

This is as true in Gestalt therapy as in any other therapy. Michael Vincent Miller said:

> Present moments can become random and discontinuous unless they are grounded in a larger perspective that includes the past and the future, which is to say a view of human development, and a way of understanding how people make their experience, which is to say a theory of character. (Miller, 1985, p. 53)

Interaction Between Gestalt Therapy and Other Systems

I believe that case material, including diagnostic and treatment considerations, along with other published research results, are quite relevant to Gestalt therapy. And such material from Gestalt therapy would be quite useful to the field. The movement in the psychological literature in the United States in the last few years has stressed the utilization of material from various frameworks and de-emphasis on the exclusive efficacy of any one school of thought. This movement toward convergence and eclecticism could be much aided by Gestalt therapy as Gestalt therapy is aided by it. I believe that Gestalt therapy is still the best framework for utilizing the wisdom of the various approaches. In reading Les Greenberg's work, one can see how a Gestalt therapy influence can be useful in sophisticated eclectic research (Greenberg, 1986, 1988).

It is unfortunate that the diagnostic potential of Gestalt therapy theory has not been more exploited, and I am pleased and excited by various efforts to develop such throughout the world at the present time. In the meantime, before such efforts mature and are tested, I use any diagnostic wisdom that is available. I do not limit myself to what is already done within the Gestalt therapy framework or already translated into Gestalt therapy terms. I am a psychologist practicing psychotherapy from a Gestalt therapy perspective, but my commitment is not just to what has been elaborated in the Gestalt therapy literature. Wherever there is descriptive material based on actual experience that will enrich my background, I utilize this material and recommend it to those I train. I discuss how to do this in #9 (Assimilating Diagnostic and

Psychoanalytic Perspectives into Gestalt Therapy) and also later in this chapter.

Uses of Categorization, Diagnosis and Assessment

A good diagnostic description is not just a categorization, but imparts information. Using a common diagnostic language facilitates the exchange of information, so we can learn from each other. The resultant picture should have more whole person-oriented understanding and descriptions. It permits more attention to the issue of continuity of personal identity, i.e., in addition to the here-and-now moment. It eases the explicating of the patient's psychological structure. It aids the learning of the therapist and using the patient's developmental and clinical history to the patient's advantage.

Diagnosis enables the therapist to be more precise, discriminating and articulate in understanding the particular and differing reality of each individual patient and each type of patient. It enables the therapist to make better guesses about what the patient might be experiencing, how he or she might react to a particular intervention, what other behaviors are likely to accompany that which is presented to the therapist in the therapeutic hour, to recognize key developmental events that have to be worked through, etc.

Assessment and diagnosis is a process by which the therapist's experience enables him or her to make discriminations based on the recognition of patterns. Although therapeutic decisions are made based on many factors, e.g., observation, dialogue, emotional response of therapist, intuition, etc., these decisions are informed by diagnostic discriminations. Decisions that need to be diagnostically informed include: which patients to accept into treatment, assignment of therapist to patient in clinics and hospitals, choice of intervention, criteria for knowing whether one is making progress.

Questions arise when seeing a new patient: What are the chief issues being presented? Which one do I address first? What does this patient need? Is the person's story believable? Is the patient manipulating, and if so how and for what purpose? Do I inquire about developmental history, or do I insist on staying here and now? Do I share my emotional reaction, or do I share observations of the patient's behavior, or do I ask about the patient's awareness, or do I suggest an experiment?

Is it safe to confront the patient? Is the patient sane? Is there need for medical referral for a possible organic condition? Is the patient suicidal? Why does it seem that my intervention is having a negative impact? Is the patient decompensating or going into profound impasse work? Or maybe reacting to a narcissistic wounding? Why is the patient not understanding what I am saying? Is it because the patient is "playing dumb," or does not have a background that would support understanding, or has a learning disability, or lacks sufficient intelligence? Or is the patient hostile, or scared, or secretly trying to make a fool out of the therapist? Or maybe the therapist is not being clear?

What are the life patterns of this patient? What is likely to be in the developmental background that would enable us to be clearer about the patient's path, the meaning of the patient's current behavior?

Diagnostic understanding enables the therapist to know better what interventions, what sequence, what timing to use, to be able to relate these with the prior experience in treatment with patients that are similar to the one presently being worked with. It enables the therapist to be forewarned about what precautions need to be taken. For example, a patient talks of having an increase in energy, and in fact an almost inexhaustible supply of energy. Is this a normal, or better than normal, phenomena to be encouraged — or is it the beginning of the manic phase of someone with a bipolar depression and cause for some concern?

It also facilitates the therapist in understanding patients who are very different from himself or herself. Patients who are similar to the therapist are relatively easy for therapists to understand and have an empathic response to, i.e., for therapists who have had sufficient therapy of their own. But patients who are very different require more effort. Diagnosis helps. It facilitates an exchange of information between therapists and a honing of the therapist's perception. Do we need to reinvent the wheel ourselves?

It also helps in being aware of that which is not immediately obvious, especially long term implications. We will see this below when we discuss differential treatment of the narcissistic personality disordered compared with treatment of borderline patients.

Defining Diagnosis

The word *diagnosis* goes back to two Greek words, meaning "to know" and "through or between." In its most general meaning it refers to distinguishing or discriminating. Webster defines it as:

> The act or process of deciding the nature of a diseased condition by examination, OR A careful investigation of the facts to determine the nature of a thing, OR The decision or opinion resulting from such examination or investigation.

I use the term diagnosis in the latter two senses, referring to careful investigation of the facts or the result of such an examination, and do not limit the term to the examination of diseased conditions.

The English and English psychological dictionary (1958) gives two definitions of diagnosis:

> Identification of disease or abnormality from symptoms presented, and from a study of its origin and course,   O R
> Any classification of an individual on the basis of observed characters.

Clearly in the general meanings of both Webster and English and English, diagnosis must be ubiquitous in any competent psychotherapy.

Again according to English and English: A differential diagnosis is a distinguishing between two similar-appearing conditions by searching for a significant symptom or attribute found in only one. It is extended by analogy from its medical use to conditions of any sort. It seems to me that this is the sort of discrimination that good therapists always make.

Diagnosis through a Gestalt Therapy Lens

The diagnostic process is a search for meaning. In Gestalt therapy theory meaning is the relationship between figure and ground.

The Figure-Ground Invariant

The figure/ground formation and meaning construction process is an invariant in human functioning (Spinelli, 1989). The quality of this process determines the quality of a person's consciousness and self-regulation. The person is self-regulating in an organismic manner to the extent that the figure that is formed in this process is continually shaped by the dominant organismic need of the person and the environment. A careful phenomenological study of the process of a person's figure/ground meaning formation generates an understanding of the person's personality organization.

Any clear and lively figure is meaningful, for it stands out at a moment meaningfully against the background of someone's experience. However, if the figure/ground constellation is defined merely by the excitement of the moment, without connection to larger gestalten, it is a very narrow sense of meaning. A narrow sense of meaning is of insufficient consequence for good therapy. Good therapy requires a much more substantial sense of meaning, a gestalt defined by its place in the larger gestalt of the person's ongoing existence and that of the rest of the human environment.

To the extent that a person's phenomenological ground is shallow, to that extent the person's sense of meaning is also shallow. To the extent that a person's phenomenological figure is not crisp, sharp and energetic, to that extent the person's sense of meaning will also be reduced.

The Figure Ground Process in Therapy

In psychotherapy what configures the figure/ground process for the therapist is not just random excitement or just any need or interest of the therapist, but rather a particular mission, one of considerable moment. To be effective, the therapist must construct meaning by connecting the moment to larger gestalten that are vital to the task of the therapy.

In the theory of Gestalt therapy the "self" is always an interrelationship of person and environment, a current organismic/environment field. A person's selfhood can only be understood as person-in-relation, and never apart from the organismic/environment field. However, while the context — hence the organism/environment field — changes moment to moment, each person has characteristic and unique ways of relating that change very little over time, space, and context, and that the person brings to each new field. This pattern of existence that is brought to each field includes behavior, sensing, perceiving, thinking, feeling, believing, etc.

Diagnosis is the process of the therapist seeking meaning or insight into the structure of the character and personality of a patient, differentiating the similarities and differences of that patient's patterns from those of different types of patients and devising an intervention approach based on this knowledge. This is a process of the therapist relating what emerges at a moment to a larger gestalt, especially to the invariants of a person's interactions with multiple organism/environment fields, for the purpose of creating the best psychotherapeutic intervention that is possible given the global circumstances.

We seek to understand the unique person. But one cannot fully understand the uniqueness of a person, if the person is not understood in comparison with others. If a patient has a thought disorder, the therapist will not understand that unique person unless he or she knows about the thought disorder and what a thought disorder is. And, understanding a thought disorder is meaningful only in comparison with the thought processes of people who don't have a thought disorder.

Clinically we often need to distinguish between a depression stemming from the loss of another autonomous and important person from a depression stemming from the emptiness and collapse attendant on narcissistic failure. In the former case an "I" statement by the therapist might likely be experienced by the patient as reaching out in a caring manner. In the latter case an "I" statement by the therapist might well be experienced by a narcissistic patient as an intrusion, as a demand to respond, and result in narcissistic injury and, if this occurs early in the therapy, can even lead to premature termination.

At any one moment, some aspects of that overall, ongoing pattern will be manifest in an organism/environment field. In diagnosing, the therapist tries to apprehend the overall pattern from the first manifestations of that pattern in the particular therapeutic organism/environment field. Diagnosis is not only an attempt at insight into how the structure operates, but it is an attempt to do so early in the treatment process so it can inform the therapist in his or her attitudes and interventions. Differential diagnosis is being able to use early manifestations of a pattern, to distinguish it from other patterns, while the therapist can still modify his or her response.

Meaning, Contact and Unawareness

There are infinite potential figure/ground possibilities, varying with person, biology, place, time, culture, etc. However, there can only be one clear figure at a time. Much of the time the larger meaning is out of a person's focal awareness, i.e., the relationship between a figure that is manifest and the background against which the fullest meaning could be experienced, is kept out of the foreground. This can be useful, since if we were only aware of the ultimate meaning of very large or long range gestalten, we would miss more immediate, concrete and emerging realities. If we only saw the stars, we would miss the smell of the roses and the pits in the road.

Gestalt therapy addresses the person's awareness of his or her awareness process so that what is systematically kept out of awareness can become aware as needed. To do this most effectively, the therapist's figure has to take the larger gestalten into account so that the therapist's perspective is not limited to the patient's. I am not talking here of compulsive, obsessive or intellectualized focus on diagnosis or ultimate meaning, but the richness and wisdom of the therapist's orientation.

Diagnosis, like any form of meaning, is not absolute; on the contrary, it is constructed. This construction emerges out of the contact between therapist and patient. In Gestalt therapy meaning is configured separately and jointly by both the therapist and the patient. Theory, including Gestalt therapy theory, diagnosis, and research results can help clarify what figure and what ground and what relation between the figure and the ground is most useful to concentrate on at a particular moment.

For the patient the gestalt of the moment derives its meaning primarily from its part in the larger whole of the sweep of his or her entire life. The gestalt of the moment in therapy derives its meaning from its part in the larger whole of the entire therapy, especially from the therapeutic relationship with the therapist, and ultimately from the whole of the patient's life.

402

Examples and Discussion

Out of the meeting of patient and therapist, a clear figure forms for the therapist. For example, a group therapist notices the young male member turning slightly red in coloration and holding his breathe when an attractive woman comes into the room.

Of what importance is this in the therapy? Can the therapist make direct comment on the observation? Would it be appropriate to structure an experiment of contact between group members that might find the young man and woman in joint proximity? Imagine for a moment that this is a young man who is well supported, fairly open in contact and awareness work within the group and wanting to work on his anxiety with women he is attracted to. Now imagine for a moment a contrasting scenario: the young man is a fragile, easily wounded person who gets paranoid and rageful when threatened. Now imagine that the young man is homosexual, and ambivalent about his mixed positive and negative feelings toward women and not ready to work on his feelings toward women.

I hope it is clear to all readers that these distinctions would make a difference in how the therapist intervened.

Another example: a therapist notes that when she tells the patient he has some responsibility for the fight between him and his wife the night before, that the patient does not acknowledge the therapist's statement. Is this a patient who is very shame oriented, blaming himself, and likely to be feeling shamed by the therapist? Or is the patient, perhaps, doing with the therapist what he did with his wife, i.e., not responding? Or is this a person who chronically responds without taking responsibility and needs a very firm and assertive stance by the therapist? Perhaps it is a psychotic patient and out of contact with reality altogether.

Again I assume the reader can readily see that these distinctions would make a difference in how the therapist responds. Below we will explore in more detail how the diagnostic distinctions make a significant difference in the differential treatment of patients with a narcissistic character disorder and of borderline patients.

In another example, a patient fidgets and this becomes the therapist's foreground. This must also be responded to with discrimination. Is this a narcissistically vulnerable patient who would react with shame, deflation, rage, etc., if the fidgeting is pointed out? Is this a conforming patient who would respond to any experiment on explicating the fidgeting, but all of it in an "as if" manner? Is it a patient who is bizarre and usually shows gestures more dramatically than today? Or perhaps just an uptight neurotic patient that might really be able to reown some of the disowned emotional energy being drained off by the fidgeting if it were worked with?

How does the therapist decide what to respond to, and of what importance it is in the therapy? Part of the answer is: by relating the here-and-now figure of attention to the background of both its meaning in the patient's phenomenology, the observed life pattern of the patient (the phenomenology of the patient and others who observe the patient) and that which arises out of the interaction between the two people.

As we come to anticipate what is likely to develop, and we respond according to our differential understanding of the person, i.e., the differential diagnosis discriminating how this patient is similar and different from others, we systematically note our understanding and our response. Then we test our understanding of the pattern and our response against the actual experience that emerges over time from the clinical interactions.

Do Gestalt Therapists Analyze and Diagnose?

In some of the cliché level statements, it has been claimed that Gestalt therapists do not analyze or interpret. If this kind of claim refers to not making psychoanalytic interpretation, this is conceivably defensible, although not true in how I practice Gestalt therapy. But any claim that Gestalt therapists make no analysis or interpretation at all is nonsense. Any observation adds to the data in many ways. The choice of what to observe, what to emphasize, what meanings come out of the interaction between the observer and the observed, all add to the data. Our suggested experiments, observations, homework assignments, our emotional response, all arise in part out of the meanings that arise in the phenomenological interaction, including inferences.

At least four factors make an analysis or interpretation consistent with Gestalt therapy theory and practice: First is that the statements be phenomenologically focused. This has been discussed above, but briefly this refers to bracketing, epoché, etc. Thus any statement needs explication via a phenomenological reduction to separate actual experience from sedimented preconception.

Second, in the clinical situation, the phenomenological exploration is done in a dialogic manner. This means that the patient is encouraged and trained to partake in the experimentation and the conclusion making. When the analysis is about the patient, the patient's phenomenologically aware experience is the most important test of accuracy.

Third, to be consistent with Gestalt therapy theory, the conclusions should ultimately be framed in field process language. In the clinical situation and in many preliminary discussions, the language may not yet be transformed into process terms. An interpretation in mechanistic language could be: "You are a hostile person." A field process interpretation might be: "You are acting angry without being direct."

Often the patient makes a mechanistic interpretation rather than a field process interpretation. I have often heard patients who feel empty conclude "I have no self." The patient is making a mechanistic interpretation of himself or herself. Thinking of the self as a thing that one has or lacks is an unfortunate mechanistic interpretation that can create despair and lead the patient away from important growth work. The process of experiencing emptiness is a self process. I recently had a patient talking of the illness of his elderly father. He talked about the possible disintegration of the "family unit," as if it were a thing that automatically turns into nothing with change. When he framed the family unit in process terms he realized the human behaviors that went into the family unit, that these would change upon the death of his father, and that the family was not static but always in the process of change.

Fourth, what makes an interpretation or analysis consistent with the Gestalt theory is whether it is a "structure-clear analysis" (Wertheimer, 1945). Some analyses are treated as a summation of separate monads, like a chemical formula. These analyses Gestalt psychologists referred to as "and summative" analyses. This kind of analysis does not take into account the structure of the whole.

Rather than being insightful, such interpretations are mechanistic, simplistic and misleading.

Another way of saying this is that in a Gestalt analysis the parts are an integral part of the whole. In an analysis not consistent with the Gestalt attitude the parts are derived from some outside theoretical bias. As Fuchs put it: "There are two kinds of analysis: in one a whole is divided into subdivisions already given or implied by the whole itself; in the other an arbitrary principle of division is imposed upon the whole" (Fuchs, 1938, p. 354).

An example: a man talks of his problems at work with his supervisor. His supervisor is authoritarian, arbitrary, unpredictable. The distribution of responsibilities, authority and perks are not rational and equitable. The patient is easily hurt and reacts with primitive rage. The therapist works with the transference reaction of the patient, for there are distinct similarities between the boss and the patient's father. The therapist makes the interpretation that the patient's reaction is explained by the transference phenomenon, i.e., caused by the patient's past experience with his father.

Transference is just one piece and must be related to the whole field to be structure-clear. By itself it does not account for the multiplicity of factors in the actual situation that would be necessary for a full account. A structure-clear interpretation makes clear how the patient acts, feels, perceives in the actual present situation, how he brings to foreground beliefs and attitude formed in past situations, how this behavior fits into the general functioning of the patient, how this is elicited and reinforced by the structure of the work situation and the personalities of those in that situation, etc.

I think that diagnosis in Gestalt therapy should be made with full recognition of the structure of the whole. When dealing with people this means accounting for their image of themselves and their identity over time, the context of meaning of their current interaction, the history of such interactions in various contexts that form the background of the present moment, and the like.

When dealing with diagnosis the question of what is normal and abnormal arises. I mentioned in my discussion of the definition of diagnosis that I was not restricting its use to the diagnosis of pathology. Yet questions of normality and pathology do arise when observing patterns and deciding on interventions.

Deviation from a norm means deviation from a norm. This may be subnormal or supernormal or just different. And it is essential to keep clear what the criterion is for the use of the term abnormal. What is statistically normal in a group or culture may or may not be normal either in the context of a theory of human functioning or from the standpoint of the organismic functioning of a particular individual. What is functional for a person in one context or culture might be quite dysfunctional in another.

Gestalt therapy has a theory of normality that is not content specific, but is process specific. That is, the theory advances a concept of normality that is culturally neutral; it defines normality in terms of the figure/ground formation and destruction process in the organism/environment field. This leaves unanswered many questions of philosophy and morality, but does give a standard of normality that is quite serviceable in psychotherapy. If the person's relation with the environment is such that the awareness and contact process is clear and forms a good Gestalt that accounts for what is present and what is needed in the person and environment, then this is psychological health.

From a phenomenological, field perspective, there is no absolute healthy culture or standard against which to judge individuals or cultures. However, we can observe a person's functioning and describe it in terms that make clear whether there is clarity of awareness, contact, boundaries, and so forth. This leaves a lot of room for some individuals who are deviant in "sick cultures" to be healthy, and for conforming people, even in healthy cultures, to be seen as unhealthy.

The test of diagnosis is in the phenomenology of patient and therapist and the dialogical process between them. No statistical or theoretical test, no therapist opinion or preset outcome criteria can substitute for emerging discriminations based on phenomenological focusing, dialogue and the self-determined self-regulation of the patient.

Assessment and diagnosis should not be equated with a code number in a DSM III handbook. It may be a paragraph of descriptive material. A diagnosis is what does the job described in this chapter.

No two therapies are the same. We think of the therapy relationship as relating to the unique person of the patient with the manifest unique presence of the therapist. But there are patterns of distinguishing features we can use to discriminate how people are alike and not alike. And by thinking in these terms, over time we learn from experience of these patterns so that each unique situation is not totally unique and we do not have to reinvent the wheel over and over.

How Do I Assess and Diagnose?

Before I discuss some specific considerations of differential treatment of patients with narcissistic personality disorders and with borderline conditions, I will make some general observations on how I assess and diagnose while dialogically relating to the patient.

First, whenever possible I begin any clinical interaction by centering and bracketing so that when I am with the patient I can allow the obvious (the "given") to impress me. What do I see and hear? What is the quality and way of contact? How does the patient's awareness process work? What do I observe and how am I affected?

What Do I See And Hear? The Body and Speech Pattern

I observe the person's breathing, body posture, movement and sound of voice. How tense is the patient, and what is the pattern of the tension? What is the coloration, ease of movement, liveliness? Is there grace and power in the movements? Is the pitch and rhythm of the voice easy, forced? Is it choppy, staccato? Or perhaps belabored?

Initiative

Does the patient take initiative? Does the patient give me a chance to take initiative? Does he or she react to me, or perhaps act as if I am irrelevant? Or perhaps react only to me, leaving out himself or herself as an autonomous person?

Coherence Of Story

How coherent is the patient's story? Does one aspect follow from the other in the person's account? Does it make sense, or do

I find myself asking "What's wrong with this picture?" Is it logical by consensual standards? Does the story confuse me, make me squint and shake my head? Is the story incomplete, leaving gaps?

Liveliness And Emotionality

How much vitality does the patient show? Does the emotion, both the quality of the emotion and the intensity, match the situation or story being told? What is the quality of the energy? Flat? Totally flat, as in psychotic withdrawal? Or perhaps flat as in depressed affect. Is the energy staccato, marked by quick retroflective withdrawal? Or smooth, as if everything is rehearsed? Does the energy seem exaggerated or the figure forming very quickly and changing as quickly?

Changes During The Hour

How do the gestures and other nonverbal aspects change during the hour? Does the latency of response, retroflections, emotional quality change during the course of the hour? Does this move in linear fashion, e.g., the patient improving mood during the course of the hour, or more likely, does it change depending on the subject of the moment and the meaning it has for the patient?

Listen To The Patient's Story

Gestalt therapy was part of the humanistic reaction against the frequently emotionless, lifeless and obsessive routine that classical psychoanalysis had evolved to, including free associating (sometimes pejoratively called "free dissociation" by Gestalt therapy wiseguys), and recounting of history past and current. Gestalt therapy groups, sensitivity groups and similar endeavors discovered the excitement and vitality of here-and-now activities. The point of this new fashion was the focusing of attention on what was of felt importance to the patient rather than spending time on that which was not organismically involving.

Unfortunately many Gestalt therapists in the late 1960s treated any discussion of the patient's life as an avoidance of reality, i.e., "here and now" (see discussion in #1 — "Recent Trends in Gestalt Therapy"). This radical position wrought stimulation, tumult, passion and elation. It was this radical and simplistic position that was most publicized and most emulated. It was simpler than the theoretically sounder Gestalt therapy position that required discrimination of what was actually important to the patient at the moment.

Proficient Gestalt therapists did not stay long with this radical position. Actual experience as well as a better understanding of theoretical considerations led to following what the dialogue and patient concern dictated. Those who oversimplified Gestalt therapy theory and treated it as rigid dogma were faced with the choice of being narrow and following what they thought was orthodox Gestalt therapy principles, techniques and clichés or rebelling against them and rejecting Gestalt therapy. Many of these went from Gestalt therapy into other therapies because of the perceived limitation. A better understanding of Gestalt therapy theory and the role of theory (and distinguishing this from cliché level verbalizing) made obvious to many of us that this Hobson's choice was unnecessary.

Recently Erv Polster (1987) made a clear statement of the importance of the person's life history, and how to bring out the drama of that story.

I believe it is impossible to do competent, comprehensive, long term psychotherapy without respecting the importance of the patient's story. The answer to the compulsive beginning of therapy with a long diagnostic phase and history gathering is not to discard diagnosis and history, but rather to work with it as it arises and is relevant to the phenomenological and dialogical clinical work.

How Is The Therapist Affected?

Do I react with interest or apathy? If I am not touched by what the patient says, why not? Am I untouchable? Are other matters in my life intruding on my availability? Or is the patient not expressing anything of organismic value to him or her? Or perhaps something of organismic value is being expressed, but with the energy retroflected and withheld? If I am touched, in what way? What is stirred up in me? Do I respond sadly, compassionately, angrily, with joy? What memories, associations, metaphors emerge?

How the therapist is affected is important for several reasons. It is important for therapists to be aware of their own reactions so that they can be responsible for them, center themselves, bracket, and prevent unaware contamination of interventions. Moreover, to be able to enter into a dialogue, knowing one's reaction and whence it comes is absolutely essential. It is also important to know one's reaction for its diagnostic value.

There is a tendency for many therapists to blame the patient for the therapist's own reaction. In psychoanalysis the concepts of resistance and projective identification have sometimes been used in that way. Unfortunately, this has also occurred in Gestalt therapy. In both systems, good practice requires that therapists take responsibility for their own emotional reactions.

In Gestalt therapy we do not regard all emotional reactions of the therapist as countertransference. A reaction is counter-transferential when it is projected without insight into the current field and when it is residue from another field, i.e., another time, place or person. When the emotional response of the therapist is made with insight and mainly in reaction to the patient in the here and now, it is not transferred. It may still be another kind of parataxic distortion (or not), and it may or may not be good to share this with the patient. Of course all of these discriminations depend on being aware of how one is affected as well as the make-up of the patient.

Let A Figure Form

When I center and bracket and let myself be affected, I am letting a figure form. I am letting myself be impressed by the obvious. This means allowing something to come into awareness, allowing the figure to sharpen, and so through the whole cycle of figure formation and destruction. This makes room for spontane-ous reaction, curiosity, etc. and allows a relationship to form between the here-and-now interaction and a broad background. The emerging figure forms a spontaneous answer to questions such as: "How do I understand this?" "What interests me about this?" "What makes this work?" "What is important about this?"

Patterns In the Hour and Parallels with the Patient's Story

Observing parallels between what is happening in the therapy hour and the theme or story that the patient is working on is particularly valuable for differential treatment. If the patient is

411

working on a pattern of behavior that does not emerge during the session, why not? If it does emerge in the session, bringing this to the attention of the patient often causes surprise and new perspective. Awareness of this enables the therapist not to willingly be part of a repetitive pattern of interrelationships of the patient that have not been satisfying.

For example, a 25-year-old man complains of the lack of emotional responsiveness of the women he dates. As he talks of the lack of warmth, excitement, caring, sensitivity, etc., of the women in the relationships, he sounds flat, intellectualized. The content contains a lot of rationalizing, obsessive circles. What emerges for the therapist is an awareness of the avoidance of feelings in the interaction in the session and that was a clue to what was happening in relationship with the women also. This gave the therapist and patient two vantage points to the same problem.

When the therapist shared observations of this, or shared his own reaction or suggested experiments, the patient became hurt, increasingly defensive, distressed and unable to do any significant psychological work. When the therapist listened empathically, slowly making very small correlations with previous patient statements, the patient increased his sense of well-being, increased his openness and the depth of his psychological work. This paralleled the patient's report of well-being when his friends or lovers showed caring response to his feelings.

The observations in the session helped speed the understanding of how the patient was outside the hour, and the reports of the patterns outside the therapeutic hour helped speed the understanding of what was happening in the hour. Sometimes the clarification comes from the lack of similarity.

A 37-year-old married woman with two young children reported feeling safe in the intimacy of the therapeutic encounter and feeling better after sessions. In the sessions she seemed bright, had a good sense of humor, was open, showed a good deal of common sense, and did her exploratory work. What she reported with her husband was seeming to be stupid (by self-observation and husband's observation), dour, rigid, brittle, closed. Why the discrepancy?

At the beginning of the therapy she was very defensive, but over time learned that the therapist would respond with caring, would listen, would not attack, and would be straight with feedback. At home she experienced her husband as attacking, sarcastic, isolating himself, rejecting affectionate advances, and so forth. While she was able to feel some cohesion and self-esteem in the good contact with the therapist, she felt fragmented, rageful, and sometimes panicky when the situation was not safe. This was especially so with her husband, and their relationship that was very contaminated by both of their transferences from early developmental experiences with their own parents.

What Makes This Understandable?

I ask myself what makes that which is being told to me or that which I observe work, what makes it understandable. If it is important, what makes it important. In this the therapist's task is like that of the researcher. How do I account for what I observe? Many years ago I treated a couple who, at that time, had been married for twenty years. During that time they had a contract that he could have affairs with other women, which he never did. Now she demanded a change in the contract, and he was ready to get a divorce over that change. What made that change so important to each of them, when it did not signal any intention of changing the external behavior? He did not intend to have an affair. What made this so important?

It was vitally important to him to maintain the symbol of his freedom so that he didn't feel captured and enmeshed as he had experienced with his suffocating mother. The wife had grown increasingly insecure about her looks as she grew older and wanted the change of contract as a sign of his continuing interest in her.

Diagnostic Background Questions and Correlations

When I am working well with a patient I do not think about interpretations or diagnoses or theory. However, sometimes I do think about these issues. Sometimes this occurs after sessions, sometimes before, sometimes it intrudes on the hour. Sometimes the figure of the moment is informed by these more abstract issues without my personally breaking my contact with the patient. In these cases the figure of the moment is spontaneously informed by the more abstract information in my background. Sometimes when I am stuck I will remind myself of what I know of the patient and our history and will thus center myself.

The following is not meant to be an exhaustive or even systematic list, but rather some indication of some of the relevant factors I consider.

Level Of Support

I make discriminations as to the level of patient personality organization (psychotic, character disorder, neurotic, "normal neurotic"), biological, cultural and ethnic factors. Of most importance: the nature of the character structure of the patient.

Contact Ability ?What Is the Patient's Current Capacity for Contact?

Empathy: To what extent is the patient able to give and receive empathy, i.e., the understanding of the phenomenological reality of another person.

Intimacy: Contact ability includes the ability to be open, vulnerable and intimate.

Dialogue: Various forms of dialogue ability need to be assessed. This includes the ability to negotiate, fight, compromise, debate, to express one's point and also listen to the other and to stay in contact with another person or an issue when it becomes difficult or frustrating. Sometimes overlooked is also the healthy and necessary ability to let go, to withdraw, to give up.

Aggression: To what extent is the patient able to use psychobiological aggression assertively and in a manner that is integrated and takes the needs and limits of others into account? Does the person show a concern for self and other in the use of aggression. Does the person have control of the application of aggression, e.g., to consider consequences?

Joy: To what extent is the patient able to have fun, experience excitement, play, sensuality, sexuality?

Awareness Process

A most central area of consideration is exploring how the person's awareness process works. How does the person sense, perceive, feel, infer, imagine, wish? How does the stream of consciousness flow, or how is it blocked? What is allowed into awareness and what is kept out of awareness? How is awareness avoided, i.e., by what means?

The awareness process is most important in figuring the capacity of the person for self-support and for contact of various sorts.

Figure/ground formation and destruction process: How does the person typically move through the stages of the figure/ground formation and destruction, i.e., fore-contact, contacting, final contact, postcontact? Does the person let go enough for a new figure to emerge into awareness? Are a variety of stimuli allowed to have an effect? Which ones are and are not? Can the person be stimulated by his or her own needs and the needs of those around? Does the person let the emerging figure sharpen? Does the person surrender to the final contact and complete spontaneity and unitary action? Finally does the person move into the postcontact interaction of diminished self?

Healthy functioning requires that the figure change according to need. If it changes too slowly, the person stays stuck in a rigid state, unable to complete the figure, let go and proceed to new figures. If it changes too rapidly, the figure does not deepen and results in superficiality. Does the figure change so quickly that nothing deepens, as in the hysteric? Or does the person keep the figure unchanging so long, that final contact or postcontact is avoided?

Ability to discriminate: Does the person discriminate accurately? How finely? Does the person only discriminate into either-or discrete categories (competent-needy; good-bad; wonderful-rubbish)? Or does the person make such deliberate and fine distinctions that no flowing action occurs? Can the person discriminate between his parents and his current significant others? Can the person distinguish between legitimate authority and authoritarian control? Between freedom and license? Between responsibility and blame? Between tasty and tasteless or disgusting? Between levels of importance? Between hopeless and possible?

Owning and feeling: Does the person acknowledge his or her own actions, feelings, thoughts? Does the person actually feel that, or just intellectually observe or infer self-responsibility? What boundary disturbances does the person usually engage in (for example, projection)?

Expressing the awareness: Does the person express his or her emotions, wishes, thoughts? Is the expression from a person to a person? Or is it deflected, displaced, converted into gossip? Does the person convey the emotional energy and meaning associated with the feelings, wishes and thoughts, or is it merely talked about?

Personal Relationships

What is the person's history of relationships? Are they inevitably brief? Or perhaps the opposite, hanging on to relationships that are unsatisfying or even abusive? Does the person consider the needs of his partners and his own, or only the needs of one person, self or other? Or perhaps considers the needs of no one? Is the person able to meet new people? To have meaningful interactions with people who are known? Can the person separate and support him or herself? Can the person move toward loving merger and support him or herself? Does the person move between healthy confluence and withdrawal, or do they get stuck in a narrow range along the continuum of contact and withdrawal?

Work

Does the person show a dedication and commitment to achievement and accomplishment appropriate to age, background, intelligence and value system? Does the person have work that is relatively satisfactory emotionally and adequate for financial support? Is the person able to sacrifice for the good of a cause or project? Sacrifice for personal advancement? Is the person able to cut back on commitment and achievement in order to balance out his or her life? Is the person able to move toward and away from work?

Further Professional Issues about Assessment

There are several issues of ethics and competence that arise in connection with diagnosis. I believe that not being systematic about diagnosis is equivalent to not doing the best possible therapy, thus not fulfilling the calling of our profession. For Gestalt therapists this requires taking into account the behavioral as well as other phenomenological data, i.e., that no data is systematically excluded.

At the same time, diagnosing for its own sake is not an enhancement of the therapeutic work. It may have intellectual value, or may be useful for research, but it is not useful for therapy, and in fact ensures that the therapist (and perhaps the patient as well) will be attending to gathering information for or making diagnoses that compete with rather than augment the treatment.

At the heart of the professional obligation for accurate diagnosis is something that is also at the heart of the phenomenological discipline: knowing the difference between hypothesis and fact. What is the source of information, how much is known, what is the data and to what degree is this confirmed? If the therapist does not have sufficient education, therapy, discipline and humility to be accurate about what is known in general (state of the art) and what the therapist knows, the patient may well be led into excessive trust of the therapist's opinions or else be cheated by paucity of shared wisdom by the therapist.

The therapist who does not have good training in research or philosophic analysis will not be able to do this well. By the same token the therapist who is too engaged in narcissistic inflation will not be able to do this, and in fact may actively, albeit often unconsciously, seek more adulation than appropriate.

And lastly, diagnosis is systematic pattern recognition useful for a task. It is not putting people into cubbyholes. It is certainly not dividing people into good or bad, into valuable and not valuable, capable of growing or not growing.

14

TREATING PEOPLE WITH CHARACTER DISORDERS

Commentary

*This 1990 article, together with #13, The Differential Applica-
tion of Gestalt Therapy, was written as a single unit for this book.
In #13 the general topic of diagnosis is discussed. In this essay I
discuss diagnosis and treatment of the character disorders, with
detailed illustrative discussion of the Narcissistic and Borderline
Personality Disorders.*

Scope of this Essay

Intuition Is Not Enough

I believe therapy is better now than it was twenty years ago. I
think it is more effective, with fewer patients suffering ineffective
or harmful therapy experiences. This is especially true of patients
with character disorders. I certainly experience this improvement
in my practice. Some of my personal improvement as a therapist
comes from what the general professional community has learned.
I have benefited from the shared experience of clinicians of
various kinds. I believe that sharing experience makes such a
difference that therapists cannot do a state-of-the-art job by

following only their own intuition, feelings, or the teachings of a single mentor, or even having the perspective of only one system. The sharing of many clinicians is needed to temper generalizations and biases, add multiple perspectives and enable us to learn from the treatment of many more patients than any one of us could see alone.

Some of my improvement as a therapist also comes from my own personal aging and growth, including about 40,000 hours of doing individual, conjoint and group Gestalt therapy, as well as time spent thinking, teaching, consulting and writing about that experience. I want to share some of what I have learned.

In this essay I intend to illustrate how a differential understanding of overall character structure leads to differential application of Gestalt therapy and improved treatment. After a general discussion, I will do so by discussing the comparative treatment of narcissistic and borderline personality disorders. My purposes in doing this are several fold. Most important, I want to illustrate in some detail how differential diagnosis makes a difference in my practice of Gestalt therapy, to show what is possible by way of improving treatment via differential understanding.

I chose the comparison of borderline and narcissistic personality disorders because they are common in clinical practice, I have a lot of personal treatment experience with them, and the diagnosis makes a big difference in the course of their therapy, choice of intervention, understanding the supports and needs of the patient. Without adequate understanding, at best the treatment of these patients meanders, i.e., without focus on what is essential, without a necessary sense of sequence and timing. With the right understanding these patients can be successfully treated, and without that understanding treatment can make these patients worse. For me, this adds some urgency. Moreover, without adequate perspective, therapy with these patients becomes dangerous for the therapist's mental health.

There Is No "Right" Intervention

While I hope this discussion will be useful to practicing Gestalt therapists, I also hope that the reader will show due caution. I sometimes read in the psychoanalytic literature statements saying, for example, in response to a clinical situation, that there is "Only one correct analytic attitude" (Kohut). There is no one right way. There is no "correct" response or style either in Gestalt therapy or in psychoanalysis. There is no clear consensus about the treatment of choice with the character disorders, although many write as if they do have an agreed-on truth. The conclusions in this essay are also not correct in any absolute way. The conclusions are mine based on my experience in treating the kind of patients I attract, considering my personality and strengths and weaknesses, etc.

General discussions of the patient's characteristics and treatment options must be adapted to the particular context of therapist, patient, system of therapy, mode of therapy, agency, community, etc. To maintain holistic integrity, any generalization from psychoanalysis should be assimilated and not introjected piecemeal into the Gestalt therapy system (see #9, Assimilating Diagnostic and Psychoanalytic Perspectives into Gestalt Therapy). For example, in much of the discussion in the psychoanalytic literature, e.g., the work of Masterson, they are talking about a minimum treatment frequency of three times a week and even six times a week. The discussion may assume two years to get to the middle phase of treatment (not a bad estimate), which in such a psychoanalysis would mean 300 hours of treatment. If the treatment is in a context of once a week treatment, or even twice a week, the actual treatment situation must be taken into account in assimilating any statement.

Frequency is not the only variable. In my opinion, Masterson's discussion of treatment of the borderline and narcissistic character disorders is too valuable to ignore. Yet Masterson states that when the patient wants an emotional response from the therapist he or she is showing resistance and acting out. To Masterson this is acting out since the analyst's task is an intellectual one (Masterson, 1981, p. 78). Since this attitude is so contrary to the Gestalt therapy attitude, obviously, his descriptions of the therapeutic task cannot be taken into Gestalt therapy without a thoroughgoing assimilation. Kohut similarly shows how large the differences between therapeutic attitudes can be when he talks of an analysis being hopelessly stalemated because the analyst made an irretrievable error in allowing the patient to discover that he was a Roman Catholic.

I believe that excellent Gestalt therapy treatment requires the kind of background understanding of the patient that psychoanalytic discussions can be extremely helpful with, AND an accurate and deep self-understanding by the therapist, AND also a good theoretical and practical understanding of the Gestalt therapy system, including the centrality of dialogue and phenomenological focusing and how this can be lived out in therapy.

I make an effort to take into consideration general professional information, including diagnosis, psychodynamics, treatment from other perspectives, outcome and process studies, etc. But in this essay I am not explicitly and systematically discussing all of this. This is just one of the limitations of this essay that needs acknowledging.

My conclusions are not scientifically tested. I am not even setting out operationalized criteria that would directly lead to such studies. Moreover, many fine and important distinctions of diagnosis, developmental background, etc., are not included in this discussion. Not all character disorders are being discussed. I do not set out a typology or complete consideration of diagnosis or treatment of the character disorders. I do not try to duplicate or summarize the DSM III, nor to translate it into Gestalt therapy language. This is not an exposition on diagnostic criteria.

All of the above are important for the reader to keep in mind. I hope we in Gestalt therapy fill in some of those gaps. My purpose here is preliminary to that, to share current experience hoping it will lead later to more complete systematizing and testing and in the meantime be of some help to those presently on the firing line.

I especially want to emphasize that Gestalt therapy is not, cannot, and should not be a manualized or cookbook kind of therapy. It requires that the clinician make contact with the unique person who is the client with an openness based on centering, bracketing, focusing, dialoguing by the person who is therapist. It requires art and dialogue, not application of technique or dogma. It is within this spirit that I share my treatment experience.

But we can learn from past experience and the experience of others. To do artful therapy does not mean generating understanding or intervention without reference to the distilled wisdom of the field.

On the Need to Distinguish Levels of Character Disturbance

It was my turn to work. It was 1965 and I was at Esalen for an advanced workshop for therapists with Fritz Perls and Jim Simkin. For that workshop the participants had counted off numbers and were to do 1-1 work in front of the group in the order of the number that was picked.

At the time I was to work, group members were being distracted by their concern about the absence of a group member who was extremely unhappy and fairly disturbed. Some of them wanted to leave the group to go and find him.

Jim was peeved at the group and at the missing person. Jim was in one of his well-known self-righteous and unyielding moods. He held the errant group member responsible for himself and wanted to give no quarter. Fritz disagreed and said that this particular participant was too sick to be held responsible. Indeed, as I remember it 25 years later, that participant might have been psychotic.

Fritz recognized that psychotic patients needed different interventions. This incident was one example. I had noticed in prior contact with Fritz that he clearly distinguished who he confronted, who he left alone, who he approached lightly. At the hospital in which I worked and met Fritz, he demonstrated an extraordinary ability to establish contact with psychotic, backward patients who had not been reached by others. However, in demonstration workshops using dreams, when the patient showed no signs of any life in the dream, he believed that this pointed toward psychosis and he would not work with that person. In clinical work, as in life, he advocated discrimination. Of course, he was not always successful in making these discriminations.

In the 1960s and early 1970s there was recognition in Gestalt therapy of patterns of the moment, a little recognition of repetition at a trait level. But there was very little systematic attention to typology, except at the very crude level of Fritz and Jim's disagreement at Esalen. But individual Gestalt therapists, e.g., those treating psychotic patients, knew that diagnosis and differential treatment were necessary and proceeded accordingly.

However, in most practices there were (and are) patients who were not psychotic, but were more disturbed and problematic than neurotic. Of course, I am talking about the character disorders, now often referred to as self disorders. Frequently these patients are frustrating for the therapist, the therapy troublesome, and in the past the outcome was frequently negative. Please note that this was true not only in Gestalt therapy, but in all forms of therapy. Classical psychoanalysis had the same difficulty with the same kind of patients. Sometimes these patients would be in full analysis, five times a week, for seven, ten or more years and getting worse. Or see a series of analysts, without improvement and often with deterioration. The problem was a general one in the state of the psychotherapy art, and not just a problem with Gestalt therapy or psychoanalysis.

Jerry Greenwald (1973) illustrated one kind of reaction to such patients. He started writing about N (Nourishing) and T (Toxic) people. This crude dichotomizing was one of the reactions to the frustration of treating such patients. This approach was pejorative and did not help discriminate the level or nature of the disturbance or what the therapist needed to do differently. It did not adequately account for the structured deficits in the psychological organization of patients with character disorders. This attitude made the situation worse, leading to trying to improve the outcome by frustrating the patient. It seemed logical, but no attempt was made to verify that the patient-therapist process was described accurately, it was not checked with patient phenomenology, long-term results were not considered, and so forth.

Many times patients became paranoid, rageful, and wounded, and left workshops or therapy with such therapists with their wounds opened in a way that was not healing. And, in the course of this practice, we learned some things.

424

There are some obvious discriminations that any competent and responsible clinician makes, e.g., whether the patient is psychotic, dangerous to self or others, in need of medical treatment or at least the need for medical consultation to rule out a possible medical condition or need for psychopharmaceuticals. One set of such discriminations is whether the overall character structure of the patient is at a mild neurotic, severe neurotic or at a character disordered level and then the nature of the self-structure within those levels. This must be done, and if the details are not elaborated in the Gestalt therapy literature, then the Gestalt therapist must use whatever professional knowledge is available. This discrimination of the quality of the overall personality organization is vital and always relevant, regardless of formal diagnosis.

The therapist needs to know that the functioning of character-disordered patients is easily disrupted in most organism/environment fields in which they live. The etiology and treatment of these patients with their characterological weaknesses was not adequately accounted for in classic therapy theory, either Gestalt or classic psychoanalytic. In noting recent improved descriptions of these patients in self psychology and object relations, some Gestalt therapists were led to abandon the beauty of the Gestalt therapy process theory for a Newtonian, mechanistic frame. In that frame these patients could be said to have a fractured or broken core self. Of course, I prefer not to conceptualize it as: people "have" a self, but rather prefer a process view — they are themselves, they are living processes and not things that can be broken and mended. In my reply to Tobin, I discuss the theoretical difficulty of using the mechanistic terminology.

In field process terms the patient who is suffering from a character disorder doesn't and can't yet maintain a cohesive sense of self through a succession of here-and-now moments, especially in certain kinds of interpersonal contacts. There is need to be clearer about these patients, as I will try to be later in this essay, but there is no need to depart from the phenomenological, dialogical, field process framework of Gestalt therapy.

Regardless of the presence or absence of other physical, social, psychological conditions or symptoms, the therapist needs to know if the patient's character structure is cohesive, if the cognitive processes are intact and operating within the normal range, if the patient is oriented in time, space and person, if the patient is delusional, if the patient has a thought disorder, etc.

General Characteristics of the Character Disorders

Neurotics show reduced awareness, elevated anxiety, depression and internal conflict. But they continue to manifest an interest in and a capacity for understanding consensual reality, including the phenomenological reality of others. They also show a continuity of personal identity, at least some minimal sense of self-esteem and esteem of others, and make a creative adjustment to their context.

All of this is different with the character disorders. They don't, can't yet, maintain this kind of boundary activity and personal cohesion. They have some disturbance in the achievement of a sense of personal cohesion and/or failure to relate to context in a manner that takes context as consensually perceived into account and/or failure to make adequate intimate or dialogical interpersonal contact, that is, contact that recognizes different phenomenological realities and allows for emergence rather than instrumentally aiming for an outcome. The therapist needs to recognize this and alter his or her interventions accordingly.

A character disorder is a level of personality organization that is more disturbed than the neurotic and less disturbed than the psychotic. In the psychosis the very foundation of accurate perception, logic, and orientation to time, place, person is disturbed. By contrast, the neurotic maintains the capacity for accurate perception and thought and self-reflection, even under stress. These functions remain at least minimally intact in neurosis. In the character disorders the functions of orientation are not as disturbed as in psychosis, but other ego functions are more disturbed than in neurosis, including the capacity for regular self-reflection, especially in situations of stress or conflict.

In general they do not maintain the ability to continue selfobservation that takes responsibility for behavior, meets others when there are differences or conflict, struggles with awareness of that which is threatening or painful, or connects the person they

426

are in their present experience with other moments (past or probable) in which they experience themselves differently.

In the character disorders there is a marked deficiency in the ability of the person to exercise the ego functions of self-regulation, to contain, channel, assimilate and integrate varying intensities of emotion and desire, to soothe, calm and center him or herself, and support the total absorption into an emerging spontaneous figure in the current field. They have special difficulties forming a gestalt that takes others and self into account. Typically these patients are not able to maintain a cohesive background sense of who they are, to feel at least a minimum background level of trust both in their self-support and possible forthcoming environmental support. There is a deficit in feeling at least a minimal amount of goodwill toward self and others, including positive valence, love, and a healthy, balanced sense of entitlement (also self and other). Often their perceptions and cognitions do not adequately gauge the actual situation and the possibilities for creative adjustment. They are often deficient in present-centered awareness in which the current figure connects to and emerges from the past and that experimentally moves toward emerging but not yet clear future possibilities.

The personality disorders all exhibit a dichotomy of personality functions, i.e., to some degree have a deficit in the ability to integrate polarities into wholes. The degree and type of this differs with the different types of disorders, which we will discuss below. Some examples: the integration of expectation and disappointment, of need and competence, of positive and negative, of distance and closeness, of present and past.

I will discuss two of the most common of the character disorders and their treatment: the narcissistic personality disorder and the borderline personality disorder. Then I will compare their treatment needs. I will not try to give a complete description of each disorder, but merely enough to set the stage to demonstrate my point about differential application of Gestalt therapy.

The concept of narcissism has a long and confusing history in psychotherapeutic theory. Differences of theory over innate drives, developmental progression, and such have dominated the psychoanalytic discussions. In this discussion I will not deal with these differences. Rather I will describe the appearance, phenomenology and treatment of these patients through the lens of my practice.

Narcissistic Personality Disorders

Description
The popular image that is called to mind when the word narcissism or narcissist is used is a picture of a thoroughly self-centered, self-loving person who, with an inflated sense of self, ruthlessly pursues his or her own selfish needs without care about other people. To some extent this picture is supported by the description in the DSM III.

The following are taken from the DSM III description of the Narcissistic Personality Disorder (Quick Reference, pp. 178-179):

A. Grandiose sense of self-importance or uniqueness.

B. Preoccupation with fantasies of unlimited success, power, brilliance, beauty, or ideal love.

C. Exhibitionism: the person requires constant attention and admiration.

D. Cool indifference or marked feelings of rage, inferiority, shame, humiliation, or emptiness in response to criticism, indifference of others, or defeat.

E. At least two of the following:

(1) entitlement: expectation of special favors without assuming reciprocal responsibilities ...

(2) interpersonal exploitiveness: taking advantage of others to indulge own desires or for self-aggrandizement; disregard for the personal integrity and rights of others.

(3) relationships that characteristically alternate between the extremes of overidealization and evaluation.

(4) lack of empathy: inability to recognize how others feel, e.g., unable to appreciate the distress of someone who is seriously ill.

An apparently different picture arises when a sympathetic therapist describes the narcissistic person as one who is easily wounded, has low self-esteem, is very dependent on the attention, approval, respect and love of others in order to maintain a sense of themselves. This description is at least different in emphasis, weighing item D. more heavily.

In this description, the narcissistically disturbed require external support to maintain any semblance of equilibrium. They have difficulty maintaining a sense of safety and cohesive identity over time, especially in difficult situations, e.g., situations with possibilities of conflict, competition, failure, deprivation. Thus the narcissistic person fills with shame and erupts in rage, despair and/or panic and at those times appears inconsolable, with contact apparently impossible. I would hesitate to call this self-love.

Are the narcissists people who truly regard themselves as superior, or are they really insecure? Are these conflicting pictures, or do they fit into a more comprehensive picture that encompasses both descriptions? Or perhaps the term covers multiple subtypes. While I think there are multiple types of narcissists, I also think that there is a comprehensive picture that encompasses the multiplicity.

The narcissistic person is "self-centered," but not centered on his or her "true self." The true self is of the organism-environment field. As Perls, Hefferline and Goodman (p.235) say:

> Let us call the "self" the system of contacts at any moment....The self is the contact-boundary at work; its activity is forming figures and grounds.

Healthy self-functioning is not self-centered, but self-othercentered. Healthy awareness is not awareness of oneself, but of other and self.

Narcissists are confluent and field dependent. They are very dependent on smooth and positive reception by others. While they are dependent on the field, they are not appropriately differentiated from the rest of the field. They treat the environment as existing in order to support them. They do not truly see others as autonomous, different, worthy as they are, an end in and of themselves. They do not see the needs of others as important as their own, often not perceiving the needs of others at all.

If narcissistic persons felt as wonderful as their cover story, and if the healthy self is self-other oriented, why are they so field dependent and self-centered? We shall see later that one of their characteristics is contempt for others. Why would a secure, wonderful person need to be contemptuous of others? Why do they not regard the needs of others with more respect?

The inflated self-image of the inflated narcissists helps them avoid the shameful experience of being depleted and deflated. When the shameful mode is predominant, the sympathetic picture of the narcissist is more in evidence. It is my point of view that with the narcissistic patient both the inflated and deflated pictures always exist together as true polar opposites. The deflated patient has a conscious or unconscious grandiose self-picture — that is the background that makes the deflated experience understandable. So too, the deflated picture gives meaning to the inflated or grandiose picture that is so tenaciously defended.

Paul is a 48-year-old psychologist. When he is with a patient or in front of a group, his face is alive with energy, his eyes clear, sparkling, expressive. He moves with fluidity and grace. His speech is articulate. He talks authoritatively and with great presence. Many of his patients feel personally touched, led, inspired, cared about. Is this not a picture of excellent contact and caring for others?

All is not what it seems to be. For Paul uses the other person as a means to his glorification. It is important to Paul's sense of himself both that his patients adore him and that he move them somewhere. His attitude precludes being fully satisfied with horizontal contact in which the patient is affirmed as they are and in which Paul gets his confirmation from that task and from other situations.

Out of their presence, he often refers to patients in either a depreciatory or inflating way, not horizontal and balanced. One often gets the impression that self-inflation is central to Paul's attitude. Patients who are successful reflect on how great a therapist he is to treat such successful people; patients that he is pejorative about reflect how great a therapist he is to accept such "assholes" (his word). When patients try to leave therapy before he thinks they are ready, he has frequently let them know that they could not get along without him.

Without Paul or the patient's realizing it, to Paul the patient is an extension of Paul's need, not really a source independent of Paul. When a patient does not agree with him, or refuses to follow a particular suggestion, or wants to stop therapy before Paul believes the patient is ready, a fuller picture of Paul emerges and his underlying lack of treating the patient as a self-regulating unique "other" becomes clear. Paul's previous self-inflation deflates, like a balloon losing air. Variously he feels depressed, rageful, spiteful, ruthless.

In his social relations one sees the same inflation-deflation, and contact that looks interpersonal, but actually disguises a projected self-centeredness. He is on a perennial search for the right woman. With each new woman he weighs, judges, compares — he screens for her looks, spirituality, intelligence, independence. Most of his love relationships start with the woman adoring and flattering him. At times it starts with his adoring her. Of course, with time there is some inevitable disappointment in either case. And with disappointment, Paul decides that she is not the right woman, not "Ms. Right." With that, the glow totally disappears for him, she is of no value. At 48 and never married, he starts each new relationship with inflation, convinced that this time it is different.

In his own therapy, Paul needs to believe his therapist is wonderful, the best, "very spiritual." At the beginning of therapy he was very vulnerable to any sign that the therapist might be anything less than "very advanced" in all respects. I know of many patients like Paul who chose therapists that would collude with the patient's narcissism, flatter them, etc. I have found that the best prognosis for narcissistic patients is for those who insist on respect for their experience and do not insist on the illusion that the therapist is perfect ("the best") nor adulatory of the patient.

Babette is a 40-year-old nurse. Much of the time she is depressed and experiences herself as mistreated, helpless, unhappy,

431

impotent. While she consistently has no sense of being responsible for any plight she is in, she also has very little respect or compassion for herself. She picks men who are charming and glamorous, without regard for their caring, psychological honesty, etc. He always turns out to be a "bastard" — the powerful man who swept her away and made her feel great and now disappoints and abandons her and leaves her depleted and deflated.

Babette is easily hurt, cries easily, and "expresses anger." Actually she rages rather than contacts the other person with anger. In her therapy she requires that the focus be only on her experience, her phenomenological reality without new data, contrary observations or feelings, phenomenological refinement of her awareness process or experimentation. When hurt she becomes rageful, then sullen and spiteful. With good empathic and sympathetic responses from the other person, she recovers quickly from these incidents. However, without a capitulation, apology or agreement from the offending person, she does not recover well at all.

What I call "forced confluence," she calls "understanding" — and has very little concept that her experience may be real and intense, but not an absolute truth. If she feels "like I was stabbed in the back," she believes she is as incapacitated as if she was literally stabbed in the back. No other perspective is relevant to her. In that mood, even her own prior feelings, or the fact that she might see things differently tomorrow, are not relevant to her.

Babette and Paul appear to be opposites, but their mode of personality organization is more alike than different. He appears to be on top of the world and she appears to be on the bottom. But in her heart there is a grandiosity she rarely lets herself know about, let alone reveal to others. Paul protects himself from any possible sudden drop into depletion that comes when the balloon of grandiosity is punctured.

Both Paul and Babette are self-centered, field dependent, confluent. For both, the grandiosity-deflation polarity is central to their personality organization. However, they lead with different aspects of that polarity. One would have to look to the ground to see the other half of the polarity. A naive therapist might be surprised by how vulnerable Paul is to deflation, that is, how weak his self-support is, also surprised by how inflated a self-picture

Babette would have to live up to before she would not feel deflated.

Image Centered and Alienated

Narcissistic patients are twice alienated. They are alienated from other people because they are so self-centered. They are alienated from their true selves because they are centered on their self-image rather than on who they really are and what they actually experience. With other people also, they tend to be in contact with with image, rather than the person. Typically a narcissistic person will be in touch with how attractive (or unattractive), prestigious (or unprestigious) the other person is. Contempt or idealization marks much of the lens through which the narcissist sees others.

Much of what passes for person-to-person contact and self-awareness in patients with a narcissistic personality disorder is not person-to-person contact at all and is not awareness of their inmost feelings or the nature of how they relate to people. The charismatic type of narcissist may look interpersonally contactful and the depleted type of narcissist may look emotionally expressive, but neither is really in contact with other people.

Moreover, they are often alienated from their own past and feel shame to be associated with how they were before their improved state. As they focus on their current experience, especially in the grandiose mode, they do not make their past experience part of the meaningful background. In addition to the disidentification with who they were, they also tend to be contemptuous of who they were and blame who they were on others.

It is difficult for these patients to imagine being in any mood other than the one they are in, and difficult also for them to imagine the differing emotional experience of others. This makes empathy very difficult for them. It also makes it difficult for them to maintain equilibrium over time when they cannot keep an emotional constancy, which requires being able to imagine and identify with moods and situations other than the one they are in presently.

Need to be Special

People with narcissistic personality disorders frequently think, feel and act in ways resembling a preschool child. They show a grandiosity that sometimes appears similar to that which is so normal in preschool youngsters, as well as exhibiting an inability to consider the needs of others which is similar to that seen in very young children. Of course, the adult narcissist is not the same as a preschool child. The grandiose, and self-centered demeanor of a Three-year-old is very different than a charismatic or depleted adult presenting themselves in a similar manner.

Their view of themselves is often distorted — seeing themselves as extraordinary (talented, brilliant, even extraordinarily sick, etc.). They need to be special. They often feel entitled to special treatment or products, which ordinarily have to come through effort, risk, learning over time, but without the effort. This alternates with the polar opposite attitude of no entitlement at all.

They are manipulative and exploitive, although often feeling like a victim, misunderstood or insufficiently recognized for the superior persons they are (star, genius, etc.). They lack empathy, the ability to see life as the other person does. In fact the other person often is just not relevant to them except as an extension of their own needs and fantasies. Narcissistic vulnerability alone is not enough to justify the narcissistic personality disorder diagnosis: the inability to react with empathy to the needs and feelings of others is an essential part of the diagnosis. It is only in the later phases of therapy that this really changes in a patient with a narcissistic personality disorder.

These patients usually have a history of being used in the service of their parents' needs, rather than been seen as separate people whose real self needs are valued. The parents model a lack of true empathy. Even the achievements of the narcissistic patient have been used for the parent's glorification. The true self of an autonomous child is just treated as if it were not there. There is such parental impingement in these families that children who later become narcissist protect their true self by subjectively living in images, especially images of grandiosity and idealization.

Field Dependent

People do not exist apart from a field of which they are a part. However, existentially we exist by differentiation from the rest of the field. While people depend on the rest of the psychological and physical field for all kinds of nutrients (food, respect, love, feedback, etc.), most adults, even neurotic adults, can maintain a sense of their own cohesion, a sense of safety and a positive feeling about themselves even when these needs are not being met.

The narcissistically disturbed person is even more field dependent than this. It is normal to feel deprived when one *is* deprived, but nevertheless to feel compassion and respect for oneself as well as a continued clear sense of oneself. But narcissistic persons have a lot of shame, and use something external to give themselves a feeling of safety, cohesion and self-warmth. Before treatment they lack the developed capacity to accept, nurture and respect themselves as they are.

All people need nourishment from the outside, but not to substitute for their internal sense of personal identity, cohesion, continuity over time. The neurotic can relate to external reality as an "external" reality, with whatever blinders they have, but as an external reality. The narcissistic personality disorder treats the outside as an extension of self and its needs.

Narcissistic patients often feel invisible. When they are not recognized, when their feelings and beliefs are not mirrored back to them, they often feel invisible and their psychological existence as well as their well-being is threatened.

The Four Ds

Therapy requires making and learning how to make real contact and learning to be in touch with how one really is. The pretherapy narcissists live in a system of confluence and fantasy wherein they can only value themselves when their accomplishments match their fantasies. There is no acceptance of themselves when aspects of their self-experience are discrepant from their fantasies of who they "should" be. For instance, the narcissistic system does not take development over time into account. Thus, narcissists typically feel an exaggerated sense of pride at what they can do, and do not assume they can learn what is difficult for them. They do not assume that struggle is normal, do not assume they should have to struggle, and do not feel a confident and loving feeling toward themselves as they go through the pain that is involved in learning.

It is not only narcissists who have shame reactions to learning situation. Shame-oriented people in general tend to feel shame when they become aware of what they do not yet know. This is true whether that which is not known is a real deficit or not, and whether or not the awareness comes through their own efforts or it is pointed out by others or a social test.

But the difficulty is much greater with the narcissistic personality disorders. The neurotic shame-oriented person proceeds to deal with this with a cohesive sense of personal identity over time, without the inflation-deflation that marks the narcissistic personality disorder, and is usually able to stay with the task at hand. As with any neurotic, the neurotic shame-oriented patient maintains the capacity for self-reflection that is often lost in the narcissistic personality disorders.

Frustration, conflict, failure, deprivation, difficulty, criticism and feeling shame all lead narcissistically disturbed persons to the four Ds: deflation, depletion, depression and despair. With the narcissistic personality disorder confrontation, interpretation, experimentation suggestions or even contact exposure usually results in an equilibrium defeating deflation, feeling of complete depletion, depression and despair. They lose the sense of themselves, the sense of relative safety, the sense of well being, structural cohesion and temporal stability.

They feel depleted, as if empty inside — as if they "have no self." They feel deflated, as if without the energy to fly, like a balloon without air. They feel depressed: retarded biopsychological energetic functioning, lowered self-esteem, avoidance of primary emotions, e.g., being depressed rather than feeling their loneliness and sadness. They feel despair, not maintaining any hope or faith in movement beyond the present crisis.

I believe human recovery requires human contact. The narcissist who experiences the four Ds requires empathic bonding. But his/her pretherapy adjustment system depends on not treating the other as a separate person, which precludes real contact (dialogue, intimacy). Neither grandiosity nor depletion is being in contact with an accurate picture of how one is. This makes therapy a very risky business for the narcissist and difficult for the therapist. Therapy has an inherently confrontive effect on these patients, even if done gently, empathically and lovingly.

Of course effective therapy has to bring to the patient the demands of the organism/environment field, including their own organismic needs and capacities, the needs of others, limits, etc. Like any learning, this involves frustration, conflict, difficulty. In order to successfully go through this process, the narcissist needs a therapeutic relationship in which for a long time the therapist consistently attunes to the needs of the patient in order to protect the patient against feelings of overwhelming deflation and depletion.

The Narcissistic Teeter-totter

The narcissistically disturbed are caught in a phenomenological teeter-totter. One end of the teeter-totter is inflation, the other deflation. The inflated pole is the pole of grandiosity, of being a star, Mr. Wonderful, etc., and is often accompanied by contempt, spoiling, devaluing of others. The deflated end of the teeter-totter ("If I am not great, I am rubbish") often manifests as a hungry, lost, powerless infant who feels envy, shame and rage. The grandiosity helps the person avoid awareness of the deflated state.

When the person feels threatened, when the bubble of inflation is pierced, when there is conflict, etc., he/she often experiences a narcissistic injury. This is a change of state that is immediate and total, experienced as if without any internal psychological processing is relatively long lasting. All sense of safety or self-worth is lost, and often the sense of temporal continuity also. There may be no phenomenological access to strengths otherwise available to the person.

It is instructive to compare the neurotic shame experience with the narcissistic injury of a person with a narcissistic personality disorder. The neurotic shame-oriented person can continue to reflect and self-examine. In response to a negative experience, competition or conflict they often ask the question: "What is wrong with me?" In this neurotic shame experience the person loses a sense of the love of the other person for them, wanting to hide from being seen as flawed as they feel at that moment, but they don't totally lose the sense of self or totally lose the other person. They don't lose a sense of their own identity, they don't totally lose the discrimination between self and other (although there is a great deal of introjection and retroflection), they are often still able to cope with the task at hand (although perhaps impeded by the shame), and they are able to recover. When performance is impeded by the shame reaction, the shame-oriented neurotic tends to blame himself as much as circumstance and other.

The narcissistic personality disorder experiences a more globalized emotional loss of the other person. They may experience it with defensive grandiosity, or more often with sudden and global deflation or rage. During this phase they often cannot or do not cope with tasks, have very slow recovery and tend to blame their plight on treatment by others rather than either blaming themselves or taking responsibility for their own inadequacies. In this state they can be ruthless and are quite capable of justifying irresponsibility, unethical or illegal behavior, outrageous demands. They treat as totally unfair, worthless or vindictive any contrary opinion or frustrating treatment.

But these maneuvers still leave them feeling shame and a diminished sense of self-worth, since their self-worth is so dependent on how they are treated by others. However, since they do not support themselves by taking responsibility for their situation, they feel a narcissistic injury. This is true of both the predominantly inflated and the predominantly deflated narcissists.

Summary of the two poles

Inflation (I am great!)	*Deflation (I am rubbish)*
Contempt	Hungry, lost, powerless infant
Spoiling	Envious
Devaluing	Shame, rage or panic

Disappointment

One of the deficits maintaining the narcissistic personality disorder is the manner in which disappointment is dealt with. The narcissists usually do not have a sense of assimilable disappointment — they don't experience "a little bit of disappointment."

438

Their expectations are inflated, in an all-or-nothing manner. Inevitably, experience does not completely match their expectations. Their expectations are like a bubble, and a little disappointment breaks the film keeping the bubble intact. When the bubble bursts, the inflated narcissist shows contempt, spoils or devalues that which is disappointing or competing. The deflated narcissists show their hungry, lost, powerless infant mode. This is marked with envy, shame and rage. The envy is as spoiling as the contempt of the inflated mode.

The narcissist assimilates to the grandiose-deflated self, not the self as is. Any glow of warmth, excitement and safety that they experience is not associated with ordinary living. They identify with extraordinary, with special. For them, ordinary necessarily means flawed, flat, dull, uninteresting, unpredictable, unsafe and worthless. Who would love an ordinary person? Someone who could love and be interested in an ordinary person must be quite flawed himself or herself.

I hypothesize that normal people have a warmth, or glow or good feeling about themselves, and with disappointment this feeling continues, albeit somewhat diminished. In other words, they can be disappointed without plunging into shame and depletion. This is part of what happens during the process of narcissistic injury. There is no middle between the inflated bubble of expectations met and the fallen position that is without worth, grace, importance, and so forth. It is not a system of continuities, but rather of dichotomies.

When there is disappointment, upset feelings, pain, loss, failure, the young child learns a style of coping. If a parent is able to attend to the child lovingly and stay reasonably calm, and is able to contain and "hold" his feelings and allow him to feel upset while the emotions are expressed, understood, allowed to run their course in a healthy manner, the child can feel understood and soothed and the negative affect can be mediated and completed. As this process occurs in relationship with the empathic parent, the child assimilates the process and learns to do this for himself/herself. Narcissistically disturbed patients are usually lacking in this skill of recognizing, holding and mediating their feelings and soothing themselves.

Developmental Background

Much has been written of the developmental background of narcissistic patients, unfortunately very little within the Gestalt therapy framework. I will only mention a few items that go along with the present discussion. An amplified developmental theory in the Gestalt therapy framework awaits later formulation.

The early childhood experience of every narcissistic patient I have worked with has been marked by a lack of authentic contact between them and their parents. However, they often do not enter therapy presenting that history. They are often focused on more current concerns, and will say their childhood was fine, wonderful, uneventful. They will often say their families, especially their mother, did an excellent job. Sometimes they will say they had an unusually close relationship with their mother. Paul, the patient who was a therapist, said that of him and his mother. The depleted narcissists often say they don't understand how they can be so insecure when they had such a good mother.

One patient, a bright and handsome professional man, early in his treatment said of his mother: "She was the best little mother in the world." Later in therapy it was slowly revealed that she was so narcissistically deprived herself, so self-centered, so lacking in insight that she could not attend to his needs even minimally. She drank to excess, laid out her problems for him to emotionally hold, created an impression of being a woman long suffering from the mistreatment of her husband (my patient's father). With any confrontation she would collapse into a state of great and inconsolable pain. Story after story emerged in which the therapist was aware, and at first the patient was not, that the mother's behavior was outrageous. The patient had introjected the mother's self-picture and had his own need to have at least one parent he could idealize in order to maintain any sense of having an ordered, loving family.

The most important aspect in the childhood of the narcissistic adult is usually not being accurately perceived and appropriately responded to in a manner that recognized their true self, including their emotional experience, their needs, their abilities and weaknesses. Starting in the preschool years, the parent(s) treated the youngster as secondary to the emotional needs of the parents. The feelings of the child were not acknowledged and respected.

They were seldom praised for developmental achievements except as they reflected on the parents' self-esteem. They were often inordinately praised when there was no real achievement, or the achievements were minimized or attributed to the parents. In short, the patient was treated as not at all special.

One variation is the youngster who was treated as so special that he could do no wrong. The "Young Prince" was frequently inordinately praised for doing very little. He didn't have to struggle, he didn't really earn the praise. This results in the same lack of realistic sense of themselves as if he received no recognition at all. For in fact it is the same his true self is not recognized.

Preschool children naturally seem to go through phases of grandiosity and idealization. It seems to go with the developmental process to naively assume safety and competence. I remember my daughter shortly after learning to walk and walking off any surface confident that she would do fine, survive, and if there was any problem someone would be there to catch her. So too, it is normal to go through phases of idealization. I remember my son asking me to do something impossible. When I said "No," he looked up at me with wide innocent eyes and said "Yes," meaning "Of course you can do it."

It is assumed that in normal development in those early years the child learns that his parents are flawed, and still wonderful, and that he or she (the child) is also flawed, and still wonderful. Children learn that small disappointments are not catastrophic and that the ordinary can be thoroughly enjoyed and loved. The future narcissistically disturbed persons' experience with disappointment is such that they cannot assimilate it. In their adult life disappointment brings on loss of the good stuff, loss of the self-structure. In the developmental years the narcissistic patients experienced too much disappointment (or at least too suddenly) or else were so sheltered and catered to that they have a grandiose sense of themselves and insufficient experience with disappointment. Patients who start therapy saying they were "indulged" and they never suffered disappointment, struggle, disillusionment, etc., later in therapy often report having actually felt misunderstood, used, deprived and invisible for who they really were.

One important need that was not met in the earlier years of the future narcissist is that of going through upset and being effectively soothed by an emotionally responsive parent.

Boundary Disturbances

Narcissistic patients are confluent with their grandiose and idealized images. Those who are usually in the deflated mode are also confluent with the grandiose and idealized images, identifying themselves with being essentially flawed for not being as the images would have them be. They have many introjects, including family myths and beliefs about what is lovable and worthy of respect.

They are usually deficient in being able to retroflect in a healthy manner when there is disappointment — to contain and hold their feelings, express and channel them into socially constructive ways, and soothe and maintain good feelings about themselves.

They also use a lot of projection and projective identification. They project their self-critic onto others and interpret communications through a lens that attributes to the other negative judgments, values and emotions that are true of themselves and may or may not be true of the other person. Any smile, joke, observation, emotional expression, gesture of the other person is often seen as meaning the other person was either being negative toward them or else flawed himself or herself. On exploration, either of these often turn out to be projections.

By projective identification I mean projection in which the person alienates or disowns some aspect of him or herself, attributes it to another person, but instead of moving away from the person on whom the aspect is projected (or instead of moving against them), instead identifies with the other person. Thus a bright person who does not own her own intelligence might see her lover as brilliant. Then she may become confluently attached to the lover, often clinging and allowing herself to be badly treated. One very bright narcissistic woman saw her husband as competent and intelligent and herself as ordinary (not a good thing to be in her vocabulary). He would criticize her, sometimes reasonably and sometimes in a very disrespectful manner. She would believe there was something wrong with her, he must be right in his criticism, and believe that she couldn't get along without him.

I do not use the term "projective identification" to mean that someone can put a feeling or trait into another person. I never use the term projective identification to explain why in the presence of a hostile patient I might be angry. I do not use the term to mean the patient "made me angry by projective identification." However, if I am frustrated with a patient, he might stay in therapy with me because of identifying my frustration with his internal self-critic, allowing himself to fight with me and feel better about himself. The frustration would be my responsibility, and playing that role for the patient would be a therapeutic error, usually based both on misunderstanding the situation clinically and also countertransference.

There is a paranoid flavor to the functioning of these patients. Because of their self-centeredness, they often believe that what is happening in the environment is a statement about them, i.e., they personalize it. When people in their environment are withdrawn, negative, grumpy, they will often assume it has to do with them. Of course, sometimes it does. The paranoid stance assumes that one is the center of attention of the other person or people.

There is also the projection of self-rejection and the current residue of past experiences of being invisible or poorly treated that is brought into the situation by the narcissistically wounded patient. Thus, the person often experiences not only that he is the object of the other person's state, but assume that the reaction to him is one of rejection, hostility, contempt, and the like.

Part of this paranoid reaction is suspiciousness of any positive reception. The depleted narcissist will often just not believe that the positive feedback is honest, or if honest, will assume it is misguided. The inflated narcissist will often regard with contempt the person who gives them the positive strokes they crave. According to Lynne Jacobs, this distrust of the positive is partly based on the narcissist's belief that they must support the other's narcissistic needs in exchange for which the other agrees to support his or her grandiosity. When human interactions are viewed in this way, positive reactions are no more than an instrumental social contact (Jacobs, personal communication).

Treatment of Narcissistic Personality Disorders

In this essay I make suggestions about the practice of Gestalt therapy with patients who are moderately to severely narcissistically disturbed. I assume the reader is familiar with the principles and methodology of Gestalt therapy that are discussed elsewhere in this volume and I will not repeat them here.

Allowing and Empathic Attunement

First and foremost in doing therapy with this type of patient is to really respect and trust the patient's phenomenological reality. Take their experience seriously! "Start where the patient is," a good old social work motto, and "stay with" the awareness of the patient, a good old Gestalt therapy concept, are illustrations of this attitude. With this kind of patient, it is important that the therapist have an attitude that on balance emphasizes inclusion or empathic responding more than being personally expressive, actively insisting on overt dialogue, suggesting experiments and exciting enactments, interpreting or teaching phenomenological focusing.

Witness, verify and authenticate the patient's experience at each moment. Do not try to move the patient to better awareness or better contact, be very slow to defend a position, but rather follow the patient's awareness continuum.

Many ordinary and useful therapy interventions are experienced by narcissistic patients as demands that they meet the needs of the therapist rather than their needs being foreground. When this happens the world is experienced as not safe enough for their true self to enter and their resources are devoted to psychological survival.

The relationship with an empathic therapist may be the first time in their lives that they experience someone really listening to them, to the message of their true self, understanding how they experience the world — someone who doesn't give them the message that they should be experiencing something other than what they do actually experience. It may be the only experience they have with a significant other that does not covertly or overtly insist on the patient giving themselves up to the needs, beliefs, interests of the other. This experience of having one's experience validated by a caring other is vital in the development of a cohesive sense of oneself, caring for self and other and trust of interpersonal contact.

Therefore it is important that patients with narcissistic personality disorders be allowed to develop a therapeutic relationship relatively free of interventions they experience as intrusive or invalidating their phenomenological experience, such as clarifying the actual manifest person or phenomenological experience of the therapist, sharing life experiences or feelings by the therapist, therapeutic observations or suggestions, clarifying remarks, suggesting options that can be experimented with, etc. Some interventions are even more offensive, such as aggressively structuring a session or insisting on attention to the therapist rather than to the patient.

Ellen was an intelligent Jewish woman with extremely low self-esteem. She was easily hurt, frequently resentful, and tight almost to the point of physically hunkering down. When she related an event in which she regarded herself as helpless, blameless, impotent and put upon, she exhibited retroflected anger all over her body, her face and in her voice. The air reeked with bitterness. She talked with sarcasm about her victimizer. When she was not talking of victimization, she spoke with contempt of anyone who was different from her.

It was natural to suggest expressive experiments to her. The bitter angry energy was retroflected. But she felt hurt that I would even suggest such an experiment, she hated experimenting or doing anything that would expose her to others. She was impatient with how slow her therapy went, but would not do any experiment. Even sharing observations (such as about her holding her breath), suggesting she had any part in the development of her unfortunate relationships, fantasy experiments, etc. was received the same way. The only interventions that didn't increase her sense of shame and not being understood were reflections like: "That felt like he stabbed you with a knife." "When she said she didn't think your paper was up to par, it seemed like being with your mother and nothing was ever good enough." "Of course you could not regard yourself as an attractive woman when he said he didn't have a romantic interest in you." "It felt like you couldn't work in the group, because it wasn't safe enough for you if Joe might criticize you."

445

Josephine gave an entirely different appearance. She often felt helpless, victimized — but she thought it meant something wrong with her. She didn't reek of bitterness as Ellen did. She looked resigned, depressed. She would entertain a different interpretation by me with the same resignation. She did not need me to be perfect, nor did she need me to constantly mirror her experience. What she did need was a sympathetic hearing, to "hang out" and be able to talk about things.

She looked up to her husband, who was easily hurt and protected himself by attacking and keeping a distance. At first any suggestion that her husband was part of the problem — by being easily injured and by the ruthlessness of his attacking defenses — was greeted with a naive, incredulous attitude. It had to be something wrong with her. But she left feeling better from a respectful hearing of her experience, something she never got from her family and rarely from her husband. However, when I suggested she tell her husband that she felt hurt and ashamed when he criticized her, or any other simple expression of her feelings or how she was affected, she replied: "What, are you kidding?"

Over a period of months she was gradually able to see her husband's contribution to their interaction and became much more discriminating about his and her contributions. She was a narcissistic patient who could slowly consider my presentation of a differing viewpoint — in part because of the warmth and regard I felt toward her, in part due to my practicing inclusion and in part due to her idealization of me. She developed more self-cohesion and differentiation from her husband. She was able to maintain some minimum self-esteem and detachment when he distanced or attacked. Her increased sense of self-cohesion inevitably resulted in increasing her boundary skills. And she moved from very primitive emotional outbursts, clinging and isolating, to more contactful behavior. To date the marital situation is cyclical, but on balance not much improved. It is not very satisfying to either of them, and remains at an impasse. Short of leaving the marriage, improvement at this point would also require therapy for the husband, who is resistant.

Of course, all patients will sometimes experience disappointment, fear, narcissistic injury, wounding, etc. When this does happen with narcissistically vulnerable patients, the therapist need

446

not and generally should not either defend their intervention or apologize for it (unless the therapist truly feels guilt) or actively try to change the patient's experience as experienced. It is precisely in the circumstance of such a clinical situation that the attitude I am describing is most clearly called for: Explore the patient's experience and simply acknowledge your part in the interaction, along with affirming that their experience has validity.

Often therapy with these patients requires a relatively long period of focus on the patient's experience without explicit attention to improving phenomenological focusing, experimentation, dialogue, or even clarifications or interpretations unless these arise spontaneously from the patient. But as the patient receives the kind of attention in therapy that is organismically needed for personal cohesion and autonomy to emerge for the first time, they gradually acquire the self-support to gain from more traditional therapeutic work, such as: dialogue, phenomenological focusing, experimentation and interpretation.

As the therapist attends to the experience of the patient with empathy and caring, the relationship will develop according to the kind and degree of self-support and personality organization of the patient, according to the actual feelings, potentials, true self of the patient. As a result the patient gains in self-support and usually comes to a sufficiently integrated sense of himself or herself that there are timely opportunities to improve second-order awareness, clarify the actual relationship of therapist and patient, discuss options for experimentation, dialogue, etc.

It is hardly surprising that narcissistic patients often form relationships based more heavily on narcissistic transferences rather than on interpersonal contact. That means that the transference is likely to be one in which the patient reduces the therapist to being a mirror for the patient's actual or grandiose self-experience, the latter a mirror-image transference in Kohutian terms, or else one in which the patient idealizes the therapist. A third possibility is one in which the narcissistic patient forms what Kohut calls a twinship transference, in which the patient needs to "hang out" with the therapist. This may be exactly what the patient needs to do, although it may not appear to be doing therapeutic work.

When the therapist makes contact based on this empathic attunement, patients may come to feel safe enough to show their grandiosity and/or depletion. Then as patients show their reactions to disappointment and frustration, an opportunity emerges for further using the therapeutic relationship of empathic bonding and therapeutic technical work on awareness so that unfinished business is worked through. Also patients show more consistent cohesion, safety and positive feelings toward themselves. Patients' awareness processes become more accurate and used in the service of organismic needs of self and other, and they become more attuned to other people as separate people while at the same time being less field dependent for their own safety and well being. Thus more and more the patients come to have more resilient contact.

There has been a growing awareness that all people are narcissistically vulnerable to some degree. The work with narcissistic patients has led to an awareness of the extent to which people in general are narcissistically vulnerable. Thus in dialogic Gestalt therapy there has been some movement toward greater emphasis on inclusion, balancing an earlier emphasis on presence.

Serving the patient's need for empathic attunement has been so effective that some therapists have been led to purposely foster an idealizing or mirror-image transference with narcissistic patients. They do this by being overly solicitous, always agreeing with the patient's view that a situation couldn't be safe because of narcissistic dangers, not holding the patient at all responsible for his own behavior. Some have even gone so far as to treat all patients like this, as if they all suffer from a narcissistic personality disorder, and even structure training groups in the same manner. This is manipulative rather than authentic contact.

I think this is very unfortunate. Allowing is not the same as controlling. The therapist must continue his or her work as usual, albeit with modification of the work according to the patient's support, so that the patient can feel minimally safe enough to continue the therapeutic relationship — but this does not mean to modify the interventions and manifest presence of the therapist in order to control, encourage or manipulate the transference.

In training, a good attitude means that the personal experience of the trainees is valued, the safety factors in the groups are considered vitally important, the person of the trainee is valued, not just demonstrated competence. But it does not mean suspending the requirements of the training or testing situation. Treating trainees as if they are too fragile to face honest requirements and limits and function according to high standards is extremely condescending and ultimately reinforces the narcissistic system of being either wonderful or rubbish.

In traditional Gestalt therapy and psychoanalysis the patient insisting on an idealizing or mirror-image transferential relationship became the object of therapeutic interventions such as interpretation, dialogue, suggested enactment experiments, etc. When the patient failed to adhere to the therapeutic frame and do the work of therapy according to the preexisting bias of the therapist, this became the focus of comment, interpretation, encounter, suggestions for experimentation. In psychoanalysis this meant interpreting the narcissistic transference. In Gestalt therapy this meant sharing with the patient observations on issues such as responsibility, working, dialogue, willingness to experiment, and the like. This therapeutic attitude took insufficient account of the actual self-support of the patient and the nature of the therapeutic relationship. If the therapist were really practicing bracketing, as called for in the phenomenological model of Gestalt therapy, this would occur infrequently and would be corrected quickly by adherence to the actual experience of the patient.

Often the narcissistic patient will come in week after week and tell the story of this week in his or her life. In more traditional therapy work this was considered only an impediment to therapeutic work, a waste of time, a manipulation, etc. From our present perspective we can see that this activity is an important one in which the patients get the attention of an important and respected person who can hear, understand and respond to their experience and help them integrate any hurts, celebrate any victories, etc.

When the therapist wants more active or emotionally intense therapeutic work and is frustrated with the narcissistic patient's activity, it is often because the therapist does not understand the necessity and utility of this for the patient, and doesn't acknowledge and take responsibility for his or her own frustration. The patient often senses the lack of responsiveness, openness, positiveness, and warmth, from the therapist. When the therapist then gets defensive, denies any difficulty or any part in the difficulty, and projects this onto the patient, the patient feels unsafe, wounded, etc. Under these conditions the work that is needed — on grandiosity, depletion, disappointment — can not be done.

Disappointment

Disappointment is inevitable in any relationship. At some time during the course of therapy every patient will feel somewhat disappointed in the therapist. For the narcissistic patients this will often result in a vivid display of their lack of cohesion and integration, manifest in states of intense rage, panic, contempt, spoiling and envy. The bottom falls out of their grandiose or idealizing defenses and they have difficulty feeling OK about the ordinariness of a less than perfect therapist or therapeutic relationship or about themselves being less than perfect.

I had a group therapy patient in her middle twenties. Her father was intrusive, physically and psychologically, and her mother not even minimally protective or empathic. During group she often felt disappointed in my interventions. While I clarified each interaction, and explored the ways in which she did not feel heard, this was not enough. It did help, but eventually she left therapy with me. What I missed and didn't clarify was the effect on her when she perceived that I wasn't perfect, when I wasn't the best therapist in the world in all respects. When this happened, she lost any sense of being OK, soothed, safe or satisfied.

The situation is commonly made worse by a defensive reaction on the part of the therapist, manifested in the form of interpretation, confrontation, character assassination or negative judgments. This is often disguised in the form of humor or of a suggestion for an experiment, a confrontation about "responsibility," or attention to the contact boundary.

Norman was a patient in individual and group therapy. He frequently told stories in the "check in" part of the group that did not make any contact with others, did not show "real" here-and-now based feelings, did not take others into account and was repetitive. The therapist as well as the group was frustrated. While the group was relatively straight about their frustration, the therapist maintained a more open demeanor. On one night, however, the therapist's frustration showed in his clipped voice, a sharpness and lack of softness in how he shared observations. On that night an observer would see the therapist's curt responses followed by a depressed look on the patient's face. Norman left the group that evening feeling ashamed, depressed and thinking of leaving the group.

The next session the therapist observed that Norman seemed to be negatively affected by the last session. Norman didn't identify much about his mood or the cause. Luckily the therapist was able to realize and share that the effect might be a reaction by the patient to the apparently negative reaction of the therapist the previous session. Norman was able to hear, recognize and confirm that this guess of the therapist was accurate. And Norman felt more centered with the realization of what had occurred. He left the session with some appreciation for the therapist's attending to the relationship issues and to his (Norman's) feelings, and taking responsibility for his part in the interaction.

Another example did not work out as well. It was a training workshop. The trainee working as patient had shown an inability or unwillingness to compromise when there was conflict, was rageful when any feedback was less than adulatory, was very demanding. His therapist, a therapist in training working in a technique oriented style, suggested that the trainee stand up and imagine being a prison camp guard. The trainee said he did not want to do that, and looked upset at the suggestion. The therapist pressed, asking what his objection was. The patient trainee gave stock objections: it was silly, it wouldn't accomplish anything, etc. They reached an impasse, and the work never really progressed any further.

The therapist made that suggestion without having first made a good connection with the patient. So, to start with there was not the conditions of trust and good contact — not even a minimally adequate therapeutic relationship. Moreover, the suggestion was made not out of a sense of experiment, but the therapist was actually frustrated with the self-protection of the patient, seeing it as tyrannical. So, the tone and manner of presentation was not experimental, but confrontive in a hostile manner. The most pregnant opportunity that presented itself during this unfortunate work was when the patient's feelings were showing, although the nature of these feelings were not elicited by the question: "What was your objection?"

It was only later, when the patient worked with a second student therapist, that the actual nature of the patient's protectiveness became clear. He discovered a sense of being made a fool of by the previous therapist. The truth or falsity of this was less important than the fact that this was the actual experience of the patient, and it had not been recognized. The technique and the frustration of the first therapist predominated over the patient's need.

The trainee patient was frightened, and at times of conflict went into a panic. Conflict threatened the patient's sense of wholeness, and the rigidity of his response was an attempt to "stay together." In the context of empathic contact with the second therapist, being aware of the panic and expressing the underlying fear in the group, the patient actually was able to soften and move away from the belligerence he had been showing.

The minor error of the first therapist trainee was choosing the technique in the first place. It was based on countertransference, bad timing and not recognizing the patient's vulnerability. A more major error was not recognizing the strength and type of reaction of the patient and working with that with more respect and caring for the patient than for his own preconceptions.

Even without these countertransference-based interventions, doing what one would naturally do with a patient who is not narcissistically disturbed often exacerbates the situation. In many situations my natural tendency is to dialogue, hearing and acknowledging the other person and responding by expressing what I experience. This needs to be modified with moderately or severely narcissistically disturbed patients. With most patients authentic dialogue is an effective way to behave, and it is often not so with these patients. At least, in my experience, this kind of contact must follow a period of intervening based on the recognition of the inadequacy of the patient's self-support.

Marsha was a 35-year-old graduate student in individual therapy. Periodically she would call between sessions tearful, depressed, upset or else angry with me. The upset usually started or was exacerbated by something in the last session that seemed quite ordinary to me. In our telephone conversation I would often clarify the situation from my perspective, and after hearing her point of view I would often tell her my memory, intent and feelings. This somewhat settled things down, but was not very therapeutically effective. It did not result in recentering by the patient. While the patient was generally satisfied with our work and appreciated my caring response, progress was slow. Part of the reason for this was that during the phone conversations I frequently committed the same therapeutic error. Being supportive, open, dialogic, etc., was not enough. I did not respond to the experiences underlying the upset. So no real insight ensued, that is, a clear figure making sense of the central issue. For example, when she felt despairing and hopeless and bitter about her treatment by others and contemptuous of them, she did not sense my understanding of her feelings. I did not stay long enough with reflecting back how bleak things seemed, how awful her treatment by others felt to her.

The narcissistic patients need the therapist to attend to their (the patients') experience, the meanings these have for them, and to relevant developmental experiences. During the beginning phases of the therapy it is more important to explore what these disappointments mean to the patient than it is to build more accurate awareness by the patient (such as, hearing the therapist's phenomenological description of the patient) or more explicit statements by the therapist of how the patient affects the therapist. Later in therapy there will be support for these other avenues of therapeutic activity.

If the diagnosis is accurate and the intervention following the disappointment or "narcissistic injury" establishes an empathic attunement, the patient will feel better. This is easily observed and usually willingly acknowledged by the patient, although the improvement in mood is usually somewhat mystifying and not well understood by the patient. When such patients feel better, they are able once again to contain, regulate and channel their feelings and to resume their life and therapeutic activities. This same sense of feeling better follows ordinary sessions with these patients when they tell the story of the week, and no therapeutic work seems to have been done. The patients leave more centered, feeling better about themselves, with more of a chance to interact in the world in a manner that results in growth.

Make it Ordinary

The narcissistic patient lives in a world of greatness and rubbish, and the ordinary is equivalent to rubbish. They do not experience any glow or warmth with a little disappointment or being a little disappointing. If there is deviation from their fantasy picture, the good feeling from it is totally lost. If not wonderful, they are nothing. "Being nothing" threatens their psychic existence. They lose any sense of being unique or special.

One of the tasks these patients face in therapy is "making it ordinary." Being able to stay centered in the face of inflation and deflation, to keep perspective: to be able to be competent, without being the best; to continue to love when a flaw is perceived in the beloved; to be loved without the image of perfection of self.

My experience in working with these patients is that in their childhood they lacked the experience of adequate repair and soothing; they were not appropriately responded to in a manner that was well matched in intensity to their support level and were not responded to with needed empathic attunement that would have enabled assimilation rather than being overwhelmed. Disappointment with equanimity requires soothing, and it is that which is most lacking in most of their early history. If they don't maintain the grandiose position, they have no developed skills for soothing themselves. The upset becomes major because they cannot make it minor. When the soup is hot, they don't know how to blow on it to cool it down. Frequently their parents, especially the mothering person, also lacked this ability.

And conversely, when they received compliments, they were frequently not matched to what was an actual achievement for the developmental stage and intelligence of the child. When receiving an exaggerated response — a compliment — for something that is not an accomplishment, it is the same as being invisible or not seen for who one really is. The child who "can do no wrong," the little prince or princess, is not seen for who they really are, but rather given the message that only the grandiose self is worthy of love, attention and respect. They are not expected or allowed to be ordinary or just competent.

Often these patients were subject to massive disappointment (or disappointment that came on too suddenly); they were not allowed to experience realistic disappointment or else had to suffer disappointment without needed empathically based contact. To grow adequately a child needs to take risks, to fail sometimes, to learn about success and failure, skills and weaknesses. They need to learn about learning — being less than perfect and getting better. To do this they need to be able to look up to parents, and find them somewhat lacking and still wonderful. They need the parents to be able to acknowledge the child's weaknesses and still regard them as wonderful.

Individualize

While these suggestions are for narcissistic patients in general, this is most vital: You must understand the individual patient and individualize your treatment approach. In my opinion, good therapy does not happen by applying cookbook-type rules. For me, Gestalt therapy is an art based on clear phenomenologically based awareness and dialogic contact and any suggestions based on group data, such as diagnosis, are only suggestive and helpful for the therapist's growth in perspective.

The need to individualize was brought home to me during one time period when I had two patients with narcissistic problems start therapy at the same time. They had very similar character structures. Both had mental health backgrounds, one being a therapist and the other an advanced graduate student. And, as chance would have it, I saw them both on the same day.

The one I saw earlier in the day clearly insisted on the therapy following her experience only. She was able to verbalize clearly what so many patients feel but are not able to articulate. Most of her life she had taken care of the needs of others, and she wanted this to be her time. Knowing anything about me personally would risk that she give herself over to my needs rather than hers. For some time her therapy was experiential, even experimental, but not revealing of anything personal about me. As she grew, this changed. After a year and a half the relationship started to become more overtly interactional, and eventually her finding out about me became an important part of therapy: Would I turn out to be a disappointment? Would I invade her? Or abandon her? Or would she find out that I did awful things when not being a therapist?

During the first couple of sessions with the second patient I started with the reflecting, mirroring, empathic responding that the earlier patient thrived on. During the second or third session he exclaimed in frustration: "Don't tell me what I experience. I know that already. Tell me what you experience!" And, when I did, he did respond well to what he said he wanted. He needed to know that I was really present and impacted — and also that I was sufficiently supported to provide a safe framework for him.

My message is that we have to work with the connection between the unique individuals that the patient is and that we are, using our general professional information to sensitize ourselves to major themes, probable superior sequences, possible variations, etc. Taking seriously what the patient says he experiences (and of course what the therapist experiences as well) is our most valuable guide.

Grieving the Loss

When the fantasy of perfect confluence is explored, and the disappointment accepted, it will become clearer and clearer to the patient that the world of contact will only approximate that which is sought in fantasy. The idealized fantasy parent who is perfect and selfless and who mirrors and perfectly cares more about the child's needs than their own, the parent who is always there when wanted and absent when the child needs space, the parent who knows what the child wants even without it being asked for, is not possible even in infancy. In adulthood it is even less possible.

Lynne Jacobs points out the importance of timing, or who initiates discussion of the fantasy as a fantasy. She states that her narcissistic patients often describe "an experience of exquisite, perfect attunement from me. In early stages, their experiencing is dominated by their contacting fantasy. After experiences with me where I fail them and we repair it, they begin to identify a wish or fantasy which differs from direct experience. But when I challenged the experience of confluence by calling it fantasy, before they did, I often lost the patient" (Personal communication, September 1990).

Contact only approximates that desire, at best. What is not possible must be mourned. To heal, one must acknowledge the loss, the limits of what is possible, grieve that loss, and go on. The pace of this with the narcissistic patient must be determined by the patient.

"God grant us the serenity to accept what we cannot change, the courage to change what we can, and the wisdom to know the difference."

Final Note

My discussion of the treatment of the narcissistic patient is not concluded until the end of the discussion of treatment of the borderline patient and the discussion comparing treatment of the two types of patients.

Borderline Personality Disorder

Contrasting Pictures

People often perceive patients with a narcissistic personality disorder as immature, overemotional kids, or alternatively as condescending, charismatic, manipulative and/or power-oriented leaders. The borderline is often received with bafflement, appearing to be "crazy." The narcissist often appears normal on the surface, and problems emerge with certain interpersonal situations, such as conflict, failure or intimacy.

Although at times borderlines seem to function impressively well, they frequently fall apart. Better functioning borderline patients at work often appear to do their job very well, but without enjoyment, or joie de vivre. In such cases, their intimate lives are often either nonexistent or characterized by extremely entangled relationships marked by poorly defined boundaries. They are very labile, and when upset, function very poorly. They lose basic ego functions that the narcissists do not lose, that is, their basic perceiving, thinking, self-identity is at risk. They usually have a very poorly developed sense of object constancy, and, under stress, lose time, space and person boundaries.

When disturbed they often seem crazy, dangerous or unbelievable. This can be brought on by all of the situations that can evoke primitive responses in the narcissistic patient, but in addition any kind of separation or close contact is threatening. Any separation can elicit a feeling of threat of abandonment to the borderline. Even success can bring on that fear of abandonment panic.

Confluence is also highly charged for borderlines. They avidly seek confluence. In fact, they have an underlying fantasy of being taken care of and merging that is compellingly attractive — and terrifying. Their desire for confluence and avoidance of separation makes close contact psychologically dangerous for them. If a borderline were to get the confluence he seeks, he would lose any autonomous sense of himself.

Some borderlines, frequently those functioning in a better range ("north borderlines"), fear abandonment even more than confluence, and defend against it by being very confluent.

The borderline often presents a picture of either multiple unsuccessful prior therapies or a long previous therapy without change. They often start each therapy by denigrating the past therapist, talking as if that therapist were without redeeming virtue. Their desperate wish for rescue often results in unrealistic assumptions about how much the new therapist will do for them.

Whereas the narcissist often starts therapy showing a kind of paranoia — a suspiciousness of the therapist — the borderline wants salvation. The borderline's history in therapy is often one of this great hope followed by great disappointment, then denigration of the therapist. Whereas the narcissist seeks perfection and will idealize and then spoil the icon or hero when there is disappointment, the borderline will not only idealize but actually expect to be taken care of and his problems solved (magic solution), and turn against the fallen wizard. The narcissist wants a hero or to be recognized emotionally, the borderline has an underlying fantasy of merging with the wizard. The narcissist wants the therapist to be at one with his grandiose images; the borderline wants to merge into the therapist. Narcissists want affirmation of the validity of their experience; borderline patients want soothing and rescue.

Whereas the person with a narcissistic personality disorder feels alienated and wants his existence validated, the borderline feels helpless, fragmented and abandoned (Giovacchini, 1979) and wants to be taken into the protective arms of the therapist.

Narcissists often have no emotional connection with their past, and will maintain a grossly idealized picture of their family. They need to be encouraged to talk about their background. The borderline will frequently start with meaty psychological background material talked about freely, but without assimilation. It would not be unusual for the borderline patient in the first session to be relating the most apparently intimate factors or genetic material, often pathogenic material, when there is little support for dealing with this material either in the self-support of the patient or in the relationship between therapist and patient (which has just now barely begun).

In my paper on assimilating psychoanalytic perspectives into Gestalt therapy, #9, I discuss a patient I called Bundini. Bundini had a long line of therapists and came to me directly from a psychiatric hospitalization. At the beginning of the very first session he told me he knew I would make him a champ, since he heard how good I was. He had not met me, had not sized me up, did not know my approach or how the chemistry would be between us. But he made clear that unlike his previous therapists, some of which were well known in the general psychiatric community, I would be successful.

The course of treatment with borderlines, like their lives, is marked with frequent crises, with poor resolution even when treated appropriately, and with limited capacity for rapid recovery of equilibrium. They will show severe regression, fragmentation and loss of connection with the therapist between sessions. For example, if the narcissist is really heard by the therapist when upset, they will usually recover and proceed with the therapy on the next occasion as if nothing had happened. The borderline that is heard, acknowledged and respected may come in unaffected or worse.

In short, where the narcissist wants mirroring and empathic attunement, the borderlines want the therapist to accept them when they wish to merge and also wants to be taken care of and their problems made to disappear. Where the narcissist is self-image absorbed, the borderline is fragmented. And where the narcissist alternates between inflation and deflation, the borderline shatters, often going into rage, panic and sometimes into temporary psychosis. When hospitalized, the borderline with a temporary psychosis is very vulnerable to long-term deterioration and states of permanent dysfunction.

Diagnosing the Borderline

There are several lists of criteria for the borderline diagnosis, in addition to the DSM III. I found Kernberg (1975) and Gunderson (undated) useful. Rather than discuss the similarities and differences of these criteria, the validation research, the populations studied, etc., I offer a tentative amalgamated list I derived from my experience doing Gestalt therapy with borderline patients and from Kernberg and Gunderson. This has no research validation whatsoever and is offered only to suggest possibilities.

(1) Polysymptomatic. One of the first clues to a borderline diagnosis is a patient that has a range of symptoms that is either much wider than usually found and/or that seldom occurs in the same person. For example, when I find a patient who is obsessive, hysterical, and depressive (often these patients also have multiple medical health problems as well) a borderline diagnosis comes to mind.

(2) Impulsive, addictive and acting out behavior. They often take premature action, without regard to consequences, ethics, safety or legality. These patients are not sociopathic and without guilt — but rather carry intense affect into behavior to rid themselves of the experience of an emotional energy that is too intense for their self-support system. The acting out often includes chemical addiction. Sexually they often use others without regard to their personhood and are promiscuous (and often have polymorphous perverse sexual trends).

(3) Manipulative and suicidal. Perhaps it goes without saying that acting out and addictive patients are also manipulative. Borderline patients often manipulate through suicidal gestures and threats. Please note this does not mean these threats can be treated lightly.

(4) Heightened and labile affectivity, especially dysphoric moods. Borderline patients usually have intense emotions and are emotionally labile. They are rarely emotionally flat. They especially manifest dysphoric moods, having very little ability to experience positive affect, and are frequently anhedonic. Anger, rage, bitterness and depression predominate.

(5) Mild psychotic experiences. Borderlines sometimes have stress related, transient and ego-dystonic psychotic experiences. They often show a drug-free paranoid ideation and a history of becom-

ing worse in prior therapy. They often have dissociative experiences, although they do not typically have hallucinations or delusions.

(6) Disturbed close relationships. Borderline patients often have very intense attachments. They knowingly, repeatedly and avoidably get hurt in intimate relationships and complain, that is they experience themselves as "victims." An alternative pattern involves having only superficial relationships with no intimacy. They often are very dependent and demanding, but devalue their partner. They are manipulative and often appear masochistic. This relates to losing themselves in the confluence and to their swings between split modes (see #7).

(7) Nonspecific manifestations of ego weakness. They often have the personality structure of the classical prepsychotic personality, functioning in the range of a low level character disorder, with infantile narcissism, masochism and primitive defensive operations. Their tendency to use the mechanism of splitting (discussed below) is particularly noteworthy.

Ego Deficits
Object Constancy

An important developmental task is to learn object constancy. If the person is biologically intact and has even a minimally adequate caring environment in the first few years of life, this develops as a naturally occurring maturational process. This is essential for integration and the development of a reasonably stable and accurate picture of the interpersonal world. This is a part of our holistic perceptual functioning. We do not have to be taught that the table is square, even though we may be looking at it from an angle in which it mechanically registers on the retina as a rectangle. Beyond a certain age, we can imagine an object that is partially or fully out of view. Below that age, it is literally not only "out of sight, out of mind," but "out of sight, out of existence."

We also learn that people continue to exist when they are out of sight. Not only that, we learn that they reappear. Mom leaves, and then she returns. When the child becomes a toddler, he learns that he can leave, and then return. Thus he can test his independence, and return for support as needed. Mother will be there (or at least that is the ideal picture; we will see below that this often is

461

not true for the early childhood experience of the adult border-line). And the child learns to carry the expectation of the coexis-tence of independence/autonomy and appropriate environment support.

The child also learns emotional object constancy, that parents do things he or she (the child) likes, and they also do things he or she does not like. Good parents sometimes do bad things. Good children do bad things. The child makes mistakes, is hurtful, and learns that love continues to be available. The picture of the good parent (and the good child) is kept constant even though at the moment the air may be filled with anger.

The developmental maturational task of achieving object constancy has not been completed for the borderline patient and he or she has not developed a good sense of object constancy. It is very difficult for them to hold the image of a person when they are separated as it is for a young child. They have difficulty experi-encing constancy across boundaries of time, space, person. If it is not concretely represented in the current sensory field, they have trouble relating to it. This is not true of the narcissistic patient who is not borderline.

Since borderlines have such a limited ability to keep a sense of relationship when they are separated, separations mean abandon-ment and threaten the patient with disintegration and psychologi-cal death. In fact, with any threat, there is a propensity for disinte-gration, fragmentation and loss of basic ego functions.

Splitting

In Gestalt therapy dichotomizing is considered a basic aspect of all psychopathology and of the pathological aspects of modern life. This was discussed clearly in *Gestalt Therapy* (Perls, et. al., 1951). We have already stated that the character disorders in general have difficulty putting opposites together into integrated polarities rather than polarizing them into dichotomies.

The difficulty achieving a gestalt that deals with contradictions and polarities is especially important in the borderline personality organization. The borderline assiduously avoids awareness/ of opposites. When they do become aware of opposites they experi-ence havoc, panic and anxiety. Moreover, they have a particular way of dichotomizing that is usually called "splitting."

Parts of the self-experience that together constitute a whole are kept apart in awareness without influencing each other. The person is aware of both, but never at the same time. This contrasts with repression. With repression, that which is kept out of awareness, is kept out of awareness. That which is in awareness, is readily available to awareness. This does not alternate from moment to moment. With splitting, half of the polarity is "repressed," the other part available. When the "repressed" part comes into awareness, the other part is "repressed."

The unavailable side of a borderline split is unavailable to varying degrees. Sometimes the unavailable side is totally repressed at a particular time. More often the borderline can "remember" the other side if pressed — but the emotional meaning is lost. The meaning and importance the other side had for him or her is changed, often beyond recognition. When the sides reverse, the meaning reverts.

This splitting also happens with the borderline's picture of others. Parts of the other person that together would constitute a reasonably accurate picture of the other person, are kept separate in the perceiver's awareness, thus creating a very misleading and inaccurate picture. Thus when the borderline is angry with another, he or she often he/she cannot remember ever feeling anything good about them. And, when feeling loving, not remember anything negative.

The borderline cannot keep an accurate picture of the whole. To do this the person would minimally need a sense of object constancy and ability to see opposites and other differences that coincide in the same person group of people.

The narcissists will dichotomize to the extent of their inflation-deflation pattern, and occasionally even to the extent of splitting. However, typically they will remember both sides, but be able to feel only one. In fact some of the rage and panic of the narcissistic injury reaction is just because of awareness of the loss of the constantly held idealized image of the now disappointing one. This narcissistic pattern can be seen in both narcissistic and borderline personality disorders. There is a lack of integration in both kinds of dichotomizing, but the awareness block is much more severe with the borderline splitting.

Connection *or* Separation: Twin Dangers

The split of good and bad is noted throughout the psychoanalytic literature. In fact, at times splitting is defined solely in terms of the split of good and bad. I believe the process of the splitting has to do with all of the basic ego functions and is not at all confined to good and bad. Borderline splitting is more basic than the content of the split of good and bad and the good-bad split is not the essence of splitting.

I look at the process of splitting, rather than the content. When looking at the phenomenon in this process way, the splitting seems ubiquitous in the borderline and covers many areas of thinking, perceiving and emotional feeling. In fact, another split emerges for me that I believe is more significant than the good-bad split, and in this split the Gestalt therapy concept of contact and contact boundaries is a very useful starting place.

The title of this section stresses the word *or*. The borderline splits connecting and separating. Of course, anyone with any knowledge of Gestalt therapy theory at all knows that contact consists of both connecting and separating. This basic Gestalt theory is a very useful conception in understanding and treating the borderline. The emphasis on contact as a concept and as a principle of therapy is part of why I say that Gestalt therapy, at least a psychoanalytically informed Gestalt therapy, is the therapy of choice for the borderline.

The borderline thinks of "contact" or "connectedness" as being equivalent to confluence, fusion, regression, loss of autonomy and competence. They can conceive of emotional closeness and can conceive of competence and autonomy, but cannot conceive of the two together. They split the two. Being close means being taken care of, being incompetent.

Connectedness is equated with fusion; separation or autonomy is equated with abandonment, isolation and starvation. Being competent and autonomous means being separated. Separated means no connection at all (remember the borderline lacks object constancy and splits the phenomenological field). Being competent means not needing help. For the borderline dependence and competence cannot be integrated, even as a mental possibility. Therefore competence means being abandoned, and that means getting nothing emotionally.

Thus for them the choice becomes: to starve (alone and competent) or be fed (merged and incompetent). Hence, one of the danger points in therapy that requires good perspective on the part of the therapist is occurs the patient is beginning to demonstrate increased competence. At this point many borderline patients will prematurely leave therapy, without being aware that they are doing so because to stay would mean taking nourishment from the therapeutic relationship, and that would mean giving up competence. Unfortunately, this split-off state of competence is not sustainable since it does not take interdependency needs into account.

Borderlines both seek and fear this confluence. But with their splitting, they do not recognize that both exist. Thus one moment they feel as if their survival depends on having no separation or differences, and at another moment they are terrified of the loss of their self in the merger. When intimacy looms close, the borderline will often disturb the relationship, e.g., by running from therapy.

Because of the splitting they have an infinite capacity for regression. When they have a fantasy of being taken care of, they do not retain a background sense of the reality of their autonomous status and the impossibility of the merger. Thus, with the borderline, regression is not in service of the ego. Their fantasies of actually being take care of by the other is often more grossly inappropriate and primitive than it appears. When regressed, they do not have access to the observing ego, which is split off. There is insufficient observing ego. This is the reason that, in working with the borderline, too much "support" backfires, as I will discuss below.

When they are in the split-off mode of competence, they have an observing ego that does not observe the merger-hungry, fearful, incompetent, dependent self. Thus when the borderline patient is in that state, the therapist needs to keep the unavailable part of the patient's phenomenology in mind.

The Borderline Sequence

The separation and individuation of the "I" from confluence (symbiotic fusion) leads to a loss of any sense of connectedness, i.e., abandonment. This is true even if it is the borderline who is voluntarily doing the separating or leaving. This usually leads to the defense of clinging, although sometimes to the defense of distan-cing (isolating). If the clinging is responded to confluently, it leads to more confluence and to the terror of loss of the "I," and thus to separating, and the cycle repeats itself. If the confluence is met with differentiated contact, the borderline patient will feel abandoned and react with primitive negative emotions.

Good contact is not established by a dichotomized alternating between the extremes of confluence and isolation that jumps over any middle ground. Contact is maintained by moving between separation and connecting, between the withdrawal and contact phases of the contact-withdrawal cycle. But the contact function is lost when the withdrawal moves into static isolation with the concomitant loss of the connecting function of the boundary; it is also lost when connecting moves into a static position where there is loss of the separating function of the boundary,

Working through the borderline's sense of abandonment and its defenses is a lengthy, difficult, arduous and necessary task. This process strengthens the patients' true sense of "I" and connection and separation from the therapist. This tends to set off another round of the cycle we have been discussing.

The therapist needs to know in advance that the borderline patient will typically go through these cycles repeatedly in the course of living and in the course of therapy.

The distancing defenses usually appear as a competence that denies any problems, and is sometimes accompanied by leaving therapy prematurely because they are doing so well. The problem is that this is a split off state. The patient feels a sense of competence split off from any sense of needing to take in nourishment from the outside. It is a starvation position and as such it is not sustainable.

The borderline who is in this state will often suddenly deteriorate under certain kinds of interpersonal pressure, usually sticky, intimate relations in which boundaries have not been respected, or difficult interactions with authorities. In love relationships there is often tempestuous and stormy intimacy in which the patient has very primitive fusion fantasies stirred up, and acts out to get separation. At work this often means power battles with authorities, and often acting out in the form of inappropriate intimate and even sexual relations with a key figure at work.

Masterson (1972, 1976, 1981) describes in detail this separation of competence and dependence. He also has a useful discussion of the treatment implications. Unfortunately, his particular psychoanalytic bias, e.g., the therapist's task being an intellectual one, requires a lot of transformation of the material into the Gestalt therapy framework. Also, his etiological theory is marred by his narrowly linear, historical, mechanistic sense of causality.

He also presents a thesis that I think is useful, interesting and also false and dangerous. He believes that the etiology of the borderline condition is in the 18 to 36 month stage of development (Mahler's rapproachment subphase of the separation individuation stage) and due entirely to the mother not supporting, or even actively frustrating, the child's movement into separation and autonomy. According to him, the mother either totally withdraws so that the toddler who is experimenting with challenging the world comes back to find that mother isn't there emotionally or else she attacks and more actively interferes with autonomy. In either case this inhibits the development of a sense of object constancy, makes likely a splitting of competence and dependence on mom, and forces the child to be totally independent or merged with mom.

While Masterson's discussion captures the essence of the borderline dynamic, he also makes the claim that the condition is solely caused by the mother-child relations during this period, i.e., that this treatment by mother during this particular period is both sufficient and necessary for the later development of the borderline condition. For me this viewpoint is theoretically marred because I reject his linear, historical, one-way, mechanistic sense of causality. There are also empirical reasons for rejecting this aspect of Masterson's theory.

Many, myself included, believe that the problem begins at an earlier period and manifests itself during the developmental period Masterson claims is the origin of the disorder (for example, Horner, 1984, pp. 34, 76, 133). There is evidence that the borderline condition doesn't just relate to that period. Supporting her view that the condition starts earlier, Horner cites Mahler, who had patients with great disturbance in this period and but did not later become borderlines and other borderlines without great disturbance in this developmental period.

A more general objection to this has to do specifically with whether an adult characterological issue is caused by a particular genetic period. Even more eclectic psychoanalysts share this belief in its broad outline, and I do not think that this is good Gestalt therapy theory. This linear causality model and its attribution of all the variance to the mother's behavior and none to genetics, behavior of the child or general societal conditions, is contrary to Gestalt therapy theory.

However, I do find that the background of borderline patients that I have treated is generally marked by a family history of punishing independence, or else dichotomizing so that independence means total independence and nothing to come back to, which makes it prohibitively difficult for the young child to make the move. I just find this interaction to be a mutual interaction and one that precedes the 18 month developmental period and also continues for many years past 18 months.

Treatment Suggestions
(Comparison of Treatment of Borderline and NPDO Patients)

The prescriptions for treatment of the borderline patient vary from one end of the spectrum to the other. Within psychoanalysis it has been advocated that straight psychoanalysis be used, psychoanalysis with parameters has been recommended, psychoanalysis with increased regression, psychoanalysis with increased support, and it has been claimed by some analysts that psychoanalysis is not possible with the borderline. Some psychiatrists advocate psychopharmaceutical treatment, a practice I find useless and destructive (strengthens the fantasy of a magic solution, provides constant distraction for the patient, and brings on more side effects than useful).

Masterson advocates a more dialogical treatment — that the patient be confronted in a realistic and firm way with responsibility for stopping the acting out and taking responsibility for his or her share of the therapeutic learning tasks. He states that there is need for boundaries and "confrontation," and that empathy alone does not heal the borderline.

A strong presence by the therapist is needed to halt regression and establish clear boundaries and to establish the conditions that make successful therapy possible. A necessary concomitant of this is that many borderlines will leave therapy early if treated this way. Those who remain have a chance of getting well. If an effort is made to use support and empathy alone to hold the borderline patient in therapy regardless of the acting out or the lack of taking even minimal responsibility for the therapeutic work, the therapy is doomed to failure. Typically therapy started that way will blow up with extremely negative transference (and countertransference), acting out and occasionally even a psychotic episode or transference. I had one patient who came to me after attacking her previous therapist (who did use a regressive approach) with a knife.

Here are nine suggestions for treatment of borderline patients:

ONE: Contact With Actuality-based ("Reality") Contact Boundaries

The reader may well wonder why it is necessary to devote a section discussing a special role for contact in the treatment of the borderline patient in particular when the Gestalt therapy methodology in general emphasizes contact. The thoughtful reader might also wonder about the use of the word reality, when Gestalt therapy's phenomenological viewpoint is that reality is always through some person's phenomenology and the patient and therapist have different and equally valid views of reality.

Although the "default value" in Gestalt therapy is person-to-person contact, the borderline patient needs an especially disciplined, consistent and professionally informed application. There are important differences in how this contact needs to be applied in treatment of the borderline patient (compared to other kinds of patients).

Growth emerges from contact and experimentation in the organism/environment field. This means the therapist and patient as separate persons contact each other and growth emerges from this "broad spectrum" contact. The quality of the psychotherapy is largely a function of the quality of the contact established with the patient. Good therapy with the borderline patient depends on the qualities of contact shown by the therapist: caring, empathy, authenticity, commitment over time, and the clarity and adequacy of the therapist's clinical knowledge, personal awareness and contacting process. In addition there are specific requirements that are the object of this discussion.

The therapist with the borderline patient must be especially diligent in emphasizing verbal and nonverbal contact that is explicitly present-centered and in which the realities of the borderline patient, the therapist and other persons present are affirmed. In this kind of grounding contact, all people in the encounter are present as separate persons, impacting each other. This may be confrontive, or as simple as taking the time for effective eye-to-eye contact between therapist and patient.

Therapeutic contact in Gestalt therapy takes different form in different contexts. Different patients, therapists, modalities, cultures, institutions call for differential applications. Sometimes a session in Gestalt therapy will emphasize expression of affective energy, or exploring developmental history or the current interaction, or the mode of thinking of the patient, or a reconsideration of introjects, etc. Sometimes the contact between people in a group may predominate and the contact between therapist and patient may not be foreground. Sometimes the focus will be educative, as when contact skills are emphasized. All of this is sometimes appropriate and competent treatment using Gestalt therapy. We discussed this differential application of therapeutic contact in the last section when we covered treatment of those with a narcissistic personality disorder.

Narcissists need a narrower range of dialogue and the borderline a wider range. The therapy of the borderline must be weighted more heavily in the direction of the presence and emergence aspects of dialogue. Often the borderline patient requires more disclosure by the therapist. The therapist may need to say more energetically how he or she is being affected, or believes, or thinks — or to be present as guardian of the needs of all the members of a system of which the borderline is part.

Beginning narcissistic patients primarily need an empathic bond established with the therapist. Whereas it is usually therapeutic if the therapist relates to narcissistic patients by empathically following their current experience and stories of their life, with borderlines a more active and two-sided dialogue is the order of the day. I believe that just following the subjective experience of the borderline patient is insufficient at best and possibly dangerous.

The borderline patient needs the empathic bonding quite as much as the narcissistic patient, but cannot benefit unless other issues in the therapeutic frame are carefully attended to, the acting out is interrupted, and the relationship based on contact is strengthened before going too far into any exploration that leads to primitive emotionality. Empathic immersion without sufficient outside perspective by the therapist can be dangerous in the treatment of the borderline. This will be spelled out in more detail below.

Therapy with the borderline patient not only calls for the therapist to be caring and empathically attuned, but also to make person-to-person contact that emphasizes the borderline's phenomenological actuality in the borderline's various emotional states (one might say the various selves). For example, the therapist may need to take the initiative in reminding the borderline patient who is experiencing one part of a split whole of the now avoided aspects of his on-going experience.

This can be done in a caring and empathic manner that confirms and clarifies the patient's current experience and makes the reminder a form of caring disclosure by the therapist. Lynne Jacobs (personal communication) gives this example: "Therapist: I can see this state you're in seems so endless, boundless to you now. Other qualities of your life means nothing to you in this state. I feel sad as I sit with your anguish, and wish I could lend you some of my perspective of you, which is broader than what you can access now."

The borderline patient is often emotionally expressive without being in contact with the present context, and the effective therapist must be sensitive to this "contact" by the borderline. Frequently, the borderline patient's awareness process is heavily sedimented, that is, centered on repetitive thoughts not based on perception of the obvious or given in the current situation. Thus the borderline may not even note the limits in a situation, consequences, competing needs in the situation, facets of his/her own personality that are in the background rather than being salient at the moment, the fact that the therapist is both important to him or her and also a separate person.

Emphasizing contact in which the actuality of self and other is salient is consistent with two aspects of the awareness goal in Gestalt therapy: establishing dialogic contact between therapist and patient and improving the patient's awareness of his or her own awareness process. To do this with the borderline patient requires autonomous and vigilant awareness by the therapist, and often that the therapist struggle with the borderline patient in addition to being empathically attuned.

The therapist needs to establish a relationship that constantly builds for the borderline patient a sense of "and," the holistic joining of self and other, different and same, connected and separated, loving and hating, independent and dependent. Often the borderline splits asunder the differentiated wholes of self-other, of connecting-separating, of different-same. This is one of the central characterological processes of the borderline. Contact, the healing encounter, is the meeting of the "I" and the "You," an awareness of differences.

Self-other awareness and contact produces growth. Self-other is also the kind of differentiated whole that the borderline has trouble with. Awareness that is pointed only to oneself apart from the field is not dialogic and generally not growth enhancing. Awareness that is pointed only toward the other is also not dialogic and usually is not growth enhancing.

If the therapist allows the borderline to focus on the self only, i.e., only on the self aspect of the self-other, the borderline fails to grow and maintains a very immature style. This allows a regression that is not reparative, not in the service of growth, but rather infantalizing.

The borderline patient will not achieve a differentiated unity unless the therapist persistently, firmly and repetitively focuses on self *and* other in most of the borderline's work (which most often starts with a focus on something else). If the borderline patient continues in the belief that taking the reality of another person into account means that he or she will have to give up themselves to the other, they must necessarily not take the other into account. Then they cannot and will not have growth-producing awareness and contact. It is a long struggle for the borderline patient to learn that it is possible to take into account what they themselves need *and* what the others need.

The borderline patient needs a therapist who energetically, reliably, explicitly, consistently and insistently presents the demands of the environment for consideration. This encounter is not to impose change on the patient or convince the patient of the need to change, but to have the patient deal with that which is essential to the patient in his human environment which the patient does not allow into awareness, and then ultimately to enable the patient to be aware of his or her own awareness process.

"Presenting for consideration" does not mean imposed on the patient. The utmost respect must be given for the phenomenological reality of the patient. The borderline patient needs this to be presented for consideration in a nonmoralistic, nonjudgmental, matter-of-fact manner, rather than authoritatively imposed.

This is often an issue of bringing to the borderline patient's awareness options that would otherwise not be available to him. For example, logical consequences of a behavior are often out of the patient's awareness when the behavior is being enacted, although at other times the patient suffers from these consequences. And when consequences are considered, the borderlines often get stuck making either/or choices because they have no idea that there may be any other option. So too, the demands of the situation and of the other people in the situation is often assumed to be diametrically opposed to their own interests. Reconciliation based on contact is not possible unless the borderline faces their own reality *and* that of others. The therapist can present the needs of self-other for their consideration and thereby open up new possibilities.

Much of the work done in psychotherapy has to do with contact boundaries. It is even more so with treatment of the borderline patient. The therapist must constantly refocus on the contact boundary between the patient and the therapist. When the work focuses on the relationships of the patient outside of therapy, generally that work should also emphasize contact boundary awareness in that relationship as well as the contact boundaries between patient and therapist in doing the work about the other relationships.

We are taught that usually good psychotherapy interventions are based on appreciating reality as experienced by the patient. An established and useful clinical attitude recommends that work focus on what is ego-dystonic to the patient and leaving that which is ego-syntonic until it starts to cause discomfort for the patient. A modification in therapeutic attitude is often needed with the borderline patient.

With the borderline patient, work often needs to be done on behavior, thoughts, feelings, beliefs, etc., that are still ego-syntonic. The patient is not pressured to give up his "reality," what is ego-syntonic, but rather to broaden the lens through which he or she views the world to take into account the different awareness of the therapist and relevant others. That results in dialectical transcendence via expanded awareness rather than choosing between their own reality and that of the therapist. Growth emerges from this interaction. For the borderline growth does not emerge from empathic attunement without struggle and conflict. Growth also does not emerge from overriding the patient's reality by aiming at conformity with the therapist's reality.

This is a most difficult task made more difficult by the urgency of the patient's felt need for support and regressive caretaking by the therapist and frequent inability to form a Gestalt taking into account his or her own needs and the needs of others and the limits of the situation.

The borderline patient who sticks to destructive but ego-syntonic behavior does so for important reasons. The behavior that is destructive from one perspective may enable a kind of psychic survival. The therapist has the job of both explicating and acknowledging with the patient the function of this behavior in the patient's experience and also bringing into the perceptual field of the patient other aspects that are systematically excluded from the patient's awareness. This includes the need to be aware of the multiplicity of his or her own needs, the needs of others, the limitations, resources and needs of the situation, and the possibility of meeting those needs in other ways. Above all, it is the borderline's therapist who must have the faith and trust to overcome the borderline's despair and discover new options. This is a gradual and lengthy process.

The point here is that the therapist must, with good timing and judgment, in some way bring that which is excluded by the borderline patient in his self-centered and split state into the phenomenological field for consideration.

Good therapy with the borderline patient requires therapeutic empathy as an underpinning for a wide range of responsiveness, including: self-disclosure, limit setting, case management, education, experimentation, struggling with the patient. The goal is not patient conformity with the therapist's reality, but rather that the patient and the therapist take into account the awareness of the other.

Responsibility and the Process of Learning

Actuality-based contact also applies to the process of learning. Whereas with the narcissist one might follow the patient's awareness and then encourage patient reporting about genetic material, with the borderline the responsibility for learning and the awareness process must be stressed early in the therapy. The borderline must be made aware of the responsibility for the learning process, or else it is very possible, even likely, that the magical thinking will be out of control at a fantasy level.

Jacobs (personal communication) points to an attitude in doing this work that is often quite useful: "I tend to focus not on their assuming responsibility but on how their statements reflect a view that they do not feel responsible, often feel unable to be responsible. A subtle difference, but leads to growing interest in feeling responsible for the pleasure of being agents of their lives, rather than response to therapist moralism." While I find this to be true, I still maintain the necessity for nonmoralistic confrontation in dealing with the "I can't" belief of many borderline patients.

The idea of the patient doing the work is foreign to the borderline, although the words may have been learned from previous therapy, like the trick vocabulary of a parrot. The idea of the work being done together, you and I, is even more foreign to them. Yet, the actuality is that if they don't take responsibility for their part of the learning process, the therapy cannot go well in the long run. With the borderline patient one cannot take the learning for granted.

Masterson advocates confrontation of the borderline patient early in therapy on the issue of their taking responsibility for their therapeutic work. I agree. If the patient is either unwilling or unable to take this responsibility, and demands excessive support from the therapist, Masterson advises to let him go. He states that he does not know of any case in which the patient leaves therapy because of the therapist not feeding the regressive self, and later working successfully with another therapist (Masterson, 1981, p. 196). Of course this reflects a limitation of the state-of-the-art of psychotherapeutic knowledge as well as a limitation of the state of development of the patient.

Our ability to help is not infinite, but rather must operate on certain minimal conditions. I believe that at least a minimal patient self-responsibility for the learning process, achieved early in therapy, is a necessary condition for successful therapeutic treatment of the borderline patient.

If the regressive fantasy of the borderline patient is acted out in the patient's therapeutic behavior, and if the therapist colludes with this by an excess of "support" and empathy, there will come crises a year or two down the line in which the patient feels overwhelmed, increases the acting out, increases demands on the therapist and has intense negative transference reactions. The patient cannot support themselves better in these situations because during the early days in therapy the therapist did not insist on the building of the patients' responsible attitude, relationship and boundary skills, etc. (The spouse of the therapist will recognize these periods in the borderline's therapy by the midnight calls and emotional upset of their therapist spouse!)

Stressing awareness training and responsibility early in therapy leaves the narcissist feeling not understood and intruded upon. The borderline must be confronted, although they are also very prone to narcissistic wounding. It is best done with love, empathy, sympathy — but with firmness in insisting on the actual. I believe the treatment has no chance of success with a borderline patient without this confrontation.

Not only must borderline patients be made aware of their mutual responsibility for their own therapy, but also the responsibility and necessity for controlling the acting out. No borderline therapy can be successful if the acting out is not limited, preferably early in the therapy, and eventually stopped. If the patient gets drunk or engages in other chemical abuse, or promiscuous sex, or violence, etc., whenever he or she is stressed, the therapy cannot succeed. Not only will the stresses of the borderline's life overrun the pace of the therapeutic development, in part since the acting out makes the situation worse, but the normal crises of therapy will result in more acting out and prevent working through.

Some forms of acting out only end in the middle phase of therapy. Usually the borderline patients learn to feel responsible only late in the therapy. As therapy proceeds, articulating their fantasy of merger and being taken care of, and their belief in merger as the only meaningful way to connect, despite the inherent loss of autonomy, does help clarify that their identity and responsibility is separate from those of the therapist (Jacobs, personal communication). Of course, this must be done over and over again. Meanwhile, the therapist can avoid colluding with regressive fantasies and confront gross acting out behavior without expecting the patient to feel fully responsible for himself or herself. Gross acting out and the experiencing of a mature sense of personal identity and responsibility are somewhat separable.

Limits

Along the same lines, the issue of limits is often the initial battle-ground with the borderline patient on the issue of boundaries and self-responsibility. The borderline patient who is allowed to miss appointments (especially without paying), not pay bills, call after agreed-on hours, etc., is doomed in that therapy.

The patient I mentioned above who had taken a knife to her previous therapist started therapy by calling me at 6:00 a.m., talking of suicide or hospitalization. In fact, she had already contacted a local psychiatric hospital. After some talk, I told that patient that I would be glad to treat her, but only under certain conditions. I told her the hours she could call, and told her I would not see her in the hospital (at that particular time I did not want to do hospital work, and I didn't believe hospitalization was good for this particular patient), and that if she believed she could not follow these limits that I would help her get to another therapist. I also had to tell her that her living or suicide was her responsibility, although I very much hoped she would not kill herself before we even got to know each other.

I was very, very firm in the way I told her this. I was lucky in that she agreed to the terms and kept them. This was an excellent sign for her therapy, which was rather successful. This was not the last time this patient was suicidal, but she never made another attempt (and had made four previous very serious suicide attempts). She also kept her contract on the hours. It turned out with her that hospitalization was only considered by her in panic, that she absolutely wanted as little to do with hospitalization as possible.

I was not as lucky with Bundini. I saw him much earlier in my career and made more mistakes, including not being fully cognizant of the borderline process and therefore my interventions were not as crisp and accurate as they could have been. Also, I did not make clear that there were limits on the phone calling, and he did not manifest an ordinary capacity to contain his impulse to call me frequently and at all hours. When I became more confrontive, he would frequently call and hang up. I presume that he got some support from hearing my voice, making some connection, ascertaining that I was alive, and perhaps also punishing me by his intrusive behavior. An interesting contrast with Bundini was that I was very firm from the beginning about not treating him for free, insisting that my fee be paid in full and on time. I was firm, and he never gave me a problem on his bill.

TWO: Do Not Feed the Regressive Self

I discussed the contrasting situations with Bundini and the Gatekeeper's Daughter in the paper on assimilation (#9). In general, with Bundini I did not feed his regressive tendencies, in fact sometimes being rather abrasively confrontive, except for tolerating his phone calling. With Gatekeeper's Daughter I did feed the regression by being overly supportive and not confronting some of her acting in (acting out in the therapy hour and therapy group). Bundini had the longest period of good functioning and nonhospitalization of his life during the five years of treatment with me. On the other hand, Gatekeeper's Daughter left therapy in a rage, based on a transference reaction that could perhaps be called psychotic. During the first year and some months we had what appeared to be a good relationship. However, this was an

478

erroneous perception on my part because I did not understand borderline characteristics at that point. My lack of firmness, limit setting and support of regression, set up the unfortunate outcome.

I believe that not being firm and contactful in the way I have been discussing sets up a long but unsuccessful therapy, or a blowup of therapy (often a year or two after the beginning) in the form of an extreme and unmanageable negative transference. I think my experience with these two patients is typical. The blowup may come from the therapist improving and finally doing his or her job, or merely from not doing the beginning phase well without any change on the therapist's part.

Advice: do the job needed for growth and healing. Know your own limits. Let the patient go if that is what happens.

THREE: Countertransference

If there is ever a patient in your practice that you respond to by being defensive, upset, having a strong countertransference reaction, it is likely to be a borderline patient. These patients regularly elicit feelings of guilt, shame and inadequacy, and resentment from their therapist. Regularly therapists want to rescue them or commit mayhem on them, or both.

With the narcissistic patient things go slowly, and that may elicit some therapist self-doubt, impatience, etc. There are also narcissistic outrage attacks by the narcissistic patient. However, by understanding the process and responding with empathic reflections, the therapist is likely to see positive results and get some believable reinforcement from the patient.

However, the borderline will frequently strike at the very core of the therapist's self-esteem. The many crises often result in the therapist fearing disaster, e.g., successful suicide.

"Forewarned is forearmed." Know yourself and your limits. Know when you need to yell for help, either from consultant or therapist.

One should also note that because of the borderline's ability to stimulate bad feeling in others and their tendency to project one aspect of their intense feelings on one person and another aspect on another, they have a tendency to stir people into fighting with each other. One person would unknowingly be led to represent one aspect of the borderline patient's intrapsychic conflict, and another person would be led to represent another. For example, two staff members may wind up feeling resentful of each other, each having been led to know only a part of the patient's story. Borderline patients frequently split professionals one against the other, and can be destructive to agencies and to groups. In groups they will often establish an alliance system dichotomizing the group. This often happens outside the group, with divisive consequences for the group as a whole. I know one group that was destroyed by a borderline patient stirring up the women into a frenzy against the men and the male therapist. Unfortunately, the therapist was not sensitive to the emotional undercurrents in the group until it was too late.

I had one borderline patient who, when angry with me, would regularly call other therapists. Unfortunately, there are an infinite number of therapists in Los Angeles. He would tell a story that would make me seem like a fool at best. When he finally told me he had talked with another therapist, he told the story of the other therapist as if that therapist had told him outright what an incompetent I was and that he should leave therapy with me. The first couple of times I felt resentful of the other therapists, whom I did not know personally, until I realized that this was part of the borderline system of splitting and getting other people to fight their intrapsychic battles in an interpersonal field.

FOUR: Genetic Material

The narcissistic patient can use discussion of childhood material and will usually be slower about getting into this material than most patients and slower than useful for their therapy work. Thus, the therapist may fruitfully inquire of associations into their past history, and do some gentle probing beneath idealized stories of ideal childhood and "the best little mother in the world."

However, this is not true with the borderline patient. With the borderline the material must be carefully titrated against the strength of their self functions, such as contact boundaries, the health and strength of their relationship with the therapist, their awareness strengths, their ability to contain primitive emotions and their ability to integrate opposites. If this is not done, two things tend to happen.

The more innocent of the outcomes from not properly titrating this material is a lot of meaningless talk that is disguised as meaningful. This is a common weakness with beginning therapists. The patient will to be able to gain in "awareness" and nothing changes. The more dangerous route is a significant risk of fragmentation, regression, decompensation. For example, if primitive rage is stirred up before the patient's self-support system is strengthened, he or she may need to act out, go crazy, make midnight calls to the therapist, but certainly will not be able to assimilate and integrate.

The genetic material must be dealt with in pieces that are no greater than the patient's ability to assimilate.

FIVE: Need For Therapist Clarity

The borderline patient will engage in a lot of spurious talk and emotionality. For example, one patient at the beginning of therapy came in and immediately started talking of oedipal issues. He told of the seductive quality of his relationship with his mother and hostility between him and his father. His details, the age at which he said these events took place, consistently indicated oedipal issues. But this patient's issues were very much preoedipal. The issues that were related to his core functioning were dyadic issues of maternal intrusion and abandonment. No matter how we discussed these "oedipal" issues no improvement would occur they were simply the wrong issues.

I heard Harold Searles discuss a borderline patient's reaction to him after a separation. "Sorry I missed you, Doc," said the patient. Searles had an immediate image of a sniper who was saying he was sorry he missed in shooting him. Then Searles concluded that either he (Searles) was very hostile and projecting it or the patient was resentful while talking as if friendly.

Of course, this kind of incongruity is not an unusual one for a therapist to face. But the borderline will usually keep the incongruous aspects split and not spontaneously work on it or easily respond to reflections on this by the therapist. The easy offhand joke prevailing one day, the rage erupting at a different time. Since the borderline patient splits, expects rescue and does not take responsibility for the therapeutic work, the therapist must be all the more alert to inauthenticity. Special attention should be paid to expressed emotions that do not represent the most central of the patient's actual emotions.

With most patients, following the patient's experience will be a good compass point. If the therapist is off center, the interaction with the patient will return the therapist to the real issue. Thus with the narcissistic patient, the patient's experience is an excellent guide to what is the issue of the moment and good results flow from following the patient's experience.

However, this is not true with borderline patients. They will talk of an unimportant issue, distraction or interpretation that is based solely on an inaccurate interpretation or self-interpretation as if it were true, central and relevant to their here-and-now work. They are often taken up with their own distraction and even show the emotionality that one would expect with the content being discussed. With the borderline, the intuition and clinical acumen of the therapist is strained, the therapist has to have his or her own compass point. With the borderline, if the therapist is off center, tangential to the real issue of the moment, the patient will follow the tangent with the therapist right off into space.

SIX: Polar Responses

Because of the splitting and unusual need for therapist clarity, it is recommended that the therapist express both sides of polarities that are usually assumed. With the narcissistic patient, following the patient's experience will usually lead to the patient broadening his perspective and take in the polarity. This may take time, but is fairly reliable. With the borderline, it is wise to always make the bipolarity explicit.

For example, when having a direct dialogue, it is good practice with the borderline patient to pedantically state the patient's view and your own. "You don't want to leave, and I need to end the hour now." "I think you made a mistake in walking off the job, and I don't think you are an incompetent person who always makes mistakes — and you think that if you make a mistake once, then you are just an incompetent who shows bad judgment."

Neither frustration and firmness alone nor empathy alone are enough to help the borderline. Sometimes I will make a statement of my caring for the patient — only if true, never just as a technique — and will sometimes couple it within the same sentence with "and I don't want to take care of you." If I do care, feel warm or loving, I will say so. But if I think there is still a regressive fantasy of my taking care of him or her, I will do my best not to have my sharing of good feelings reinforcing any confusion about the limits of the relationship.

When discussing competence, it is wise to couple it with statements of the normal dependency on others. And when talking of the needs of the patient from others, it is wise to couple it with an affirmation of autonomy and competence.

Issues of blame, shame and responsibility for the borderline patient and the people they interact with are very touchy and difficult. When making statements of responsibility one has to be very careful to distinguish responsibility from blame or shame. It is also necessary to be very clear that when talking about responsibility for something involving someone other than the borderline person, that it be made clear that it is not only the borderline patient who is responsible.

For example, I had a borderline patient with whom I had worked for weeks about her marriage. In previous sessions I had made very clear about the responsibility of her husband for his part in their interactions (Perhaps I had not made her equal responsibility clear). In one session I observed that she was responsible for some aspect of an interaction she was discussing. She left the session feeling blamed, shamed and accused of being solely responsible for their marital difficulties.

Now this message she left with was in no way related to my actual verbal or nonverbal message. In the context of our long-standing discussion of her husband's responsibility this would have been even clearer to most other patients. But she was a borderline and it would have been better to make explicit mention of the fact that while she was responsible for x and y, that her husband also bore responsibility for a and b. She had trouble not blaming herself totally for all of their difficulty or on another day blaming her husband totally and taking no responsibility.

Empathizing with the patient's feeling of despair without sharing the patient's lack of faith in the future and dire predictions about the future is another polarity that needs stating. In the assimilation paper I mention a borderline patient who almost committed suicide when I went on vacation. The therapist who took my emergency calls showed beautiful empathy in staying with the feeling of despair, but did not express that she (the therapist) did not herself despair about the patient's future. The patient almost killed herself, but had a strong enough connection with me to hold on until I came back. She had needed some simple statements like "I want to sit with you, with your feelings, although I don't feel hopeless about you."

SEVEN: Contact Before and After Everything

Before any work begins, and after any work ends, I make whatever person-to-person contact is possible with the borderline patient. This is true in group and in individual. When a group leaves and people mill around, I usually say good night to each. But sometimes this is either perfunctory or a person slips out without a connection. This is dangerous with the borderline. I try very hard to get effective eye contact as a grounding and reconnecting at key transition points.

I noticed that if a borderline patient leaves in an emotional state and is not returned to good contact with me, there is a much increased likelihood that the patient will make an emergency call to me later that day or the next.

EIGHT: Watch Separations

Because of the centrality of the abandonment issue to borderline patients, and because of their splitting and their deficit in maintaining object constancy, every separation and parting is a potential crisis in the treatment of the borderline. The end of each hour may raise issues of a total emotional discontinuation of the relationship, of a sense of being interpersonally connected, for the patient. Separation without object constancy means loss of the person, and separation means never connecting again. It is hard for the borderline patient to believe that he or she will be real for the therapist between sessions.

Sometimes the patient will defend against this with total denial of the importance of the separations, leaving it for the therapist alone to express any feelings about separation. The patient will disown also by projection onto the therapist, maintaining an identification with the therapist who is perceived as doing the missing: "Gee, Gary, you make a big deal of your going away." This reaction will frequently happen during a phase when the borderline patient feels autonomous and competent. The autonomy is protected by denial of the importance of the connection. At this stage they are likely to use distancing defenses rather than work through the separation or termination. This is connected with some of the premature terminations of the borderline patients. They will protect the feeling of competence, although they will be leaving with much of the transference not brought into awareness and without integrating their need and their competence.

Masterson's discussion of the feelings of abandonment (Six Horseman of the Apocalypse) is useful in what to look for in working with abandonment with the borderline (1976, p.78):

(1) Depression and mourning [and grief]

Something is lost with abandonment, either the exaggerated abandonment that comes with each separation or the significant abandonment that the borderline patient felt in relation to his family. Something was lost and grief and mourning are appropriate and healing emotions. When the sadness is not experienced, stayed with, expressed and let go of, then depression rather than mourning sets in. This is frequent with the borderline since abandonment is such a traumatic experience for them.

(2) Anger [and rage]

The emotional reaction to abandonment is frequently anger or rage. Borderline patients tend to have a high level of anger of all sorts anyway and have trouble letting go of negative emotions in general.

(3) Fear [and panic]

Being alone in the world is quite frightening for the young preschool child. It is during this time period that the borderline condition starts. The borderlines doubt their capacity for self-support and the capacity of the rest of the environment to provide adequate nourishment. So they are fearful. And if they become more hysterical about the fear, they frequently convert the ordinary fear into panic. When patients are in a panic, as when they are in a rage, they need to move to a more centered position of just being scared or angry, rather than the exaggerated and unsupportable position of panic and rage.

(4) Guilt [and shame]

Although Masterson lists guilt only, my experience is that shame is a more predominant experience with abandonment. Children in general assume that abandonment is because there is something wrong with them. Borderline patients are filled with shame. They are often also guilt ridden.

(5) Passivity [and helplessness]

The abandoned person often feels lost, and helpless and passive. They are shocked, resigned, despairing. So it is with the borderline patient when they are allowing themselves to acknowledge their abandonment and feel their emotional reaction.

(6) Emptiness [and avoidance]

The impasse level feeling of being empty inside, the void, the empty-bottomless-pit feeling is very intense with borderline patients. They need the contact, empathy, confidence in them by the therapist in order to get through that impasse. Trying to fill the emptiness is an endless task destined to fail. However, staying with the feeling, using the awareness continuum, imagery, good breathing, etc., can lead to a sense of serenity.

NINE: R and R (Rage and Revenge)

The borderline patient has a great many intense rageful, vengeful feelings. They have mucky boundaries, multiple intense, crazy and tenacious transferences (with therapists, lovers, bosses, physicians, etc.). Their boundaries are foggy and filled with bitter stuff that is "in the air." Searles' patient who missed him like a sniper is an example.

The borderline cannot heal without giving up revenge. Revenge and bitterness permeates and ruins all endeavors of the borderline, and ultimately is turned against the self. R and R is another reason for premature termination by the borderline patient. They terminate prematurely to protect competence, to avoid the threat of merger that arises with real contact with the therapist, and also to punish the therapist for not taking care of them and performing magic.

They feel deprived, despairing, dissatisfied and envious. When they see others, they want what the others have — especially the prosperity and ease the borderline imagines other people have. They feel dependent on the largess of others, rarely satisfied, and unable to earn for themselves that which they want. Since they want to be taken care of, often they do not want to work for what they want either. They feel their dissatisfaction intensely and their envy is often bitter and filled with malice and desire to hurt the prosperous other.

They fear emotional starvation if they autonomously work for what they want, and weakness, inadequacy and incompetence as the necessary price of any dependence. With relation comes the twin sets of fears: intrusion, control, manipulation, merger on one hand and being alone, starving, abandoned on the other.

They blame others for their plight. Each succeeding new rescuer is hailed with inflated hope and contrasted with the terrible person responsible for their misery. When the rescuer becomes another disappointment, the borderline wants to punish, hurt, humiliate and get revenge on the newest failed parent figure — as they want to do to their parents and past parent figures.

Lacking the ability to integrate opposites, they have trouble letting go of negative feelings, such as disappointment, fear, anger, etc. Avoiding limits, they have trouble stopping their impulsive movement in one direction and come to a zero point. Blaming others and not taking responsibility, they have trouble making the changes they would need to make in order to get where they would like to be.

Rage and revenge function to maintain the status quo by directing the borderline's thinking, feeling and behaving toward impotent blaming and away from constructive action. It is based on an attitude of "I am not OK as I am," and "They (or you) are to blame." "If only he or she would feel the humiliation I feel, I would feel better." But no amount of revenge or raging can get the borderline what he/she hungers for, and rage and revenge are ultimately futile.

Only by moving beyond rage and revenge can borderline patients grow into forgiving their parents, therapists, lovers, and themselves. To feel OK, to feel some modicum of balance and serenity, the borderline must ultimately accept the unchangeable past, the invariant fact of limits and show the courage to change that which can indeed be changed. Rage and revenge are not compatible with wisdom or serenity.

Summary

The quality and safety of therapy depend in part on the quality of the discriminations made by the therapist. A therapist whose contact is guided by clear awareness can make discriminations that will maximally match the patient's therapeutic needs.

The gross discrimination between neurosis, character disorder, psychosis and conditions requiring medical intervention are vital for safety as well as for guiding the therapist toward therapeutic effectiveness. In my opinion, without this minimal diagnostic sorting no counseling or psychotherapy can be considered professional or competent.

If the therapist is aware of the state of cohesion, self-esteem and consistency of identity of the patient's self-functions, he or she will be able to direct his or her own attention in the best sequence, with the best size steps, with the best amount and type of support.

Just as a good therapist discriminates between an obsessive neurotic who needs to experience sensations and emotions with less mental ruminating and a hysteric neurotic who needs to slow the rapid jump from feeling to feeling and be more deeply in touch with what is meaningful to him or her, the good therapist discriminates between a narcissistic personality disorder who needs to start therapy with maximal empathic attunement and a borderline personality disorder who needs empathic attunement in a context of steady, persistent and firm insistence on patient awareness of the needs of self and other.

A phenomenological and dialogic therapy such as Gestalt therapy requires bracketing and genuine response to the uniqueness of the person being treated. This does not require being ignorant of or ignoring the known descriptive data of how certain kinds of patients, such as patients with narcissistic and borderline personality disorders, are characterologically organized, their developmental history, and how they need to be treated. On the contrary, when the therapist has knowledge of the key issues in a person's pattern of relating to the world, he or she is in a better position to be accurately empathic and to be able to respond with a minimum of counterproductive attitudes.

15

SHAME

Commentary

This essay was written in 1991 especially for this book. I believe that the recognition and treatment of shame, distinguishing it from guilt, knowing the implications for treatment are vital to Gestalt therapy and to the improvement in clinical attitudes in Gestalt therapy over the last decade. I believe that no single clinical subject could have a more salutary effect on the practice of Gestalt therapy than could the concept of shame if it were to become assimilated into the functioning of Gestalt therapists.

Shame

Shame and guilt are two major forms of negative self-reaction to the process of enculturation. Shame is the feeling that accompanies the experience of being "not OK" and/or "not enough." Guilt is the feeling that accompanies the experience of doing something bad, of hurting someone, of breaking some moral or legal code.

Although shame is ubiquitous in our culture, in my opinion it is seldom noticed and well treated in therapy. It is one of the most common and least understood experiences in therapy. Shame can be a reaction to specific traits, behaviors, thoughts or feelings —

489

or can be about one's global sense of self. Often specific shame reactions, and also guilt reactions, are merely the leading edge of more enduring, deep-seated and intense reactions to one's entire sense of self. These intense reactions can be triggered by apparently innocuous stimuli. One can feel bad, inadequate, or unworthy in one's essence, and it is this sense of not being OK at one's core that is the central interest in this paper.

In this article I concentrate on shame rather than guilt since I find that guilt with no shame base is relatively easy to understand and treat and most therapists know how to do so. On the other hand, it is my experience that as common as shame experiences are, many clinicians do not recognize the many manifestations and nuances of the shame process, nor do they know how to work with it. Often the therapist also experiences shame, and doesn't recognize it in himself or herself. In my experience, this can be true even of experienced clinicians.

Shame and its Origins

Shame reactions are negative emotional and evaluative reactions to oneself, to what one is, how one is, what one does. Most frequently these feelings are experienced in an inchoate, misty, unclear, mysterious and puzzling mode. Often the shame is successfully hidden from awareness by automatic maneuvers that function to avoid experiencing exposure to self and others. For the shame-ridden person, exposure, especially as inadequate or bad, brings up an intense affective energy that is almost intolerable.

The presence of a patient's shame reaction is typically first known and labeled by the therapist rather than the patient; the therapist is typically first informed by inference or intuition based on clues overlooked by the patient — rather than by direct patient report. Often the mechanisms of avoidance are so strong that patients know about their shame indirectly rather than by directly and consciously feeling it. Only gradually do patients come to have enough support to be aware of their feelings of shame. Ever so gradually the intense shame can become moderated and the patients' sense of self-esteem rise.

Initially the patient might be aware that he or she regards himself or herself as inadequate, unworthy, not a joy, or just plain not ok. But sometimes even this is not in focal awareness. Shame-prone people frequently heap a host of personal insults and hateful invective on themselves. Words that frequently refer to this shame process are: not entitled, weak, humiliated, incompetent, inadequate, silly, dumb, awkward, stupid, exposed, naked, not enough and so on. But these invectives are self-accusations treated as fact, rather than being a direct and insightful expression of the shame affect.

In the beginning of therapy patients may be aware of some aspect of shame, but with neither awareness of the central unifying process underlying these negative attitudes nor a vocabulary to express it. Vocabulary is a difficult problem in working with shame. Although we do have many English words to describe aspects of the shame process, the key word "shame" is frequently not used and the aspects that are known are not insightfully connected with the central self-process.

Shame often functions as a background process that seems so natural as to not come into foreground without specific therapeutic work. The sense of shame in a shame-oriented person usually goes back before the age of clear memory. It is based in the earliest strivings and interpersonal experiences of the infant and toddler. Since the shame process starts before awareness becomes verbal, shame feelings are often either not in verbal awareness or at least are only diffusely so. Shame-based gestalten are largely experienced in fore-contact, with later phases of the figure/ground cycle being interrupted.

To understand this, let us briefly review some basic Gestalt therapy theory about personality functioning and human development.

Identifying with figures as they emerge at the contact boundary in the organism/environment field is a pivotal Gestalt therapy personality and developmental concept. Through this important self-process novelty is assimilated and adjusted to and new Gestalten are created (creative adjustment). Although figure formation is a biologically given self-function, it is fundamentally the structure of experience. As experience, it inevitably and inexorably exists, functions and is developed in an interactional matrix of the person and the rest of the organism/environment field. In this interactional field people learn to support, enhance or interfere with their self-functions.

In Gestalt therapy theory the self is the system of contacts in the organism/environment field. The sense of self develops in contact between members of the family system. As figures arise and sharpen in fore-contact and the early stages of contact during infancy and early childhood, there are constant verbal and nonverbal interactions between the child and others in the family system. When the child acts, observes, feels, senses, thinks and so forth and this becomes known to others, the interpersonal contact, whether in awareness or not, helps shape both the child's response repertoire and sense of self. The family informs the child about cultural, ethnic, religious, familial expectations about how to act, think, talk and so forth. The family also informs the child about which affects are welcomed in that system and also about preferred emotional and communication styles.

This social shaping process can be done with a message of love, respect and acceptance for the whole person of the child (e.g., "You are a good boy, and we don't allow you to hit your sister — it hurts her"). On the other hand, this enculturation process may engender a pathological sense of personal shame or guilt. The early family interactions may support the formation of a self that identifies with its forming figure, one which values the contact and differences between the person and others, or it may be one that interrupts the forming figure and the entire forming sense of self and leaves the child with a negative reaction to one's self as a whole.

In the right environment shame comes in like mother's milk, automatically and naturally. It seeps in by osmosis, like the sounds in the room, the look on a parent's face, the sound of his or her voice, the rhythm of parental movements, how he or she is touched or not touched, and so forth. The youngster does not feel as if he or she is a joy or a gift to his or her parents. Although this shame process often runs throughout a shame-oriented person's personality, and can be very intense and brutal, especially in the case of character disorders or psychotics, it is usually subtle — as befitting a process that starts so young.

492

Shame includes a sense of defect or inferiority and a sense of being unlovable and unworthy of respect as a person with that defect. Shame usually carries the belief or sentiment that with such a defect one does not truly belong in human company. People experiencing this sense of shame often describe themselves as: alien, not human, toxic, untouchable, "yucky." Some ideal self would be worthy of love and respect, but not the self as is. This is an area where the Gestalt therapy paradoxical theory of change is particularly valuable, since identification with one's state is the heart of that change theory.

The sense of defect or inferiority may be based on almost any aspect of human life. Sometimes there is indeed a specific defect, as when there is a biological deficit, learning disability, etc. On the other hand, sometimes this sense of inferiority comes because of an inordinately high criterion for competence, as in the obsessive or perfectionistic neurotic ideal self and also in the case of narcissistic grandiosity.

The sense of unentitlement, of not being worthy of love, respect or achievement grows in interaction with significant others in the person's environment. It is in this context that the sense of shame comes in so automatically to the young person. When the parent coldly looks away, or looks disgusted, or overreacts with anger or insult to a small event, the confused youngster does not understand the overreaction and naturally assumes that "there must be something wrong with me." When it is not clear what this "something wrong" is, then the person is mystified: "There must be something wrong with me, but I don't know what it is." This sense of mystification is a prime ingredient in the shame process.

Although some believe that these matters are entirely environmental, evidence indicates that there may be a genetic component. Anxiety, insecurity, compulsivity, perfectionism and so forth may well have a genetic component. And some shame reactions to inferiority seem to arise regardless of parental treatment.

However, what is perfectly clear is that a sense of shame that endures over the years develops in an environmental context in which the child does not receive a sense of being known, accepted, loved and respected for who he or she is, including "deficits." With a physical disability or other form of defect, with some kind of inferiority, and the right parental attitudes, the child has an excellent chance of growing with pride in self rather than shame.

All forms of unrequited love bring up shame. Abandonment, especially by parents, is an especially potent case in point. Since chronic shame reactions start so young, the relationship with the mothering person is especially important in its induction. The shame reaction is bred in the child's need to have the parent be someone who can be counted on, and therefore when there is difficulty there is a tendency to assume that "mom is OK, and the problem is me." The four-year-old whose parents divorce says to himself or herself: "What is wrong with me, what did I do, to cause mommy and daddy to break up?"

Identification with oneself as one is, especially identification with one's state and one's experience is the opposite of shame-based self-regulation. Shame and organismic self-regulation based on the paradoxical theory change are mutually inconsistent. In essence shame rearing gives the message of an ideal self that is competent and acceptable, whereas the actual self is not.

In the United States the image of the ideal self usually excludes feeling or showing strong emotions, vulnerability or human weakness. Shame oriented societies often teach that control is worthy of pride and failure to "control oneself" is shameful. The young child is not only taught to control his bladder, feces, emotions and anything else society emphasizes, but is taught in a way that also teaches the young child to be ashamed of his or her very essence.

Introjection and confluence are important mechanisms in this shame process. The introjected message is usually: "Never enough!" "Your impulses, emotions and wishes are not acceptable. They show you are socially incompetent. Mistakes are intolerable. Keep control, look good and try to be competent — although you will fail because you are not competent enough."

Often the "you are not enough" message is given as a tag line. I remember getting straight A's for the first time in my life. I was pretty proud. My mother responded with some appropriate congratulations, then adding: "I got straight A's all through high school." The tag line said to me that I was not yet enough to be proud of. Sometimes the tag line was a gesture, for example flicking a microscopic piece of lint off my sweater. This communi-

494

cated to me that to mom appearance had to be perfectly in order before being acceptable, and my appearance was not good enough.

An example: a therapist in a training group related that when she was ten-years-old she made up by herself a complex contract for negotiating an important issue with her parents. It was important to her that this be done in writing because they didn't take her issue seriously and dismissed her childhood wants. When she showed it to her parents, they ridiculed her in front of others for misspelling a word. Never enough. Most parents would be proud that a ten-year old could be so competent and independent. However, in this family shame was induced by dismissing her wants and ridiculing her in front of people.

Comparing Guilt and Shame

Perhaps shame can be more sharply understood by comparing and contrasting it with guilt. Both feelings are negative reactions to the self. Shame refers to a person's basic nature and existence. While shame tends to be a feeling about the whole self "not being enough," guilt is the feeling that accompanies the experience of doing something bad, of hurting someone, of breaking some moral or legal code.

In contrast with the linguistic problem with shame, English speakers referring to guilt feelings often use the word "guilt." However, it is most often used when the actual experience of the patient is fear of punishment or resentment of "shoulds" and expectations either introjected and now self-imposed or else imposed by others. Authentic guilt, i.e., a sense of responsibility, regret and remorse about inflicting injury on others, requires a more mature sense of integrated personal values and empathy with others.

Guilt feelings are most often elicited by behaviors and feelings of aggression (hostile or nonhostile aggression) and sexuality. If these are acted on, there is often guilt because of damage to others (real or imagined) and/or violations of the forms of sexuality and aggression allowed in that particular culture. Guilt feelings are often present even for impulses felt and not acted on.

The sanction for guilt is punishment. Archetypically the punishment is mutilation. The sanction for shame is abandonment, varying from significant people looking away from the person being shamed, to physical abandonment, or even banishment.

Both shame and guilt can be based on a mature and assimilated sense of oneself, which might be called authentic, or on the other hand they can be based on introjected standards that bring on reactions that are more or less inauthentic or not organismic. Both guilt and shame call for discriminating what is reasonable to expect, hence for what it is reasonable to feel ashamed or guilty about and to what degree. Generalized and specific guilt and shame reactions can be reasonable or unreasonable, assimilation-based or introjection-based.

Sometimes what people call "guilt" is not a real sense of doing something harmful, but rather fear of being punished for breaking rules imposed by another. When the guilt is introjection-based it tends to be exaggerated, i.e., phenomenological exploration finds that it is ill fitted to the situation, and the phenomenological exploration also reveals that the feeling the patient is experiencing is more accurately labeled as resentment. This experience is more a fear of prosecution than a fully developed feeling of personal responsibility and guilt. This is usually associated with an ongoing power battle interpersonally, especially with authority figures, and between aspects of the person's psychological system, especially topdog-underdog conflicts. Of course introjection and projection play heavily in this process.

In such cases of introjected guilt there is a neurotic loss of ego functions that can be recovered with Gestalt therapy. The work of clarifying introjects, reowning projections, spotlighting the topdog - underdog dialogue, expressing resentments, and feeling through to organismically based choices are familiar to any well-trained Gestalt therapist. A good therapeutic outcome in such cases involves the recovery of the lost ego functions and either continuing the behavior without guilt or else discontinuing the behavior based on the person's now integrated sense of what is fitting for him in his context.

Sometimes another kind of mislabeling results in the patient "feeling guilty" when a careful phenomenological exploration finds that the actual experience is one of regret, sadness and caring for the other person's pain, but not a sense of guilt since the hurtful behavior was either necessary, unavoidable, not deliberately chosen or the injury not foreseeable. In these cases merely discriminating between guilt and these other feelings can result in a real *aha!* experience and a sense of relief. For example, sometimes I am called upon to review or evaluate a piece of professional writing or therapy practice and I see the work as clearly deficient and must say so. Even when this review or evaluation was requested by the person and done in a sensitive and sympathetic manner, some people feel injured. I used to label my affective response as "feeling guilty" when I actually felt regret, sadness and compassion.

Feelings of guilt are appropriate to the degree that they are based on an assessment of doing harm to another, to a relationship or to the environment. It is pathological if the harm is not real, if the assessment is not an assimilated one (i.e., is based on introjection), or if the feelings are more extreme, unyielding, overgeneralized or punitive than called for by the circumstances. It is also pathological not to feel guilt when one's chosen behavior results in such harm. Of course in both cases the discrimination is not objective, but is made through someone's judgment.

When the guilt is authentic, "existential guilt" and also not shame-based, the behavior that induces the guilt usually ceases. Unless the circumstances are unusual, people with a mature value system do not continue behavior they genuinely regard as wrong. When the offending behavior does occur, then awareness, confession, and repair are spiritually and therapeutically indicated.

Authentic guilt may be relieved by confession, repentance, repair and forgiveness. Neurotic guilt may be relieved by exploring the introjected basis of the code being broken and by bringing into awareness the emotions of resentment and anger, undoing projections, and mobilizing a channel for the expression of the aggression toward the environment and allowing the emergence of a code based on organismic self-regulation.

If the guilt is authentic and intense, it often leads to shame. For when one commits bad deeds, it does mean that one is the kind of person who can and did do that offending behavior. This leads to feelings of shame in people with any inclination toward shame.

Shame refers to a person's basic nature and existence. Mere punishment or forgiveness or repair to others would not make a person feel like they were "enough," e.g., competent and lovable. Relief from shame is therefore much more long term, gradual and difficult.

The Shame-Guilt Bind

If someone acts on their aggressive or sexual impulses they will often feel guilt. However, note that if a person avoids feelings of guilt by not acting on them, the person often regards himself or herself as inadequate and is often so regarded by others. In this case, the person is caught in a "shame-guilt bind."

The little boy who goes out on the playground and hits back when attacked may be told by the adults that he is bad for doing so. In the primary school grades this is often an interaction between a female teacher and a boy. If the boy does not hit back, he becomes labeled by himself and others as weak, sissy, etc. This can also be true of sexual behavior. In the United States a sexually active teenager is often labeled as promiscuous or bad by adults; however, teenagers who are not sexually active are often labeled as inadequate by their peers.

Often the experience of guilt is used to avoid the experience of shame, and the experience of shame is used to avoid the experience of guilt. Some patients come in complaining of sexual inadequacy, but would rather die than admit that they have moralistic, puritanical, Victorian attitudes about sex. After all, one is supposed to be liberated. So a person confesses to shame and inadequacy, disguising the conflict between sexual desires and the attitude that this is wrong. On the other hand, some will come in and say that they regard sex as distasteful, dirty, bad or else that they are just "not interested," when in fact they are avoiding their fear or sense of inadequacy. Sometimes the moralism is disguised as idealism or romanticism. I have seen this most often in adolescents.

Any rupture in the basic family bond has a tendency to result in guilt. Separating from mother may well cause mother to feel some grief, pain or hurt. Nevertheless, if the child is in fact to be competent, he or she must individuate from mother and establish his or her own values, competence, beliefs, feelings and interests. Failure to separate and individuate from the family at developmentally appropriate times has a tendency to result in inadequate functioning and feelings of shame.

Within the guilt-shame system there is often no way out, short of interrupting, exposing and interfering with the system that leaves the individual with no options other than being bad or inadequate.

Piers and Singer (1971), who clearly describe this shame-guilt bind, also discuss cultures as shame or guilt oriented. For years I have been very suspicious of the anthropological accuracy or utility of characterizing whole cultures as shame or guilt cultures. However, as I travel and train therapists in various countries, there does seem to be a marked difference on this dimension from one country to another. I have noticed, for example, that the ambience in the group and the dominant issues of the individuals in this regard are very different, say, in Finland, a "shame culture," and Brazil, a "guilt culture."

The Appearance of Shame

A person feeling shame may have a hot, flushed, embarrassed look. More often, the appearance is marked by both the feeling of shame, the impulse to hide, and efforts to avoid knowing or showing either. This may appear as a rigid, isolated manner in which there is little movement. The shame itself may be shown in the form of a physical shrinking, head hanging and looking away and avoiding eye contact. Cognitively, the patient will often experience going blank or numb. Attacking, rationalizing, raging and self-righteousness are often used to avoid the feeling of shame. It is as if the person were saying: "I have to be right and adequate and you have to be wrong and inadequate so that I don't have to feel ashamed."

The polar opposite of shame is pride. The person who is proud of himself or herself has a good, glowing, warm, confident feeling about self. Whereas the person feeling shame wants to hide, the person feeling pride puffs out the chest and feels: "Look at me,

I'm OK." The shame reaction is to shrink and hide, and the pride reaction is to expand and be heard and seen. At the extreme pride can be a matter of narcissistic grandiosity. In such cases the pride is not well supported, is not based on full appreciation of who they are and not well matched to their actual accomplishments and weaknesses. Moreover, in the case of grandiosity in persons with narcissistic personality disorders, the pride is accompanied by a contempt for others. This is not necessarily present in all cases of pride. Sometimes when people start to feel pride, they have a reaction of shame or guilt since they were taught that pride is bad and that only inferior, ill-bred persons are prideful. Some ministers preach "Pride goes before destruction and a haughty spirit before a fall."

Most of this shame process is not conscious, and only comes into awareness as a result of ongoing therapy, with a good relationship, and in which the therapist gradually introduces awareness of shame. By good relationship I include the therapist: (1) having an accurate empathic understanding of the patient; (2) expressing this understanding in a manner in which the patient can confirm its the accuracy or inaccuracy; and (3) the therapist feeling warmth, acceptance and respect for the patient and manifesting it in a manner the patient can recognize; and (4) the therapist is both congruent and authentic. We will speak of this therapeutic aspect later.

Self and Ideal Self

The ideal self refers to an image or picture of self as one would like to be, or feels one has to be in order to be acceptable. Although the ideal image can be assimilated or introjected to varying degrees, it is frequently more assimilated or ego-syntonic than mere "shoulds."

Shame-oriented people compare themselves to this ideal self, and identify more with that ideal than with their actual experience of themselves. They feel shame to the degree that they identify with the ideal image and experience a discrepancy from it. I find it ironic that later in therapy patients often discover that they do not even like people who match their ideal self and when they experiment phenomenologically with being that ideal self they often do not like being it.

The ideal self-image of shame-ridden people is usually rigid and allows only a narrow range of traits, often not even mutually consistent; it excludes a broad range of behavior and experiences. These nonacceptable behaviors and experiences are such that they are seen as reflecting on the overall character of the person, on the adequacy and competence of the person. For example, the ideal self may be smooth and graceful, and the experience of being awkward does not fit that ideal self; the person feels ashamed whenever he or she starts to experience awkwardness. Of course, the paradox is that when the shame experience sets in, awkwardness is very likely to increase. Thus shame can be a circularly self-increasing process.

Hiding and Embarrassment

"I don't want to be seen" is frequently heard in working with shame-oriented people. They often have trouble looking or being looked at. They disown their eyes, usually by projection. This is both because of injunctions against looking ("Don't stare, it isn't polite.") and because looking means making real the social contact. They might see the other person looking at them, thus raising the interpersonal exposure and intensity.

To be seen means exposed, and shame-oriented people project their own judging eyes and expect to be found wanting. It is as if one's own eyes are staring back, looking with the projected disgust and imagining that the others feel as much disgust as the self-disgust. With the projection of one's eyes, a person feeling shame shrinks away from looking and then experiences being exposed and looked at by the other and their own projected eyes. Because they have trouble actually looking, they are to varying degrees in touch with their own projected expectations, not what their eyes would tell them.

In the face of the judging eyes they expect, they feel exposed and naked. Being seen means no shield, no hiding, no mask, no privacy. In shame they are filled with an emotional energy of blushing, rising temperature, shrinking, head hanging. Of course, this is worse in a critical, unsafe, shame-inducing environment.

The experience of shame is always accompanied by a desire to hide. Sometimes, persons feeling ashamed may say that they wish the ground would just swallow them up. This hiding can be accomplished by a stony facial mask, by overuse of words, by physical withdrawal, by being quiet and not moving, by avoiding having attention called to oneself, and so forth. When one feels shameful, inadequate and unworthy, one does not want to be seen, does not want to have his shame exposed to the world.

The shame-ridden person also often feels untouchable, unworthy of being touched or that if someone touches him or her they would find it a burden or unpleasant or even toxic. This is often expressed with sentences like "I don't want to be touched," or "I don't deserve to be touched." They are embarrassed by being seen or touched, or even by the realization that they desire to be seen or touched.

The hiding isolates the person and creates an endless loop. Without interaction and feedback, the person has no input to contradict the sense of shame. Each awareness leads to shame, shame leads to wanting to hide, then the shame leads to shame at being ashamed and being ashamed of wanting to hide. The more one needs or desires contact, the more intense the feeling of shame. This leads to more hiding and isolation. This can be an infinite regress.

Embarrassment can be the leading edge of shame and is often the feeling that is observed by the therapist and also reported by the patient who is feeling shame and doesn't know it. Let us contrast embarrassment as the leading edge of shame and simple embarrassment.

At its heart embarrassment is the emotion that is felt when current experience is not accounted for in a person's "I boundary." For example, when thrust into a role or status that is not integrated into the self-image, whether the role is better, worse or parallel with the person's usual status, the person usually feels embarrassment. When noticing an emotion or desire that is not part of one's self-image, or showing an emotion that is not part of one's selfimage to show, then the feeling of embarrassment often results. Embarrassment is usually accompanied by flushing, the experience of self-consciousness and feeling shy.

Erv Polster calls embarrassment "curdled delight." In the simple case, embarrassment is both warm aliveness and also a sense of it not being what is customary, not quite what is allowed. Often a patient will not have the cognitive and emotional support for this embarrassment and it is then experienced by the patient as a negative feeling. When this is the case, the person will often hold his/her breath, shrink, and want to hide or disappear. But this is not inherently so with embarrassment.

Embarrassment is not inherently negative. When the person can stay "soft" and in contact, support the excitation with their breathing, stay present-centered and identify with their current experience, the feeling of "curdled delight" can even be enjoyable. People can learn to "make friends" with their embarrassment. Embarrassment usually accompanies growth and expansion and it is important that patients learn to be friends with their embarrassment so that they can move ahead with changes that are accompanied by simple embarrassment.

It is different when embarrassment is the leading edge of shame. Simple embarrassment in the context of general self-acceptance can be merely a warm uncomfortable feeling. In the context of shame, embarrassment is only the leading edge, the feeling that is most easily felt by the patient who is in a shame state. Shame embarrassment is often accompanied by a very painful feeling of humiliation.

This shame embarrassment is not a feeling one can easily become friends with. It is accompanied by a deeply held sense of not being worthy of being seen and an intense need to hide. Although when one is simply embarrassed there is always some tendency to hide, the prideful delight may be strong enough to override it. One often sees this in the peek-a-boo contact that shy people often make. In the case of shame the sense of being not OK and needing to hide is much more deeply and intensely felt.

Hiding is accomplished in part by retroflection. This is the mechanism of substituting oneself for the environment, and is used by the shame-prone person to avoid the exposure and sense of shame that comes with social contact. Self-directed feelings are retroflected and substitute for interpersonal contact. Anger originally aimed at someone else may be retroflected into shrinking.

Shame is marked by rage, disgust and disapproval of the self. Oedipus' tearing out of his eyes on discovering he had bedded his mother is a classical example of retroflecting guilt and shame.

Retroflection in shame is part of a marked isolation, often denying needs from the outside. The shamed person needs love and approval from the outside, but often adopts a defense of self-sufficiency. It is an open question to what degree this is based on a felt sense of not deserving and to what degree it is merely a result of hiding the shame by minimizing interaction.

As we have discussed, awareness of feeling ashamed often results in feeling ashamed of being ashamed. The realization of wanting to hide is also often accompanied by a feeling of shame of needing to hide. Each of these is experienced as evidence of inferiority. Of course, this increases the shame and the need to hide and the closed loop effect continues. The person isolates and does not assimilate the needed novelty from the outside. One of the ironies of shame is that the natural tendency to hide is one that leads one away from the cure, which is loving encounter.

Of course, the hiding was probably quite appropriate in the environment in which the shame originated. In that environment, further exposure often meant a continuation of the interaction that caused or maintained the shame. Ideally the therapy environment is much more loving and not shaming compared to the patient's internal environment, which is based on early childhood experience (especially introjects and unfinished business). Unfortunately this is often not true enough.

Shame reactions in neurotic patients are different than for those who are character disordered. This has been noted elsewhere in this volume, in discussing the treatment of patients with narcissistic and borderline personality disorders. While the reaction to shame is always one of reduced self-esteem, as discussed previously in this section, there is not a collapse of the sense of self in the neurotic. The neurotic doesn't lose the ability to reflect (except momentarily), doesn't lose the sense of personal cohesion, doesn't lose the ability to function (although it will be impaired by the shame reaction), and isn't reduced to an "all bad" state (except momentarily).

Therapeutic Approach to Shame

The Goal and Timeline in the Treatment of Shame

The general therapeutic goal in Gestalt therapy is: (1) to know and *identify with one's own primary experience* while in contact with the rest of the organism/environment field, especially the primary experience of other people in that field; (2) to take *action* based on that identification; and (3) to trust that *growth emerges from interaction.* Primary experience includes awareness of limitations and strengths, effectiveness and ineffectiveness, and concern about morality, immorality and amorality. It is important that people learn from experience by recognizing their mistakes, weaknesses and limitations and still have a good sense of self-esteem.

Generally my specific goal in therapy with shame-oriented patients is to increase their awareness of and choice over the shame and guilt process, help them become free from the automatic and excessive self-attacking process of shame, to achieve a cohesive, safe and generally positive and compassionate sense of self, and finally to have a sense of guilt and shame that is sensibly and rationally directed by their own spirituality, values and needs, in a process of self-other contact, awareness and epoché. A part of that goal would be awareness and acceptance of their need to hide and transform defensive hiding into healthy withdrawal.

Accomplishing this requires long, repeated, gradual work. This is in part because of the preverbal, conditioned sense of self that is so diffuse, ubiquitous, primitive and ego-syntonic. The slow pace of work with shame is determined not only by the inherently gradual nature of altering such ingrained attitudes, but also shame continues to be evoked in the patient's ordinary life during the course of treatment. Moreover, shame is evoked by the mere process of being in therapy, an obvious weakness or flaw to the shame-oriented patient. When such a patient learns something in therapy, there is a propensity to feel the shame reaction that "If I were adequate, I would have already known that." And when therapy brings the shame itself into awareness, the inveterate reaction of being ashamed of being ashamed sets in.

Moreover, I question whether the total elimination of shame or guilt is a good therapeutic outcome. Authentic guilt feelings about causing harm is an inherent part of being a complete person. Feeling guiltless would mean either doing no harm to anyone, a suspicious claim, or not feeling appropriate guilt at the harm. I am not here judging what one should feel guilty about, just that the therapist should not try to eliminate all guilt, treat all guilt as neurotic or believe that guiltlessness is a desirable therapeutic goal.

So too, note the word *shameless*. A person who acts shamelessly is thought to lack an appropriate sense of context and of their own limits. Again, I am not making a case for what should cause shame or to what degree, but merely making a case for the therapist not believing that the healthiest mode, hence the goal in therapy, is to be without any sense of shame.

The choice of what is appropriate guilt or shame is the patient's choice and not the therapist's. The therapist's job is to accept and bring awareness to all aspects of the patient's awareness process and facilitate the emergence of a healthier, more integrated sense of self from the phenomenological and dialogical interplay of these conflicting forces.

Healthy guilt and shame are experiences that go through the figure/ground cycle, starting in forecontact and ending in the letting go of postcontact. In health the feelings of shame or guilt arise from and are determined by actual conditions in the organism/environment field. In contrast to more vulnerable neurotic and character disordered patients, healthy people have a wide, discriminated range of guilt and shame reactions. They neither deny shame or guilt when their values and standards are violated, nor do they suffer self-annihilating misery at every failure to meet their values and standards. They have mild shame or guilt reactions at infractions which they consider minor, and more severe reactions at grosser violations of their standards. The whole person is not condemned for small transgressions and self-esteem is not entirely lost for specific personal weaknesses. As the contact intensifies, appropriate action is taken and fully engaged (final contact). This includes restitution for damages and acknowledgment of limits.

For me the goal of the growth work in this area is not merely to eliminate the shame, but for the patient to grow into a more loving, reasonable, productive sense of themselves. Working for an assimilated, integrated, positive sense of self is not a sudden process, but one that happens in small increments or approximations. This process is complicated by the fact that the therapeutic goal must be a realistic positive sense of self in which inherent limits in self and the self-other field are recognized and the patient develops an ongoing process of sensible discrimination rather than a largely grandiose positive sense of self that is without this discrimination.

The Relationship In Shame Treatment

Shame cannot be successfully treated unless the relationship between therapist and patient is one in which the therapist truly understands, accepts and confirms the patient as well as practices inclusion. It is vitally important that the therapist be congruent and show this in nonverbal as well as verbal ways.

The shame-oriented patient cannot heal except in the context of person-to-person contact. The shame must be expressed in the presence of others who accept the person with a genuinely horizontal attitude. The quality and quantity of contact is vital. In groups the patient needs to be facilitated toward such contact with others in the group during and after working or other forms of exposure.

For optimal healing, the shame-oriented patient also needs to know that people he or she respects, especially the therapist, also have feelings of shame and are also willing to expose them. In a sense, the shameful patient needs the therapist to be exposed also. Of course, this requires a therapist with enough self-support to be able to be so exposed and also maintain a good and loving sense of himself and also requires a therapeutic theory and methodology in which "I statements" by the therapist are a regular and recognized part of the treatment. This is difficult to reconcile with the traditional psychoanalytic methodology. Of course, self-awareness, timing, discrimination, tact, dedication to the welfare of the patient, understanding the individual patient's character and treatment needs are all essential and immutable responsibilities of the therapist who does use I statements as a part of the treatment methodology.

It is of vital importance that there be no shaming or humiliation of the patient. Sarcasm, teasing, contempt, pity, condescension and other similar attitudes on the part of the therapist can be devastating in the treatment of any patient, but this is especially true of shame-prone patients. This is true whether the offending behavior is direct or indirect, verbal or nonverbal. For example, a Gestalt therapy experiment can be devised based on a disrespectful and negative attitude toward the patient and this will inevitably evoke shame in a patient prone to shame. The problem here is usually not the technical aspect of the intervention, but rather the attitude of the therapist toward the patient. Therapists who do this shame stimulation frequently do not know they are doing it and would themselves feel shame if they were to realize it, for it is usually not in their picture of themselves to cause shame in their patients.

Person-to-person encounters can be respectful and horizontal or vertical and shame-invoking. The statements "You want a lot from me" or "You have to take care of yourself" may actually communicate: "You are too needy a person." These have a different impact than "You want me to take care of you and while I care about you, I do not want to take care of you, and in fact cannot really take care of you in the way you wish." The first statements categorize the patient as a deficient person, while the last statement may be based on accepting the other person, and distinguishes both the limitations of the situation and the therapist's reaction to an aspect of the patient from the patient as a whole. It should be noted that an intervention that verbally appears straightforward and respectful may in fact be shaming. Of course, even with a nonshaming message, the patient may still with shame. But in the case of the more respectful attitude from the therapist, it may be safe enough for the patient to work on this shame.

One of the temptations that is not useful is the temptation to talk the patient out of his or her feelings in an attempt to be loving or accepting. While it is important that the therapist not agree that the patient is shameful or bad, and indeed therapists usually feel much more compassionate and respectful of their patients than patients feel toward themselves, talking patients out of their feelings of shame is doomed to failure and only elicits the feeling of being ashamed of the continuing failure to be rid of the shame, i.e., being ashamed of being ashamed. Then, instead of just being generally ashamed, in their own eyes they become inadequate patients.

Beginning the Treatment of Shame

The initiative in identifying the presence of a shame process rests largely with the therapist. Typically the therapist will observe signs that suggest the possibility that a shame process is operating. These signs can be quite subtle and require sensitivity and intuition on the part of the therapist. Some of the obvious signs include changes in coloration indicating autonomic changes (e.g., flushing or becoming pale), sudden blanking or going numb, looking down, hanging the head, sudden defensive reactions, facial masking, becoming very still and quiet, self-conscious or apologetic statements. Characterological and situational indicators alert the therapist who is knowledgeable about and sensitive to shame issues to the probable presence of shame and the need to inquire about the possibility.

The therapist can initiate this exploration by asking about the patient's experience, reflecting, sharing observations, sharing the therapist's own present reaction, sharing a relevant past experience of the therapist or making an interpretation. Since the patient's shame vocabulary may be either nonexistent or very different than the therapist's, the therapist needs to find a language that makes communication possible. The therapist may also have to explain or teach the patient something about the shame process before the patient can respond. My experience has been that patients generally welcome this teaching and respond with feelings of relief at being understood and in suddenly understanding this mystifying aspect of themselves.

The test of the accuracy of all of these interventions is confirmation by the patient. The guide and final authority is not the therapist, is not any clinical theory, but the patient's experience. As the clinical interactions proceed, the patient's experience often becomes clarified and the patient's ability to separate immediate experience from past expectations grows. Then the patient may confirm what he or she had either not been able to confirm earlier or had denied. But I believe that the experience of the patient at each moment should be the guide and respected by the therapist. The therapist has the job of respecting and even protecting the patient's experience, while simultaneously using his or her own experience to guide the clinical interventions.

This may be done by putting a very explicit and positive emphasis on differences between their present experiences. "Our experience is very different on this point. In this situation I would feel ashamed. You have a very different experience; you do not experience shame." If the patient is shame-oriented there is a fair chance of a shame reaction by the patient to this interaction: "What is wrong with me that I don't feel shame now?" This gives the therapist and patient another chance to work with the shame reaction.

The therapist may also hold his own experience in the background while time and further clinical interactions clarify the situation and the patient's self-support grows. The evidence revealed over time may show that the therapist's earlier framing was inaccurate; on the other hand further evidence may support the therapist's earlier framing. But it is only when the patient's support reaches a certain level that this information can be used by the patient. It is only when the patient's self-support in the awareness and contact modes are sufficient to authoritatively affirm or deny the existence of the shame reaction that there is any trustworthy way to verify the therapist's empathic guess.

The Here-and-Now Manifestations

When the patient knows and can acknowledge the shame reaction, then it is possible to become clear about what aspect of the current field led to the shame reaction. Although the patient may carry a propensity to feel shame, something in the present provides the context for that reaction. Some contexts make shame reactions likely even in patients who are not especially shame-oriented.

It is helpful for people to know what is observed, said or done to them that led to the shame reaction. One patient would feel shame whenever I would tighten between my eyes and look upward. The patient interpreted the non-verbal cue as disapproval, which was the look her father had when he disapproved. When she was finally able to identify this look of mine, we could dialogue. My actual reaction was not disapproval, but rather being thoughtful. The patient believed my report of my experience, and stopped feeling the shame reaction in that context. This interaction did lead to some rather useful work on the shame reaction elicited by her relationship with her stern, aloof and disapproving father.

It is useful for the patient to recognize the sensory, cognitive and affective components of his or her shame reaction. Knowing the physical signs of shame is one way of recognizing that something is amiss and that vigilance rather than automatic functioning is needed. For example, I recognize a certain tension, freezing across my chest, tightening around my eyes, flushing, and a flurry of other sensations as physical manifestation of my shame reaction. Sometimes I am first aware of the shame affect, sometimes I first become aware of the physiological cues and then tune into the affective and cognitive components.

The cognitive aspects have to do with thoughts of not being enough, being unworthy, inadequate, unfavorable comparisons with other people and with ideal self images, etc. This process of self-rejection, and even disgust at self, coincides with physiological aspects: flushing, tightening, shrinking in the body, wanting to hide, i.e., not to be seen or heard in this shameful state. The impulse to retreat, be silent, hide, disappear, be small, often feels inborn and very intense.

The shame reaction to being spotlighted — by criticism, or even neutral or positive attention — is often indiscriminate shrinking and turning aggression against the self. When shame-oriented people are self-justifying, self-righteous and attacking or contemptuous of others, they are defending against the deeper and more centrally held feeling of shame. This socially difficult form of self-protection is made necessary by the lack of trust in themselves and lack of complete loving identification with their actual self. It is ineffective in that it usually alienates people, seldom contributes to dealing effectively with whatever task is at hand and does not actually lessen the shame.

Self: Now and Then
Developmental Work with Shame

A complete Gestalt therapy with shame requires exploration of the roots of the shame process in early childhood relationship experiences, especially in the family. I discern at least three goals in this aspect of the Gestalt therapy work:

1. To explore the induction of shame in the family of origin so that the patient can understand his or her own shame process in the present. This is use of the past as background to understand the present, and does not involve the assumption that the distant past causes the present.

2. To complete unfinished business and freeing the patient from emotional energy that has not been released. The objects of this present-centered exploration are feelings that are still lively but based on old gestalten that have not been completed. Included in this work is undoing retroflections, especially by expressing the emotions that are being suppressed, repressed and deflected.

3. To re-experience and assimilate/reject introjected parental figures and beliefs from this early childhood period. Again with this goal, the past is worked with in Gestalt therapy only insofar as it arises in the present-centered existential work and not for its own sake.

I do not regard this work with developmental material in a present-centered mode as new in Gestalt therapy.

As a result of this work the patient can live a full, present-centered existence unencumbered by figures that more accurately pertain to past fields. This means being able to observe his current field with minimal distortion from projections, to regulate based on organismic self-regulation and the needs of the environment rather than based on introjections, to have a more accurate picture of self and others (including parents), and to have more flexibility to contact, act, create, emote, and so forth.

I have found two very different modal shame induction family systems. In one system the shaming is done overtly and harshly. This occurs in families with harsh, punitive regulatory systems, that give little attention to the emotional needs of the family members and that have boundaries that are either inflexible or extremely sticky and porous. Here I refer to families in which child abuse is common and the parents characterologically disordered. The result is often an adult patient with serious narcissistic or borderline disturbances and the shame work then needs to follow the principles of treatment discussed in my essay on that subject (above) and suggestions here assimilated to that context.

In the second type of system the shaming is often more subtle and indirect. In this kind of family the shaming is often embedded in interactions that are thought to be caring, for example, I do this "for your own good." Whereas in the first kind of family the message is delivered with intensity and overt hostility, in the second type the message is often hidden, indirect, cloaked. In this second type of system, there is usually a discrepancy between the underlying nonverbal message and the verbal message. The verbal message is often something positive or objective, and the underlying message is shame inducing. "I know you can do better" can be encouraging or can be expressing the sentiment: "You are not enough."

In this system, there is a subtle abandonment. It can be as subtle as the disappearance of warmth in the mother's eyes or the "heavenly shot" of father's eyes looking at the ceiling. The bond that connects the child with the parent and lets the child know that he or she is ok, is loved and safe, is gone. The child is left mystified. Sometimes there is a mystification of the feeling, and even when the child is older and might identify the feeling, there is a mystification of "What did I do to deserve that?" or "Why is mom reacting so strongly?" The answer the child creates is usually "It is not a specific thing. There must be something inherently wrong with me."

While at a very general level work with shame is not essentially different than most other intensive therapeutic work in Gestalt therapy, i.e., a variety of ways of exploring are used until the unfinished business is finished, the introjects are assimilated, and the present situation understood, this essay does includes some specific treatment suggestions and cautions for working with shame. In discussing this treatment I have been thinking primarily of the neurotic shame resulting from this second type of family. For shame work with patients with serious character pathology, the primary character pathology must be emphasized and that provides the matrix within which the shame work proceeds.

Development of Positive Self-Parenting

A variety of metaphors are used to express aspects of the self functions. Self-regulation can be done in a manner in which the person takes his or her own emotions and needs into account, has warm positive feeling about self, shows trust of and compassion for self, gives permission to work for conditions within which his or her needs can be reasonably met and allows the person to take in nourishment and enjoy life. One way of referring to this is good self-parenting. When a person regulates himself or herself with an attitude of self-rejection or disgust, does not honor his or her feelings and needs, and does not mobilize healthy aggression for one's goals or even feel entitled to do so, one can refer to this as poor self-parenting (punitive, harsh, neglectful, smothering, and so forth).

It is thought that when a biologically intact child is raised in an environment that is at least minimally healthy, and parenting is "good enough," that the child learns these good self-parenting traits. They learn this by all forms of social learning — imitation of and identification with the parents, by introjection, by active teaching by the parents, and so forth. They watch what the parents do, they absorb the parental attitude at a very young age. When children are treated with respect, love, empathy and good limits there is a reasonably good chance that their self-regulatory processes will be healthy.

Shame-oriented patients to varying degrees regulate themselves in a manner that is not well described as good self-parenting. One of the tasks of therapy with such patients is to bring this self-regulatory or self-parenting system into awareness so it does not continue to operate at a merely habitual level. Then the possibility of good self-parenting is modeled by the good and loving contact that is a spontaneous part of the therapeutic relationship in the Gestalt therapy methodology. Within this matrix of a positive therapeutic relationship the negative residue of the past is worked through and the patient learns new skills and attitudes about the self.

At a basic level the new skills are the contact and awareness skills that are part of the Gestalt therapy process: knowing what one senses and observes, appreciating differences, bringing I and you together. At a more complex level, there is a learning about a whole new pattern of self-regulation. This is learned through the processes we have been discussing, and also by imitating and identifying with the therapist, benefiting from the empathy of the therapist, active learning about new models for self-care, interacting with others in groups, trial-and-error phenomenological

514

experimentation, and actively applying insight in programs of self-care.

The relationship between therapist and patient is vital in this regard. It is important that the therapist have a positive attitude toward and faith in the patient's gradual growth. We all need to be a joy to significant others. The shame-ridden patient who was considered a burden rather than a gift to his or her parents needs the therapist to feel like the patient is a joy, for the therapist to really like the patient.

The patient also needs the therapist to have good perspective on how long it takes, how gradual the work. He or she needs the therapist to model self-disclosure as well as empathic connecting. It is advisable for the therapist to keep checking with the patient to see what the patient is experiencing, rather than for the therapist to assume that he or she knows what the patient is experiencing or should be experiencing. And most of all, the patient needs the therapist to acknowledge all aspects of the patient and accept and respect the patient as a whole.

Self-care may start with behaviors suggested in therapy and initially practiced in a mechanical manner, which then become assimilated into the self-regulatory processes and become authentic. For example, an anxious person may mechanically follow suggestions about breath and thought control, meditation-like relaxation procedures, etc. At first this may be done with skepticism and without much enthusiasm. However, the patient may discover that such good self-care feels good and develop genuine enthusiasm for the particular self-care activities that were experimented with. As they are practiced they may become part of the habitual activities the person engages in and then no longer need to be the object of focal awareness. In short, they become assimilated and transform the functioning of the self.

Specific Interventions

It is imperative in Gestalt therapy practice to accent the virtue of identifying with one's experience. Therefore a most important aspect of the treatment of shame has to do with a relationship based on an attitude of empathic understanding and respectful warmth in which the patient is indeed encouraged to clarify and identify with his/her actual experience. The atmosphere should be one in which the pace can be gradual, the attitude reassuring, and in which there is safety and room for the full range of feelings, including fear, resistance, shame, and the like.

Within this context we may discuss some specific interventions (experiments). But these are merely illustrative applications that are useful only insofar as they apply this basic attitude rather than replace or violate it.

It is vital in this situation to remember that these experiments are phenomenological experiments, not exercises, that the purpose is for the patient to learn something, that in Gestalt therapy they are not used to recondition the patient. There is nothing for the patient to achieve, he cannot pass or fail these experiments. Whatever happens informs both patient and therapist and provides guidance for further work. The Gestalt therapist is expected to borrow or create other experiments as clinically indicated.

Repeated careful checking on the here-and-now experience of the patient allows them to share the data that is the object of the experimentation and also to maintain the shame-reducing connection between therapist and patient and to guard against inadvertent shame inducement. Shame work requires time and space and not pressure.

Contact Experiments

Experiments in which the patient is guided toward contacting are very useful. Sometimes this needs to be very structured, e.g., having the patient look at the therapist or others in a group and then give guidance in slowing up, inhaling and exhaling while looking, and so forth.

When patients can do this, then it can be suggested that they tell the therapist, or other participants in a group context, what they experience. Sometimes this can be done without a lot of structure from the therapist, and sometimes it is useful for the therapist to "feed a sentence" to the patient to say out loud or express to other people in a group. These sentences might express things such as: "I feel ashamed of ...," "I am hanging my head in shame," "I can hold my head up" or "I need to hide." While these interventions are based on empathic interpretations of the therapist, using them as explicit experiments puts the emphasis squarely on the phenomenological experience of the patient rather than on the therapist telling the patient what he feels.

Allowing themselves to be seen, and to stay with the continuum of their awareness, may follow next. This usually means feeling embarrassed. Hearing how others react to the shame-oriented patient may be healing, if the environment is believably supportive.

Embarrassment can be effectively worked on with contact experiments, if the patient has or develops sufficient support. The patient who has learned to control breathing and muscle relaxation can experiment with this in connection with embarrassment. Being able to stay "soft" and in contact while embarrassed helps the patients "become friends with their embarrassment." If the patients can look and be seen, feel the embarrassment, and not tense themselves, the simple embarrassment may be experienced as a warm and joining feeling in the context of a good therapeutic relationship or a cohesive group.

The embarrassed shame-oriented patient usually has a lot of trouble accepting positive feedback or strokes from other persons, especially if the feedback or strokes are sincere, deserved and desired. One aspect of the contact work is to encourage them to acknowledge the positive strokes, acknowledge that they are desired and needed, acknowledge that they are sincerely given or deserved and to "take them in." This means to let themselves feel warm, full, safe, good (and embarrassed) by the unexpected good stuff they are given.

Obviously we all have needs from others, and good self-parenting would be to take it when needed and offered. In these interactions good self-parenting is encouraged. I remember being at a meeting in which I was given a hearty round of applause for some hard work done and things accomplished, and was shrinking with embarrassment. Someone in the group said in a loving way: "Take it!" I did, and it felt wonderful.

Focus on Cognition

Focusing on the thinking processes of the shame patient is frequently useful. One finds a lot of negative self-talk, negative futurizing, remembering past failures without letting go, devaluing successes, and so forth. It is useful for the patient to become aware of this process, and then to become acutely aware as these thoughts habitually arise. If the awareness becomes sharp and current, the patient will often gain control of these cognitions. Some technical interventions may be of help here, for example, as a form of feedback. For example the patient might count the negative cognitions (as a way of being aware).

I have found it extremely useful for the patient to learn to be aware of the earliest signs of the shame process, e.g., the negative cognitions, and then to practice a pause. The pause can be something simple like taking a long, slow breath with good releasing exhale. Longer pauses (e.g., three long, slow breathes), or longer pauses using meditative imagery, can be used as needed. The purpose of the pause is to allow the patient to be aware rather than to automatically continue the well rehearsed pathway into deeper shame. It can be seen as a compassionate way of interrupting the patient's interruption of organismic self-regulation.

Sometimes it is useful for the patient to focus on positive self-talk. This is not to propagandize the patient out of his or her old beliefs or to "think positive," but to interrupt the automatic negative self talk and open the patient's awareness to the possibility of authentically feeling something positive about the self. Experimentation can give patients the feel of positive self-talk and they can find out what they experience.

Often this raises a lot of resistance to seeing themselves in a positive light and this can quicken the therapeutic work. It is important for the therapist to keep in mind that this is psychotherapy and these are experiments, and that "resistance" and work about difficulties is not an impediment to psychotherapy but is the valuable substance of which therapy is made and about which the therapeutic relationship is concerned.

One danger is that shame patients will often feel ashamed that they are not reaching a goal that they think a superior person would reach, such as feeling positive about themselves. If the therapist also has this behavioristic focus, the patient's shame may be exacerbated. This often happened in the past in technique- and expression- oriented Gestalt therapy ("boom-boom-boom therapy").

Movement

Shame can be thought of as a dance. It has a pattern of movement that can be pictured, experienced and enacted. This particular dance has a polar quality of shrinking and expanding. The shame pole is often experienced, pictured or danced as shrinking, retreating, being small, being hidden, making no sound. Eventually this can become a dance of no movement or sound, of utter stillness. This can be a profound spiritual experience.

At the other pole, the movement is expansive. The patient can move with expanded chest, head held high, taking up space in the room, making strong energetic connections with the ground and pushing upward and outward. The movements can be free, proud. Sound may accompany the expansive movement. At this pole other people may be engaged.

The movement back and forth between the two energies of expansion and shrinking gives the patient some sense of activity rather than paralysis and of being able to accept the shame as the feeling of a moment and not a characterological indictment.

People who are not touched as a child often have trouble with free movement and shame-ridden adults often have a childhood history in which there was very little touching, even in infancy. Touch, bodies, feelings and so forth were treated as disgusting and to be minimized. Sometimes there is confirmation of this reconstructed picture when the shame-oriented person's parents are observed playing with grandchildren.

While movement and touch (massage) are difficult for the shame-ridden patient, they can be quite powerful in enhancing healing and growth. Structured experiments and homework, such as those used in sex therapy, are sometimes useful.

Hiding and Masking

The need to hide requires expression and experimentation. This can be the focus of contact, movement or cognitions experiments. Some of the enactment or movement experiments can be to verbally or nonverbally express the impulse to hide. Being allowed to play with the hiding, especially in a group context, can make the impulse to hide less heavy and onerous to the patient. Sometimes it is both fun and freeing to hide behind the couch in the context of enacting the need to hide. Sometimes it brings up early childhood memories that can then be shared and worked with.

The hiding may take the form of a stony face. Sometimes the term "mask" describes it well. I have experimented with patients actually covering their faces with an external mask and making contact. For some patients this makes no difference, nothing happens and they learn nothing. When this happens it is usually very quick and I discard the experiment, having learned that this experiment is not useful for this patient.

However, for some patients there is a very interesting immediate effect of being able to look without tension when the face is covered by the mask. The external mask seems to replace the need for the biological mask. Not being seen seems to enable such people to look without tension and shame. This can make more concrete for the patient the shame aspects of not being seen, tensing and hiding, etc.

Ideal Self

Comparison to the ideal self is another aspect of the shame process that needs to be made explicit. Often this can be done just by contactful talking. At other times it is useful to do more active phenomenological focusing, e.g., to give the ideal self a more concrete symbolic expression. Sometimes I suggest that the patients imagine in front of them a self they would not be ashamed of and ask them to describe it. Sometimes I use the image of an old-style theater marquee with one of the lifesize cardboard pictures of one of the actors as a model and ask them to describe their own picture of the self that would be acceptable.

When they can describe the person, the dress, the manner, the voice, etc., then I inquire how they feel in response to this picture. The responses are more varied than one might imagine. Sometimes I use an empty-chair format with the ideal self being in the empty chair.

One common theme is for shame-oriented patients to identify more with the ideal self than with who they really are. It sometimes comes as a surprise to patients that the ideal self might be obnoxious, contradictory and only real as a concept and not as an existent — while they themselves are real as an existent.

520

Sometimes I have asked patients to play the ideal self. When they are not too inhibited to do so, they often find that they don't even like being that self. I am thinking of one earthy woman who wanted to be a "Beverly Hills Lady," very sophisticated, chic, polished. She was able to do the role playing, and create a credible image for herself and the others in the group. When she played that role she experienced it as empty; her phenomenological experience in that role was one of emptiness and meaninglessness.

Undoing Retroflections

There is so much retroflected anger and rage in shame, that it needs to be straightened out — directed at the actual environmental target of the anger before it became turned against the self. Since so much of this process goes back to such a young age and is so preverbal, expressive techniques often have to be used. The child who was shamed rarely has the external support or self-support to express it against the parents. One aspect of the therapy is to provide an opportunity to do just that, when it applies.

Frequently this can be done only after the subtle shaming behaviors are exposed and understood by the patient. A patient may remember shrinking when patted on the head, but not know why and may feel bad about himself or herself for shrinking away: "Why did I make so big a deal out of it?" When the condescension involved in the original context is explicated, when the putting the child out of view with minimal and inauthentic contact is explicated, the patient may be aware of anger rather than shame.

A period of expressive techniques may be useful at this time. For example, patients may vigorously push their arms outward — pushing against their parents while expelling air and feeling their anger. I remember one patient backhanding the parent in the empty chair saying "Away with you!"

Good Self-Parenting

Specific experiments and exercises are sometimes useful in developing self-acceptance and good self-esteem — when used in the context of a good relationship and after the patient has developed some support (as discussed above). These may provide a taste of what was missing and needed in childhood and of what is still possible for them to experience. Over time this taste of what is possible and practice with the exercises may lead to new, authentic and assimilated self processes. Here I discuss only one of many possibilities.

This exercise is a series of three. Usually one must be mastered before the patient has enough support to do the next.

1.

The patient is asked to picture a "metaphorical good parent" (MGP), a fantasy parent who is ideal in responding to the early childhood (now "inner child") needs of the patient. This is the figure of a person who responds with empathy and sympathy and wisdom without being smothering. This MGP, usually the "good mother," is defined as one who is always present, who looks at the patient with love and joy, who always says "I am here for you," and means it. This may also be a "good father," as feels most fitting to the patient. Some images include Grecian goddess, old man of the woods, woman in the kitchen, etc. One image patients have spontaneously fantasied is of a big, plump woman who would be able to hold them on her lap with ease, and whose softness they would feel. Sometimes the picture includes the images of a lot of kids playing around the woman. In the fantasy this woman is oriented to the children, and not concerned about losing weight, building a career, impressing the neighbors, or being sexy.

The use of a metaphorical person rather than another person in the patient's actual sense world meets several needs. It uses the richness of fantasy. It is possible to make the symbol more emotionally evocative by describing looks, dress, sound, home, geography, ethnicity, and so forth that tap into the patient's fantasy life.

What the MGP can do in fantasy is not possible in actual life. Outside of the womb, and perhaps not even there, no one can be totally present and meet these needs of the other person without regard to differing needs of their own. The use of metaphor makes clear that this isn't what a real person in the person's past, present or future life can give. The fantasy can only be approximated in interaction with other persons. The bulk of this process of constant caring and so forth is what a person can do for themselves. The metaphor is a symbol that can facilitate the internalization of the caring into the processes of the self. That which cannot be obtained from self or others must be grieved for.

Then the patient is asked to put this MGP in the empty chair and to make the image as real as possible. Then dialogue from the MGP to the patient is attributed to the MGP from the empty chair, usually the therapist saying the sentence (as one would in psychodrama when "doubling"). These sentences are along the order of "I love you just the way you are." "I will always be there for you."

Then the phenomenological work begins in earnest and the focus is on the patient's reaction to this. The therapist helps the patient begin to hear the loving sentiment, to "take it in," to breathe with it, to be warmed by it. If the therapist's timing is right, this phase of the experiment continues the work on the patient's picture of self, on past experiences with parents, and dialogue between the therapist and patient. It can be a valuable part of the working through process. It is easy for the therapist at this point to lose the discipline of the phenomenological experimental process and make "taking it in" a should or a goal. The patients must identify with their actual experience, and sometimes this means not "taking it in."

2.

When the patient can do this receptive function fairly well, then the patient is asked to play the MGP. Passively receiving the good parent message is hard for the shame-oriented patient, but saying the message himself or herself is even harder. This is another step toward assimilating the self-affirming message into the actual functioning of the self.

3.

The final phase occurs when the patient is asked to feel this good feeling without going through steps one and two. The sense memory of the good feeling and affirming thoughts are used as stimuli to prompt the simple glowing feeling within. This phase of the experiment is usually not effective until late in therapy.

There is no magic to this exercise, nor is it vital to the methodology. It illustrates using enactment, experimentation and program to develop a positive self-attitude that wasn't present before. It goes along with such exercises as meditation, journal writing, poem writing, drawing and other experiential activities that may intensify the therapeutic work and decrease the number of sessions and the length of therapy.

Summary

The effectiveness of psychotherapy rests on the quality of the relationship and the adequacy of the understanding and interventions of the therapist. Identification with one's actual state and with one's experience is a characteristic of health and must be central in the therapist's treatment of the patient if the therapy is to be successful.

It is important that the therapist understand the way shame and guilt are induced, maintained and healed. It is important that the therapist understand the difference between healthy and unhealthy shame and guilt. The treatment of neurotic shame requires that the therapist have an empathic connection with the patient, have a warm and positive feeling about the patient and also work with the shame in a technically appropriate manner. In shame work this means gradual long-term work in which the self-esteem functioning of the patient is strengthened and matched to the patient's actual personal virtues and positive self-parenting build up.

BIBLIOGRAPHY

Appelbaum, S. (1976). A psychoanalyst looks at Gestalt therapy. In C. Hatcher & P. Himelstein (Eds.). *The Handbook of Gestalt Therapy*. New York: Jason Aronson.

Bach, G. (1961). Comments. In C. Buhler. *Values in Psychotherapy*. New York: Free Press.

Barnwell, J. (1968). Gestalt methods and techniques in a poverty program. In J. Simkin (Ed.). *Festschrift for Fritz Perls*. Los Angeles: Author.

Beisser, A. (1970). The paradoxical theory of change. In J. Fagan & I. Shepherd (Eds.). *Gestalt Therapy Now*. New York: Harper. (pp. 77-80)

Bentov, I. (1977). *Stalking the Wild Pendulum*. New York: Bantam Books.

Bergin, A. E., & Suinn, R. M. (1975). Individual psychotherapy and behavior therapy. *Annual Review of Psychology*, 26, 509-556.

Berne, E. (1964). *Games People Play*. New York: Grove Press.

Bevan, W. Contemporary psychology: a tour inside the onion. *American Psychologist*, 46, 5 (May 1991), 475-483.

Brown, G. Teaching creativity to teachers and others. *Journal of Teacher Education*, 21, 210-216.

Brown, G. (1974/1977). The farther reaches of Gestalt therapy. *Synthesis*, 1, 27-43.

Brown, R. & Lunneberg, E. (1961). A study in language and cognition. In S. Saporta (Ed.)., *Psycholinguistics*. New York: Holt, Rhinehart & Winston.

Brunnink, S. & Schroeder, H. Verbal therapeutic behavior of expert psychoanalytically oriented, Gestalt and behavior therapists. *Journal of Consulting and Clinical Psychology*, 47, 567-574.

Buber, M. (1965a). *Between Man and Man*. New York: MacMillan.

Buber, M. (1965b). *The Knowledge of Man*. New York: Harper & Row.

Buber, M. (1967). A believing humanism. In R. Anshen (Ed.), *Gleanings by Martin Buber*. New York: Simon & Schuster.

Buber, M. (1970). *I and Thou*. New York: Scribner's Sons.

Buhler, C. (1962). *Values in Psychotherapy*. New York: Free Press.

Capra, F. (1975). *The Tao of Physics*. Berkeley: Shambhala Publications.

Capra, F. (1976). *Quantum Paradoxes and Eastern Mysticism.* Big Sur: Esalen Workshop Cassettes.

Chessick, R. (1977). *Intensive Psychotherapy of the Borderline Patient.* New York: Jason Aronson.

Davies, P. (1983). *God and the New Physics.* New York: Simon & Schuster.

Dolliver, R. (1981). Some limitations in Perls' Gestalt therapy. *Psychotherapy, Research and Practice*, 8, 38-45.

Dublin, J. (1976). Gestalt therapy: Existential-Gestalt therapy and/versus `Perls-ism.' In E. Smith (Ed.). *The Growing Edge of Gestalt Therapy.* New York: Brunner/Mazel.

Edward, D. (1977). Self-hood: Bright figure of the Gestalt. *Journal of Contemporary Psychotherapy*, 9, 89-94.

Einstein, A. (1950). *Out of My Later Years.* New York: The Wisdom Library.

Einstein, A. (1961). *Relativity.* New York: Crown Publishers.

Ellis, A. (1962). *Reason and Emotion in Psychotherapy.* New York: Lyle Stuart.

Ellis, W. (1938). *A Source Book of Gestalt Psychology.* London: Routledge & Kegan Paul.

Emerson, P. & Smith, E. (1974). Contributions of Gestalt psychology to Gestalt therapy. *The Counseling Psychologist*, 4, 4-7.

English & English. (1958). *A Comprehensive Dictionary of Psychological and Psychoanalytic Terms.* New York: David McKay.

Ennis, K. & Mitchell, S. (1970). Staff training for a day care center. In J. Fagan & I. Shepherd (Eds.). *Gestalt Therapy Now.* Palo Alto: Science and Behavior Books.

Enright, J. (1970a). An introduction to Gestalt therapy. In J. Fagan & I. Shepherd (eds.), *Gestalt Therapy Now.* Palo Alto: Science and Behavior Books. (pp. 140-219). Also in (1975) F. Stephenson (Ed.), *Gestalt Therapy Primer.* Springfield, IL: Charles C. Thomas. (pp. 13-33)

Enright, J. (1970b). Awareness training in the mental health professions. In J. Fagan & I. Shepherd (Eds.), *Gestalt Therapy Now.* Palo Alto: Science and Behavior Books. (pp. 263-273)

Enright, J. (1975). Gestalt therapy in interactive groups. In F. Stephenson (Ed.)., *Gestalt Therapy Primer: Introductory Readings in Gestalt Therapy.* Springfield, IL: Charles C. Thomas.

Fagan, J. (1970). Gestalt techniques with a woman with expressive difficulties. In J. Fagan & I. Shepherd (eds.), *Gestalt Therapy Now.* Palo Alto: Science and Behavior Books.

Fagan, J. (1974). Personality theory and psychotherapy. *The Counseling Psychologist*, 4, 4-7.

Fagan, J. & Shepherd, I. (1970). *Gestalt Therapy Now*. Palo Alto: Science and Behavior Books.

Feder, B. & Ronall, R. (Eds.). (1980). *Beyond the Hot Seat*. New York: Brunner/Mazel.

Frew, J. (1988). The practice of Gestalt therapy in groups. *The Gestalt Journal*, 11, 1, 77-96.

Friedman, M. (1976a). Healing through meeting: a dialogic approach to psychotherapy and family therapy. In E. Smith (Ed.), *Psychiatry and the Humanities*, Vol 1. New Haven: Yale University Press.

Friedman, M. (1976b). *Martin Buber: The Life of Dialogue*. Chicago: University of Chicago Press.

From, I. (1978). Contact and contact boundaries. *Voices*, 14, 1, 14-22.

From, I. (1984). Reflections on Gestalt therapy after thirty-two years of practice: A requiem for Gestalt. *The Gestalt Journal*, 8, 1, 23-49.

Fuchs, W. (1938). Completion phenomena in hemianopic vision. in W. Ellis, *A Source Book of Gestalt Psychology*. London: Routledge & Kegan Paul. (pp. 344-356)

Geller, L. (1982). The failure of self-actualization theory: A critique of Carl Rogers and Abraham Maslow. *Journal of Humanistic Psychology*, 22,2 (Spring 1982), 56-73.

Geller, L. (1984). Another look at self-actualization. *Journal of Humanistic Psychology*, 24, 2 (Spring 1984), 93-106.

Gergen, K. (1991). Emerging challenges for theory and psychology. *Theory and Psychology*, 1, 1 (February 1991), 13-36.

Ginsburg, C. (1984). Toward a somatic understanding of self: A reply to Leonard Geller. *Journal of Humanistic Psychology*, 24, 2 (Spring 1984), 66-92.

Giovacchini, P. (1979). *Treatment of Primitive Mental States*. New York: Jason Aronson.

Glasser, W. (1965). *Reality Therapy*. New York: Harper & Row.

Greenberg, L. (1979). Resolving splits: Use of the two-chair technique. *Psychotherapy, Theory, Research and Practice*, 16, 316-324.

Greenberg, L. (1986). Change process research. *Journal of Consulting and Clinical Psychology*, 54, 1 (February 1986), 4-9.

Greenberg, L. & Higgins, H. (1980). Effects of two-chair dialogues and focusing on conflict resolution. *Journal of Counseling Psychology*, 27, 221-224.

Greenberg, L. & Johnson, Susan. (1988). *Emotionally Focused Therapy for Couples*. New York: Guilford Press.

Greenwald, G. (1969a). The art of emotional nourishment. Santa Monica, California: Distributed by author.

Greenwald, G. (1969b). The art of emotional nourishment: Self-induced nourishment and toxicity. Santa Monica, CA: Distributed by author.

Greenwald, G. (1973). *Be The Person You Were Meant To Be.* New York: Simon & Schuster.

Gunderson, J. Formulation of the Borderline Personality. Continuing Education Series (CES) tape. Tape #1.

Guntrip, Harry. (1969). *Schizoid Phenomena, Object Relations and the Self.* New York: International Universities Press.

Harman, R. (1984). Recent developments in Gestalt group therapy. *International Journal of Group Psychotherapy,* 34, 3, 473-483).

Harré, R. (1991). The discursive production of selves. *Theory and Psychology,* 1, 1 (February, 1991), 51-64.

Hatcher, C. & Himelstein, P. (Eds.). (1976). *The Handbook of Gestalt therapy.* New York: Jason Aronson.

Hawking, S. (1988). *A Brief History of Time.* New York: Bantam Books.

Heidbreder, E. (1933). *Seven Psychologies.* New York: Century Company.

Henle, M. (1978). Gestalt psychology and Gestalt therapy. *Journal of History of the Behavioral Sciences,* 14, 23-32.

Herman, S. (1972). The Gestalt orientation to organizational development. In *Contemporary Organization Development.* Bethel, ME: National Institute of Applied Behavioral Science.

Horner, A. (1984). *Object Relations and the Developing Ego in Therapy.* New York: Jason Aronson.

Hycner, R. (1985). Dialogical Gestalt therapy: An initial proposal. *The Gestalt Journal,* 8, 1 (Spring 1985), 23-49.

Ihde, D. (1977). *Experimental Phenomenology: An Introduction.* Albany: State University of New York.

Jacobs, L. (1978). I-thou relations in Gestalt therapy. Unpublished doctoral dissertation. California School of Professional Psychology.

Jacobs, L. (1989). Dialogue in Gestalt theory and therapy. *The Gestalt Journal,* 12, 1 (Spring 1989), 25-67.

Jourard, S. (1967). Psychotherapy in the age of automation: From the way of a technician to the way of guru. Paper presented to the Cleveland Institute of Gestalt Therapy, May 19, 1967.

Kahn, E. (1989). In Heinz Kohut and Carl Rogers: Toward a constructive collaboration. *Psychotherapy,* 26, 4 (Winter 1989), 555-563).

Kaufman, W. (1956). *Existentialism from Dostoevsky to Sartre.* New York: Meridian Books.

Kelly, G.A. (1955). *The Psychology of Personal Constructs.* New York: Norton.

Kempler, W. (1965). Experiential family therapy. *International Journal of Group Psychotherapy,* 15, 57-71.

Kempler, W. (1966). The moving finger writes. *Voices,* 2, 73-74.

Kempler, W. (1967). The experiential therapeutic encounter. *Psychotherapy: Theory, Research and Practice,* 4, 166-172.

Kempler, W. (1968). Experiential psychotherapy with families. *Family Process,* 7, 88-89.

Kempler, W. (1973). Gestalt therapy. In R. Corsini (Ed.), *Current Psychotherapies,* Edition One. Itasca, IL: F.E. Peacock.

Kempler, W. (1974). *Principles of Gestalt Family Therapy.* Costa Mesa, CA: Kempler Institute.

Kernberg, O. (1975). *Borderline Conditions and Pathological Narcissism.* New York: Jason Aronson.

Keutzer, C. (1984). Power of meaning. *Journal of Humanistic Psychology,* 24, 1 (Winter 1984) (pp. 80-94).

King, J. (1976). Discussion of Quantum Theory. Big Sur: Esalen Workshop Cassettes.

Koffka, K. (1931). Gestalt. *Encyclopaedia of the Social Sciences.* New York.

Koffka, K. (1935). *Principles of Gestalt Psychology.* New York: Harcourt, Brace & World.

Kogan, G. (1976). The genesis of Gestalt therapy. In C. Hatcher & P. Himelstein (Eds.). *The Handbook of Gestalt Therapy.* New York: Jason Aronson.

Kogan, G. (1980). *Gestalt Therapy Resources* (3rd ed.). Berkeley: CA: Transformation Press.

Köhler, W. (1938a). Physical Gestalten. In W. Ellis (Ed.). *A Sourcebook of Gestalt Psychology.* London: Routledge & Kegan Paul. (pp. 17-54).

Köhler, W. (1938b). Some Gestalt problems. In W. Ellis (Ed.). *A Sourcebook of Gestalt Psychology.* London: Routledge & Kegan Paul. (pp. 55-70).

Köhler, W. (1947). *Gestalt Psychology.* New York: Mentor Books.

Köhler, W. (1969). *The Task of Gestalt Psychology.* Princeton, NJ: Princeton University Press.

Kohut, H. (1971). *The Analysis of the Self: A Systematical Approach to the Psychoanalytic Treatment of Narcissistic Personality Disorders.* New York: International Universities Press.

Kohut, H. (1984). *How Does Psychoanalysis Cure?* Chicago: The University of Chicago Press.

Kutash, I. & Wolf, (1990). *Group Psychotherapist's Handbook.* New York: Columbia University Press.

Lambert, M. J. (1989). The individual therapist's contribution to psychotherapy process and outcome. *Clinical Psychology Review*, 9, 469-485.

Latner, J. (1973). *The Gestalt Therapy Book*. New York: Julian Press.

Latner, J. (1983). This is the speed of light: Field and systems theory in Gestalt therapy. *The Gestalt Journal*, 6, 2 (Fall 1983), 71-90.

Lederman, J. (1970). Anger and the rocking chair. In J. Fagan & I. Shepherd (Eds.), *Gestalt Therapy Now*. Palo Alto: Science and Behavior Books.

Levitsky, A. & Perls, F. (1969). The rules and games of Gestalt therapy. In H. Ruitenbeek (Ed.). *Group Therapy Today: Styles, Methods and Techniques*. New York: Atherton. 221-230. Also (1972) (1974). G. Davidson & K. Price (Eds.) *Contemporary Readings in Psychopathology*. New York: John Wiley.

Levitsky, A. & Simkin, J. (1972). Gestalt therapy. In L. Solomon & B. Berzon (Eds.). *New Perspectives on Encounter Groups*. San Francisco: Jossey-Bass.

Lieberman, M. A., Yalom, I. D., & Miles, M. B. (1973). *Encounter Groups: First Facts*. New York: Basic Books.

Lewin, K. (1938a). Will and needs. In U. Ellis (Ed.), *A Sourcebook of Gestalt Psychology*. London: Routledge & Kegan Paul. (pp. 283299.)

Lewin, K. (1938b). The Conflict Between Aristotelian and Galilean modes of thought in contemporary psychology. In K. Lewin, *A Dynamic Theory of Personality*. London: Routledge & Kegan Paul.

Masek, R. (1989). The overlooked problem of consciousness in psychoanalysis: Pierre Janet revisited. *The Humanistic Psychologist*, 17, 3 (Autumn 1989), 474-279.

Masterson, J. (1972). *Treatment of the Borderline Adolescent: A Developmental Approach*. New York: John Wiley.

Masterson, J. (1976). *Psychotherapy of the Borderline Adult: A Developmental Approach*. New York: Brunner/Mazel.

Masterson, J. (1981). *The Narcissistic and Borderline Disorders*. New York: Brunner/Mazel.

Melnick, J. (1980). The use of therapist-imposed structure in Gestalt therapy. *The Gestalt Journal*, 3, 4-20.

Miller, M. V. (1985). Some historical limitations of Gestalt therapy, *The Gestalt Journal*, 8, 1 (Spring 1985), 51-54.

Miller, M. V. (1988). Introduction. In F. Perls, *Gestalt Therapy Verbatim*. New York: The Gestalt Journal Press.

Misiak, H. & Sexton, V. (1966). *The History of Psychology*. New York: Grune and Stratton.

Naranjo, C. (1975). I and thou, here and now: Contributions of Gestalt therapy. In F. Stephenson (Ed.)., *Gestalt Therapy Primer: Introductory Readings in Gestalt Therapy*. Springfield, IL: Charles C. Thomas. (pp. 34-53).

Nevis, E. (1968). Beyond mental health. Paper, Cleveland: Gestalt Therapy Institute of Cleveland.

O'Connell, V. (1970). Crisis psychotherapy: Person, dialogue and the organismic approach. In J. Fagan & I. Shepherd (Eds.), *Gestalt Therapy Now*. Palo Alto: Science and Behavior Books.

Parlett, M. (1990). Reflections on field theory. Lecture at the 4th British Gestalt Conference, Nottingham, July 1990.

Perls, F. (1947). *Ego, Hunger and Aggression*. Woking, Great Britain: Unwin Brothers. (1966 edition) San Francisco: Orbit Graphic Arts. (1969 Edition) New York: Vintage Books.

Perls, F. (1948). Theory and technique of personality integration. *American Journal of Psychotherapy*, 2, 565-586. Also in (1975) J. Stevens (ed.), *Gestalt Is*. Moab, UT: Real People Press.

Perls, F. (1950). The anthropology of neurosis. *Complex*, 2, 19-27.

Perls, F. (1953/1954). Morality, ego boundary, and aggression. *Complex*, 9, 42-52.

Perls, F. (1965). Big Sur: Esalen Institute. Also in (1966) H. Otto (Ed.), *Explorations of Human Potentialities*. Springfield, Ill: Charles C. Thomas. Also in (1975) F. Stephenson (Ed.), *Gestalt Therapy Primer: Introductory Readings in Gestalt Therapy*. Springfield, IL: Charles C. Thomas.

Perls, F. (1966). Group vs. individual therapy. Paper presented at the American Psychological Association, New York, September 1966. In *ETC*, 24 (1967), 306-312. Also in J. Stevens (ed.), *Gestalt Is*. Moab, Utah: Real People Press. (pp. 9-15).

Perls, F. (1969). *Gestalt Therapy Verbatim*. Moab, UT: Real People Press.

Perls, F. (1973). *The Gestalt Approach*. Palo Alto: Science and Behavior Books.

Perls, F. (1975). Resolution. In J. Stevens (Ed.) *Gestalt Is*. Moab, UT: Real People Press.

Perls, F. (1976). Gestalt therapy verbatim: Introduction. In C. Hatcher & P. Himelstein (Eds.), *The Handbook of Gestalt Therapy*. New York: Jason Aronson.

Perls, F., Hefferline, R. & Goodman, P. (1951). *Gestalt Therapy: Excitement and Growth in the Human Personality*. New York: Julian Press. Also (1965) New York: Dell (A Delta Book).

Perls, L. (1950). The psychoanalyst and the critic. *Complex*, 2, 41-47.

Perls, L. (1953/1954). Notes on the psychology of give and take. *Complex*, 9, 24-30.

Perls, L. (1956). Two instances of Gestalt therapy. *Case Reports in Clinical Psychology*, 3, 139-146.

Perls, L. (1961). The Gestalt approach. In J. Barron & R. Harper (Eds.), *Annals of Psychotherapy*, 1 & 2.

Perls, L. (1973). Some aspects of Gestalt therapy. Manuscript presented at Annual Meeting of the Orthopsychiatric Association.

Perls, L. (1976). Comments on the New Directions. In E. Smith (Ed.). *The Growing Edge of Gestalt Therapy*. New York: Brunner/Mazel.

Perls, L. (1978). Concepts and misconceptions of Gestalt therapy. *Voices*, 14, 3, 31-36.

Piers, G. & Singer, M. (1971). *Shame and Guilt*. New York: Norton.

Polster, E. (1957). Techniques and experience in Gestalt therapy. Paper presented at the Ohio Psychological Association Symposium. In (1975) F. Stephenson (Ed.), *Gestalt Therapy Primer: Introductory Readings in Gestalt Therapy*. Springfield, IL: Charles C. Thomas. pp. 147-150.

Polster, E. (1966). A contemporary psychotherapy. *Psychotherapy*, 3, 1-6. Also in (1968) P. Pursglove (Ed.), *Recognitions in Gestalt Therapy*. New York: Funk & Wagnalls.

Polster, E. (1976). Trends in Gestalt therapy. Paper presented at Ohio Psychological Association, February 22, 1967. In (1975) F. Stephenson (Ed.), *Gestalt Therapy Primer: Introductory Readings in Gestalt Therapy*. Springfield, IL: Charles C. Thomas. (pp.151-160).

Polster, E. (1985). Imprisoned in the present. *The Gestalt Journal*, 8, 1, 5-22.

Polster, E. (1987). *Every Person's Life is Worth a Novel*. New York: Norton.

Polster, E. & Polster, M. (1973). *Gestalt Therapy Integrated*. New York: Brunner/Mazel.

Polster, M. (1981). The language of experience. *The Gestalt Journal*, 4, 1 (Spring 1981). (pp. 19-2).

Pursglove, P. (Ed.). (1968) *Recognitions in Gestalt Therapy*. New York: Funk & Wagnalls.

Quick Reference to Diagnostic Criteria from DSM-III (Mini-D), American Psychiatric Association.

Resnick, R. (1970). Chicken soup is poison. *Voices*, 6, 75-78. Also in (1975) F. Stephenson (Ed.) *Gestalt Therapy Primer*. Springfield, IL: Charles C. Thomas.

Resnick, R. (1984). Gestalt therapy East and West: Bicoastal dialogue, debate or debacle? *The Gestalt Journal*, 7, 1, 13-32.

Robinson, D. (1991). Might the self be a substance afer all? *Theory and Psychology*, 1, 1 (February 1991), pp. 37-50.

Rogers, C. (1956). Training individuals to engage in therapeutic process. In C. Strother (Ed.), *Psychology and Mental Health*. Washington, DC: American Psychological Association, 1956.

Rogers, C. (1960). Two divergent trends. In R. May. (Ed.). *Existential Psychology*. New York: Random House.

Rogers, C. (1967). *The Therapeutic Relationship and Its Impact: A Study of Psychotherapy With Schizophrenics*. With E. T. Gendlin, D. J. Kiesler, & C. Louax. Madison, WI: University of Wisconsin Press.

Rosanes-Berret, M. (1970). Gestalt therapy as an adjunct treatment for some visual problems. In J. Fagan & I. Shepherd (Eds.), *Gestalt Therapy Now*. Palo Alto: Science and Behavior Books.

Rosenblatt, D. (1980). Introduction. in D. Rosenblatt (Ed.), *A Festschrift for Laura Perls*. *The Gestalt Journal*, 3, 1 (Spring 1980) (pp. 5-15).

Rosenfeld, E. (1978). An oral history of Gestalt therapy: Part I: A conversation with Laura Perls. *The Gestalt Journal*, 1, 8-31.

Rosenfeld, E. (1981). The Gestalt bibliography. *The Gestalt Journal*, 1981, 1, 8-31.

Sachs, M. (1973). *The Field Concept in Contemporary Science*. Springfield, IL: Charles C. Thomas.

Sartre, J. (1946). Existentialism is a "humanism." In (1956) W. Kaufman, *Existentialism from Dostoevsky to Sartre*. New York: Meridian Books.

Sartre, J. (1966). *Being and Nothingness*. New York: Washington Square Press.

Satir, V. (1964). *Conjoint Family Therapy: A Guide to Theory and Technique*. Palo Alto: Science and Behavior Books.

Schutz, W. (1967). *Joy: Expanding Human Awareness*. New York: Grove Press.

Shafer, R. (1976). *A New Language for Psychoanalysis*. New Haven: Yale University Press.

Shapiro, K. (1990). Animal rights versus humanism: The charge of speciesism. *Journal of Humanistic Psychology*, 30, 2 (Spring, 1990), 9-37.

Shepherd, I. (1970). Limitations and cautions in the Gestalt approach. In J. Fagan & I. Shepherd (Eds.), *Gestalt Therapy Now*. Palo Alto: Science and Behavior Books.

Sherrill, R. (1974). Figure/ground: Gestalt therapy/Gestalt psychology relationship. Unpublished doctoral dissertation, The Union Graduate School.

Shostrom, E. (1966a). *Manual for the Caring Relationship Inventory.* San Diego: Educational and Industrial Testing Service.

Shostrom, E. (1966b). *Manual for the Personal Orientation Inventory.* San Diego: Educational and Industrial Testing Service.

Shostrom, E. (1967). *Man the Manipulator.* Nashville: Abingdon Press.

Shostrom, E. (1969). Group therapy: Let the buyer beware. *Psychology Today*, 2, (12), 36-40.

Simkin, J. (1962). Contributions. In C. Buhler, *Values in Psychotherapy.* New York: Free Press.

Simkin, J. (1960s). An introduction to Gestalt therapy. Big Sur: Esalen Institute. Also Cleveland: Paper #6, Gestalt Institute of Cleveland. In (1973) *Direct Psychotherapy: 28 American Originals* (Vol. 1). Coral Gables, FL.: University of Miami. (pp. 423-432). Also in (1975) F. Stephenson (Ed.), *Gestalt Therapy Primer: Introductory Readings in Gestalt Therapy.* Springfield, IL: Charles C. Thomas. (pp. 3-12).

Simkin, J. (1968). *Festschrift for Fritz Perls.* Los Angeles, CA: Author.

Simkin, J. (1969). *In the Now.* A training film. Beverly Hills, CA.

Simkin, J. (1970). A session with a passive patient. In J. Fagan & I. Shepherd (Eds.), *Gestalt Therapy Now.* Palo Alto: Science and Behavior Books.

Simkin, J. (1974). *Mini-Lectures in Gestalt Therapy.* Albany, CA: Wordpress.

Simkin, J. (1976). *Gestalt Therapy Mini-lectures.* Millbrae, CA: Celestial Arts.

Simkin, J. (1979). Gestalt therapy. In R. Corsini (Ed.), *Current Psychotherapies* (2nd Ed). Ithasca, IL.: F. E. Peacock.

Simkin, J. & Yontef, G. Gestalt Therapy (1984). In Corsini, R. (Ed.). *Current Psychotherapies, (3rd Ed.)* Ithasca, IL: Peacock Publishers.

Smith, E. (1976). *The Growing Edge of Gestalt Therapy.* New York: Brunner/Mazel.

Spinelli, Ernesto. (1989). *The Interpreted World.* Newbury Park, CA: Sage Publications.

Stewart, R. (1974). The philosophical background of Gestalt therapy. *Counseling Psychologist*, 4, 13-14.

Tobin, S. (1982). Self-disorders, Gestalt therapy and self psychology. *The Gestalt Journal*, 5, 2 (Fall, 1982), 3-44.

Van Dusen, W. (1960). Existential analytic psychotherapy. *American Journal of Psychoanalysis*, 20, 35-40. Also in (1968) P.

Pursglove (Ed.). *Recognitions in Gestalt Therapy*. New York: Funk & Wagnalls.

Van Dusen, W. (1975a). Invoking the actual. In J. Stevens (Ed.), *Gestalt Is*. Moab, UT: Real People Press.

Van Dusen, W. (1975b). The phenomenology of schizophrenic existence. In J. Stevens (Ed.), *Gestalt Is*. Moab, UT: Real People Press.

Van Dusen, W. (1975c). The perspective of an old hand. In J. Stevens (Ed.), *Gestalt Is*. Moab, UT: Real People Press.

Wallen, R. (1957). Gestalt psychology and Gestalt therapy. Paper presented at Ohio Psychological Association Symposium. In (1970) J. Fagan & I. Shepherd (Eds.), *Gestalt Therapy Now*. Palo Alto: Science and Behavior Books. (pp. 8-13)

Webster's New Twentieth Century Dictionary of the English Language (1962). New York: World Publishing.

Wertheimer, M. (1938a). Gestalt theory. In W. Ellis (Ed.), *A Sourcebook of Gestalt Psychology*. London: Routledge & Kegan Paul.

Wertheimer, M. (1938b). The general theoretical situation. In W. Ellis (Ed.), *A Sourcebook of Gestalt Psychology*. London: Routledge & Kegan Paul.

Wertheimer, M. (1945). *Productive Thinking*. New York: Harper and Brothers.

Wheeler, G. (1991). *Gestalt Reconsidered*. New York: Gardner Press.

Whitaker, C. (1965). The psychotherapy of marital couples. Lecture presented to Cleveland Institute of Cleveland.

Wolfe, B. (1989). Heinz Kohut's self psychology: A conceptual analysis. *Psychotherapy*, 26, 4 (Winter 1989), 545-554.

Wolfe, F. (1981). *Taking the Quantum Leap*. NY: Harper & Row.

Wysong, J. & Rosenfeld, E. (1982). *An Oral History of Gestalt Therapy*. Highland, NY: The Gestalt Journal.

Yontef, G. (1975). A review of the practice of Gestalt therapy. (First published 1969). Also in (1975) F. Stephenson (Ed.), *Gestalt Therapy Primer: Introductory Readings in Gestalt Therapy*. Springfield, IL: Charles C. Thomas.

Yontef, G. (1976). Gestalt therapy: Clinical phenomenology. In Binder, V., Binder, A. & Rimland, B. (Eds.), *Modern Therapies*. New York: Prentice-Hall.
  Reprinted:
  (1977) *Psihijatrija Danas*, 4, 401 - 418.
  (1979) *The Gestalt Journal*, 2, 1, 27 - 45.
  (1984) #7, Documents de l'institut de Gestalt, Bordeaux.

Yontef, G. (1981a). The future of Gestalt therapy: A symposium. with Perls, L., Polster, M., Zinker, J., & Miller, M. V. *The Gestalt Journal*, 4, 1, 3 - 18.

Yontef, G. (1981b). Mediocrity and excellence: An identity crisis in Gestalt therapy. ERIC/CAPS, University of Michigan, Ed. 214,062.

Yontef, G. (1982). Gestalt therapy: Its inheritance from Gestalt psychology. *Gestalt Theory*. IV, 1/2, 23-39 (abstract in German). Reprinted (1984) *Psihijatrija Danas*, 16, 1, 31-46.

Yontef, G. (1983a). Gestalttherapie als Dialogische Methode. *Integrative Therapie*, 9, Jg. Heft 2/3, 98-130. (First circulated 1981 as unpublished paper: Gestalt Therapy: A Dialogic Method).

Yontef, G. (1983b). The self in Gestalt therapy: Reply to Tobin. *The Gestalt Journal*, 6, 1, 55-70.

Yontef, G. (1984a). Modes of thinking in Gestalt therapy. *The Gestalt Journal*, 7, 1, 33-74.

Yontef, G. (1984b). Why I became a Gestalt therapist. In R. Resnick & G. Yontef (Eds.), *Memorial Festschrift* (for Jim Simkin). L.A.: Gestalt Therapy Institute of Los Angeles.

Yontef, G. (1987). Gestalt therapy 1986: A polemic. *The Gestalt Journal*, 10, 1, 41-68.

Yontef, G. (1988a). Assimilating diagnostic and psychoanalytic perspectives into Gestalt therapy. *The Gestalt Journal*, 11, 1 (Spring 1988), 5-32.

Yontef, G. (1988b). Comments on "boundary processes and boundary states". *The Gestalt Journal*, 11, 2, 25 - 36.

Yontef, G. (1990a). Gestalt therapy in groups. In I. Kutash & A.Wolf, A. (Eds.), *Group Psychotherapist's Handbook*. New York: Columbia University Press.

Yontef, G. (1990b). Interview. In R. Harman (Ed.). *Gestalt Therapy Discussions with the Masters*. Springfield, IL: Charles C. Thomas.

Yontef, G. (1991). Recent trends in Gestalt therapy in the U.S. and what we need to learn from them. *British Gestalt Journal*, 1, 1.

Yontef, G. & Simkin, J. (1989). Gestalt Therapy. In R. Corsini & D. Wedding, (Eds.). *Current Psychotherapies*, 4th *Ed*. Ithasca, IL: F. E. Peacock Publishers.

Zinker, J. (1966). Notes on the phenomenology of the loving encounter. *Explorations*, 10, 3-7.

Zinker, J. (1977). *Creative Process in Gestalt Therapy*. New York: Brunner/Mazel.

Zinker, J. & Fink, S. (1966). The possibility of growth in a dying person. *Journal of General Psychology*, 74, 185-199.

Zukav, G. (1979). *The Dancing Wu Li Masters*. New York: Bantam Books.

INDEX

Lightning Source UK Ltd.
Milton Keynes UK
30 August 2009

143187UK00001BA/17/P